OXFO

THE LADIES' PARADISE

ÉMILE ZOLA was born in Paris in 1840, the son of a Venetian engineer and his French wife. He grew up in Aix-en-Provence where he made friends with Paul Cézanne. After an undistinguished school career and a brief period of dire poverty in Paris, Zola joined the newly founded publishing firm of Hachette which he left in 1866 to live by his pen. He had already published a novel and his first collection of short stories. Other novels and stories followed until in 1871 Zola published the first volume of his Rougon-Macquart series with the sub-title *Histoire naturelle et sociale d'une famille sous le Second Empire*, in which he sets out to illustrate the influence of heredity and environment on a wide range of characters and milieux. However, it was not until 1877 that his novel *L'Assommoir*, a study of alcoholism in the working classes, brought him wealth and fame. The last of the Rougon-Macquart series appeared in 1893 and his subsequent writing was far less successful, although he achieved fame of a different sort in his vigorous and influential intervention in the Dreyfus case. His marriage in 1870 had remained childless but his extremely happy liaison in later life with Jeanne Rozerot, initially one of his domestic servants, gave him a son and a daughter. He died in 1902.

BRIAN NELSON is Professor of French and Head of the Department of Romance Languages at Monash University, Melbourne. His publications include *Zola and the Bourgeoisie* and, as editor, *Naturalism in the European Novel: New Critical Perspectives* and *Forms of Commitment: Intellectuals in Contemporary France*, as well as a translation of Zola's *Pot Luck* (*Pot Bouille*) for Oxford World's Classics. He is engaged at present on a book on Huysmans and the Decadent Imagination.

OXFORD WORLD'S CLASSICS

For over 100 years Oxford World's Classics have brought readers closer to the world's great literature. Now with over 700 titles—from the 4,000-year-old myths of Mesopotamia to the twentieth century's greatest novels—the series makes available lesser-known as well as celebrated writing.

The pocket-sized hardbacks of the early years contained introductions by Virginia Woolf, T. S. Eliot, Graham Greene, and other literary figures which enriched the experience of reading. Today the series is recognized for its fine scholarship and reliability in texts that span world literature, drama and poetry, religion, philosophy and politics. Each edition includes perceptive commentary and essential background information to meet the changing needs of readers.

OXFORD WORLD'S CLASSICS

ÉMILE ZOLA

The Ladies' Paradise

Translated with an Introduction and Notes by
BRIAN NELSON

OXFORD
UNIVERSITY PRESS

OXFORD
UNIVERSITY PRESS

Great Clarendon Street, Oxford OX2 6DP

Oxford University Press is a department of the University of Oxford.
It furthers the University's objective of excellence in research, scholarship,
and education by publishing worldwide in

Oxford New York

Athens Auckland Bangkok Bogatá Buenos Aires Calcutta
Cape Town Chennai Dar es Salaam Delhi Florence Hong Kong Istanbul
Karachi Kuala Lumpur Madrid Melbourne Mexico City Mumbai
Nairobi Paris São Paulo Singapore Taipei Tokyo Toronto Warsaw
with associated companies in Berlin Ibadan

Oxford is a registered trade mark of
Oxford University Press in the UK and in certain other countries

Translation, Bibliography, Notes © Brian Nelson 1995
Chronology © Roger Pearson 1993

The moral rights of the author have been asserted

First published as a World's Classics paperback 1995
Resissued as an Oxford World's Classics paperback 1998
Reissued 2008
This TV tie-in edition published 2012

BBC is a trademark of the British Broadcasting Corporation and is used under licence

BBC Logo © BBC 1996

British Library Cataloguing in Publication Data
Data available

Library of Congress Cataloging in Publication Data
Data available

ISBN 978-0-19-967596-8

3

Printed in Great Britain by
Clays Ltd, St Ives plc

CONTENTS

INTRODUCTION

ÉMILE ZOLA was born in Paris on 2 April 1840 of a French mother and an Italian father. At the time of Émile's birth his father, a civil engineer, was trying to secure government approval for the construction of a canal to bring a water supply to Aix-en-Provence. His attempts were successful, and as a result Émile spent his childhood at Aix (the 'Plassans' of his novels), where one of his close school-friends was Paul Cézanne, the painter. When he was 6 his father died suddenly, leaving Madame Zola in a precarious financial situation. In 1858 she moved with her son to Paris, hoping to gain the support of her husband's friends; but this came to nothing and, for a few months in 1860, Zola lived in desperate poverty. At the beginning of 1862 he took a job with the publisher Hachette, rising quickly to the position of advertising manager. After four years with the firm he decided to become a full-time writer. He had already published his first novel, the semi-autobiographical *La Confession de Claude*, in 1865. This book gave him a certain notoriety, which was greatly increased by his vigorous defence of Édouard Manet's paintings in a newspaper review of the Salon of 1866. Zola became the main champion of the Impressionist movement. His literary reputation was further enhanced with the publication in 1867 of *Thérèse Raquin*, a tale of adultery and murder which displayed the powerful atmospheric effects that characterize his later work.

During 1868 Zola conceived the idea of writing a series of novels about a single family, the Rougon-Macquart, whose fortunes would be followed through several generations. The subtitle of the series, 'A Natural and Social History of a Family under the Second Empire', suggests Zola's two interconnected aims: to embody in fiction certain 'scientific' notions about the ways in which human behaviour is determined by heredity and environment; and to use the symbolic possibilities of a family whose heredity is warped to represent critically certain aspects of a diseased society—the decadent and corrupt, yet dynamic and vital, France of the Second Empire (1852–70). The Rougon-

Macquart family is descended from the three children, one legitimate and two illegitimate, of an insane woman, Tante Dide. There are thus three main branches of the family. The first of these, the Rougons, prospers, its members spreading upwards in society to occupy commanding positions in the worlds of government and finance. *His Excellency Eugène Rougon* describes the corrupt political system of Napoleon III, while *The Kill* and *Money* evoke the frenetic contemporary speculation in real estate and stocks. The Macquarts are the working-class members of the family, unbalanced and descended from the alcoholic Antoine Macquart. Members of this branch figure prominently in all of Zola's most powerful novels: *The Belly of Paris*, which uses the central food markets, Les Halles, as a gigantic figuration of the appetites and greed of the bourgeoisie; *L'Assommoir*, a poignant evocation of the lives of the working class in a Paris slum area; *Nana*, the novel of a celebrated prostitute whose sexual power ferments destruction among the Imperial Court; *Germinal*, perhaps Zola's most famous novel, which focuses on a devastating miners' strike on the coalfields of north-eastern France; *The Masterpiece*, the story of a half-mad painter of genius; *Earth*, in which Zola brings an epic sweep to his portrayal of peasant life; *The Beast in Man*, which opposes the technical progress represented by the railways to the physiological fatalities embodied in the homicidal mania of a train driver, Jacques Lantier; and *The Downfall*, which describes the Franco–Prussian War and is the first important war novel in French literature. The second illegitimate branch of the family is the Mourets, some of whom are successful bourgeois adventurers. Octave Mouret is an ambitious philanderer in *Pot-Bouille*, a savagely comic picture of the hypocrisies and adulteries behind the façade of a bourgeois apartment building. Mouret's determined efforts to build a career set him apart from the failures and frustrations of the bourgeois world Zola portrays with such vehemence. In *The Ladies' Paradise*, the effective sequel to *Pot-Bouille*, he is shown making his fortune from women as he creates one of the first big Parisian department stores.

The Ladies' Paradise is an important text, for, whereas *Pot-Bouille* had concentrated on the private lives of the bourgeoisie, its sequel marks Zola's desire to broaden his social perspective and embrace the whole of socio–economic reality through his representation of the world of the department store. The model for Mouret's store is the Bon Marché, Paris's first department store and the largest single department store in the world before 1914.[1] Aristide Boucicaut took over the Bon Marché, a large drapery shop, in 1852 and quickly transformed it into a much larger shop. In 1852 it boasted four departments, twelve employees, and a turnover of 450,000 francs a year. Its turnover rose to 5 million in 1860, 7 million in 1863, 21 million in 1869, 77 million in 1877, more than 80 million in 1882, 123 million in 1888, and over 200 million in 1906. The physical expansion of the store was equally impressive. When Boucicaut stopped building in 1887, it occupied a whole city block. The establishment of the Bon Marché as a *grand magasin* was followed by that of the Bazar de l'Hôtel de Ville in 1854, Les Grands Magasins du Louvre (usually just called Le Louvre) in 1855, Au Coin de la Rue in 1864, Au Printemps in 1865, La Belle Jardinière in 1866–7, La Samaritaine in 1869, and Les Galeries Lafayette in 1895. There were parallel developments of course in the United States and England—Macy's in New York, Marshall Field in Chicago, Wanamaker's in Philadelphia, Selfridge's in London. In his preparation for the novel Zola visited the Bon Marché and Le Louvre, took notes, and consulted with various authorities, including former employees of department stores and the architect Frantz Jourdain, a pioneer designer of this sort of establishment. 'What I want to do in *The Ladies' Paradise*', Zola wrote in his notes, 'is write the poem of modern activity. Hence, a complete shift of philosophy: no more pessimism, first of all. Don't conclude with the stupidity and sadness of life. Instead, conclude with its continual labour, the power and gaiety that comes from its productivity. In a word, go along with the century, express the century, which is a century of action and conquest, of effort in every direction.'[2] Despite the destruction of many of the traditional little family shops, *The Ladies' Para-*

---

[1] For an extremely useful social history of the Bon Marché, see Michael Miller, *The Bon Marché: Bourgeois Culture and the Department Store, 1869–1920* (Princeton, NJ: Princeton University Press, 1981).

[2] Quoted by Henri Mitterand in *Les Rougon-Macquart*, ed. Henri Mitterand, iii (Paris: Gallimard, Bibliothèque de la Pléiade, 1964), 1679 (my translation).

dise is a hymn to modern business, a celebration of the entrepreneurial spirit.

In spite of his scientific attitude Zola's writing is highly romantic: the giant symbols he uses to represent modern society—the city, the market, the machine, the prostitute, the theatre, the stock exchange, the department store—are the visions of a romantic imagination. Everywhere he sees allegories and symbols. The department store in *The Ladies' Paradise* is a symbol of capitalism, the Second Empire, the experience of the city, and the bourgeois family; it is emblematic of commodity culture and new systems of fashion; and it is the site of nineteenth-century sexual attitudes and class relations. The physical space of the store is also social and cultural space. Zola's representation of the illusions that define consumer culture is as subversive as that offered by the German philosopher and cultural critic Walter Benjamin in his 'Arcades Project', an uncompleted but seminal study of the 'phantasmagoria' of urban experience and modern consumerism.[3] This project is as striking and poetic in its images as it is sophisticated and challenging in its analyses. Benjamin's dominant image is the shopping arcade itself, the *passages* built in Paris during the Restoration (1814–30) and the reign of Louis-Philippe (1830–48). The arcades, with their iron and glass roofs, were places for the display and sale of commodities, which they illuminated and enshrined in visions of abundance and luxury which gave the crowds that strolled by no clue as to the conditions of their production. These elegant centres of bourgeois life were like cities, little worlds, in miniature. They housed cafés, brothels, luxury stores, apartments, displays of food, fashion, and furniture, art galleries, bookstores, dioramas, theatres, baths, news-stands, gambling houses, and private clubs. For Benjamin they represented an extraordinary historical stage, illuminated by gaslight (first used in the arcades), through which

[3] Walter Benjamin, *Das Passagen-Werk*, in *Gesammelte Schriften*, v (Frankfurt: Suhrkamp, 1982). For an excellent reconstruction-cum-commentary, see Susan Buck-Morss, *The Dialectics of Seeing: Walter Benjamin and the Arcades Project* (Cambridge, Mass.: The MIT Press, 1989). Marina Warner has characterized Benjamin as 'this century's most acute critic of public lies and the culture of illusion' (Marina Warner, *Monuments and Maidens: The Allegory of the Female Form* (London: Picador, 1987 (1985), 144).

paraded the figures of the crowd: financiers, gamblers, bohemians, *flâneurs*, political conspirators, dandies, prostitutes, criminals, rag-pickers. They were an image of the bourgeois world, a montage of its realities and fantasies, a stage set for an allegorical representation of the origins of modern mass culture.

The development during the Second Empire of the department stores (which made use of the same iron and glass construction as the arcades) marked a further development. If commodities had first promised to fulfil human desires, now they created them: dreams themselves became commodities. In the 1850s the Boucicauts developed a new retailing policy. They realized that, whereas they could make a living from supplying a conscious need on the part of their customers, they could make an infinitely better living by supplying a desire the customer did not know she had until she entered the shop. In this way, the Boucicauts pioneered the idea of the department store as a building purposely designed for fashionable public assembly and which, by the use of display techniques, eye-catching design, and other ploys, replaced the commercial principle of supply with that of consumer seduction.

The mechanisms of seduction, all of which are described in *The Ladies' Paradise*, were multiple. They included advertising (a novel practice in the nineteenth century); the policy of 'free entry' (the freedom to enter the shop and browse without being obliged to buy, by which shopping came to be seen for the first time as a leisure activity); the establishment of fixed prices, which fostered speed and impersonality of purchase; and the system of 'returns'—the easy exchangeability of purchases that failed to satisfy, for other objects of fantasy and desire. In addition, there was the manipulation of space—the creation of deliberate disorder, disconnection, in the layout of the different departments within the store. This obliged the shoppers to travel the length and breadth of the shop to find the items they had come to purchase; as they walked through the shop, they were exposed to the display of other items they had not initially thought to acquire. Above all, there was the seduction of pure spectacle, the seduction of the eye through an almost orgiastic display of visual pleasures enticingly encased in their wrappings and sealed by the surrounding womb of warmth and light. The introduction of sheet glass and electric lighting for the ground-floor window displays not only enticed potential customers (mainly women) into the store; it made window-shopping along the boulevards a standard form of Parisian *flânerie*. To adapt a favourite Benjamin metaphor, based on his awareness that the origin of the arcades was the Eastern bazaar, department stores offered a kind of Arabian Nights world of limitless gratification in time and space. The term 'window-shopping' in French is, of course, suggestively sensual: 'lèche-vitrines'—literally, licking windows. The department store sold not just commodities, but the very process of consumption, transforming the mundane activity of shopping into a sensuous and enjoyable experience. In Zola's novel, Octave Mouret is presented as the Great Seducer. The best window-dresser in Paris, it is he who arouses and orchestrates consumer desire: 'Mouret's sole passion was the conquest of Woman. He wanted her to be queen in his shop; he had built this temple for her in order to hold her at his mercy. His tactics were to intoxicate her with amorous attentions, to trade on her desires' (p. 234).

Mouret's store is a model of the new capitalism, of an economic system based on the principle of circulation, movement, turnover, the constant and increasingly rapid renewal of capital in the form of commodities. Mouret's success is due not only to his refined understanding of the capitalist system (the principles of which he clearly expounds himself), but also to his exploitation of another new system, namely, the integrated transportation network which facilitated travel and the rapid circulation of goods both within the city and between Paris and the rest of the world. The two basic elements of the new transportation system were the railway and the new urban network of wide, straight boulevards. Each plays a role in determining both the conception and the operation of Mouret's department store.

The railway, with its speed and its far-flung network of track, promoted the economic circulation of goods, feeding Mouret's store with an endless supply of fabric from the French provinces and elsewhere. Wolfgang Schivelbusch, in his remarkable study of railway travel in the nineteenth century, has shown how the emergence of new modes of transport, together with the development of commodity culture and the concomitant replacement of use value by exchange value, produced new modes of perception.[4] The relationship between subject and object is no longer stable but evanescent and detached. In a railway journey the speed of the train blurs all foreground objects, often to such an extent that the foreground seems to disappear entirely. Near space is lost and the viewing subject on the train has the sensation of being totally detached from the distant space which contains the objects he can see. And even these distant objects are perceived only evanescently and in a dispersed manner, since the train traveller is unable either to fix the objects as he speeds by or to organize them perceptually.

The perceptions of the railway traveller can be compared with those of the shopper in the department store, in that the physical motion of the shopper, the symbolic motion of the goods (through accelerated turnover), and the presentation of these goods via their commodity (or exchange) value all combine to produce a relationship between subject and object which is analogous to that of the train traveller and the landscape that zooms past his window.[5] The descriptions of the sales in *The Ladies' Paradise*, with their swirling movement and their frenetic circulation of money, goods, and bodies, are the perfect expression of commodity culture, which, as Benjamin and others have pointed out, is a culture of speed, movement, dislocation, disorientation:[6]

The great afternoon rush-hour had arrived, when the overheated machine led the dance of customers, extracting money from their very flesh. In the silk department especially there was a sense of madness . . . In the still air, where the stifling central heating brought out the smell of the materials, the hubbub was increasing, made up of all

4 Wolfgang Schivelbusch, *The Railway Journey: The Industrialization of Time and Space in the 19th Century* (Berkeley, Calif.: University of California Press, 1987 (1977)). See esp. the chapter entitled 'Circulation', 188–97.

5 See ibid. 189.

6 See Stephen Kern, *The Culture of Time and Space*, 1880–1918 (Cambridge, Mass.: Harvard University Press, 1983) ('Speed', 109–30), and Paul Virilio, *Vitesse et politique* (Paris: Galilée, 1977).

sorts of noises—the continuous trampling of feet, the same phrases repeated a hundred times at the counters, gold clinking on the brass of the cash-desks, besieged by a mass of purses, the baskets on wheels with their loads of parcels falling endlessly into the gaping cellars. (pp. 108–9)

Technological change and the accelerated circulation of commodities not only affected man's perceptions of the world but also influenced the way he organized the space in which he lived. Urban planning was informed partly by a desire to accommodate the increasingly rapid circulation of goods and their consumers. Under Napoleon III in the 1850s Baron Haussmann (1809–91), the Prefect of the Seine, launched his massive plan of urban redevelopment for Paris. His modernization of the city by means of broad, straight, strategically placed boulevards which facilitated the movement of troops reflected the counter-revolutionary political needs of the Emperor, providing a fundamental nineteenth-century example of the links between spatial planning and the institutionalization of state power; but its purpose was also to advance the bourgeoisie's business interests by creating a more efficient transport network. Mouret longs to expand his operation so that the Ladies' Paradise will have its entrance and a palatial new façade on one of the grand new boulevards, the Rue du Dix-Décembre. He thus curries favour with the man in charge of the redevelopment, the wealthy and influential Baron Hartmann, whose name, with its phonetic resemblance to Haussmann, is clearly no coincidence. Mouret tries to convince the Baron to develop a section of the new boulevard with an extension of the department store. If he could have found a way, the narrator tells us, he would have made the street run right through his shop (p. 236). And he succeeds in a sense in doing this by the visual openness created by his use of sheet glass and electric lighting for his ground-floor window displays, and by his system of interior traffic circulation which is modelled on Haussmann's network of boulevards.

The department store, the Second Empire, and the modernization of Paris by Haussmann all form part of the same general economy. Just as Mouret is able to provide a 'healthy' retail environment (in both physical and commercial terms) by opening up the space of the store, in contrast to the cramped darkness of the old drapery shops, so Haussmann's opening up of Paris with his network of wide, bright, efficient arteries improved the physical and commercial 'health' of the city. In the modern city, the capital of the world of work, everyone is busy, everything has its function, an organic justification. For Zola, who always identified laziness and idleness with waste, the modern city's beauty comes from its being a space in which whatever has no use has no place. The sight of the city—and by the same token its microcosm the department store—at work is for Zola a beautiful spectacle.

For Michel Serres it is Mouret's understanding of imperialism as shown in his mastery over space, in his ability to use the interior space of his store to his own advantage (creating an environment where he can easily dominate his female subjects), and his ability to draw together under one roof products from all over the world (exploiting the productive capacity of far-flung regions) that accounts for his success: 'Space is necessary—and, I believe, sufficient—for control: kings, tyrants, those who have power, the ruling class, have understood, I think, that they can give up certain things, even the means of production, even energy, *provided that* they keep and maintain complete control over space.'[7] Both Mouret and Louis-Napoleon are masters at controlling space, and thereby at controlling crowds.

Although Zola was no friend of the real Imperial system, his symbol includes those aspects of it which promoted the public good as he saw it. He suggests that the placing of political power in the hands of a benevolent despot (such as Mouret could be, it is suggested, when tempered by the ideas of Denise Baudu, the working–class salesgirl whom he eventually marries) would ensure that certain Imperial preoccupations (such as greater prosperity through greater efficiency) would work to the general good. *The Ladies' Paradise* represents an attempted marriage between bourgeois individualism, rationalized efficiency, and the common good.[8]

Another symbolic (and quintessentially nineteenth-century) aspect of the store is its representation as a gigantic combustion

---

[7] Michel Serres, *Feux et signaux de brume: Zola* (Paris: Grasset, 1975), 293 (my translation).

[8] See Brian Nelson, *Zola and the Bourgeoisie* (London: Macmillan, 1983), 30.

machine, whose moving parts, the laces, the linens, the finery, the displays, seem to gain in life and vitality (as Kristin Ross has pointed out)[9] in proportion to the reification of its clientele and personnel. The first view of the giant is presented through the uplifted eyes of Denise Baudu, freshly arrived from the provinces:

Denise felt that she was watching a machine working at high pressure; its dynamism seeming to reach to the display windows themselves . . . A crowd was looking at them, groups of women were crushing each other in front of them, a real mob, made brutal by covetousness. And these passions in the street were giving life to the materials: the laces shivered, then drooped again, concealing the depths of the shop with an exciting air of mystery; even the lengths of cloth, thick and square, were breathing, exuding a tempting odour, while the overcoats were throwing back their shoulders still more on the dummies, which were acquiring souls, and the huge velvet coat was billowing out, supple and warm, as if on shoulders of flesh and blood, with a heaving breast and quivering hips. But the furnace-like heat with which the shop was ablaze came above all from the selling, from the bustle at the counters, which could be felt behind the walls. There was the continuous roar of the machine at work, of customers crowding into the departments, dazzled by the merchandise, then propelled towards the cash-desk. And it was all regulated and organized with the remorselessness of a machine: the vast horde of women were as if caught in the wheels of an inevitable force. (p. 16)

The giant machine devours, disgorges, consumes, and accelerates to the point of overheating and explosion during the sales. And the master of the machine is Mouret.

In opposition to Mouret, Master of the Machine, Emperor of Signs in his shop, and Great Seducer, stands Denise Baudu, the young working-class girl who is often seen (although I want to question this reading) as the feminist pole of the novel, the representative of the women and the workers. Denise is taken on at the Ladies' Paradise, which, on another level, is represented as a bourgeois 'home' on a hugely magnified, fantastic scale: transformation and multiplication of drawing-rooms and boudoirs, dream-like proliferation of clothing and lingerie, fabulous extension of the powers of the dominant patriarchal figure. This di-

---

[9] Kristin Ross, 'Introduction', Émile Zola, *The Ladies' Paradise* (Berkeley, Calif.: University of California Press, 1992), p. xii.

mension of the store is of central importance, and it would be useful to place it in the general context of nineteenth-century urban life and the meaning of urban life in terms of sexual relations.

As Elizabeth Wilson and others have pointed out, a cause for alarm in the nineteenth century was the way in which urban life undermined patriarchal authority. Prostitution was of course the great fear of the age: it was not only a real and ever present threat, but also (as Zola's *Nana* brilliantly illustrates) a metaphor for disorder and the overturning of the naturalized hierarchies and institutions of society. The prostitute was a 'public woman', but the problem in nineteenth-century urban life was whether every woman in the new, disordered world of the city was not a public woman. The very presence in the public spaces of streets, cafés, and theatres of unattended—that is, unowned—women constituted a threat to male power. Many commentators have described how male bourgeois society sought systems of control and regulation. Bourgeois women were largely excluded from nineteenth-century urban space, while bourgeois men were free to explore urban zones of pleasure such as the restaurant, the theatre, the café, and the brothel. The proliferation of public places of pleasure and leisure created a new kind of public person: the *flâneur*, key figure in the critical literature of modernity and urbanization, and associated with the new urban pastimes of crowd-watching and shopping (including window-shopping). The *flâneur* spends most of his day—to borrow a phrase from Rachel Bowlby—'just looking' at the urban spectacle.[10]

One of the significant features of the department store is that it shows women emerging more and more into the public spaces of the city. It functioned in the same way that the Church had previously done, by providing women with a haven outside the home, in which to sit, think, and find solace. Shopping in the late nineteenth century became a woman's natural way of entering into and occupying the public domain. In that sense the department store represents a transitional social space. Like the arcades, the boulevards, and the cafés, the department store was a

[10] Rachel Bowlby, *Just Looking: Consumer Culture in Dreiser, Gissing and Zola* (New York: Methuen, 1985).

space half-public, half-private, which women—that is, the women shoppers—were able to inhabit quite comfortably. At least for the leisured few, shopping provided the pleasures of looking, socializing, and simply strolling; in the department store a woman, too, could become a *flâneur*. Within the store, women were induced into a dream world in which they enjoyed a sense of freedom from husbands and the restraints of family life. As orthodox religion had once instructed women in the moral codes of daily life, so the department store now delineated a new ethic centred on womanhood and femininity.[11]

But the pleasures of shopping, though half-illusory, were not available to all women—largely for reasons of class. Whereas for bourgeois women the department store was the equivalent of the arcades, a protected place half-way between the home and the street, for working-class women the store was hardly different from the street: whether in the street or in the store, Denise and the other working-class salesgirls are constantly a prey, because of their subordinate social and economic status, to the masculine gaze; and they themselves are also buyable objects. In the Paris of the Second Empire, and indeed the Third Republic, a woman who was not a bourgeoise could not enjoy the pleasure and freedom, albeit limited, of *la flânerie*.

Moreover, although women enjoyed commodification, they were themselves commodified. Mouret, always a figure of power, is not only a kind of capitalist emperor, the man with the Midas touch, the Goldfinger of modern commerce; he is also, as we have seen, the Great Seducer. The store is not just a money-making machine, but, as operated by Mouret, is an instrument of sexual exploitation and domination, a male pleasure-machine: 'They all belonged to him, they were his property, and he belonged to none of them. When he had extracted his fortune and his pleasure from them, he would throw them on the rubbish heap' (p. 77). Mouret proclaims and affirms his virility through

---

[11] I am indebted to the following studies of women and urban experience: Elizabeth Wilson, 'The Invisible Flâneur', *New Left Review*, 191 (1992), 90–110; Janet Wolff, 'The Invisible *Flâneuse*: Women and the Literature of Modernity', in *Feminine Sentences: Essays on Women and Culture* (Cambridge: Polity Press, 1990), 34–50.

his machine, which functions, so to speak, as a condenser and generator of sexual pleasure, enabling him to possess all women simultaneously.

The shop, objects, things, are eroticized, transforming everything for sale into an object of desire. The store becomes not only a harem but a dream-machine, generating limitless sensual fantasies. The rhythmic structure of the descriptions, with their cascading images and rising pitch, suggests loss of control, quasi-sexual abandonment to consumer dreams, as well as mirroring the perpetual expansion that defines the economic principles of consumerism:

The crowd had reached the silk department . . . At the far end of the hall, around one of the small cast-iron columns which supported the glass roof, material was streaming down like a bubbling sheet of water . . . Women pale with desire were leaning over as if to look at themselves. Faced with this wild cataract, they all remained standing there, filled with the secret fear of being caught in the overflow of all this luxury and with an irresistible desire to throw themselves into it and be lost. (pp. 103–4)

The women shoppers themselves are shown as fragmented, reduced to distorted parts of the body, merged with the fabrics and objects in the shop, like modern advertising images: 'the mirrors made the departments recede further into the distance, reflecting the displays together with patches of the public—faces in reverse, bits of shoulders and arms' (p. 250). Furthermore the vocabulary of sexual dominance and exploitation is accompanied by images marked by a great deal of violence directed against women. Images of decapitation and pierced flesh are common. On the way up the staircase of the Ladies' Paradise, there is a curious and disturbing image of rows of mannequins, again headless: 'each one had a little wooden handle, like the handle of a dagger, stuck in the red flannel, which seemed to be bleeding where the neck had been severed' (p. 253). Woman for Mouret is reduced to a sexually throbbing body, a body that is nothing more, for him, than a source of money, a figure for money. The first window display Denise sees when she arrives in Paris features a row of mannequins, mirrored to infinity, with price tags instead of heads. The women shoppers lose their heads in that they undergo a euphoric loss of self; they are driven crazy, they go mad in ecstasies of buying, succumbing in spectacular fashion to false consciousness. In that sense they become mere bodies, manipulated and mindless.

The description of the mannequins focuses the commodity fetishism that figures so prominently in the novel. The psycho-analytical reading of erotic fetishism is usually attributed to Freud, but in fact the decisive introduction of the notion of the fetish into the psychological field took place some decades earlier in the work of Alfred Binet (whom Freud acknowledged) in a paper published in the *Revue philosophique* in 1877. Like Freud, Binet was an observer of Charcot's clinical practice and acquainted with Charcot's famous focus on hysteria. Hysteria is not irrelevant to the reaction of the fetishist and is hardly irrelevant to the behaviour of the women shoppers with their erotic fascination with the commodity objects in Mouret's store.

In Denise's first glimpse of the display windows she sees silk stockings 'displaying the rounded outline of calves', and the stockings' flesh colour and satiny texture give them 'the softness of a blonde woman's skin' (p. 5). After the first of the three sales, the lace and lingerie scattered on the floors and counters 'gave the impression that an army of women had undressed there haphazardly in a wave of desire' (p. 117). An endless array of lingerie seems strewn everywhere during the climactic sale of the final chapter, 'as if an army of pretty girls had undressed as they went from department to department, down to their satiny skin'. The mannequins themselves seem to have a 'disturbing lewdness' (p. 409).

As Peter Brooks has pointed out, the clothing—the lingerie and the lace—that speaks of the woman's erotic body is offered for sale to women themselves: there are very few male shoppers in the Ladies' Paradise. Brooks comments:

While this might seem to suggest a primal narcissism of women, or an invitation to them to possess their own bodies, there is rather an alien-ation of women from their bodies, which have been taken over by the (male-owned and -managed) market economy, defined and fetishized by that economy, and offered back to women in piecemeal form, through the cash nexus . . . Mouret's establishment figures a culture in which a woman, through the relay of the economy, commercial and erotic, established by man, is forced to accept herself as other; she is foreclosed from her own desire, never in full possession of her own body.[12]

In that sense, the women are not only headless but, paradoxically, bodyless too.

Denise is the only one of the salesgirls who refuses to be seduced, refuses to be commodified. Having refused Mouret's advances, she wins his heart; the masterful Mouret is gradually brought to his knees by his love for one of his own shop assistants. But the price of Denise's hand in marriage is the introduction of humanitarian reforms in the running of the store, for the dream-machine depends on a brutal system of labour organization. The role of Denise is thus to humanize the store, to harmonize its economic functions with the moral qualities associated with femininity. The romance plot has been read by feminist critics as an allegory of feminization and female revenge, transcendence of the commodity, and the achievement of autonomy;[13] but what is more striking is the bourgeois ideology, the enduring patriarchal structure, that informs the humanization and domestication of Mouret. Although Denise breaks the mould of masculine domination, her influence and independence are only achieved in terms of her critical presence within the existing system. She argues for her reforms in the spirit of sound business practice, and in rewriting Mouret's male narrative of sexual and economic exploitation, she uses the discourse of bourgeois ideology—the discourse of reason, logic, control, and order:

She could never do anything herself, or watch a task being carried out, without being obsessed with the need to put method into it, to improve the system . . . She would plead the cause of the cogs in this great machine, not for sentimental reasons, but with arguments based on the employers' own interests. (p. 355)

[12] Peter Brooks, *Body Work: Objects of Desire in Modern Narrative* (Cambridge, Mass.: Harvard University Press, 1983), 154.

[13] See e.g. Naomi Schor, 'Devant le château: femmes, marchandises, et modernité dans *Au Bonheur des Dames*', in Philippe Hamon and Jean-Pierre Leduc-Adine (eds.), *Mimésis et sémiosis: littérature et représentation* (Paris: Nathan, 1993), 179–86.

The domestication of Mouret and his machine is identified, moreover, with an idealization of the bourgeois family, the final figuration of the store. As Michelle Perrot has written: 'The founders of the large department stores raised the "happy household" to the pinnacle of honor.'[14] At the beginning, the store is seen as a threat to the family, that is, to the small family business represented by the Baudus (victims of the economic Darwinism of the new system); but in the end the family is restored, so to speak, in a form better adapted to the new capitalism—in the form of Octave and Denise, the capitalist and worker united as man and wife, watching paternally over their huge, happy family of employees.

The bourgeois family is thus the social family, indeed the corporate family/society, and the dream-machine assumes ideological significance if we identify its 'dream state' with the insidious blurring of social difference, the suppression of oppositional relations within the system, the suppression of the political. As Pierre Bourdieu points out in *Language and Symbolic Power*,[15] the suppression of signs of social conflict is a tactic of dominant forces in liberal societies. The department store played a leading role in the marketing of life-styles that simultaneously demarcated and blurred class distinctions, encouraging everyone to aspire to a middle-class way of life. Whereas, for the working class, the displays of luxury were signs of their own misery, of the fact that the new social wealth which their own labour was producing had become the source of their impoverishment, there was a danger that the glamour of the scene would blind them to the reality of their self-alienation, that this new worship of commodities and the spectacle of their display would function, like the old religion, as an opiate of the masses. As we have seen, commodities possess a fetish character, they cast a spell; they are dream-symbols of a world of material abundance. Thus, the false harmony of this society is closely related to the formidable structures of manipulation that define modern consumer

---

[14] Michelle Perrot (ed.), *A History of Private Life*, v: *From the Fires of Revolution to the Great War* (Cambridge, Mass.: Harvard University Press, 1990), 121.

[15] Pierre Bourdieu, *Language and Symbolic Power* (Cambridge: Polity Press in association with Basil Blackwell, 1991) (originally published as *Ce que parler veut dire* (Paris: Fayard, 1982)).

culture. The department store, in Zola's depiction of it, is an ambiguous symbol of progress. It helped women to establish themselves historically in the public sphere, and it may appear to have increased the customer's power and autonomy; but, as Zola shows, the new codes of social behaviour and social discourses which it entailed for the shopper simultaneously organized a powerful network of constraints, providing a mere illusion of freedom and fulfilment. The department store, in its embodiment of consumer culture, was—and is—a giant, precision-made dream-machine.

TRANSLATOR'S NOTE

THE text on which the translation is based is that included in vol. iii of Henri Mitterand's Bibliothèque de la Pléiade edition of *Les Rougon-Macquart* (Paris: Gallimard, 1964), although a number of other editions were consulted.

The main challenge facing any translator of Zola is how to capture the rhythm, balance, and colour of the many descriptive passages, with their proliferating detail. I hope I have succeeded in capturing the spirit of these passages without sacrificing precision. I hope also that I have written dialogue that is unstilted. My task was greatly facilitated by the help of Jocelyne Mohamudally and Marie-Rose Auguste, to whom I am most grateful. My thanks too, for different reasons, to Ilona Chessid, Joanne Finkelstein, Françoise Gaillard, Pamela Genova, and Rosemary Lloyd.

SELECT BIBLIOGRAPHY

The Ladies' Paradise (Au Bonheur des Dames) was first published in book form by the Librairie Charpentier in Paris in 1883 (having been serialized in *Le Gil Blas* between 17 December 1882 and 1 March 1883). It is included in volume iii of Henri Mitterand's superb scholarly edition of *Les Rougon-Macquart* in the 'Bibliothèque de la Pléiade' (Paris: Gallimard, 1964). Paperback editions exist in the following popular collections: GF-Flammarion (ed. Colette Becker, Paris, 1971); Folio (ed. Henri Mitterand, Paris, 1980); Livre de Poche (ed. Bernadette and Auguste Dezalay, Paris, 1984); Presses Pocket (ed. Robert Sctrick and Claude Aziza, Paris, 1990). The University of California Press reissued in 1992 the old nineteenth-century (1886) translation of the novel, with an introduction by Kristin Ross.

General studies of Zola and Naturalism in English include:

Baguley, David (ed.), *Critical Essays on Émile Zola* (Boston: G. K. Hall & Co., 1986).

Baguley, David, *Naturalist Fiction: The Entropic Vision* (Cambridge: Cambridge University Press, 1990).

Hemmings, F. W. J., *Émile Zola* (2nd edn., Oxford: Oxford University Press, 1966).

Lethbridge, R. and T. Keefe (eds.), *Zola and the Craft of Fiction* (Leicester: Leicester University Press, 1990).

Schor, Naomi, *Zola's Crowds* (Baltimore: Johns Hopkins University Press, 1978).

Walker, Philip, *Zola* (Routledge & Kegan Paul, 1985).

Wilson, Angus, *Émile Zola: An Introductory Study of his Novels* (London: Secker & Warburg, 1952; rev. 1964).

Articles and chapters of books in English on The Ladies' Paradise *include:*

Bell, David, 'The Play of Fashion: *Au Bonheur des Dames*', in *Models of Power: Politics and Economics in Zola's 'Rougon-Macquart'* (Lincoln, Nebr.: University of Nebraska Press, 1988), 96–124.

Bowlby, Rachel, ' "Traffic in her Desires": Zola's *Au Bonheur des Dames*', in *Just Looking: Consumer Culture in Dreiser, Gissing and Zola* (New York: Methuen, 1985), 66–82.

Brooks, Peter, *Body Work: Objects of Desire in Modern Narrative* (Cambridge, Mass.: Harvard University Press, 1993), 149–54.

Felski, Rita, 'Imagined Pleasures: The Erotics and Aesthetics of Consumption', in *The Gender of Modernity* (Cambridge, Mass.: Harvard University Press, forthcoming 1995).

Gay, Peter, *The Bourgeois Experience: Victoria to Freud*, ii: *The Tender Passion* (Oxford : Oxford University Press, 1986), 312–19.

Kamm, Lewis, *The Object in Zola's 'Rougon-Macquart'* (Madrid: José Porrúa Turanzas, 1978), 8–25.

Niess, Robert J., 'Zola's *Au Bonheur des Dames*: The Making of a Symbol', in Marcel Tétel (ed.), *Symbolism and Modern Literature: Studies in Honor of Wallace Fowlie* (Durham, NC: Duke University Press, 1978), 130–50.

Saisselin, Remy G., 'Enter Woman: The Department Store as Cultural Space', in *The Bourgeois and the Bibelot* (New Brunswick: Rutgers University Press, 1984), 31–49.

Viti, Robert M., 'A Woman's Time, a Lady's Place: *Nana* and *Au Bonheur des Dames*', *Symposium*, 44/4 (Winter 1990–1), 291–300.

On the background of the department store and consumer culture generally, the following are very useful:

Abelson, Elaine S., *When Ladies Go A-thieving: Middle-Class Shoplifters in the Victorian Department Store* (Oxford: Oxford University Press, 1989).

Adburgham, Alison, *Shops and Shopkeeping, 1800–1914: Where and in What Manner the Well-Dressed Englishwoman Bought her Clothes* (London: George Allen & Unwin, 1981).

Bowlby, Rachel, *Shopping with Freud* (London: Routledge, 1993).

Campbell, Colin, *The Romantic Ethic and the Spirit of Modern Consumerism* (Oxford: Basil Blackwell, 1987).

Chaney, David, 'The Department Store as a Cultural Form', *Theory, Culture and Society*, 1/3 (1983), 22–31.

Featherstone, Mike, *Consumer Culture & Postmodernism* (London: Sage, 1991).

Finkelstein, Joanna, *The Fashioned Self* (Oxford: Polity Press, 1992).

Friedberg, Anne, *Window Shopping: Cinema and Postmodernism* (Berkeley, Calif.: University of California Press, 1993).

Lancaster, W., *The Department Store: A Social History* (London: Pinter Publishers, 1992).

McCracken, Grant, *Culture and Consumption: New Approaches to the Symbolic Character of Consumer Goods and Activities* (Bloomington, Ind.: Indiana University Press, 1990).

Miller, Michael, *The 'Bon Marché': Bourgeois Culture and the Department Store, 1869–1920* (Princeton, NJ: Princeton University Press, 1981).

Morris, Meaghan, 'Things to Do with Shopping Centres', in Susan Sheridan (ed.), *Grafts: Feminist Cultural Criticism* (London: Verso, 1988), 193–225.

Mukerji, Chandra, *From Graven Images: Patterns of Modern Materialism* (New York: Columbia University Press, 1983).

Reekie, Gail, *Temptations: Sex, Selling and the Department Store* (Sydney: Allen & Unwin, 1993).

Sennett, Richard, *The Fall of Public Man* (New York: Vintage, 1974), 141–6.

Shields, Rob (ed.), *Lifestyle Shopping: The Subject of Consumption* (London: Routledge, 1992).

Williams, Rosalind, *Dream Worlds: Mass Consumption in Late Nineteenth-Century France* (Berkeley, Calif.: University of California Press, 1982).

Wilson, Elizabeth, *Adorned in Dreams: Fashion and Modernity* (Berkeley: University of California Press, 1985).

Further Reading in Oxford World's Classics

Zola, Émile, *L'Assommoir*, trans. Margaret Mauldon, ed. Robert Lethbridge.

—— *The Belly of Paris*, trans. Brian Nelson.

—— *La Bête humaine*, trans. Roger Pearson.

—— *The Fortune of the Rougons*, trans. Brian Nelson.

—— *Germinal*, trans. Peter Collier, ed. Robert Lethbridge.

—— *The Kill*, trans. Brian Nelson.

—— *The Masterpiece*, trans. Thomas Walton, revised by Roger Pearson.

—— *Nana*, trans. Douglas Parmée.

—— *Pot Luck*, trans. Brian Nelson.

—— *Thérèse Raquin*, trans. Andrew Rothwell.

A CHRONOLOGY OF ÉMILE ZOLA

1840   (2 April) Born in Paris, the only child of Francesco Zola (b. 1795), an Italian engineer, and Émilie, née Aubert (b. 1819), the daughter of a glazier. The Naturalist novelist was later proud that 'zolla' in Italian means 'clod of earth'

1843   Family moves to Aix-en-Provence

1847   (27 March) Death of father from pneumonia following a chill caught while supervising work on his scheme to supply Aix-en-Provence with drinking water

1852–   Becomes a boarder at the Collège Bourbon at Aix. Friendship with Baptistin Baille and Paul Cézanne. Zola, not Cézanne, wins the school prize for drawing

1858   (February) Leaves Aix to settle in Paris with his mother (who had preceded him in December). Offered a place and bursary at the Lycée Saint-Louis. (November) Falls ill with 'brain fever' (typhoid) and convalescence is slow

1859   Fails his *baccalauréat* twice

1860   (Spring) Is found employment as a copy-clerk but abandons it after two months, preferring to eke out an existence as an impecunious writer in the Latin Quarter of Paris

1861   Cézanne follows Zola to Paris, where he meets Camille Pissarro, fails the entrance examination to the École des Beaux-Arts, and returns to Aix in September

1862   (February) Taken on by Hachette, the well-known publishing house, at first in the dispatch office and subsequently as head of the publicity department. (31 October) Naturalized as a French citizen. Cézanne returns to Paris and stays with Zola

1863   (31 January) First literary article published. (1 May) Manet's *Déjeuner sur l'herbe* exhibited at the Salon des Refusés, which Zola visits with Cézanne

1864   (October) *Tales for Ninon*

1865   *Claude's Confession*. A *succès de scandale* thanks to its bedroom scenes. Meets future wife Alexandrine-Gabrielle Meley (b. 1839), the illegitimate daughter of teenage parents who soon separated, and whose mother died in September 1849

1866   Forced to resign his position at Hachette (salary: 200 francs a month) and becomes a literary critic on the recently launched daily *L'Événement* (salary: 500 francs a month). Self-styled 'humble disciple' of Hippolyte Taine. Writes a series of provocative articles condemning the official Salon Selection Committee, expressing reservations about Courbet, and praising Manet and Monet. Begins to frequent the Café Guerbois in the Batignolles quarter of Paris, the meeting-place of the future Impressionists. Antoine Guillemet takes Zola to meet Manet. Summer months spent with Cézanne at Bennecourt on the Seine. (15 November) *L'Événement* suppressed by the authorities

1867   (November) *Thérèse Raquin*

1868   (April) Preface to second edition of *Thérèse Raquin*. (May) Manet's portrait of Zola exhibited at the Salon. (December) *Madeleine Férat*. Begins to plan for the Rougon-Macquart series of novels

1868–70 Working as journalist for a number of different newspapers

1870   (31 May) Marries Alexandrine in a registry office. (September) Moves temporarily to Marseilles because of the Franco-Prussian War

1871   Political reporter for *La Cloche* (in Paris) and *Le Sémaphore de Marseille*. (March) Returns to Paris. (October) Publishes *The Fortune of the Rougons*, the first of the twenty novels making up the Rougon-Macquart series

1872   *The Kill*

1873   (April) *The Belly of Paris*

1874   (May) *The Conquest of Plassans*. First independent Impressionist exhibition. (November) *Further Tales for Ninon*

1875   Begins to contribute articles to the Russian newspaper *Vestnik Evropy* (*European Herald*). (April) *The Sin of the Abbé Mouret*

1876   (February) *His Excellency Eugène Rougon*. Second Impressionist exhibition

1877   (February) *L'Assommoir*

1878   Buys a house at Médan on the Seine, 40 kilometres west of Paris. (June) *A Page of Love*

1880   (March) *Nana*. (May) *Les Soirées de Médan* (an anthology of short stories by Zola and some of his Naturalist 'disciples', including Maupassant). (8 May) Death of Flaubert. (September) First of a series of articles for *Le Figaro*. (17 October) Death of his mother. (December) *The Experimental Novel*

1882   (April) *Pot-Bouille*. (3 September) Death of Turgenev

1883   (13 February) Death of Wagner. (March) *The Ladies' Paradise* (*Au Bonheur des Dames*). (30 April) Death of Manet

1884   (March) *La Joie de vivre*. Preface to catalogue of Manet exhibition

1885   (March) *Germinal*. (12 May) Begins writing *The Masterpiece* (*L'Œuvre*). (22 May) Death of Victor Hugo. (23 December) First instalment of *The Masterpiece* appears in *Le Gil Blas*

1886   (27 March) Final instalment of *The Masterpiece*, which is published in book form in April

1887   (18 August) Denounced as an onanistic pornographer in the *Manifesto of the Five* in *Le Figaro*. (November) *Earth*

1888   (October) *The Dream*. Jeanne Rozerot becomes his mistress

1889   (20 September) Birth of Denise, daughter of Zola and Jeanne

1890   (March) *The Beast in Man*

1891   (March) *Money*. (April) Elected President of the Société des Gens de Lettres. (25 September) Birth of Jacques, son of Zola and Jeanne

1892   (June) *The Débâcle*

1893   (July) *Doctor Pascal*, the last of the Rougon-Macquart novels. Fêted on a visit to London

1894   (August) *Lourdes*, the first novel of the trilogy *Three Cities*. (22 December) Dreyfus found guilty by a court martial

1896   (May) *Rome*

1898   (13 January) 'J'accuse', his article in defence of Dreyfus, published in *L'Aurore*. (21 February) Found guilty of libelling the Minister of War and given the maximum sentence of one year's imprisonment and a fine of 3,000 francs. Appeal for retrial granted on a technicality. (March) *Paris*. (23 May) Retrial delayed. (18 July) Leaves for England instead of attending court

1899   (4 June) Returns to France. (October) *Fecundity*, the first of his *Four Gospels*

1901   (May) *Toil*, the second 'Gospel'

1902   (29 September) Dies of fumes from his bedroom fire, the chimney having been capped either by accident or anti-Dreyfusard design. Wife survives. (5 October) Public funeral

1903   (March) *Truth*, the third 'Gospel', published posthumously. *Justice* was to be the fourth

1908   (4 June) Remains transferred to the Panthéon

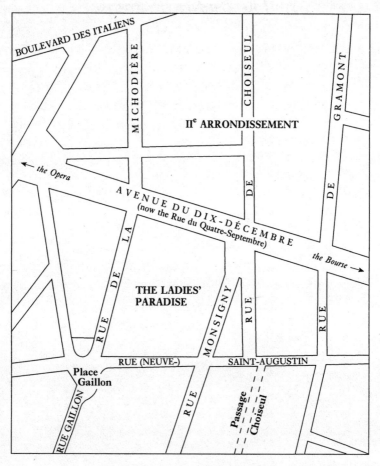

The Ladies' Paradise: plan of the area

The Ladies' Paradise

CHAPTER 1

DENISE had come on foot from the Gare Saint-Lazare. She and her two brothers had arrived on a train from Cherbourg and had spent the night on the hard bench of a third-class carriage. She was holding Pépé by the hand, and Jean was walking behind her, all three exhausted from the journey, frightened and lost in the midst of the vast city of Paris. They kept looking up at the houses, and at every intersection they asked the way to the Rue de la Michodière, where their uncle Baudu lived. But on arriving in the Place Gaillon, the young girl suddenly stopped in surprise.

'Oh!' she said, 'look at that, Jean!'

And they stood there, huddled together, all in black, in the mourning clothes bought on their father's death. Denise, rather skinny for her twenty years, and looking down-at-heel, was carrying a small parcel, while on her other side her little brother of five was clinging to her arm; her other brother, a strapping youth of sixteen, stood looking over her shoulder, his arms dangling.

'Well!' she resumed, after a pause. 'There's a shop for you!'

They were at the corner of the Rue de la Michodière and the Rue Neuve-Saint-Augustin,* in front of a drapery shop, the windows of which, on that mild, pale October day, were bursting with bright colours. Eight o'clock was striking at the church of Saint-Roch, and the streets were deserted except for early risers, office workers hurrying to their desks and housewives scurrying to the shops. Two shop assistants, standing on a step-ladder outside the door, had just finished hanging up some woollen goods, while in the window in the Rue Neuve-Saint-Augustin another assistant, on hands and knees and with his back turned, was delicately folding a piece of blue silk. The shop, still waiting for its customers—the staff themselves had only just arrived— was buzzing inside like a beehive coming to life.

'I say!' said Jean. 'That beats Valognes . . . Your shop wasn't as grand as that.'

Denise nodded. She had spent two years in Valognes, at Cornaille's, the main draper in the town; and this shop which

had suddenly appeared before her, this building which seemed
so enormous, brought a lump to her throat and held her rooted
to the spot, excited, fascinated, oblivious to everything else. The
high plate-glass door, facing the Place Gaillon, reached the
mezzanine floor and was surrounded by elaborate decorations
covered with gilding. Two allegorical figures, two laughing
women with bare breasts thrust forward, were unrolling a scroll
bearing the inscription: *The Ladies' Paradise*. The shop windows
stretched along the Rue de la Michodière and the Rue Neuve-
Saint-Augustin, where, apart from the corner house, they occupied four other houses which had recently been bought and
converted, two on the left and two on the right. With its series of
perspectives, with the display on the ground floor and the plate-
glass windows of the mezzanine floor, behind which could be
seen all the intimate life of the various departments, the spectacle
seemed to Denise to be endless. Upstairs a girl in a silk dress was
sharpening a pencil, while near her two other girls were unfolding some velvet coats.

'The Ladies' Paradise,' read Jean with his soft laugh—the
laugh of a handsome adolescent who had already had an affair
with a woman in Valognes. 'That's nice, isn't it? That must pull
the crowds!'

But Denise stood transfixed before the display at the main
door. There, outside in the street, on the pavement itself, was a
mountain of cheap goods, placed at the entrance as a bait, bargains which stopped the women as they passed by. It all cascaded
down: pieces of woollen material and fabric, merino, cheviot,
flannelette, were falling from the mezzanine floor, flapping like
flags, their neutral tones—slate grey, navy blue, olive green—
broken up by the white of the price cards. Close by, framing the
doorway, strips of fur were hanging down, straight bands for
dress trimmings, the fine ash of squirrel, the pure snow of
swansdown, imitation ermine and imitation sable made of rabbit.
And below this, on racks and tables, in the middle of a pile of
remnants, there was a profusion of knitted goods being sold for
a song, gloves and woollen scarves, hooded capes, cardigans, a
whole winter display of many colours, mottled, dyed, striped,
with bleeding stains of red. Denise saw a piece of tartan at forty-
five centimes, strips of American mink at one franc, and mittens
at twenty-five centimes. It was a giant fairground display, as if

the shop were bursting and throwing its surplus stock into the street.

Uncle Baudu was forgotten. Even Pépé, who had not let go of his sister's hand, was staring with wide-open eyes. A carriage forced all three of them to leave the middle of the square; mechanically they walked down the Rue Neuve-Saint-Augustin, past the shop windows, stopping again in front of each fresh display. First they were attracted by a complicated arrangement: at the top, umbrellas, placed obliquely, seemed to form the roof of some rustic hut, beneath which, suspended from rods and displaying the rounded outline of calves, were silk stockings, some strewn with bunches of roses, others of every hue—black net, red with embroidered clocks, flesh-coloured ones with a satiny texture which had the softness of a blonde woman's skin; lastly, on the backcloth of the shelves, gloves were symmetrically arranged, their fingers elongated, their palms as delicate as those of a Byzantine virgin, with the stiff, seemingly adolescent grace of women's clothes which have never been worn. But it was the last window, above all, which held their attention. A display of silks, satins, and velvets spread out before them in a supple, shimmering range of the most delicate flower tones: at the top were the velvets, of deepest black and as white as curds; lower down were the satins, pink and blue, with bright folds fading into infinitely tender pallors; lower down still were the silks, all the colours of the rainbow, pieces rolled into shell shapes, folded as if round a drawn-in waist, brought to life by the knowing hands of the shop assistants; and, between each motif, between each coloured phrase of the display, there ran a discreet accompaniment, a delicate gathered strand of cream-coloured foulard. And in colossal piles at each end were the two silks for which the shop held exclusive rights, the Paris-Paradise and the Cuir-d'Or, exceptional items that were to revolutionize the drapery trade.

'Oh! Look at that faille at five francs sixty!' murmured Denise, amazed at the Paris-Paradise.

Jean was beginning to feel bored. He stopped a passer-by.

'Could you tell us where to find the Rue de la Michodière, sir?'

The man pointed it out as the first street on the right, whereupon they all retraced their steps round the shop. But, as she turned into the street, Denise was struck again by one of the shop windows, which contained a display of ladies' clothes. She had had special responsibility for the clothing section at Cornaille's in Valognes, but she had never seen anything like this! She was rooted to the pavement in admiration. At the back, a long scarf worked in Bruges lace, and costing a considerable amount, was spread out like an altar cloth, its two reddish-white wings unfurled; flounces of Alençon lace were strewn like garlands; then there was a cascade of every kind of lace—Mechlin, Valenciennes, Brussels appliqué, Venetian rose-point—streaming down like a snowfall. To the right and left, rolls of cloth formed dark columns, which made the distant tabernacle seem even further away. And there in this chapel built for the worship of woman's beauty and grace were the clothes: in the centre was a most striking item, a velvet coat trimmed with silver fox; on one side was a silk cloak lined with Siberian squirrel; on the other side was a cloth overcoat edged with cock's feathers; and finally some evening wraps in white cashmere and white quilting, decorated with swansdown or chenille. There was something for every whim, from evening wraps at twenty-nine francs to the velvet coat priced at eighteen hundred francs. The dummies' round bosoms swelled out the material, their wide hips exaggerated the narrow waists, and their missing heads were replaced by large price tags with pins stuck through them into the red bunting round the collars, while mirrors on either side of the windows had been skilfully arranged to reflect the dummies, multiplying them endlessly, seeming to fill the street with these beautiful women for sale with huge price tags where their heads should have been.

'They're amazing!' murmured Jean, who could think of no other way of expressing his feelings.

Suddenly he had become motionless again, his mouth open. All this luxurious femininity was making him pink with pleasure. He had the beauty of a girl, beauty which he seemed to have stolen from his sister—dazzling skin, curly auburn hair, lips and eyes moist with love. By his side, Denise, in her astonishment, looked even thinner, her mouth too large in her long face, her complexion already sallow beneath her light-coloured head of hair. Pépé, blond too with the fairness of childhood, clung closer to her, as if overcome by an anxious need for affection, disturbed and delighted by the beautiful ladies in the shop window. These three fair-haired figures poorly clad in black, the sad young girl between the pretty child and the handsome youth, were so conspicuous and so charming as they stood there on the pavement that passers-by turned round and smiled at them.

A fat man with white hair and a big yellowish face, standing in a shop doorway at the other end of the street, had been looking at them for some time. He had been standing there with bloodshot eyes and pursed lips, beside himself with rage at the displays at the Ladies' Paradise, when the sight of the young girl and her brothers completed his exasperation. What were they doing there, those three simpletons, gaping like that at a charlatan's silly concoctions?

'But what about Uncle?' asked Denise suddenly, as if waking up with a start.

'We're in the Rue de la Michodière,' said Jean. 'He must live somewhere near here.'

They raised their heads and looked about them. Then, just in front of them, above the fat man, they noticed a green signboard, its yellow letters discoloured by the rain: *Au Vieil Elbeuf, drapery and flannels, Baudu (formerly Hauchecorne)*. The house, coated with ancient, mildewed whitewash, looked very squat next to the tall Louis XIV mansions, and had only three front windows; and these windows, square and without shutters, were decorated merely with an iron railing, two crossed bars. But what Denise found most striking among all this bareness, her eyes still full of the bright displays at the Ladies' Paradise, was the shop on the ground floor, crushed by a low ceiling, topped by a very low mezzanine floor, with prison-like, half-moon shaped windows. To the right and left, woodwork of the same colour as the signboard—bottle green, shaded by time with ochre and pitch— surrounded two deep-set windows, black and dusty, in which the heaped-up goods could hardly be seen. The door, which was ajar, seemed to lead into the dank gloom of a cellar.

'This is it,' said Jean.

'Well, we'd better go in,' declared Denise. 'Come on, Pépé.'

But all three were nervous, suddenly shy. When their father had died, a victim of the same fever which had carried off their mother a month earlier, their uncle Baudu, overwhelmed by this double bereavement, had written to his niece that there would always be room for her in his house if she should ever wish to try her fortune in Paris; but this letter had been written almost a year ago, and the young girl now felt sorry that she had left Valognes on the spur of the moment, without warning her uncle. He did not know them at all, for he had never set foot in Valognes again since he had left, as a boy, to become a junior assistant in the drapery shop of Monsieur Hauchecorne, whose daughter he had later married.

'Monsieur Baudu?' asked Denise, finally bringing herself to speak to the fat man, who was still looking at them, surprised at their behaviour.

'That's me,' he answered.

Denise blushed deeply and stammered:

'Oh, thank goodness! I'm Denise, this is Jean, and this is Pépé . . . You see, we did come, Uncle.'

Baudu seemed stunned. His big bloodshot eyes wavered in his yellow face and he spoke slowly and with difficulty. It was evident that his thoughts were miles away from this family which had suddenly descended on him out of the blue.

'What's this! What's this! You here!' he repeated several times. 'But you were in Valognes! Why aren't you in Valognes?'

In her gentle voice, which was trembling a little, she had to explain to him. After the death of their father, who had squandered every penny he had in his dye-works, she had acted as a mother to the two children. The little she earned at Cornaille's had been quite insufficient to keep the three of them. Jean had been working with a cabinet-maker who repaired antique furniture, but he wasn't paid a penny for it. However, he had developed a taste for old things: he carved figures in wood. In fact, one day he had found a piece of ivory and had amused himself by making a head out of it which a gentleman staying in the town had seen and admired; and it was this gentleman who had made them decide to leave Valognes by finding a job for Jean in Paris with an ivory-carver.

'You see, Uncle, Jean will start his apprenticeship with his new employer tomorrow. They don't want any money from me, and they'll give him board and lodging . . . So I thought that

Pépé and I would be able to manage. We can't be worse off than we were in Valognes.'

She did not mention Jean's love-affair, letters written to the young daughter of a local nobleman, kisses exchanged over a wall, quite a scandal which had made her decide to leave; and she had accompanied her brother to Paris above all to watch over him, for she felt maternal fears for this big child, who was so handsome and gay and irresistible to women.

Uncle Baudu could not get over his surprise. He began to repeat his questions. However, when he heard what she told him about her brothers, he used the familiar second person singular.

'So your father didn't leave you anything? I really thought he still had a bit left. Oh, I told him often enough in my letters not to take that dye-works! He had a good heart, but no head for business . . . And you were left with these lads on your hands, you had to feed these youngsters!'

His bilious face had lightened, and his eyes were no longer bloodshot as when he had been looking at the Ladies' Paradise. Suddenly he noticed that he was blocking the doorway.

'Well,' he said. 'Come in, now that you're here . . . Come in, it's better than gaping at that nonsense.'

And having directed a last furious scowl at the displays opposite, he made way for the children and went into the shop, calling his wife and daughter as he did so.

'Elizabeth, Geneviève, come down, there are some people here to see you!'

But the gloom of the shop made Denise and the boys hesitate. Blinded by the daylight of the street, they were blinking as if on the brink of an unknown chasm, feeling the ground with their feet with an instinctive fear of some treacherous step. Clinging even closer together in their vague fear, the little boy still clutching the girl's skirts and the big boy behind, they made their entrance gracefully, smiling and nervous. The bright morning light made the black silhouettes of their mourning clothes stand out, and a slanting ray of light gilded their fair hair.

'Come in, come in,' repeated Baudu.

In a few brief sentences he explained everything to his wife and daughter. Madame Baudu was a little woman wasted by anaemia, and quite white, with white hair, white eyes, white lips.

Geneviève, in whom her mother's physical degeneration was even more pronounced, had the debilitated, colourless appearance of a plant left to grow in the dark. And yet she had a melancholy charm which she owed to her magnificent black hair.

'Come in,' said the two women in their turn. 'Welcome!'

And they made Denise sit down behind a counter. Pépé immediately climbed on to his sister's lap, while Jean, leaning against some panelling, kept close to her. Beginning to feel more at ease, they looked round at the shop, their eyes getting used to the darkness. Now they could see it, a low ceiling blackened with smoke, oak counters shiny with use, ancient show-cases with strong iron hinges. Bales of dark-coloured goods reached up to the beams. The smell of cloth and dyes, a sharp, chemical smell, seemed to be intensified by the dampness of the floorboards. At the back of the shop two male assistants and a girl were putting away pieces of white flannel.

'Perhaps this little chap would like something to eat?' said Madame Baudu, smiling at Pépé.

'No, thank you,' replied Denise, 'we had a cup of milk in a café opposite the station.'

And, as Geneviève was looking at the small parcel she had put on the floor, she added:

'I left our trunk there too.'

She was blushing, for she knew that in polite society people did not turn up out of the blue like that. Even on board the train, as it was leaving Valognes, she had felt full of regrets; and that was why, on their arrival, she had left the trunk at the station and given the children their breakfast.

'Look,' said Baudu suddenly, 'let's be brief and to the point . . . I did write to you, it's true, but that was a year ago; and you see, my dear, business hasn't been going at all well, for a year . . .'

He stopped, choked with an emotion he did not wish to show. Madame Baudu and Geneviève, with a resigned look, had lowered their eyes.

'Oh!' he continued, 'it's a crisis that will pass, I've no doubt . . . But I've reduced my staff, there are only three here now; and it's certainly not a good time to take on someone else. In short, my dear, I can't take you on as I offered to.'

Denise listened, and turned very pale. He rubbed it in by adding:

'It wouldn't be worth it, either for you or for us.'

'All right, Uncle,' she finally said with an effort. 'I'll try to manage all the same.'

The Baudus were not bad people, but they complained of never having had any luck. When their business was flourishing they had had to bring up five boys, of whom three had died before they were twenty; the fourth had gone to the bad; the fifth, an army captain, had just left for Mexico.* They had no one left but Geneviève. Their family had cost them a great deal, and Baudu had completed his own ruin by buying a big broken-down house at Rambouillet,* his father-in-law's home town. All this was slowly embittering the fanatical old tradesman.

'You might have warned us,' he went on, gradually getting angry at his own hardness. 'You could have written to me; I'd have told you to stay in Valognes . . . Of course, when I heard of your father's death I said the usual things. But you turn up without warning . . . It's very awkward.'

He was raising his voice, relieving his feelings. His wife and daughter, submissive people who would never have dreamed of interfering, still kept their eyes on the ground. Meanwhile Jean had turned very pale, while Denise had clasped the terrified Pépé to her bosom. Two big tears rolled down her cheeks.

'All right, Uncle,' she repeated. 'We'll go away.'

At that he stopped. An embarrassed silence ensued. Then he resumed in a surly tone:

'I won't turn you away . . . Since you're here you might as well stay the night. Tomorrow we'll see.'

At that Madame Baudu and Geneviève understood with a glance that they could go ahead and make arrangements. Everything was settled. There was no need to do anything for Jean. As for Pépé, he would be well looked after by Madame Gras, an old lady who lived on the ground floor of a house in the Rue des Orties, where she took in young children for forty francs a month, full board. Denise declared that she had enough to pay for the first month. It only remained for her to find a place herself. It would be easy to find her a job in the neighbourhood.

'Wasn't Vinçard looking for a salesgirl?' said Geneviève.

'Of course!' exclaimed Baudu. 'We'll go and see him after lunch. We must strike while the iron's hot!'

Not a single customer had come in to interrupt this family discussion. The shop remained dark and empty. In the background the two male assistants and the girl continued their work, talking to each other in low hissing tones. However, three ladies eventually appeared, and Denise remained alone for a moment. She gave Pépé a kiss, her heart heavy at the thought of their impending separation. The child, affectionate as a kitten, hid his head without saying a word. When Madame Baudu and Geneviève came back they remarked how quiet he was, and Denise assured them that he never made any more noise than that; he would go for whole days without saying anything, living on kisses and caresses. Then, until lunch-time, the three women talked about children, housekeeping, life in Paris and in the country, in short, vague sentences, as relations do when they feel awkward at not knowing each other very well. Jean had gone to the shop-door, and stood there watching the passing crowd and smiling at the pretty girls.

At ten o'clock a maid appeared. Usually the first meal was served for Baudu, Geneviève, and the first assistant. There was a second meal at eleven o'clock for Madame Baudu, the other male assistant, and the girl.

'Come and eat!' exclaimed the draper, turning towards his niece.

And as the others were already seated in the cramped dining-room at the back of the shop, he called the first assistant, who was slow to join them.

'Colomban!'

The young man apologized, saying he had wanted to finish arranging the flannel. He was a big lad of twenty-five, stupid but crafty, with an honest face, a large, flabby mouth, and cunning eyes.

'What! There's a time for everything,' said Baudu, squarely installed before a piece of cold veal, which he was carving with a master's skill and prudence, weighing each meagre portion at a glance to within an ounce.

He served everyone, and even cut the bread. Denise had put Pépé next to her to make sure that he ate properly. But the dark room made her feel uneasy; she felt a lump in her throat as she looked round, for she was used to the large, well-lit rooms of her native province. A single window opened on to a little inner courtyard which communicated with the street by means of a dark alley by the side of the house. This yard, sodden and filthy, was like the bottom of a well; a circle of sinister light fell into it. In the winter the gas had to be kept burning from morning to night. When the weather allowed them to do without it, the effect was even more depressing. It took several seconds before Denise's eyes were sufficiently accustomed to the dark to distinguish what was on her plate.

'There's a fellow with a good appetite,' Baudu declared, noticing that Jean had finished his veal. 'If he works as well as he eats, he'll get really strong . . . But what about you, my dear, aren't you eating? And now that we can talk, tell me why you didn't get married in Valognes?'

Denise put down the glass she was raising to her mouth. 'Oh! Uncle, get married? How can you say that? . . . What about the little ones?'

She was forced to laugh, so strange did the idea seem to her. In any case, would any man have wanted her, without a penny, as thin as a rake and showing no signs of becoming beautiful? No, no, she would never marry, she already had enough with two children.

'You're wrong,' her uncle repeated, 'a woman always needs a man. If you'd found a decent young chap you wouldn't have landed on the streets of Paris, you and your brothers, like gypsies.'

He stopped in order to divide, once more, with a parsimony that was scrupulously fair, a dish of bacon and potatoes which the maid had brought in. Then, pointing to Geneviève and Colomban with the spoon, he continued:

'Those two will be married in the spring if the winter season is good.'

It was a patriarchal tradition in the shop.* The founder, Aristide Finet, had given his daughter Désirée to his first assistant, Hauchecorne; Baudu himself, who had arrived in the Rue de la Michodière with seven francs in his pocket, had married old Hauchecorne's daughter Elizabeth; and he intended, in his turn, to hand over his daughter Geneviève and the shop to Colomban, as soon as business improved. If that meant having to postpone a marriage which had been decided on three years earlier, he did so from scruple, from a stubborn integrity: he had received the business in a prosperous state, and did not wish to pass it on to a son-in-law with fewer customers and worse prospects than when he acquired it.

Baudu went on talking, introducing Colomban, who came from Rambouillet like Madame Baudu's father; in fact they were distant cousins. He was an excellent worker and for ten years had been slaving away in the shop and had really earned his promotions! Besides, he wasn't just anybody, his father was that old reveller Colomban, a veterinary surgeon known throughout the Seine-et-Oise,* an artist in his own line, but so fond of food that there was nothing he wouldn't eat.

'Thank God!' said the draper in conclusion. 'Even if his father does drink and chase skirts, the boy has been able to learn the value of money here.'

While he was talking Denise was studying Colomban and Geneviève. They were sitting close to each other, but remained very quiet, without a blush or a smile. Since his first day in the shop the young man had been counting on this marriage. He had passed through all the different stages, junior assistant, salaried salesman, etc., and had finally been admitted to the confidences and pleasures of the family; and he had gone through it all patiently, like an automaton, looking on Geneviève as an excellent and honest business deal. The certainty that she would be his prevented him from desiring her. And the girl, too, had grown accustomed to loving him; but she loved him with all the seriousness of her reserved nature, and with a deep passion of which, in the dull, regular, everyday life she led, she was quite unaware.

'When people like each other, and when it's possible . . .' Denise felt obliged to say with a smile, in order to seem pleasant.

'Yes, it always ends up like that,' declared Colomban, who had not yet said a word, but was slowly munching.

Geneviève, after giving him a long look, said in her turn:

'When people get on together, the rest comes naturally.'

Their fondness for each other had grown up in this ground-floor shop in old Paris. It was like a flower in a cellar. For ten years she had known no one but him, had spent her days beside him, behind the same piles of cloth, in the gloomy depths of the shop; and, morning and evening, they had found themselves elbow to elbow in the cramped dining-room, as chilly as a well. They could not have been more hidden, more lost, in the depths of the country beneath the leaves. But a doubt, a jealous fear, was to make the girl discover that, from emptiness of heart and boredom of mind, she had given herself for ever in the midst of those conniving shadows.

However, Denise, thinking that she could see a dawning anxiety in the look Geneviève had given Colomban, good-naturedly replied:

'Nonsense! When people love each other, they always get on together.'

But Baudu was keeping a sharp eye on the table. He had distributed slivers of Brie, and to welcome his relatives he ordered a second dessert, a pot of gooseberry preserves, a liberality which seemed to surprise Colomban. Pépé, who had been very good until then, behaved badly at the sight of the preserves. Jean, whose interest had been aroused by the conversation about marriage, was staring at his cousin Geneviève, whom he thought too weak and pale, comparing her in his mind to a little white rabbit, with black ears and pink eyes.

'That's enough chat, we must make room for the others!' the draper concluded, giving the signal to leave the table. 'Just because we've given ourselves a treat is no reason for wanting too much of it.'

Madame Baudu, the other male assistant, and the girl came and took their places at the table. Denise, left alone again, sat near the door, waiting for her uncle to take her to see Vinçard. Pépé was playing at her feet, while Jean had taken up his observation post on the doorstep again. She sat there for nearly an hour, watching what was going on around her. Now and again a few customers came in: one lady appeared, then two others. The shop retained its musty smell, its half-light, in which the old-fashioned way of business, good-natured and simple, seemed to be weeping at its neglect. But what fascinated Denise was the Ladies' Paradise on the other side of the street, for she could see the shop-windows through the open door. The sky was still overcast, but the mildness brought by rain was warming the air in spite of the season; and in the clear light, dusted with sunshine, the great shop was coming to life, and business was in full swing.

Denise felt that she was watching a machine working at high pressure; its dynamism seemed to reach to the display windows themselves. They were no longer the cold windows she had seen in the morning; now they seemed to be warm and vibrating with the activity within. A crowd was looking at them, groups of women were crushing each other in front of them, a real mob, made brutal by covetousness. And these passions in the street were giving life to the materials: the laces shivered, then drooped again, concealing the depths of the shop with an exciting air of mystery; even the lengths of cloth, thick and square, were breathing, exuding a tempting odour, while the overcoats were throwing back their shoulders still more on the dummies, which were acquiring souls, and the huge velvet coat was billowing out, supple and warm, as if on shoulders of flesh and blood, with a heaving breast and quivering hips. But the furnace-like heat with which the shop was ablaze came above all from the selling, from the bustle at the counters, which could be felt behind the walls. There was the continuous roar of the machine at work, of customers crowding into the departments, dazzled by the merchandise, then propelled towards the cash-desk. And it was all regulated and organized with the remorselessness of a machine: the vast horde of women were as if caught in the wheels of an inevitable force.

Since the morning Denise had felt herself being tempted. She was bewildered and attracted by this shop, which looked so vast to her, and in which she saw more people in an hour than she had seen at Cornaille's in six months; and in her desire to enter it there was a vague fear, which completed her seduction. At the same time her uncle's shop made her ill at ease. She felt an irrational disdain, an instinctive repugnance for this icy little place where the old-fashioned methods of business still prevailed. All her sensations, her anxious entry, her relations' sour welcome, the depressing lunch in the dungeon-like darkness, her long wait in the sleepy solitude of the old house doomed to decay—all this was combining to form a veiled protest, a passionate desire for life and light. And, in spite of her kind heart, her eyes kept turning back to the Ladies' Paradise, as if the salesgirl in her felt the need to go and warm herself before the blaze of this huge sale.

She let slip a remark:

'They've got plenty of customers over there, at any rate!'

But she regretted her words when she noticed the Baudus nearby. Madame Baudu, who had finished her lunch, was standing up, white as a sheet, her white eyes fixed on the monster; and, resigned though she was, she could not see it, could not catch sight of it on the other side of the street, without dumb despair filling her eyes with tears. As for Geneviève, she was anxiously watching Colomban, who, not thinking that he was being observed, stood in rapture, looking at the girls selling coats, whose department was visible through the mezzanine windows. Baudu, his face contorted with rage, contented himself by saying:

'All that glisters is not gold. You just wait!'

The thought of his family was evidently holding back the flood of resentment which was rising in his throat. A sense of pride prevented him from giving vent to his feelings so soon in front of the children, who had only arrived that morning. In the end, the draper made an effort, and turned round in order to tear himself away from the sight of the selling going on opposite.

'Well,' he went on, 'let's go and see Vinçard. Jobs are soon snatched up; tomorrow it may be too late.'

But before going out he told the second assistant to go to the station to fetch Denise's trunk. For her part Madame Baudu, to whom the girl had entrusted Pépé, decided that she would take advantage of a free moment by going over to see Madame Gras in the Rue des Orties to arrange about the child. Jean promised his sister that he would not leave the shop.

'It'll only take a couple of minutes,' Baudu explained as he walked down the Rue Gaillon with his niece. 'Vinçard specializes in silks, and he's still doing a fair trade. Oh, he has his difficulties, like everyone else, but he's artful and makes ends meet by being as stingy as he can. But I think he wants to retire, because of his rheumatism.'

The shop was in the Rue Neuve-des-Petits-Champs, near the Passage Choiseul. It was clean and light, well fitted out in the modern style, but small and poorly stocked. Baudu and Denise found Vinçard deep in conference with two gentlemen.

'Never mind us,' the draper called out. 'We're not in a hurry, we'll wait.'

And, going tactfully back towards the door, he whispered in the girl's ear:

'The thin one's at the Paradise, assistant buyer in the silk department, and the fat one's a manufacturer from Lyons.'

Denise gathered that Vinçard was talking up his shop to Robineau, the assistant from the Ladies' Paradise. He was giving his word of honour in a frank, open way, with the facility of a man who could take any number of oaths without any trouble. According to him, the shop was a gold-mine; and, resplendent as he was with good health, he broke off to whine and complain about the infernal pains which were forcing him to give up making his fortune. But Robineau, highly strung and anxious, interrupted him impatiently: he knew about the crisis the trade was going through, and named a shop specializing in silks which had already been ruined by the proximity of the Paradise. Vinçard, extremely angry, raised his voice.

'No wonder! That old chump Vabre* was bound to come a cropper. His wife spent everything he earned . . . Besides, we're more than five hundred yards away, whereas Vabre was right next door to it.'

Gaujean, the silk manufacturer, chimed in. Once more their voices were lowered. Gaujean was accusing the big stores of ruining the French textile industry; three or four of them were dictating to it, completely ruling the market; and he insinuated that the only way to resist them was to encourage small businesses, especially those which specialized, for the future belonged to them. For this reason he was offering Robineau plenty of credit.

'Look how the Paradise has treated you!' he repeated. 'They take no account of services rendered, they're just machines for exploiting people . . . They promised you the job of buyer ages ago, and then Bouthemont, who was an outsider and had no right to it, got it straight away.'

Robineau was still smarting from this injustice. All the same, he was hesitating about setting up in business himself, explaining that the money was not his; his wife had inherited sixty thousand francs, and he was full of scruples about this sum, saying that he would rather cut both his hands off on the spot than risk the money in bad business.

'No. I haven't made up my mind,' he concluded at last. 'Give me time to think it over; we'll discuss it again.'

'As you like,' said Vinçard, hiding his disappointment with a smile. 'It's not in my interest to sell. You know, if it wasn't for my rheumatism . . .'

And returning to the middle of the shop he asked:

'What can I do for you, Monsieur Baudu?'

The draper, who had been listening with one ear, introduced Denise, told Vinçard as much as he thought necessary of her story, and said that she had been working in the provinces for two years.

'And as I hear that you're looking for a good salesgirl . . .'

Vinçard pretended to be terribly sorry.

'Oh! What bad luck! I have indeed been looking for a salesgirl all week. But I've just engaged one, less than two hours ago.'

A silence ensued. Denise seemed totally dismayed. Then Robineau, who was looking at her with interest, no doubt touched by her poor appearance, volunteered some information.

'I know they want someone at our place, in the ladieswear department.'

Baudu could not suppress a heartfelt exclamation:

'At your place! My goodness—no!'

Then he stopped, embarrassed. Denise had turned very red; she would never dare to enter that huge shop! And yet the idea of being there filled her with pride.

'Why not?' asked Robineau, surprised. 'It would be a good opening for her . . . I'd advise her to go and see Madame Aurélie, the buyer, tomorrow morning. The worst that can happen is that they won't take her.'

The draper, in order to hide his inner revulsion, began to chatter vaguely: he knew Madame Aurélie, or at any rate her husband Lhomme, the cashier, a fat man who had had his right arm cut off by an omnibus. Then, suddenly coming back to Denise, he said:

'In any case, it's her affair, not mine . . . She's quite free . . .'

And he went out, after saying goodbye to Gaujean and Robineau. Vinçard accompanied him to the door, saying once more how sorry he was. The girl had remained in the middle of the shop, intimidated, anxious to get more information from Robineau. But she did not dare, and said goodbye in her turn, adding simply:

'Thank you, sir.'

On the way back Baudu did not speak to his niece. He walked fast, forcing her to run, as if carried away by his thoughts. In the Rue de la Michodière he was about to go into his shop when a neighbouring shopkeeper, standing at his door, beckoned him over. Denise stopped to wait for him.

'What is it, Bourras, old chap?' asked the draper.

Bourras was a tall old man with the head of a prophet, long-haired and bearded, and with piercing eyes under great bushy eyebrows. He sold walking-sticks and umbrellas, did repairs, and even carved handles, a skill which had earned him quite a reputation as an artist. Denise glanced at the shop-windows, where the umbrellas and walking-sticks were arranged in straight lines. But when she looked up she was astonished at the appearance of the house: it was a hovel squashed between the Ladies' Paradise and a large Louis XIV mansion; its two low storeys were collapsing at the bottom of the narrow crevice where it had somehow sprung up. Without supports on each side it would have fallen down; the roof slates were crooked and rotten, and the two-windowed façade was scarred with cracks which ran down in long rusty lines over the worm-eaten signboard.

'You know, he's written to my landlord about buying the house,' said Bourras, looking at the draper intently with his blazing eyes.

Baudu became even paler, and bent his shoulders. There was a silence, during which the two men looked at each other very seriously.

'You must be prepared for everything,' Baudu murmured finally.

At that the old man flew into a rage, shaking his hair and his flowing beard.

'Let him buy the house, he'll pay four times its value for it! But I swear that as long as I'm alive he won't have a single stone of it. My lease has twelve years to run . . . We'll see, we'll see!'

It was a declaration of war. Bourras turned towards the Ladies' Paradise, which neither of them had named. Baudu shook his head in silence, then crossed the street to his shop, his legs giving way, repeating only:

'Oh! God! . . . Oh! God!'

Denise, who had been listening, followed her uncle. Madame Baudu had just come back with Pépé, and she said at once that Madame Gras would take the child whenever they wanted. But Jean had just disappeared, which made his sister anxious. When he returned, his face flushed, talking excitedly about the boulevard, she looked at him in such a sad way that it made him blush. Their trunk had arrived and it was agreed that they would sleep in the attic.

'By the way, how did you get on at Vinçard's?' asked Madame Baudu.

The draper told her about his fruitless errand, adding that they had been told about a job for Denise; and, pointing towards the Ladies' Paradise in a gesture of contempt, he cried out:

'There—in there!'

The whole family felt hurt at the idea. In the evening, the first meal was at five o'clock. Denise and the two children took their places again with Baudu, Geneviève, and Colomban. The small dining-room was lit by a gas jet, and the smell of food was stifling. They ate in silence, but during the dessert Madame Baudu, who was restless, left the shop to come and sit down behind her niece. And then the storm which had been brewing all morning broke, and they all relieved their feelings by abusing the monster.

'It's your business, you're free to do what you want . . .,' repeated Baudu. 'We don't want to influence you . . . But the sort of place it is . . . !'

In broken sentences he told her the story of Octave Mouret. Wonderful luck! A lad from the Midi* who had turned up in Paris possessing all the attractive audacity of an adventurer; and, from the day he arrived, there had been nothing but affairs with women, an endless exploiting of women, a scandal which was still the talk of the neighbourhood, when he had been caught in the act; then his sudden and inexplicable conquest of Madame Hédouin, which had brought him the Ladies' Paradise.

'Poor Caroline!' interrupted Madame Baudu. 'We were distantly related. Ah! If she had lived things would have been different. She wouldn't have let them ruin us like this . . . And he's the one who killed her. Yes, on his building site! One morning, when she was looking at the works, she fell into a hole. Three days later she died. A fine, healthy woman, who had never had a day's illness in her life! There's some of her blood under the foundations of that shop!'

With her pale, trembling hand she pointed through the walls towards the great shop. Denise, who was listening as one listens to a fairy-tale, shivered slightly. The fear which had mingled with the temptation she had felt since the morning came perhaps from the blood of that woman, which she fancied she could see in the red cement of the basement.

'It seems as if it brings him luck,' added Madame Baudu without naming Mouret.

But the draper shrugged his shoulders, contemptuous of these old wives' tales. He resumed his story, explaining the situation from the commercial point of view. The Ladies' Paradise had been founded in 1822 by the Deleuze brothers. When the eldest died, his daughter Caroline had married the son of a linen manufacturer, Charles Hédouin; and later on, having become a widow, she had married this man Mouret. He had thus acquired a half-share in the shop. Three months after their marriage, her uncle Deleuze had died childless; so that, when Caroline had met her death, Mouret had become sole heir, sole proprietor of the Paradise. Nothing but luck!

'A man with ideas, but muddle-headed—he'll turn the whole neighbourhood upside-down if he's allowed to!' Baudu went on. 'I think that Caroline, who was a bit romantic too, must have been taken in by the gentleman's grand schemes . . . In short, he persuaded her to buy the house on the left, then the house on the right; and he himself, when he was left on his own, bought two others; so that the shop has gone on growing and growing, to such an extent that it threatens to swallow us all up!'

His words were addressed to Denise, but he was really talking to himself, brooding obsessively over Mouret's story, in an attempt to justify himself. At home he was forever irascible and violent, his fists always clenched. Madame Baudu sat motionless on her chair, no longer taking part in the conversation; Geneviève and Colomban, their eyes lowered, were absentmindedly collecting and eating crumbs. It was so hot and stuffy in the small room that Pépé had fallen asleep on the table, and even Jean's eyes were closing.

'You wait!' Baudu went on, suddenly filled with rage. 'Those swindlers will break their necks! Mouret's going through a difficult time, I know he is. He's had to put all his profits into his mad obsession with expansion and advertising. What's more, in order to raise money, he's taken it into his head to persuade most of his staff to invest their savings in his business.* So he hasn't got a penny now, and unless a miracle happens, unless he manages to triple his sales, as he hopes, there'll be a tremendous crash! Ah! I'm not spiteful, but when that day comes I'll light up my shopfront, believe me!'

He went on in a revengeful voice. One would have thought that only the fall of the Paradise could restore the slighted honour of the trade. Had anyone ever seen such a thing? A draper's shop which sold everything! Just a big bazaar! And a fine staff too: a lot of dandies who pushed things about like porters at a railway station, who treated the goods and the customers like parcels, dropping their employer or being dropped by him at a moment's notice. No affection, no manners, no art! And suddenly he cited Colomban as an example of a good tradesman: of course, he, Colomban, brought up in the old school, knew the slow, sure way one learned the real subtleties, the real tricks of the trade. The art was not to sell a lot, but to sell at a high price. And Colomban could say, too, how he had been treated, how he had become a member of the family, nursed when he was ill, his things laundered and mended, looked after paternally—loved, in fact!

'Of course!' Colomban repeated after every statement shouted out by his employer.

'You're the last, my boy,' declared Baudu with emotion. 'After you there'll be none left . . . You're my only consolation; if that mad scrambling over there is what they call business nowadays, I give up; I'd rather clear out.'

Geneviève, her head on one side, as if her thick black hair was too heavy for her pale forehead, was watching the smiling shop assistant; and in her look there was a suspicion, a desire to see if Colomban would not blush at all this praise. But, as if he was used to the old tradesman's act, he maintained his quiet manner, his bland air, and the wily pucker on his lips.

However, Baudu went on, louder than ever, accusing the bazaar opposite, those savages who were massacring each other in their struggle for existence, destroying all family ties in the process. He quoted as an example their neighbours in the country, the Lhommes, mother, father, and son, all three now employed in that infernal shop, people with no home life, always out, only eating at home on Sundays, nothing but a hotel and restaurant life! To be sure, his own dining-room was not large, and it could have done with a bit more light and air; but at least he had lived his life there, surrounded by the love of his family. As he spoke his eyes travelled round the little room; and he began to tremble at the idea, which he refused to acknowledge, that the savages might one day, if they succeeded in killing his business, dislodge him from this niche where, with his wife and daughter by his side, he felt so comfortable. In spite of the assurance with which he foretold the final crash, in his heart he was terrified; he really did feel that the neighbourhood was being gradually overrun and devoured.

'I don't want to put you off,' he resumed, trying to be calm. 'If it's in your interest to get a job there, I'll be the first to say: "Go."'

'I'm sure you will, Uncle,' murmured Denise, bewildered; all this emotion made her want more and more to be at the Ladies' Paradise.

He had put his elbows on the table, and was staring at her so hard that she felt quite uncomfortable.

'Look, you've been in the trade, do you think it's right that a simple draper's shop should start selling everything under the sun? In the old days, when trade was trade, drapery meant materials, and nothing else. Nowadays their only aim is to expand their business at the expense of their neighbours and to eat everything up . . . That's what the neighbourhood's complaining about, the little shops are beginning to suffer terribly. That man Mouret is ruining them . . . Bédoré and his sister, who keep the hosiery shop in the Rue Gaillon, have already lost half their customers. At Mademoiselle Tatin's, the lingerie shop in the Passage Choiseul, they've been forced to lower their prices in order to compete. And the effect of this scourge, this plague, is felt as far as the Rue Neuve-des-Petits-Champs, where I venture to say that the Vanpouille brothers, the furriers, can't hold out. Drapers who sell furs, it's absurd! Another of Mouret's ideas!'

'And the gloves,' said Madame Baudu, 'isn't it incredible? He's had the nerve to create a glove department! Yesterday, as I was going along the Rue Neuve-Saint-Augustin, Quinette was standing at his door looking so depressed that I didn't dare ask him if business was good.'

'And umbrellas,' Baudu went on. 'That beats everything! Bourras is convinced that Mouret simply wants to ruin him; after all, what sense does it make to have umbrellas and materials together? But Bourras is tough, he won't let himself be killed off. We'll have a good laugh one of these days.'

He talked about other shopkeepers, and reviewed the whole neighbourhood. Now and again he let slip a confession: if Vinçard was trying to sell they might as well all pack up, for Vinçard was like the rats that leave sinking ships. Then he would immediately contradict himself; he would dream of an alliance, a league of little retailers to stand up to the colossus. He hesitated a moment before talking about himself, his hands shaking and his mouth twitching nervously. Finally, he took the plunge.

'As for me, so far I haven't had much to complain about. Of course he's done me some harm, the scoundrel! But up till now he's only kept cloth for women, light cloth for dresses, and heavier cloth for coats. People still come to me for men's things, velvets for shooting outfits, liveries, not to mention flannels and duffels; I challenge him to offer such a wide assortment of those! But he still tries to get at me, he thinks he really annoys me because he's put his drapery department directly opposite. You've seen his display, haven't you? He always puts his most beautiful dresses there, set in a framework of various cloths, a real circus parade to catch the girls . . . I swear I'd be ashamed to use such means. The Vieil Elbeuf has been famous for nearly a hundred years, and it doesn't need confidence tricks like that at its door. As long as I live, the shop will stay the same as it was when I took it over, with its four sample pieces of cloth on the right and the left, and nothing else!'

The whole family was becoming affected. After a silence, Geneviève ventured to say something:

'Our customers like us, Papa. We must hope that . . . Madame Desforges and Madame de Boves were here again today, and I'm expecting Madame Marty to look at some flannel.'

'And yesterday I took an order from Madame Bourdelais,' declared Colomban. 'Though she did mention an English tweed priced fifty centimes cheaper opposite, and the same as ours, it seems.'

'And to think,' murmured Madame Baudu in her tired voice, 'that we knew that shop when it was no bigger than a pocket handkerchief! Yes, really, my dear Denise, when the Deleuzes founded it, it only had one window in the Rue Neuve-Saint-Augustin, just like a cupboard, in which there was barely room for a couple of pieces of chintz and three pieces of calico. You couldn't turn round in the shop, it was so small . . . At that time the Vieil Elbeuf, which had been here for over sixty years, was already just as you see it today . . . Ah! it's all changed, greatly changed!'

She shook her head, her few words telling the story of her life. Born at the Vieil Elbeuf, she loved it even down to its damp stones, she lived only for it and because of it; in bygone days she had been full of pride for this shop, which had been the largest, the most thriving business in the neighbourhood, but she had had the continual pain of seeing the rival shop gradually growing, at first disdained, then equal in importance, then surpassing it and threatening it. For her it was an open wound; she was slowly dying of the Vieil Elbeuf's humiliation, still living, like the shop, on the strength of its momentum, but knowing that its death throes would be hers too, and that she would never survive its final closure.

Silence reigned. Baudu was beating a tattoo with his fingertips on the oilcloth. He felt weary, almost sorry at having relieved his feelings once more in this way. In fact, the whole family, their eyes vacant, felt the effects of his despondency, and could not help turning over in their minds the bitter events of their history. Luck had never smiled on them. The children had been reared, fortune was on the way, when suddenly competition had brought ruin. There was also the house at Rambouillet, the country house to which the draper had been dreaming of retiring for the last ten years; a bargain he called it, an old shack he was obliged continually to repair, which he had reluctantly decided to let to people who never paid the rent. His last profits were being spent on it—the only vice he had ever had in his honest, upright career, obstinately attached to the old ways.

'Now then,' he suddenly declared, 'we must make room for the others . . . That's enough useless talk!'

They all seemed to wake up. The gas jet was hissing in the dead, stifling air of the little room. Everyone jumped up, breaking the gloomy silence. Pépé, however, was sleeping so soundly that they laid him down on some pieces of thick flannel. Jean, yawning, had already gone back to the front door.

'In short, you do what you like,' Baudu repeated once more to his niece. 'We're just telling you the facts, that's all. But it's your business.'

He looked at her intently, waiting for a decisive answer. Denise, instead of being turned against the Ladies' Paradise by these stories, was more fascinated by it than ever, and kept her air of calmness and sweetness, under which there lay an obstinate Norman will. She was content to reply: 'We'll see, Uncle.'

And she talked of going to bed early with the children, for they were all three very tired. But it was only just striking six, so she decided to stay in the shop a few moments longer. Night had fallen, and she found the street quite dark, soaked with fine, dense rain which had been falling since sunset. A surprise greeted her: a few moments had sufficed for the roadway to become filled with pebbles, for the gutters to be running with dirty water and the pavements to be covered in thick, sticky mud; and through the driving rain she could see nothing but a confused stream of umbrellas, jostling each other, swelling out like great gloomy wings in the darkness. She drew back at first, struck by the cold, feeling even more depressed because of the badly lit shop, which had a particularly dismal appearance at this time of night. A damp breeze, the breath of the old neighbourhood, came in from the street; it seemed as if the water streaming from the umbrellas was running right up to the counters and the pavement, with its mud and puddles, was coming into the old shop's ground floor, white with saltpetre rot, giving it a final coat of mildew. It was a vision of old Paris, soaked through, and it made her shiver, surprised and dismayed to find the great city so cold and ugly.

But on the other side of the road the deep rows of gas burners at the Ladies' Paradise were being lit. She drew nearer, once more attracted and, as it were, warmed by this source of blazing light. The machine was still humming, still active, letting off steam in a final roar, while the salesmen were folding up the materials and the cashiers counting their takings. Through windows dimmed with condensation she could make out a vague profusion of lights, the confused interior of a factory. Behind the curtain of rain this vision, distant and blurred, seemed like some giant stokehold, in which the black shadows of the stokers could be seen moving against the red fire of the furnaces. The window displays had become indistinct also, and nothing could now be seen opposite but the snowy lace, the white of which was heightened by the frosted glass globes of a row of gas jets. Against this chapel-like background, the coats were bursting with energy; the great velvet overcoat trimmed with silver fox suggested the curved outline of a headless woman, running through the downpour to some festivity in the mysterious Parisian night.

Denise, yielding to temptation, had come as far as the door without noticing the raindrops falling on her. At this time of night, the Ladies' Paradise, with its furnace-like glare, seduced her completely. In the great metropolis, dark and silent under the rain, in this Paris of which she knew nothing, it was burning like a beacon, it alone seemed to be the light and life of the city. She dreamed of her future there, working hard to bring up the children, and of other things too, she knew not what, far-off things which made her tremble with desire and fear. The thought of the dead woman under the foundations came back to her and she felt afraid; she thought she saw the lights bleeding; then the whiteness of the lace soothed her, a feeling of hope sprang up in her heart, a real certainty of joy, while the soft rain, blowing on her, cooled her hands, and calmed her after the excitement of her journey.

'That's Bourras,' said a voice behind her.

She leaned forward and caught sight of Bourras, standing motionless at the end of the street in front of the window in which, that morning, she had noticed a whole ingenious display of umbrellas and walking-sticks. The tall old man had slipped out in the dark to feast his eyes on this triumphal display; his expression was heart-rending and he did not even notice the rain beating on his bare head, making his white hair drip.

'He's stupid,' the voice remarked, 'he'll catch his death of cold.'

Then, turning round, Denise found the Baudus behind her again. In spite of themselves, like Bourras whom they thought so stupid, they always came back there in the end, to this scene which was breaking their hearts. They had a passion for suffering. Geneviève, very pale, had noticed that Colomban was watching the shadows of the salesgirls passing by the windows on the mezzanine floor; and, while Baudu was choking with suppressed rancour, Madame Baudu's eyes had silently filled with tears.

'You're going to go there tomorrow, aren't you?' the draper asked, tormented with uncertainty, but sensing that his niece had been conquered like the rest.

She hesitated, then said gently:

'Yes, Uncle, unless it pains you too much.'

CHAPTER 2

THE next day, at half-past seven, Denise was standing outside the Ladies' Paradise. She wanted to call there before taking Jean to his employer, who lived a long way off, at the top of the Faubourg du Temple. But being used to early rising, she had been in too much of a hurry to get up: the shop assistants were only just arriving and, filled with shyness and the fear of looking ridiculous, she turned away to walk up and down the Place Gaillon for a moment.

A cold wind was blowing and had already dried the pavement. From every street, lit by the pale early morning light under an ashen sky, shop assistants were busily emerging, their overcoat collars turned up, their hands in their pockets, caught unawares by this first nip of winter. Most of them hurried along alone and disappeared into the depths of the shop without addressing a word or even a glance to their colleagues striding along around them; others were walking in twos or threes, talking fast, taking up the whole of the pavement; and all, with an identical gesture, threw their cigarette or cigar into the gutter before entering.

Denise noticed that several of these gentlemen stared at her as they passed. This increased her timidity; she felt quite unable to follow them, and resolved to wait until the procession had ended before going in herself, blushing at the idea of being jostled in the doorway in the midst of all those men. But the procession continued, and in order to escape their glances she walked slowly round the square. When she came back she found a tall young man, pale and ungainly, planted in front of the Ladies' Paradise; he too appeared to have been waiting there for some time.

'Excuse me, miss,' he asked her finally with a stammer, 'are you one of the salesgirls?'

She was so overcome at being spoken to by this unknown young man that at first she did not reply.

'Because, you see,' he went on, getting more embarrassed, 'I thought I might see if they wouldn't take me on, and you might be able to give me some information.'

He was just as shy as she was, and had dared to speak to her because he sensed that she was trembling like himself. 'I'd be happy to, sir,' she replied at last, 'but I'm no better off than you are. I've come to apply for a job too.

'Oh, I see,' he said, quite disconcerted.

And they blushed deeply, faced with their common shyness for an instant, touched by the similarity of their positions, yet not daring to wish each other good luck out loud. Then, as they said nothing further, and were feeling more and more uncomfortable, they separated awkwardly and began to wait again, in separate places, a few steps apart.

The shop assistants were still going in. Now Denise could hear them joking as they passed close to her, giving her a sideways glance as they went by. She was becoming increasingly embarrassed at making an exhibition of herself in this way, and she was on the point of deciding to take half an hour's walk in the neighbourhood when the sight of a young man coming quickly along the Rue Port-Mahon made her wait a moment longer. Obviously he must be the head of a department, for all the shop assistants were greeting him. He was tall, with fair skin and a carefully trimmed beard; and his eyes, the colour of old gold, and as soft as velvet, fell on her for a moment as he crossed the square. He was already going into the shop, indifferent, while she stood motionless, deeply disturbed by his glance, filled with a strange emotion in which there was more uneasiness than pleasure. She began to feel really afraid, and started to walk slowly down the Rue Gaillon, then down the Rue Saint-Roch, waiting for her courage to come back.

It was not just the head of a department, it was Octave Mouret himself. He had not slept that night, for on leaving a party at a stockbroker's he had gone to have supper with a friend and with two women whom he had picked up backstage in a small theatre. His buttoned-up overcoat hid his evening dress and his white tie. He quickly ran upstairs, washed his face, and changed; and by the time he sat down at his desk in his office on the ground floor he was quite ready for work, eyes bright, skin fresh, just as if he had had ten hours' sleep. The vast office, furnished in old oak and hung with green rep, had as its only ornament a portrait of Madame Hédouin, who was still the talk of the neighbourhood.

Since her death Octave remembered her with affection, and he was grateful to her memory for the fortune she had showered on him when she married him. And so, before setting about signing the bills which had been placed on his blotter, he gave the portrait the smile of a happy man. After all, when his escapades as a young widower were over, when he left the bedchambers where he was led astray by the need for pleasure, didn't he always come back to work in her presence?

There was a knock at the door and, without waiting, a young man entered, a tall, skinny fellow, with thin lips and a pointed nose, very gentlemanly in his appearance, with sleek hair in which strands of grey were already beginning to show. Mouret looked up; then, continuing to sign his papers, he said:

'Did you sleep well, Bourdoncle?'

'Very well, thank you,' replied the young man, who was strutting about the room, quite at home.

Bourdoncle, the son of a poor farmer from near Limoges, had started at the Ladies' Paradise at the same time as Mouret, when the shop had been at the corner of the Place Gaillon. Very intelligent and energetic, it had seemed then as if he would easily outdo his friend, who was less serious-minded, distracted in many ways, who seemed thoughtless, and had disquieting affairs with women; but he did not have the touch of genius possessed by the ardent Provençal, nor his daring, nor his winning charm. Indeed, with the instinct of a prudent man, he had bowed to him submissively, and had done so without a struggle from the very beginning. When Mouret had advised his assistants to invest their money in the shop, Bourdoncle had been one of the first to respond, even entrusting an unexpected legacy from an aunt to him; and little by little, after working his way up through the ranks, salesman, assistant buyer in the silk department, then buyer, he had become one of the chief's lieutenants, the one he liked best and listened to the most, one of the six men who had money invested in the shop and helped Mouret to run it, forming something like a council of ministers under an absolute monarch. Each of them looked after a province. Bourdoncle was in charge of overall supervision.*

'What about you?' he resumed familiarly. 'Did you sleep well?' When Mouret replied that he hadn't been to bed he shook his head, murmuring:

'Doesn't do your health any good.'

'Why not?' said the other gaily. 'I'm not as tired as you, old chap. Your eyes are puffy from too much sleep; your good habits are making you dull . . . Have some fun, it'll liven you up a bit!'

They always had the same friendly argument. In the past, Bourdoncle had beaten his mistresses because, so he said, they prevented him from sleeping. Now he professed to hate women, no doubt having chance affairs which he did not talk about, so unimportant was the place they had in his life, and contenting himself in the shop with exploiting the customers, feeling the utmost contempt for their frivolity, which led them to ruin themselves for ridiculous clothes. Mouret, on the contrary, affected to go into raptures over women; he was entranced and affectionate in their presence, and was always being carried away by new love-affairs; and his amorous adventures were a kind of advertisement for his business: it seemed as if he enveloped all the women in the same caress, the better to bewilder them and hold them at his mercy.

'I saw Madame Desforges last night,' he resumed. 'She was enchanting at the ball.'

'But you didn't have supper with her afterwards, did you?' asked his colleague.

Mouret protested.

'What an idea! She's very respectable, my dear fellow . . . No, I had supper with Héloïse, the little girl from the Folies . . . She's a silly little thing, but so amusing!'

He took another bundle of bills and went on signing them. Bourdoncle was still strutting about. He walked over and took a look through the high window-panes at the Rue Neuve-Saint-Augustin, then came back saying:

'You know, they'll have their revenge.'

'Who will?' asked Mouret, who was not listening.

'The women, of course.'

At that Mouret became even more expansive, allowing his fundamental brutality to show through his air of sensual adoration. With a shrug of his shoulders he seemed to declare that he would throw them all away like empty sacks on the day when they had finished helping him to make his fortune. Bourdoncle, in his cold way, obstinately repeated:

'They'll have their revenge. There'll be one who'll avenge the others, there's sure to be.'

'Don't you worry!' cried Mouret, exaggerating his Provençal accent. 'That one's not yet born, my boy. And if she does come, you know . . .'

He had raised his penholder, brandishing it and pointing it in the air as if he wished to stab some invisible heart with a knife. His colleague started pacing up and down again, giving in as usual to the superiority of his chief, whose genius, flawed though it was, nevertheless disconcerted him. He who was so clear-headed, so logical and passionless, incapable of slipping, could still understand the feminine side of success, Paris yielding in a kiss to the boldest man.

Silence reigned. Nothing could be heard but Mouret's pen. Then, in reply to his brief questions, Bourdoncle gave him information about the big sale of winter fancy goods which was to take place the following Monday. It was a very important affair; the shop was gambling its fortune on it, for the rumours going round the neighbourhood had some foundation: Mouret was throwing himself into speculation like a poet, with such ostentation, such a need for the colossal, that it looked as though everything would crumble beneath him. It was quite a new style of doing business, a type of commercial imagination which had worried Madame Hédouin in the past, and which still sometimes dismayed those concerned, in spite of some initial success. The governor was blamed behind his back for going too fast; he was accused of having dangerously increased the size of the shop without being able to count on a sufficient increase in customers; above all, people were afraid when they saw him gamble all the money in the till on a single venture, loading the counters with a pile of goods without keeping a penny in reserve. Thus, for the forth-coming sale, after the payment of considerable sums to the builders, the entire capital was tied up: once more it was a case of victory or death. And in the midst of all this anxiety he kept up his triumphant gaiety, his certainty of gaining millions, like a man who, worshipped by women, cannot be betrayed by them. When Bourdoncle ventured to express fears about the undue development of departments whose turnover was still unsatisfactory, Mouret gave a splendid, confident laugh, exclaiming:

'Don't worry, old chap, the shop's too small!'

His colleague seemed flabbergasted, seized with fear which he no longer tried to hide. The shop too small! A draper's shop with nineteen departments and four hundred and three employees!

'Of course,' Mouret went on, 'we shall be forced to expand within eighteen months . . . I'm seriously thinking of it. Last night Madame Desforges promised to introduce me to someone at her house tomorrow . . . We'll talk about it when the idea's ripe.'

And having finished signing the bills, he got up, and gave his lieutenant some friendly taps on the shoulder; but the latter couldn't get over his astonishment. The terror felt by the prudent people around him amused Mouret. In one of the outbursts of sudden frankness with which he sometimes overwhelmed his close friends, he declared that basically he was more Jewish than all the Jews in the world: he took after his father,* a cheery fellow who knew the value of money, whom he resembled both physically and in character; and, if he had got his excitable imagination from his mother, it was, perhaps, his most obvious asset, for he was aware of the invincible force of his charm in daring everything.

'You know very well that we'll stand by you to the end,' said Bourdoncle finally.

Then, before going down into the shop for their usual look round, the two men settled certain other details. They examined a sample copy of a little counterfoil book which Mouret had just invented for sales invoices. Having noticed that the larger the commission an assistant received, the faster obsolete goods and junk were snapped up, he had based a new sales method on this observation. In future he was going to give his salesmen an interest in the sale of all goods; he would give them a percentage on the smallest bit of material, the smallest article they sold: a system which had caused a revolution in the drapery trade by creating among the assistants a struggle for survival from which the employers reaped the benefit. This struggle, moreover, had become his favourite method, a principle of organization he constantly applied. He unleashed passions, brought different forces into conflict, let the strong devour the weak, and grew fat on this battle of interests. The sample counterfoil book was approved: at the top, on the counterfoil and on the piece to be torn off, the name of the department and the assistant's number were printed; then, also on both sides, there were columns for the measurement, a description of the goods, and the price; the salesman merely signed the bill before handing it to the cashier. In this way, checking was extremely simple: the bills given by the cash-desk to the counting-house simply had to be compared with the counterfoils kept by the assistants. Each week the latter would get their percentage and their commission, without any possible error.

'We shan't be robbed so much,' observed Bourdoncle with satisfaction. 'That was an excellent idea of yours.'

'And I thought of something else last night,' Mouret explained. 'Yes, my dear fellow, last night at that supper . . . I'd like to give the counting-house staff a small bonus for every mistake they find in the sales counterfoils, when they check them . . . You see, we'll be certain then that they won't overlook a single error; they'll be more likely to invent them.'

He began to laugh, while his companion looked at him in admiration. This new way of applying the struggle for survival enchanted him; he had a genius for administrative systems, and dreamed of organizing the shop in such a way as to exploit other people's appetites for the complete and quiet satisfaction of his own. He often said that to make people work their hardest, and even get a bit of honesty out of them, it was necessary to bring them up against their own needs first.

'Well, let's go down,' Mouret resumed. 'We must deal with this sale . . . The silk arrived yesterday, didn't it? Bouthemont must be getting it in now.'

Bourdoncle followed him. The receiving department was in the basement, on the Rue Neuve-Saint-Augustin side. There, level with the pavement, was a kind of glazed cage where the lorries discharged the goods. They were weighed, then tipped down a steep chute; the oak and ironwork of this shone, polished by the friction of bales and cases. Everything entered through this yawning trap; things were being swallowed up all the time, a continual cascade of materials falling with the roar of a river. During big sales especially, the chute would discharge an endless flow into the basement, silks from Lyons, woollens from

England, linens from Flanders, calicoes from Alsace, prints from Rouen; and sometimes the lorries had to queue up. The parcels, as they flowed down, made a dull sound at the bottom of the hole, like a stone thrown into deep water.

As he was passing, Mouret stopped for a moment in front of the chute. It was in full activity: rows of packing-cases were going down on their own, the men whose hands were pushing them down from above being invisible; and they seemed to be rushing along by themselves, streaming like rain from some spring higher up. Then some bales appeared, turning round and round like rolled pebbles. Mouret watched without saying a word. But this deluge of goods falling into his shop, this flood releasing thousands of francs a minute, lit a brief light in his limpid eyes. Never before had he been so clearly aware of the battle he was engaged in. His task was to launch this deluge of goods all over Paris. He didn't say a word, but went on with his tour of inspection.

In the grey light which was coming through the broad ventilators a gang of men was receiving consignments, while others were un-nailing packing-cases and opening bales in the presence of the managers of the various departments. The depths of this cellar, this basement where cast-iron pillars held up the arches and the bare walls were cemented, were filled with the bustle of a shipyard.

'Have you got it all, Bouthemont?' asked Mouret, going up to a young man with broad shoulders who was checking the contents of a packing-case.

'Yes, I think it's all there,' he replied. 'But it will take me all morning to count it.'

The department-manager ran his eye over an invoice; he was standing before a large counter on which one of his salesmen was placing the lengths of silk he was taking out of the packing-case one by one. Behind them were further rows of counters, also littered with goods which a small army of assistants was examining. There was a general unpacking, an apparent confusion of materials as they were examined, turned over, ticketed, in the midst of a buzz of voices.*

Bouthemont, who was becoming a celebrity in the trade, had a round, jolly face, an inky black beard, and fine brown eyes. A native of Montpellier, noisy and fun-loving, he was a poor sales-man; but as a buyer he had no equal. He had been sent to Paris by his father, who had a draper's shop in Montpellier, and when the old man thought that his son had learned enough to succeed him in the business, he had absolutely refused to go back home. From then on a rivalry had developed between father and son, the former entirely absorbed in his small provincial trade, indig-nant at seeing a mere assistant earning three times as much as he did himself, and the latter joking about the old man's routine, boasting about his earnings, and turning the shop upside-down every time he went there. Like the other department-managers he earned, apart from his three thousand francs fixed salary, a commission on sales. Montpellier, surprised and impressed, gave it out that the Bouthemont boy had, in the preceding year, pocketed nearly fifteen thousand francs—and this was only a beginning; people predicted to his exasperated father that this figure would increase even more.

Meanwhile, Bourdoncle had picked up one of the lengths of silk, and was examining its texture with the attentive air of a man who knows his business. It was a piece of faille with a blue and silver selvage, the famous Paris-Paradise with which Mouret hoped to strike a decisive blow.

'It really is very good,' murmured his colleague.

'But above all it looks so striking,' said Bouthemont. 'Dumonteil is the only one who can make it for us . . . On my last trip, when I had my argument with Gaujean, he said he was willing to use a hundred looms to make this pattern, but he insisted on twenty-five centimes more per metre.'

Nearly every month Bouthemont would visit the factories, spending days in Lyons, staying at the best hotels, and with instructions that money was no object when negotiating with manufacturers. Moreover, he enjoyed absolute freedom, and bought as he thought fit, providing that each year he increased the turnover of his department by a ratio agreed in advance; and it was, in fact, on this increase that his commission was based. In short, his position at the Ladies' Paradise, like that of all his fellow section-managers, was that of a specialized merchant in a group of different trades, a kind of vast city of commerce.

'So, it's decided then,' he went on. 'We'll price it at five francs sixty . . . You know that that scarcely covers the purchase price.'

'Yes, yes, five francs sixty,' said Mouret briskly, 'and if I was on my own, I'd sell it at a loss.'

The section-manager laughed heartily.

'Oh! That would suit me perfectly. It would triple sales, and as my only concern is to get big takings . . .'

But Bourdoncle remained serious and tight-lipped. His commission was based on the total profits, and it was not in his interest to lower the prices. His task as a supervisor consisted precisely in keeping an eye on the price tickets to see that Bouthemont did not simply indulge his desire to increase sales, and sell at too small a profit. Besides, he was once more filled with his old misgivings when faced with publicity schemes which he did not understand. He ventured to show his distaste by saying:

'If we sell at five francs sixty it's just as if we were selling it at a loss, because our expenses must be deducted, and they're considerable . . . Anywhere else they'd sell it at seven francs.'

At that Mouret lost his temper. He banged the flat of his hand on the silk, and shouted irritably:

'Yes, I know, and that's just why I want to give it away to our customers . . . Really, my dear fellow, you'll never understand women. Can't you see they'll go mad over this silk?'

'No doubt,' interrupted his associate, obstinately, 'and the more they buy, the more we'll lose.'

'We'll lose a few centimes on these goods, I'll grant you. But so what? It won't be such a disaster if it enables us to attract all the women here and hold them at our mercy, their heads turned at the sight of our piles of goods, emptying their purses without counting! The main thing, my dear fellow, is to excite their interest, and for that you must have an article that delights them—which causes a sensation. After that you can sell the other goods at prices as high as anywhere else, and they'll still think yours are the cheapest. For example, our Cuir-d'Or, that taffeta at seven francs fifty, which is on sale everywhere at that price, will seem an extraordinary bargain, and will be sufficient to make up for the loss on the Paris-. You'll see, you'll see.'

He was becoming quite eloquent.

'Don't you understand? I want the Paris-Paradise to revolutionize the market in a week. It's our master-stroke, it's what's going to save us and make our name. People won't talk about anything else, the blue and silver selvage will be known from one end of France to the other . . . And you'll hear the groan of fury from our competitors. The small traders will lose some more of their feathers over it. They're done for, all those old clothes dealers dying of rheumatism in their cellars!'

The assistants who were checking the goods stood round their employer, listening and smiling. He liked talking in this way without contradiction. Once more, Bourdoncle gave in. In the mean time the packing-case had been emptied, and two men were un-nailing another one.

'It's the manufacturers who aren't pleased!' said Bouthemont. 'They're furious with you in Lyons; they claim that your cheap sales are ruining them. You know that Gaujean has definitely declared war against me. Yes, he's sworn to give the small shops long credit rather than accept my prices.'

Mouret shrugged his shoulders.

'If Gaujean isn't reasonable,' he replied, 'Gaujean will be left high and dry . . . What have they got to complain about? We pay them immediately, we take everything they make, the least they can do is work for less . . . Besides, the public gets the benefit, that's the main thing.'

The assistant was emptying the second packing-case, while Bouthemont had gone back to checking the pieces of material against the invoice. Another assistant, at the end of the counter, was marking the price on them and, the checking finished, the invoice signed by the section-manager had to be sent up to the central counting-house. For a moment longer Mouret continued looking at this work, all the activity surrounding the unpacking of the goods, which were piling up and threatening to swamp the basement; then, without saying another word, he went away with the air of a captain satisfied with his troops, followed by Bourdoncle.

They went slowly through the basement. The ventilators placed at intervals shed a pale light; and in the depths of dark corners, along the narrow corridors, gas jets were continually burning. Leading off these corridors were the stock-rooms, vaults shut off with wooden boards, where the different departments stowed away their surplus goods. As he passed, Mouret glanced at the heating installation, which was to be lit on Monday for the first time, and at the small firemen's post which was guarding a giant gas meter enclosed in an iron cage. The kitchen and the canteens, old cellars turned into small rooms, were on the left, near the corner of the Place Gaillon. Finally, at the other end of the basement, he came to the dispatch department. The parcels which customers did not take away themselves were sent down there, sorted on tables, and put into pigeon-holes which represented the different districts of Paris; then they were sent up a large staircase which came out just opposite the Vieil Elbeuf, and put into vans parked near the pavement. In the mechanical working of the Ladies' Paradise, the staircase in the Rue de la Michodière constantly disgorged the goods which had been swallowed up by the chute in the Rue Neuve-Saint-Augustin, after they had passed through the mechanism of the various departments upstairs.

'Campion,' said Mouret to the delivery manager, a thin-faced ex-sergeant, 'why were six pairs of sheets which a lady bought yesterday at about two o'clock not delivered in the evening?'

'Where does the lady live?' asked the employee.

'In the Rue de Rivoli, at the corner of the Rue d'Alger . . . Madame Desforges.'

At this early hour the sorting tables were bare, and the pigeon-holes contained only a few parcels left over from the day before. While Campion, after consulting a list, was rummaging among these parcels, Bourdoncle watched Mouret, thinking that this devil of a man knew everything, attended to everything, even while sitting at the supper tables of restaurants and in his mistresses' bedrooms. Finally, Campion discovered the error: the cash-desk had given a wrong number, and the parcel had come back.

'Which cash-desk dealt with it?' asked Mouret. 'What? No. 10, you say . . . ?'

And turning to his lieutenant, he said:

'Cash-desk 10, that's Albert, isn't it? . . . We'll go and have a word with him.'

But before going round the shop, he wanted to go upstairs to the mail-order department, which occupied several rooms on the second floor. It was there that all the provincial and foreign orders arrived; and every morning he went there to look at the correspondence. For two years this correspondence had been growing daily. The department had at first kept about ten clerks busy, but now already needed more than thirty. Some opened the letters, others read them, sitting at both sides of the same table; still others sorted them, giving each one a serial number which was repeated on a pigeon-hole; then, when the letters had been distributed to the different departments and the departments had sent up the articles, the articles were put into the pigeon-holes according to the serial number. It remained only to check them and pack them up in a neighbouring room, where a team of workmen nailed and tied things up from morning till night.

Mouret asked his usual question.

'How many letters this morning, Levasseur?'

'Five hundred and thirty-four, sir,' replied the chief clerk. 'After Monday's sale announcement, I was afraid we wouldn't have enough staff. It was very difficult to manage yesterday.'

Bourdoncle expressed his satisfaction with a nod of the head. He had not expected five hundred and thirty-four letters on Tuesday. Round the table the clerks continued slitting the letters open and reading, with a continuous sound of rustling paper, while in front of the pigeon-holes the coming and going of goods was beginning. This was one of the most complicated and important departments in the shop: its members worked constantly at fever-pitch, for, according to regulations, all the orders received in the morning had to be sent off by the evening. 'You'll be given the staff you need, Levasseur,' Mouret answered finally; he had seen at a glance what a good state the department was in. 'As you know, when there's work to be done we never refuse the staff.'

Upstairs, under the roof, were the little attic rooms where the salesgirls slept. But he went downstairs again and entered the central counting-house, which was near his office. It was a room shut off by a glass partition with a brass pay-desk in it, and it contained an enormous safe fixed in the wall. Here two cashiers sorted out the takings which Lhomme, the chief sales cashier, brought up to them every evening; they then settled current expenses and paid the manufacturers, the staff, and the crowd of people who lived off the shop in one way or another. The counting-house communicated with another room, lined with green files, where ten clerks checked the invoices. Then came yet another office, the clearing-house: there six young men, bent over black desks, with piles of registers behind them, drew up accounts of the salesmen's commissions by collating the sales bills. This section, which was quite new, was not running well.

Mouret and Bourdoncle had passed through the counting-house and the checking office. When they went into the other office the young men, who were laughing and joking, had a sudden shock. Mouret, without reprimanding them, explained the system of the small bonus he had thought of paying them for every error they discovered in the sales bills; and when he had left the clerks, no longer laughing, and with a cowed air, set to work with a vengeance, hunting for mistakes.

On the ground floor, in the shop, Mouret went straight to cash-desk No. 10, where Albert Lhomme was polishing his nails while waiting for customers. People often spoke of 'the Lhomme dynasty', since Madame Aurélie, the buyer in the ladieswear department, after helping her husband to become chief cashier, had managed to get a retail cash-desk for her son, a tall lad, pale and dissolute, who could never stay anywhere, and who caused her a great deal of anxiety. But when confronted with the young man, Mouret stood aside, not wishing to make himself unpopular by acting like a policeman; from both policy and taste he kept to his role of benevolent god. He nudged Bourdoncle gently with his elbow—Bourdoncle, that model of rectitude, whom he usually charged with the task of reprimanding negligent staff.

'Monsieur Albert,' said the latter sternly, 'you've taken another address down wrongly; the parcel came back . . . It's intolerable!'

The cashier felt obliged to defend himself, and called as a witness the porter who had tied up the parcel. This porter, Joseph by name, also belonged to the Lhomme dynasty, for he was Albert's foster-brother and owed his job to Madame

Aurélie's influence. As the young man wanted him to say it was the customer's mistake, he stuttered, twisting the little goatee beard which made his scarred face seem longer, torn between his conscience as an old soldier and his gratitude towards his protectors.

'Leave Joseph alone,' Bourdoncle exclaimed at last. 'Don't say any more . . . You're lucky that we appreciate your mother's good work!'

But at that moment Lhomme came running over. From his own cash-desk near the door he could see his son's, which was in the glove department. Already white-haired, overweight from his sedentary life, he had a flabby, nondescript face, as if worn away by the reflection of the money he was continually counting. The fact that he had had an arm amputated did not hinder him at all in his task, and people even came out of curiosity to see him checking the takings, so swiftly did the notes and coins slip through his left hand, the only one he had. The son of a tax-collector in Chablis,* he had come to Paris as bookkeeper to a wine-merchant in the Port-aux-Vins.* Then he had married the daughter of a small Alsatian tailor, the caretaker of the house where he was living in the Rue Cuvier; and from that day on he had been under the thumb of his wife, whose commercial abilities filled him with respect. She earned more than twelve thousand francs in the clothing department, whereas he had a fixed salary of only five thousand francs. And his respect for a wife who could bring such sums into the home extended to his son as well, for he also belonged to her.

'What's the matter?' he murmured. 'Has Albert made a mistake?'

At that, Mouret reappeared on the scene to play the part of the good prince, as was his custom. When Bourdoncle had made himself feared, Mouret would ensure his own popularity.

'A silly mistake,' he murmured. 'My dear Lhomme, your son is a scatter-brain who really should take his example from you.'

Then, changing the subject and making himself seem even more amiable, he said:

'What about the concert the other day? . . . Did you have a good seat?'

A blush spread over the old cashier's pale cheeks. Music was his only vice, a secret vice he indulged in alone, constantly doing the rounds of the theatres, concerts, auditions; in spite of his amputated arm he played the horn, thanks to an ingenious system of clamps; and as Madame Lhomme hated noise, in the evening he would wrap his instrument up in a cloth, and was nevertheless delighted to the point of ecstasy by the strangely muffled sounds he extracted from it. In the endless chaos of their domestic life he had made an oasis of music for himself. That and the money in the cash-desk was all that concerned him, apart from his admiration for his wife.

'A very good seat,' he answered, his eyes shining. 'It was really too kind of you, sir.'

Mouret, who took a personal delight in satisfying other people's passions, sometimes gave Lhomme the tickets forced on him by ladies who were patrons of the arts. And he completed the old man's delight by saying:

'Ah! Beethoven, ah! Mozart . . . What music!'

Without waiting for a reply he moved on and caught up with Bourdoncle, who was already on his tour of inspection through the departments. In the central hall, an inner courtyard covered with a glass roof, were the silks. First they went along the gallery on the Rue Neuve-Saint-Augustin side, which was filled from one end to the other with household linen. Nothing unusual struck them as they passed slowly through the crowd of respectful assistants. Then they turned into the printed cotton goods and hosiery, where the same order reigned. But in the woollen department, in the gallery which ran at right angles through to the Rue de la Michodière, Bourdoncle resumed his role of chief executioner on glimpsing a young man sitting on a counter and looking worn out after a sleepless night; the young man, Liénard by name, the son of a rich draper in Angers, hung his head as he received the reprimand, fearing nothing in his idle, carefree life of pleasure except being recalled to the provinces by his father. Admonishments now began to fall like hail, the gallery in the Rue de la Michodière bearing the brunt of the storm; in the drapery department one of those salesmen who received board and lodging but no salary, who were starting their careers and slept in their departments, had come in after eleven o'clock; in the haberdashery department the assistant buyer had just been caught in the basement finishing a cigarette. But the storm broke with especial violence in the glove department, over the head of one of the few Parisians in the shop, a young man known as Handsome Mignot, the illegitimate son of a lady who taught the harp: his crime was that he had made a scene in the canteen by complaining about the food. As there were three meal services, one at half-past nine, one at half-past ten, and one at half-past eleven, and he went to the third service, he tried to explain that he always had the left-overs, the worst of everything.

'What! The food isn't good?' asked Mouret innocently, opening his mouth at last.

He only gave one franc fifty a head per day to the chef, a real terror from Auvergne,* who still managed to make a profit for himself; and the food really was awful. But Bourdoncle shrugged his shoulders: a chef who had to serve four hundred lunches and four hundred dinners, even in three sittings, could scarcely linger over the refinements of his art.

'Never mind,' said the chief good-naturedly, 'I want all our employees to have good food and plenty of it . . . I'll have a word with the chef.'

Mignot's complaint was shelved. Then, back at their point of departure, standing near the door among the umbrellas and ties, Mouret and Bourdoncle received the report of one of the four shopwalkers who supervised the shop. Old Jouve, a retired captain who had been decorated at Constantine,* a handsome man still, majestically bald, and with a big sensual nose, told them of a salesman who, at a simple remonstrance from him, had called him 'an old fool'; the salesman was immediately dismissed.

The shop was still empty of customers, except for a few local housewives who were going through the deserted galleries. At the door the inspector who clocked in the staff had just closed his book and was making a separate list of those who were late. This was the moment when the salesmen took up their positions in their departments, which porters had been sweeping and dusting since five o'clock. They all put their hats and overcoats away, stifling yawns as they did so, still half asleep. Some exchanged a few words and gazed about the shop, as though to be preparing themselves for another day's work; others were leisurely removing the green baize with which they had covered the goods the evening before, after they'd been folded up. The piles of material were beginning to appear, symmetrically arranged, and the whole shop was clean and tidy, sparkling in the gay early morning light, waiting for the rush of business once more to choke it and dwarf it beneath an avalanche of linen, cloth, silk, and lace.

In the bright light of the central hall, at the silk counter, two young men were talking in a low voice. One of them, small and handsome, sturdy-looking and with a pink complexion, was trying to blend different coloured silks for an indoor display. His name was Hutin and he was the son of a café owner in Yvetot; in eighteen months he had succeeded in becoming one of the principal salesmen, thanks to a natural flexibility of character and a continual flow of flattery, which concealed a ravenous appetite, a desire to eat up everything, to devour the world without even being hungry, for the sheer pleasure of it.

'Listen, Favier, I'd have hit him if I'd been you, honestly!' he was saying to the other, a tall, morose-looking lad with dry, sallow skin, who came from a family of weavers in Besançon and who, though lacking in charm, possessed a disquieting strength of will beneath his reserved manner.

'Hitting people doesn't get you anywhere,' he murmured phlegmatically. 'It's better to wait.'

They were talking about Robineau, who was in charge of the assistants while the head of the department was in the basement. Hutin was secretly undermining the assistant buyer, whose job he coveted. Already, to hurt his feelings and make him leave, he had brought Bouthemont in from outside to fill the vacant job of first salesman which had been promised to Robineau. However, Robineau was holding his own, and there was now an unending battle between them. Hutin dreamed of setting the whole department against him, of hounding him out by means of ill will and little humiliations. He was conducting his campaign, moreover, with his pleasant manner, inciting Favier especially, for he was the salesman next to him in seniority, and seemed to let himself be led on, although he would suddenly express reservations through which a whole, silently waged private campaign could be felt.

'Ssh! Seventeen!' he said sharply to his colleague, to warn him with this customary exclamation of the approach of Mouret and Bourdoncle.

These two were going through the hall, continuing their inspection. They stopped Robineau about a stock of velvet piled up in boxes which were cluttering up a table. And when the latter replied that there wasn't enough room, Mouret exclaimed with a smile:

'I told you so, Bourdoncle, the shop's already too small! One day we'll have to knock down the walls as far as the Rue de Choiseul! You'll see what a crush there'll be next Monday!'

And with regard to the sale, the object of preparations at every counter, he again questioned Robineau and gave him various orders. But for several minutes, while continuing to talk, he had been watching Hutin, who was lingering behind in order to put some blue silks next to grey and yellow ones, then stepping back to see how the colours blended. Suddenly Mouret intervened.

'But why are you trying to make it easy on the eye?' he said. 'Don't be afraid, blind them . . . Here! Some red! Some green! Some yellow!'

He had taken the pieces of material, throwing them together, crumpling them, making dazzling combinations with them. Everyone agreed that the governor was the best window-dresser in Paris, a revolutionary window-dresser in fact, who had founded the school of the brutal and gigantic in the art of display. He wanted avalanches, as if they had fallen at random from gaping shelves, and he wanted them blazing with the most flamboyant colours, making each other seem even brighter. He used to say that the customers should have sore eyes by the time they left the shop. Hutin, on the contrary, belonged to the classic school of symmetry and harmony achieved by shading, and watched Mouret lighting this conflagration of materials in the middle of a table without venturing the slightest criticism, but his lips pursing like an artist whose convictions were hurt by such an orgy.

'There!' exclaimed Mouret when he had finished. 'Leave it like that . . . Let me know if it doesn't attract the women on Monday!'

Just as he was rejoining Bourdoncle and Robineau, a woman appeared; she remained for a few seconds rooted to the spot, entranced by the display. It was Denise. She had waited for nearly an hour in the street, paralysed by a terrible attack of shyness, and had at last made up her mind to come in. But she was still so beside herself with shyness that she could not follow even the simplest directions; the assistants, when she stammeringly enquired for Madame Aurélie, pointed out the mezzanine staircase to her in vain; she would thank them, and then turn left if she had been told to turn right; so that for ten minutes she had been wandering round the ground floor, going from one department to another, surrounded by the ill-natured curiosity and sullen indifference of the salesmen. She felt a desire to run away and, at the same time, a need to stop and admire. She was so lost and small inside the monster, inside the machine, and although it was still idle, she was terrified that she would be caught up in its motion, which was already beginning to make the walls shake. And the thought of the shop at the Vieil Elbeuf, dark and cramped, made this vast shop appear even bigger to her; it seemed bathed in light, like a town, with monuments, squares, streets, in which it seemed she would never find her way.

She had not dared before to venture into the silk hall; its high glazed ceiling, sumptuous counters, and church-like atmosphere frightened her. Then, when she had at last gone in, to escape the grinning salesmen in the linen department, she had stumbled straight into Mouret's display; and though she was scared, the woman in her was aroused, her cheeks suddenly flushed, and she forgot herself as she gazed at the blazing conflagration of silks.

'Hey!' said Hutin crudely in Favier's ear, 'It's that tart we saw in the Place Gaillon.'

Mouret, while pretending to listen to Bourdoncle and Robineau, was secretly flattered by this poor girl's sudden fascination with his display, as a duchess might be by a brutal look of desire from a passing drayman. But Denise had raised her eyes, and she was even more confused when she recognized the young man she took to be the head of a department. She thought he was looking at her sternly. Then, not knowing how to get away, quite distraught, she once again approached the nearest assistant, who happened to be Favier.

'Could you tell me where I can find Madame Aurélie, please?'

Favier gave her an unpleasant look and replied curtly:

'On the mezzanine floor.'

Denise, anxious to escape from all these men who were
staring at her, thanked him and was once more walking away
from the staircase she should have climbed, when Hutin yielded
to his natural instinct for gallantry. He had called her a tart, but
it was with his most amiable salesman's smile that he stopped
her.

'No, this way, miss . . . If you would be so good as to . . .'

He even went with her a little way to the foot of the staircase
in the left-hand corner of the hall.

There he bowed slightly, and smiled at her with the smile he
gave to all women.

'Upstairs, turn left . . . The ladieswear department is straight
ahead.'

This tender politeness moved Denise deeply. It was
like a brotherly hand extended to her. She had raised her
eyes, she was gazing at Hutin, and everything about him touched
her, his handsome face, his smiling look which allayed her
fear, his voice which seemed to her sweet and consoling.
Her heart swelling with gratitude, she expressed her friendship
in the few disjointed words her emotion allowed her to stammer
out.

'You're too kind . . . Please don't trouble . . . Thank you so
much, sir . . .'

Hutin had already rejoined Favier, to whom he said under his
breath, in a crude tone:

'She's skinny, eh!'

Upstairs the girl found the ladieswear department straight
away. It was a vast room with high cupboards of carved oak all
round, and plate-glass windows facing the Rue de la Michodière.
Five or six women in silk dresses, looking very smart with their
chignons curled and their crinolines* sweeping behind them,
were moving about, talking to each another. One of them, tall
and thin, with an elongated head which made her look like a
runaway horse, was leaning against a cupboard, as if she was
already tired out.

'Madame Aurélie?' Denise repeated.

The saleswoman looked at her without replying, with an air of
disdain for her shabby dress; then, turning to one of her com-

panions, a short girl with a pasty complexion, she asked in an artless, wearied manner:

'Mademoiselle Vadon, do you know where Madame Aurélie is?'

The girl, who was in the process of arranging long cloaks in order of size, did not even take the trouble to look up.

'No, Mademoiselle Prunaire, I don't know,' she said rather primly.

A silence ensued. Denise stood there, and no one took any further notice of her. However, after waiting a moment she plucked up enough courage to ask another question.

'Do you think Madame Aurélie will be back soon?'

Then the assistant buyer of the department, a thin, ugly woman whom she had not noticed, a widow with a prominent chin and coarse hair, called to her from a cupboard where she was checking price tickets:

'You'll have to wait if you want to talk to Madame Aurélie personally.'

And, addressing another saleswoman, she added:

'Isn't she in the reception office?'

'No, Madame Frédéric, I don't think so,' the girl replied. 'She didn't say anything; she can't be far away.'

Denise remained standing. There were a few chairs for customers, but as no one told her to sit down she did not dare to take one, although she felt that her legs might drop off with fatigue. These young ladies had clearly sensed that she was a salesgirl coming to apply for a job, and they were staring at her, stripping her naked, out of the corners of their eyes, with the veiled, ill-natured hostility of people seated at table who do not like moving up to make room for those outside who are hungry. Her embarrassment grew; she crossed the room very quietly and looked out into the street, just for something to do. Just opposite, the Vieil Elbeuf with its rusty frontage and lifeless windows seemed to her so ugly, so wretched, seen thus from the luxury and life of her present vantage-point, that her heart was wrung with something akin to remorse.

'I say,' whispered tall Mademoiselle Prunaire to little Mademoiselle Vadon, 'did you see her boots?'

'And her dress!' murmured the other.

Her eyes still on the street, Denise felt herself being devoured. But she was not angry; she had not thought either of them beautiful, neither the tall one with her bun of red hair hanging down her horse-like neck, nor the short one with the sour-milk complexion which made her flat and seemingly boneless face look flabby. Clara Prunaire, the daughter of a clog-maker in the forest of Vivet, had been seduced by the footmen at the Château de Mareuil, where the Countess employed her to do the mending; she had worked later on in a shop in Langres, whence she had come to Paris, where she was now avenging herself on men for the kicks she had received in the past from old Prunaire. Marguerite Vadon had been born in Grenoble, where her family owned a cloth business; she had had to be sent off to the Ladies' Paradise to hush up a slip she had made, a child conceived by accident; if she behaved well she would eventually return home to run her parents' shop and marry a cousin who was waiting for her.

'Anyway,' Clara resumed in a low voice, 'she certainly won't get very far here!'

But they stopped talking as a woman of about forty-five came in. It was Madame Aurélie, very stout and tightly laced in a black silk dress; the bodice, stretched over the massive curves of her shoulders and bust, shone like a piece of armour. Beneath dark coils of hair she had large, unwavering eyes, a stern mouth, and broad, rather pendulous cheeks; and in the majesty of her position as chief buyer her face was acquiring the puffiness of the bloated mask of some Caesar.

'Mademoiselle Vadon,' she said in an irritated voice, 'why didn't you put the model of that close-fitting coat back in the workroom yesterday?'

'It needed an alteration, ma'am,' the saleswoman replied, 'so Madame Frédéric kept it out.'

At that the assistant buyer took the model from a cupboard, and the dispute continued. All opposition was crushed when Madame Aurélie thought she had to assert her authority. Extremely vain—to the point of not wishing to be called by her real name, Lhomme, which annoyed her, and of not admitting that her father, whom she always referred to as a tailor in a shop, was really just a caretaker—she was friendly only to those girls who were pliable and fawning, bowing down in admiration to her. When she had tried to set herself up in the dressmaking business she had become embittered, continually dogged by bad luck, exasperated at the feeling that she was made for affluence and yet encountered nothing but a series of catastrophes; and even now, after her success at the Ladies' Paradise, where she earned twelve thousand francs a year, she still seemed to have a grudge against the world, and she was very hard on beginners just as, in the beginning, life had been hard to her.

'That'll do!' she said tartly. 'You've got no more sense than the others, Madame Frédéric . . . Have the alteration done straight away!'

During this discussion Denise had stopped looking at the street. She thought this woman must be Madame Aurélie but, alarmed by the anger in her raised voice, she remained standing, still waiting. The saleswomen, delighted at having set their two superiors against each other, had gone back to their work with an air of complete indifference. Several minutes passed, and no one had the kindness to extricate the girl from her embarrassment. In the end, it was Madame Aurélie herself who noticed her and, surprised at seeing her standing there without moving, asked her what she wanted.

'Madame Aurélie, please?'

'I am Madame Aurélie.'

Denise's mouth was dry and her hands cold; she was as frightened as when, as a child, she'd been terrified of being whipped. She stammered out her request, and then had to repeat it to make herself understood. Madame Aurélie looked at her with her large, unwavering eyes, and not a single fold of her imperial mask deigned to relax.

'How old are you?'

'Twenty, ma'am.'

'What, twenty? You don't look more than sixteen!'

Once more, the saleswomen were looking up. Denise hastened to add:

'Oh, I'm very strong!'

Madame Aurélie shrugged her broad shoulders. Then she declared:

'Oh well, I don't mind putting your name down. We put down the names of all those who apply . . . Mademoiselle Prunaire, give me the book.'

But the book could not be found: Jouve, one of the shop-walkers, probably had it. Clara, the tall girl, was going to fetch it when Mouret arrived, still followed by Bourdoncle. They were just finishing their tour of the mezzanine floor; they had been through the laces, the shawls, the furs, the furniture, the underwear, and were winding up with the dresses. Madame Aurélie left Denise for a moment to speak to them about an order for some coats she hoped to give to one of the big Parisian contractors; usually she bought direct, and on her own re-sponsibility; but for important purchases she preferred to con-sult the management. Bourdoncle then told her about her son Albert's latest lapse, which seemed to fill her with despair: that boy would be the death of her; his father, though not a man of talent, was at least reliable. The whole Lhomme dynasty, of which she was the undisputed head, sometimes gave her a great deal of trouble.

Mouret, surprised at seeing Denise again, bent down to ask Madame Aurélie what the girl was doing there; when the buyer replied that she had come to apply for a job as salesgirl, Bourdoncle, with his contempt for women, was staggered at such pretension.

'Surely not!' he murmured. 'It's a joke! She's too ugly.'

'It must be said there's nothing very beautiful about her,' said Mouret, not daring to defend her, although he still felt touched by her rapture downstairs before his arrangement of silks.

But the book was brought in and Madame Aurélie came back to Denise, who had certainly not made a good impression. She looked very clean in her thin black woollen dress; they did not dwell on her poor get-up, as a uniform, the regulation silk dress, was provided; but she seemed very weak and puny, and her face was sad. Without insisting on the girls being beautiful, they wanted them to be attractive for the sales rooms, and beneath the gaze of all these ladies and gentlemen who were studying her, weighing her like a mare being haggled over by peasants at a fair, Denise finally lost what was left of her composure.

'Your name?' asked the buyer, pen in hand, ready to write at the end of a counter.

'Denise Baudu, ma'am.'

'Your age?'

'Twenty years and four months.'

And she repeated, risking a glance at Mouret, at the man she took to be the head of a department, whom she kept on meeting and whose presence disturbed her:

'I don't look it, but I'm very strong.'

They smiled. Bourdoncle was studying his nails with impatience. Her words fell, moreover, in the middle of a discouraging silence.

'What shop have you worked in in Paris?' resumed Madame Aurélie.

'But I've just arrived from Valognes, ma'am.'

This was a fresh disaster. Usually, the Ladies' Paradise only took saleswomen with a year's experience in one of the small shops in Paris. On hearing this, Denise thought all was lost, and had it not been for the children she would have turned on her heel in order to bring this useless interview to an end.

'Where did you work at Valognes?'

'At Cornaille's.'

Mouret let slip a remark: 'I know it, it's a good firm.'

Usually he never interfered in the engagement of personnel, as the heads of departments were responsible for their own staff. But, with his sensitive flair for women, he felt a hidden charm in this girl, a quality of grace and tenderness of which she herself was unaware. The good reputation of the shop in which an applicant had started was very important; often it was the deciding factor in engaging someone. Madame Aurélie went on in a gentler tone:

'And why did you leave Cornaille's?'

'For family reasons,' Denise replied, blushing. 'We've lost our parents; I had to follow my brothers . . . Here's a testimonial.'

It was excellent. Her hopes were reviving, when a final question embarrassed her.

'Do you have any other references in Paris? Where are you living?'

'At my uncle's,' she murmured, hesitating to name him, fearing that they would never take the niece of a competitor. 'At my uncle Baudu's, over there, opposite.'

At that Mouret intervened a second time.

'What! You're Baudu's niece! Did Baudu send you here?'

'Oh! no, sir!'

And she could not help laughing, so odd did the idea seem to her. She was transfigured. She became quite rosy, and the smile on her rather large mouth seemed to light up her whole face. Her grey eyes shone with a tender light, delightful dimples appeared in her cheeks; even her fair hair seemed alive with the frank and courageous gaiety of her whole being.

'She's really pretty!' whispered Mouret to Bourdoncle.

His colleague, with a gesture of annoyance, refused to agree. Clara pursed her lips, while Marguerite turned away. Only Madame Aurélie nodded in approval as Mouret continued:

'Your uncle should have brought you himself; his recommendation is sufficient. They say he bears us a grudge. We're more broad-minded, and if he can't find a job for his niece in his own shop, well, we'll show him that she only needs to knock at our door to be taken in. Tell him I'm still very fond of him—it's not me he should blame, but the new business conditions. And tell him that he'll end up ruining himself if he insists on sticking to all those ridiculous, old-fashioned ideas.'

Denise turned quite pale again. It was Mouret. No one had pronounced his name, but he had revealed who he was, and she guessed it now; she understood why this young man had caused her such emotion in the street, in the silk department, and again now. This emotion, which she could not understand, was oppressing her more and more, like a burden that was too heavy. All the stories her uncle had told came back to her, enlarging Mouret, surrounding him with a legend, establishing him as the master of the terrible machine which, since the morning, had been holding her in the iron teeth of its gear-wheels. And behind his handsome face, his well-trimmed beard, and his eyes the colour of old gold she saw the dead woman, Madame Hédouin, whose blood had helped to cement the stones of the shop. The cold shiver she had felt the day before seized her once more, and she thought she was simply afraid of him.

Meanwhile, Madame Aurélie had closed the book. She only wanted one saleswoman, and she already had ten applications. But her anxiety to please her employer was too great for her to hesitate. However, the application would still be treated in the usual way: Jouve, the shopwalker, would make inquiries and draw up a report; then the buyer would decide.

'Very well, Mademoiselle Baudu,' she said majestically, to preserve her authority. 'We'll write to you.'

Embarrassment held Denise rooted there for a moment longer. Surrounded by all these people, she did not know how to take her leave. At last, she thanked Madame Aurélie; and when she had to pass in front of Mouret and Bourdoncle she said goodbye to them. But they had already forgotten about her, for they were busy examining the model coat with Madame Frédéric, and did not even reply. Clara looked at Marguerite and made a gesture of annoyance, as if predicting that the new salesgirl would not have a very good time in the department. No doubt Denise felt this indifference and malice behind her back, for she went down the staircase as uncomfortably as she had gone up it, prey to a strange feeling of anguish, wondering whether she should be in despair or delighted at having come. Could she count on the job? In her anxiety, which had prevented her from understanding clearly, she was again beginning to have doubts about it. Of all her sensations, two remained and gradually replaced the others: the impression made on her by Mouret, so deep as to make her afraid; and Hutin's kindness, the only pleasure she had had that morning, a memory of charm and gentleness which filled her with gratitude. When she went through the shop to go out she looked for the young man, happy at the thought of thanking him again with her eyes; and she felt quite sad not to see him.

'Well, miss, were you successful?' asked a timid voice when she finally reached the street.

She turned round and recognized the tall, pale, ungainly lad who had spoken to her in the morning. He too had just come out of the Ladies' Paradise, and he looked even more frightened than she was, totally bewildered by the interrogation he had just been through.

'Oh! I've really no idea, sir,' she replied.

'You're in the same boat as me, then. What a way they've got of looking at you and talking to you in there! I'm trying for a place in the lace department; I was at Crèvecœur's in the Rue du Mail.'

They were once more standing facing each other; and, not knowing how to say goodbye, they began to blush. Then the young man, just for something to say to allay his extreme shyness, ventured to ask her in his awkward, good-natured way:

'What's your name, miss?'

'Denise Baudu.'

'My name's Henri Deloche.'

They were smiling now. Recognizing the similarity of their positions, they held out their hands to each other.

'Good luck!'

'Yes, good luck!'

CHAPTER 3

EVERY Saturday, between four and six, Madame Desforges served tea and cakes to those of her close friends who might wish to visit her. Her flat was on the third floor, at the corner of the Rue de Rivoli and the Rue d'Alger;* and the windows of both drawing-rooms overlooked the Tuileries Gardens.

On that particular Saturday, just as a servant was about to show him into the large drawing-room, Mouret, standing in the hall and gazing through an open door, glimpsed Madame Desforges crossing the small drawing-room. She stopped on seeing him, and he went in that way, greeting her very formally. Then, when the servant had closed the door, he quickly seized the young woman's hand, and kissed it tenderly.

'Be careful! I've got company!' she said in a whisper, glancing towards the door of the large drawing-room. 'I went to fetch this fan to show them.'

And she playfully tapped him on the face with the tip of the fan. She was dark and rather buxom, with large, jealous eyes. Still holding her hand, he asked:

'Will he come?'

'Yes, of course,' she replied. 'I have his word.'

They were referring to Baron Hartmann, director of the Crédit Immobilier.* Madame Desforges's father had been an important civil servant, and she was the widow of a stockbroker who had left her a fortune—a fortune denied by some, exaggerated by others. It was rumoured that even while her husband was alive she had shown her gratitude to Baron Hartmann, who, as an important financier, had given useful advice to the family; and later on, after her husband's death, the liaison had probably continued, though always discreetly, without imprudence or scandal. Madame Desforges never courted notoriety, and all doors were open to her in the upper middle class into which she had been born. Even now, when the passion of the banker, a sceptical, crafty man, was turning into a simple paternal affection, if she did permit herself certain lovers to whom he turned a blind eye, she displayed in her love-affairs such delicate restraint and tact, and a knowledge of the world so skilfully applied, that appearances were saved, and no one would have dared to question her virtue openly. Meeting Mouret at the house of some mutual friends, she had at first detested him; but she had yielded to him later on, as if carried away by the sudden passion of his attack, and while he was manœuvring in order to meet the Baron through her, she had gradually fallen truly in love with him, adoring him with the violence of a woman already thirty-five, but only admitting to twenty-nine, for she was in despair at the thought that he was younger than herself, terrified that she might lose him.

'Does he know about it?' he went on.

'No, you must explain the affair to him yourself,' she answered, no longer addressing him with the familiar 'tu'.

She looked at him, thinking to herself that he could not know anything or he would not use her influence with the Baron like this, while pretending to consider him simply as an old friend of hers. But he still held her hand, calling her his sweet Henriette, and she felt her heart melting. Silently, she offered her lips to him, pressed them against his, then whispered:

'Shh! They're waiting for me . . . Follow me in.'

Female voices, muffled by the heavy curtains, were coming from the large drawing-room. She pushed the double door, leaving it wide open, and handed the fan to one of the four ladies who were sitting in the middle of the room.

'Here it is,' she said. 'I didn't know where it was; my maid would never have found it.'

And, turning round, she added gaily:

'Do come in, Monsieur Mouret, come through the little drawing-room. It won't be so ceremonious.'

Mouret bowed to the ladies, whom he knew. The drawing-room, with its Louis XVI furniture upholstered with flowered brocade, its gilded bronzes, and huge green plants, had a tender feminine intimacy, in spite of its high ceiling; and through the two windows the chestnut trees in the Tuileries Gardens could be seen, their leaves blowing about in the October wind.

'This Chantilly isn't bad at all!' exclaimed Madame Bourdelais, who was holding the fan.

She was a small, fair woman of thirty, with a delicately shaped nose and sparkling eyes, one of Henriette's old school-friends, who had married an assistant undersecretary in the Ministry of Finance. She came from an old middle-class family, and ran her house and her three children with efficiency, good grace, and an exquisite flair for the practical side of life.

'And you paid twenty-five francs for it?' she resumed, examining every stitch of the lace. 'You say you got it in Luc,* from a local craftswoman? No, no, it isn't expensive. But of course you had to have it mounted.'

'Of course,' Madame Desforges replied. 'The mount cost me two hundred francs.'

Madame Bourdelais began to laugh. So that was what Henriette called a bargain! Two hundred francs for a plain ivory mount with a monogram on it! And for a simple little piece of Chantilly on which she had saved five francs! Similar fans could be found already mounted for a hundred and twenty francs. She named a shop in the Rue Poissonnière.

However, the fan was handed round by the ladies. Madame Guibal hardly gave it a glance. She was tall, thin, and red-haired, and looked utterly indifferent; though her grey eyes, occasionally penetrating her air of detachment, reflected the terrible pangs of egotism. She was never seen in the company of her husband, a well-known barrister at the Palais de Justice, who, so it was said, led a free life and was entirely devoted to his briefs and his pleasures.

'Oh,' she murmured as she passed the fan to Madame de Boves, 'I don't think I've bought more than a couple in my life. One is always given too many of them.'

The Countess replied in a subtly ironic voice:

'You are so lucky, my dear, to have an attentive husband!'

And leaning over to her daughter, a tall girl of twenty and a half, she added:

'Just look at the monogram, Blanche. What lovely work! It must have been the monogram that put up the price like that.'

Madame de Boves had just turned forty. She was a fine woman, with the figure of a goddess and a large face with regular features and big, sleepy eyes; her husband, Inspector-General of the Stud, had married her for her beauty. She appeared quite moved by the delicacy of the monogram, as if overwhelmed by desire; she turned pale with emotion. Suddenly, she said:

'Tell us what you think, Monsieur Mouret. Is it too expensive, two hundred francs for this mount?'

Mouret had remained standing in the midst of the five women, smiling, taking an interest in what interested them. He picked up the fan, examined it, and was about to give his opinion when the servant opened the door and announced:

'Madame Marty.'

A thin, ugly woman, ravaged by smallpox, and dressed with complicated elegance, came in. She was ageless; her thirty-five years looked like forty or thirty, depending on the nervous fever which agitated her. Her red leather bag, instead of being left outside, was hanging from her right hand.

'My dear,' she said to Henriette, 'forgive me for bringing my bag . . . I called in at the Paradise on the way, and as I've been extravagant again, I didn't want to leave this downstairs in my cab in case it was stolen.'

She noticed Mouret, and went on, laughing: 'Ah! Monsieur Mouret, I didn't mean to advertise for you; I didn't know you were here . . . You really have got some wonderful lace at the moment.'

This turned the attention away from the fan, which the young man put down on a pedestal table. The ladies were full of curiosity to see what Madame Marty had bought. She was known for her passion for spending, her inability to resist temptation, strictly virtuous though she was, and incapable of yielding to a lover; but no sooner did she set her eyes on the slightest piece of finery than she would let herself go and the flesh was conquered. The daughter of a minor civil servant, she was ruining her husband, a teacher at the Lycée Bonaparte* who, in order to meet the family's ever-increasing expenses, had to double his salary of six thousand francs by giving private lessons. She did not open her bag, but held it tightly on her lap, while talking about her daughter Valentine, who was fourteen and one of her most expensive indulgences, for she dressed her like herself in all the latest fashions, which never failed to seduce her.

'You know,' she explained, 'this winter, dresses for girls are trimmed with narrow lace . . . So when I saw some very pretty Valenciennes . . .'

She finally decided to open the bag. The ladies were craning their necks forward when, in the silence, the ante-room bell was heard.

'It's my husband,' stammered Madame Marty, very confused. 'He must have come to pick me up on his way from the Bonaparte.'

She quickly shut the bag, and instinctively made it disappear under her chair. All the ladies began to laugh. She blushed at her haste, and put the bag back on her lap, saying that men never understood and that there was no need for them to know.

'Monsieur de Boves, Monsieur de Vallagnosc,' the servant announced.

This was a surprise. Madame de Boves herself had not expected her husband. The latter, a handsome man, with moustaches and an imperial,* and with the stiff military bearing favoured at the Tuileries, kissed the hand of Madame Desforges, whom he had known as a girl in her father's house. He stood aside so that the other visitor, a tall pale fellow with an anaemically distinguished look, could in his turn greet the mistress of the house. But the conversation had hardly started up again when two slight exclamations were uttered.

'What! It's you, Paul!'

'Good Lord! Octave!'

Mouret and Vallagnosc shook hands. It was Madame Desforges's turn to show surprise. So they knew each other? Yes, indeed, they had grown up together, at the same school in Plassans;* and it was quite by chance that they had never met at her house before.

Still hand in hand they went into the small drawing-room, joking as they did so, just as the servant brought in the tea, a Chinese service on a silver tray, which he placed near Madame Desforges in the centre of a marble pedestal table with a light brass mounting. The ladies drew up their chairs and began talking more loudly, all speaking at once, producing an endless cross-fire of remarks; Monsieur de Boves, standing behind them, leaned forward from time to time to say a few words, with the

charm and courtesy which were part of his profession. The vast
room, so elegantly and cheerfully furnished, was made even
gayer by these chattering voices mingled with laughter.

'Well, Paul, old man!' repeated Mouret.

He was sitting close to Vallagnosc, on a settee. Left alone at
the far end of the small drawing-room—a very elegant boudoir
hung with buttercup-coloured silk—out of earshot, and with the
ladies only visible through the open door, they sat face to face,
laughing and slapping each other on the knee. They began to
recall the whole of their youth, the old college at Plassans with its
two courtyards, its damp classrooms, the refectory where they
used to eat so much cod, and the dormitories where the pillows
used to fly from bed to bed as soon as the junior master was
snoring. Paul, who belonged to an old parliamentary family,
noble, poor, and proud, had been quite a bookworm, always top
of the class, always being held up as an example by the teacher,
who had predicted a brilliant future for him; whereas Octave
remained at the bottom of the class, wasting away among
the dunces, fat and jolly, expending all his energy on violent
pleasures outside school. In spite of their different natures, a
close comradeship had made them inseparable until the
baccalauréat,* which they passed, one with distinction, the other
just scraping through after two failed attempts. Then they had
gone out into the world, and were now meeting again, after ten
years, already altered and aged.

'Tell me,' Mouret asked, 'what are you up to?'

'Oh, nothing at all.'

In spite of his delight at their meeting, Vallagnosc still retained his tired and disillusioned manner; and his friend, in
surprise, insisted, saying:

'Yes, but you must do something, after all . . . What do you
do?'

'Nothing,' he replied.

Octave began to laugh. Nothing, that wasn't enough. He
finally succeeded in extracting Paul's story from him, sentence
by sentence. It was the usual story of boys without money who
think they are obliged by their birth to remain in the liberal
professions and bury themselves under their arrogant medioc-

rity, happy to escape starvation despite having their drawers full of diplomas. He had followed the family tradition and read law; after that he had gone on being supported by his widowed mother, who was already finding it difficult to marry off her two daughters. He had finally begun to feel ashamed and, leaving the three women to live as best they could on the remains of their fortune, he had taken up a minor post in the Ministry of the Interior, where he had buried himself like a mole in its burrow.

'And how much do you earn?' Mouret resumed.

'Three thousand francs.'

'But that's a pittance! My poor chap, I'm really sorry for you . . . You were so good at school; you left us all behind! And they only give you three thousand francs, when they've had you rotting away there for five years! No, it's not fair.'

He broke off, and started to talk about himself.

'I turned my back on all that . . . You know what I'm doing now?'

'Yes,' said Vallagnosc. 'I heard you'd gone into business. You've got that big shop in the Place Gaillon, haven't you?'

'That's right . . . Calico, old chap!'

Mouret raised his head, slapped him on the knee again, and with the hearty gaiety of a fellow quite unashamed of the trade which was making him rich, repeated:

'Calico, masses of it! You know, I never really took to school, although I never thought I was any stupider than anyone else. When I'd passed the *bac* to please my family, I could easily have become a lawyer or a doctor like the rest of them; but professions like that frightened me, you see so many people become utterly frustrated in them . . . So, I ignored all that—with no regrets!—and pitched head first into business.'

Vallagnosc was smiling in a rather embarrassed way. Finally he murmured:

'It's true that your *bac* can't be much use to you for selling calico.'

'Well!' replied Mouret blithely, 'all I ask is that it shouldn't get in the way . . . And you know, when you've burdened your-self like that, it's not easy to get rid of it. You go through life at a tortoise's pace, while the others, those who are barefoot, run like hares.'

Then, noticing that his friend seemed troubled, he took his hands in his, and went on:

'Come, come, I don't want to hurt you, but you must admit that your diplomas haven't satisfied any of your needs . . . Do you know that the head of my silk department will get more than twelve thousand francs this year? Yes, really! A lad of very sound intelligence, who never got beyond spelling and the four rules . . .* The ordinary salesmen at my place make three to four thousand francs, more than you earn yourself; and their education didn't cost what yours did, they weren't launched into the world with a signed promise that they'd conquer it . . . Of course, making money isn't everything. But, between the poor devils with a smattering of learning who clutter up the professions without earning enough to keep themselves from starving, and the practical fellows equipped for life, who know their trade backwards, my word! I wouldn't hesitate, I'm for the latter against the former; I think fellows like that understand their age very well!'

He had become quite excited; Henriette, who was serving tea, looked round. When he saw her smile at the end of the large drawing-room and also noticed two other ladies listening, he was the first to laugh at his own words.

'Anyway, old chap, any counter-jumper who's just beginning has a chance of becoming a millionaire nowadays.'

Vallagnosc was leaning back indolently on the sofa. He had half closed his eyes, in an attitude of fatigue and disdain, in which a touch of affectation added to the real effeteness of his breed.

'Bah!' he murmured, 'life isn't worth the trouble. Nothing's any fun.'

And as Mouret, shocked, looked at him in surprise, he added:

'Everything happens and nothing happens. One may as well sit and do nothing!'

Then he went on to explain his pessimism, his sense of the pettiness and frustrations of existence. At one time he had dreamed of literature, but his association with certain poets had left him with a feeling of universal despair. He always came back to the uselessness of effort, the boredom of hours all equally empty, and the ultimate stupidity of the world. All enjoyment was a failure, and there was not even any pleasure in doing wrong.*

'Now tell me, do you enjoy yourself?' he asked finally. Mouret was now in a state of dazed indignation. He exclaimed:

'What! Do I enjoy myself! What's this nonsense you're saying? You're in a sorry state! Of course I enjoy myself, even when things go wrong, because then I'm furious at seeing them go wrong. I'm a passionate fellow; I don't take life calmly, and perhaps that's just why I'm interested in it.'

He glanced towards the drawing-room and lowered his voice.

'Oh! Some women have been an awful nuisance to me, I must confess. But when I've got hold of one, I keep her, damn it! It doesn't always fail, and I don't give my share to anyone else, I assure you . . . But it isn't just a question of women, for whom I don't really care much, actually. You see, it's a question of willing something and acting, it's a question of creating . . . You have an idea, you fight for it, you hammer it into people's heads, you watch it grow and carry all before it . . . Ah! yes, old chap, I enjoy myself!'

All the joy of action, all the gaiety of existence resounded in his words. He repeated that he was a man of his own time. Really, people would have to be deformed, they must have something wrong with their brains and limbs to refuse to work in an age which offered so many possibilities, when the whole century was pressing forward into the future. And he laughed at the hopeless, the disillusioned, the pessimists, all those made sick by our budding sciences, who assumed the tearful air of poets or the superior look of sceptics, amidst the immense activity of the present day. Yawning with boredom at other people's work was a fine part to play, a proper and intelligent one indeed!

'It's my only pleasure, yawning at other people,' said Vallagnosc, smiling in his cold way.

At this Mouret's passion subsided. He became affectionate once more.

'Ah, Paul, you haven't changed, you're as paradoxical as ever! We haven't met again in order to quarrel, have we? Everyone has his own ideas, fortunately. I must show you my machine in action; you'll see that it isn't really such a bad thing . . . But tell me your news. Your mother and sisters are well, I hope? And weren't you going to get married at Plassans, about six months ago?'

Vallagnosc made a sudden movement which stopped him short; and as the former had looked anxiously round the drawing-room, Octave also turned round and noticed that Mademoiselle de Boves was staring at them. Tall and buxom, Blanche was like her mother; but her face was already puffed out, her large, coarse features swollen with unhealthy fat. Paul, in reply to a discreet question, intimated that nothing was yet settled; perhaps nothing would be settled. He had met the girl at Madame Desforges's house, where he had been a frequent visitor in the past winter, but where he now only rarely made an appearance, which explained why he had not met Octave there. The de Boves had invited him in their turn, and he was particularly fond of the father, who had once been something of a man about town, but had now retired and worked in the civil service. On the other hand, they had no money: Madame de Boves had brought her husband nothing but her Junoesque beauty, and the family was living on a last, mortgaged farm, the modest income from which was, fortunately, supplemented by the nine thousand francs which the Count received as Inspector-General of the Stud. The ladies, mother and daughter, were kept very short of money by the Count, who was impoverished by amorous escapades away from home, and they were sometimes reduced to turning their dresses themselves.

'So why marry?' Mouret asked simply.

'Well! I can't go on like this for ever,' said Vallagnosc, with a weary movement of his eyelids. 'In any case, we have prospects, we're waiting for an aunt to die soon.'

Mouret was still staring at Monsieur de Boves, who was sitting next to Madame Guibal and paying her a great deal of attention, laughing affectionately like a man on an amorous campaign. Octave turned towards his friend and winked in such a meaningful way that the latter added:

'No, not her . . . Not yet, at any rate . . . The fortunate thing is that his work takes him all over France, to different stud-farms, and so he always has pretexts for disappearing. Last month, when his wife thought he was in Perpignan, he was living in an hotel in an out of the way district of Paris, with a piano teacher.'

There was a silence. Then the young man, who was now also watching the Count's attentions to Madame Guibal, went on in an undertone:

'I think you're right . . . Especially as the dear lady is not exactly shy, if what they say is true. There's a very funny story about her and an officer . . . But just look at him! Isn't he comical, hypnotizing her out of the corner of his eye! There's the old France for you, my friend! I really adore that man, and if I marry his daughter he can say I did it for his sake!'

Mouret laughed, greatly amused. He questioned Vallagnosc again, and when he discovered that the idea of a marriage between him and Blanche had originally come from Madame Desforges, he thought the story better still. Dear Henriette took a widow's pleasure in marrying people off; so much so that when she had taken care of the daughters, she would sometimes let the fathers choose their mistresses from her circle; but this was done in such a natural and becoming way that no one ever found any food for scandal. And Mouret, who loved her with the love of an active, busy man, calculating in his affections, would then forget all his ulterior motives for seduction, and have feelings of purely comradely friendship for her.

At that moment she appeared at the door of the small drawing-room followed by an old man of about sixty, whose entrance the two friends had not noticed. Now and again the ladies' voices became shrill, and the light tinkle of spoons in china teacups formed an accompaniment to them; from time to time, in the middle of a short silence, the sound of a saucer being put down too roughly on the marble of the pedestal table could be heard. The setting sun was just coming out from behind a thick cloud, and a sudden ray gilded the tops of the chestnut trees in the garden and shone through the windows in reddish-gold dust, illuminating the brocade and the brasswork of the furniture with its fire.

'This way, my dear Baron,' Madame Desforges was saying. 'May I introduce Monsieur Octave Mouret, who's longing to tell you how much he admires you.'

And, turning towards Octave, she added:

'Baron Hartmann.'

A smile played subtly on the old man's lips. He was a short, vigorous-looking man, with the large head typical of people from Alsace, and a heavy face which would light up with a flash of intelligence at the slightest curl of his mouth, the lightest flicker of his eyelids. For a fortnight he had been resisting Henriette's wish that he should consent to this interview; it was not that he felt particularly jealous for, being a man of the world, he was resigned to playing a father's part; but this was the third of Henriette's men friends she had introduced to him and he was rather afraid, in the long run, of appearing ridiculous. Therefore, as he approached Octave, he wore the discreet smile of a rich protector who, though willing to be charming, is not prepared to be duped.

'Oh! sir,' said Mouret, with his Provençal enthusiasm, 'the Crédit Immobilier's last deal was really remarkable! You can't imagine how happy and proud I am to shake your hand.'

'Too kind, sir, too kind,' the Baron repeated, still smiling.

Henriette, quite unembarrassed, was watching them with her clear eyes. She stood between the two of them, raising her pretty head, looking from one to the other. She wore a lace dress which exposed her slender wrists and neck; and she seemed delighted that they were getting on so well.

'Gentlemen,' she said at last, 'I'll leave you to talk.'

Then, turning towards Paul, who had risen to his feet, she added:

'Would you like a cup of tea, Monsieur de Vallagnosc?'

'With pleasure, madam.'

And they both went back to the drawing-room.

When Mouret had resumed his place on the sofa beside Baron Hartmann, he showered fresh praise on the Crédit Immobilier's operations. Then he broached a subject which was close to his heart; he spoke of the new thoroughfare, the extension of the Rue Réaumur, of which a section, under the name of the Rue du Dix-Décembre, was about to be opened between the Place de la Bourse and the Place de l'Opéra. It had been declared available for public purposes eighteen months ago; the expropriation committee had just been appointed, and the whole neighbourhood was very excited about this enormous space, anxiously waiting for the construction work to begin and taking an interest in the condemned houses. Mouret had been waiting almost three years for this work, first because he could see that business would be brisker as a result, and secondly because he had ambitions to expand which he dared not admit openly, so far did his dreams extend. As the Rue du Dix-Décembre was to cut across the Rue de Choiseul and the Rue de la Michodière, he visualized the Ladies' Paradise taking over the whole block of houses surrounded by these streets and the Rue Neuve-Saint-Augustin, and he already imagined it with a palatial façade on the new thoroughfare, dominating and ruling the conquered city. From this had sprung his keen desire to meet Baron Hartmann, for he had heard that the Crédit Immobilier had signed a contract with the authorities to open up and build the Rue du Dix-Décembre, on condition that it was granted ownership of the land bordering the new street.*

'Really,' he repeated, trying to put on an ingenuous air, 'you're handing over a ready-made street to them, with drains, pavements, and gaslights? And the land bordering it is enough to compensate you? Oh! that's odd, very odd!'

Finally he came to the delicate point. He had found out that the Crédit Immobilier was secretly buying up houses in the same block as the Ladies' Paradise, not only those which were to fall under the pickaxes of the demolition gangs, but others too, those which were to remain standing. And, suspecting in this a plan for some future building scheme, he was very worried about the expansion he dreamed of, filled with fear at the idea of one day coming up against a powerful company owning property which it would never sell. It was precisely this fear which had made him decide to establish a bond between the Baron and himself as soon as possible, the agreeable bond of a woman, which can be such a close one between men of a passionate nature. No doubt he could have seen the financier in his office, and discussed at leisure the big deal he wanted to propose to him. But he felt more confident in Henriette's house; he knew how much the possession of a mistress in common brings men together and softens them. For them both to be in her house, within the beloved perfume of her presence, to have her near to win them over with a smile, seemed to him a guarantee of success.

'Haven't you bought what used to be the Hôtel Duvillard, that old building next to my shop?' he finally asked bluntly.

Baron Hartmann hesitated for a moment, and then denied it. But looking him straight in the eye, Mouret began to laugh; and from then on he played the part of a good-natured young man, his heart on his sleeve and straightforward in business.

'Look here, Baron, since I've had the unexpected honour of meeting you, I must make a confession . . . Oh! I'm not asking you to tell me your secrets, but I'm going to confide mine to you, because I'm sure I couldn't put them in wiser hands . . . Besides, I need your advice, I've wanted to call and see you for a long time, but I never dared to.'

He did make his confession, he described his start in business; he did not even hide the financial crisis through which he was passing in the midst of his triumph. He covered everything, the successive expansions, the profits continually ploughed back into the business, the sums contributed by his employees, the shop risking its very existence with each new sale, in which the whole capital was staked, as it were, on a single throw of the dice. However, it was not money he wanted, for he had a fanatical faith in his customers. His ambition ran higher; he proposed to the Baron a partnership in which the Crédit Immobilier would provide the colossal palace of his dreams, while he, for his part, would give his genius and the business already created. The extent of each party's contribution could be valued; he thought nothing could be easier to do.

'What are you going to do with your building sites and land?' he asked insistently. 'You must have an idea. But I'm quite certain it isn't as good as mine . . . Just think about it. We'll build a shopping arcade on the sites, we'll demolish or convert the houses, and we'll open the most enormous shops in Paris, a bazaar which will make millions.'

Then he allowed this heartfelt cry to escape him:

'Oh! If only I could manage without you! But you hold the aces now. In any case, I'd never get the necessary loans . . . We really must come to an agreement; it would be a crime not to.'

'You do get carried away, my dear sir,' Baron Hartmann contented himself with replying. 'What imagination!'

He shook his head, and continued to smile, determined not to repay confidences with confidences. The Crédit Immobilier's plan was to create in the Rue du Dix-Décembre a rival to the Grand Hotel,* a luxurious establishment whose central position would attract foreigners. In any case, since the hotel would only occupy the sites bordering the street, the Baron might very well have welcomed Mouret's idea, and negotiated for the remaining block of houses, which was still a vast area. But he had financed two of Henriette's friends already, and he was getting rather tired of playing the part of complacent protector. Besides, despite his passion for activity, which made him open his purse to every intelligent and courageous young man, Mouret's commercial genius surprised him more than it attracted him. Wasn't it a fantastic, rash speculation, this gigantic shop? Wouldn't he risk certain ruin in wishing to expand the drapery trade beyond all bounds? In short, he didn't believe in it; he refused.

'No doubt the idea's attractive,' he said, 'but it's the idea of a poet . . . Where would you find the customers to fill a cathedral like that?'

Mouret looked at him for a moment in silence, as if stunned by his refusal. Was it possible? A man of such flair, who could smell money at any level! And suddenly, with a gesture of great eloquence, he pointed to the ladies in the drawing-room, exclaiming:

'There are the customers!'

The sun was fading, the reddish-gold dust had become nothing but a pale light, dying away in a farewell gleam on the silk of the hangings and the panels of the furniture. With the approach of dusk a sense of intimacy filled the large room with a mellow warmth. While Monsieur de Boves and Paul de Vallagnosc were chatting at one of the windows, gazing far into the distance of the garden, the ladies had drawn closer together, forming a tight circle of skirts in the middle of the room, from which laughter was ascending, and whispered remarks, eager questions and answers, all the passion felt by women for spending and for clothes. They were discussing fashions; Madame de Boves was describing a costume she had seen at a ball.

'First of all, a mauve silk underskirt, and then, over it, flounces of old Alençon lace, thirty centimetres deep . . .'

'Oh! Really!' Madame Marty interrupted. 'Some women have all the luck!'

Baron Hartmann, who had followed Mouret's gesture, was looking at the ladies through the open door. He was only half listening to them, for the younger man, inflamed with the desire to convince him, was talking away, explaining how the new type of drapery business worked. It was now based on the rapid and continuous turnover of capital, which had to be converted into goods as many times as possible within twelve months. Thus, in the present year, his initial capital of only five hundred thousand francs had been turned over four times and had produced business worth two million francs. And that was a mere trifle, which could be increased tenfold, for he felt sure that in some departments he could eventually turn his capital over fifteen or twenty times.

'You see, that's the essence of it. It's very simple, once you've thought of it. We don't need a large amount of working capital. All we want is to get rid of our stock very quickly, in order to replace it and make the capital earn interest each time. In this way we can be content with a small profit; as our general expenses reach the enormous figure of sixteen per cent and we seldom deduct more than twenty per cent profit on stock, it means there's a net profit of four per cent at most; but if we operate with a large stock and continually renew it we'll end up making millions . . . Do you follow me? It's quite obvious.'

The Baron shook his head again. He, who had in his time welcomed the most audacious schemes, and whose boldness at the time when gas lighting was a novelty was still talked about, remained apprehensive and obstinate.

'I quite understand,' he replied. 'You sell cheaply in order to sell a lot and you sell a lot in order to sell cheaply . . . But you must sell, and I repeat my question: whom will you sell to? How do you hope to keep up such colossal sales?'

A sudden burst of voices coming from the drawing-room cut short Mouret's explanations. Madame Guibal was saying she would have preferred the flounces of old Alençon lace at the front of the dress only.

'But, my dear,' Madame de Boves was saying, 'the front was covered with it as well. I've never seen anything finer.'

'You've given me an idea!' Madame Desforges went on. 'I've got a few metres of Alençon somewhere . . . I must look for some more to make a trimming.'

And the voices dropped again, becoming only a murmur. Prices were quoted, a regular haggling was going on and was arousing desires, the ladies were buying lace by the handful.

'Ah!' said Mouret, when he could speak, 'you can sell as much as you like when you know how to sell! There lies our success.'

Then, with his Provençal zest, he described the new kind of business at work in warm, glowing phrases which conjured up whole pictures. First, its strength was multiplied tenfold by accumulation, by all the goods being gathered together at one point, supporting and boosting each other; there was never a slack period, seasonal goods were always available; and, as she went from counter to counter, the customer found herself snared, buying some material here, some thread further on, a coat somewhere else; she bought a whole set of clothes, then got caught by unforeseen attractions, yielding to the need for all that is useless and pretty. He then extolled the system of marked prices. The great revolution in drapery had started from this new idea. If the old-fashioned small shops were in their death throes, it was because they could not keep up in the struggle to offer low prices, which had been set in motion by the system of marking prices on goods. Now competition was taking place before the public's very eyes, people had only to walk past the shop-windows to ascertain the prices, and every shop was reducing them, content with the smallest possible profit; there was no cheating, no attempts planned well in advance at making money on a material sold at double its value, there was just continuous business, a regular profit of so much per cent on all goods, a fortune put into the smooth running of a sale, which was all the larger because it took place in full view of the public. Wasn't this an astonishing creation? It was revolutionizing the market, it was transforming Paris, for it was based on the flesh and blood of Woman.

'I've got the women, I don't care about anything else!' he said, in a brutal admission wrung from him by passion.

Baron Hartmann seemed moved by this exclamation. His smile lost its touch of irony, and as he looked at the young man, gradually won over by his confidence, he began to feel growing affection for him.

'Shh!' he murmured paternally, 'they'll hear you.'

But the ladies were now all talking at once, so excited that they were no longer even listening to each other. Madame de Boves was concluding her description of the evening dress: a mauve silk tunic, draped and caught back by bows of lace; the bodice cut very low, with more bows of lace on the shoulders.

'You'll see,' she was saying, 'I'm having a bodice like that made with a satin . . .'

'And I,' Madame Bourdelais interrupted, 'I wanted some velvet. Oh! it was such a bargain!'

Madame Marty was asking:

'Well, how much was the silk?'

And off they went again, all talking at the same time. Madame Guibal, Henriette, Blanche were measuring, cutting, discarding. Materials were being looted, shops ransacked, the women's lust for luxury running riot as they dreamed of dresses, coveted them, feeling so happy in the world of clothes that they lived immersed in it, as they did in the warm air necessary to their existence.

Mouret glanced towards the drawing-room, and in a few phrases whispered in Baron Hartmann's ear, as if he were confiding to him one of those amorous secrets men sometimes venture to reveal when they are alone, he finished explaining the techniques of modern big business. Of supreme importance, more important than the facts he had already given, was the exploitation of Woman. Everything else led up to it, the ceaseless renewal of capital, the system of piling up goods, the low prices which attracted people, the marked prices which reassured them. It was Woman the shops were competing for so fiercely, it was Woman they were continually snaring with their bargains, after dazing her with their displays. They had awoken new desires in her weak flesh; they were an immense temptation to which she inevitably yielded, succumbing in the first place to purchases for the house, then seduced by coquetry, finally consumed by desire. By increasing sales tenfold, by making luxury democratic, shops were becoming a terrible agency for spending, ravaging households, working hand in hand with the latest extravagances in fashion, growing ever more expensive. And if, in the shops, Woman was queen, adulated and humoured in her weaknesses, surrounded with attentions, she reigned there as an amorous queen whose subjects trade on her, and who pays for every whim with a drop of her own blood. Beneath the very charm of his gallantry, Mouret thus allowed the brutality of a Jew selling Woman by the pound to show through; he was building a temple to Woman, making a legion of shop assistants burn incense before her, creating the rites of a new cult; he thought only of her, ceaselessly trying to imagine even greater enticements; and, behind her back, when he had emptied her purse and wrecked her nerves, he was full of the secret scorn of a man to whom a mistress had just been stupid enough to yield.

'Get the women,' he whispered to the Baron, laughing impudently as he did so, 'and you'll sell the world!'

Now the Baron understood. A few sentences had sufficed, he guessed the rest, and such gallant exploitation excited him, stirring memories of his dissolute past. His eyes twinkled knowingly; he was overtaken by admiration for the inventor of this machine for devouring women. It was very clever. He made the same remark as Bourdoncle, a remark prompted by his long experience:

'You know, they'll have their revenge.'

But Mouret shrugged his shoulders in a gesture of crushing disdain. They all belonged to him, they were his property, and he belonged to none of them. When he had extracted his fortune and his pleasure from them, he would throw them on the rubbish heap for those who could still make a living out of them. He had the calculated disdain of a southerner and a speculator.

'Well, sir,' he asked in conclusion, 'will you join me? Does my proposal for the building sites seem possible to you?'

The Baron, half won over, did not wish to commit himself yet. He still felt some doubt about the charm which was gradually having an effect on him. He was about to give an evasive answer, when an urgent summons from the ladies saved him the trouble. In the midst of laughter voices were calling:

'Monsieur Mouret!'

And since the latter, annoyed at being interrupted, was pretending not to hear, Madame de Boves, who had been standing up for a moment, came to the door of the small drawing-room.

'They're asking for you, Monsieur Mouret . . . It's not very chivalrous of you to hide in a corner to talk business.'

At this, he decided immediately to join the ladies, and with such apparent good grace and air of delight that the Baron was quite amazed. They both stood up and went into the large drawing-room.

'I am entirely at your service, ladies,' he said as he went in, a smile on his lips.

A hubbub of triumph greeted him. He had to go further in, and the ladies made room for him in their midst. The sun had just set behind the trees in the garden; the light was fading, and a soft shadow was gradually filling the vast room. It was the tender hour of twilight, that minute of discreet voluptuousness in Parisian apartments when the light in the street is dying and the lamps are still being lit in the pantry downstairs. Monsieur de Boves and Vallagnosc, still standing at the window, cast a pool of shadow on the carpet; while Monsieur Marty, who had entered discreetly a few minutes earlier, stood motionless in the last ray of light coming from the other window, displaying his thin profile, his skimpy, clean frock-coat, and his face grown pale from teaching. The ladies' conversation about dresses made him look even more distressed.

'That sale is going to be next Monday, isn't it?' Madame Marty was asking.

'Indeed it is, madam,' Mouret replied in a flute-like voice, an actor's voice which he affected when speaking to women.

Then Henriette interposed.

'We're all coming, you know . . . They say you're preparing wonders.'

'Oh! Wonders!' he murmured with an air of modest self-complacency. 'I simply try to be worthy of your patronage.'

They pressed him with questions. Madame Bourdelais, Madame Guibal, even Blanche, wanted to know all about it.

'Come on, give us some details,' Madame de Boves repeated insistently. 'You're making us die of curiosity!'

They were surrounding him, when Henriette noticed that he hadn't yet had a cup of tea. This provoked consternation; four of them began to serve him, but on condition that he would answer them afterwards. Henriette poured, Madame Marty held the cup, while Madame de Boves and Madame Bourdelais contended for the honour of putting in the sugar. Then, when he had declined to sit down and had started to drink his tea slowly, standing in their midst, they all drew closer, imprisoning him in the closed circle of their skirts. Heads raised and eyes shining, they all sat smiling at him.

'Your silk, your Paris-Paradise, which all the newspapers are talking about?' resumed Madame Marty impatiently.

'Oh!' he replied, 'it's quite exceptional, a coarse faille, supple and strong . . . You'll see it, ladies, and you'll only find it in our shop, for we've bought the exclusive rights.'

'Really! A fine silk at five francs sixty!' said Madame Bourdelais, quite enraptured. 'That's incredible!'

Ever since the advertisements had appeared, this silk had occupied a considerable place in their daily life. They discussed it and promised themselves some of it, tormented by desire and doubt. And, beneath the chattering curiosity with which they overwhelmed the young man, their different temperaments as customers could be seen: Madame Marty, carried away by her mania for spending, taking everything indiscriminately from the Ladies' Paradise, simply buying at random from the displays; Madame Guibal, walking round the shop for hours without ever making a purchase, happy and satisfied by merely feasting her eyes; Madame de Boves, short of money, constantly tortured by some immoderate desire, bearing a grudge against the goods she could not take away; Madame Bourdelais, with the sharp eye of a careful, practical middle-class woman, making straight for the bargains, using the big shops with such calm housewifely skill that she saved a great deal of money there; and finally Henriette, who, because she dressed with such extreme elegance, only bought certain articles there, such as gloves, hosiery, and all her household linen.

'We have other materials which are amazingly inexpensive and yet very sumptuous,' continued Mouret in his melodious voice. 'For example, I recommend our Cuir-d'Or, a taffeta with an incomparable sheen . . . Among the fancy silks there are some charming patterns, designs chosen from thousands of others by our buyer; and as for velvets, you'll find an extremely rich collection of shades . . . I can tell you that woollen clothes will be very popular this year. You'll see our quilts and our Cheviots . . .'

They had stopped interrupting him, and had narrowed the circle even further, their mouths half open in a vague smile, their faces close together and leaning forward, as if their whole being was yearning towards their tempter. Their eyes were growing dim, a slight shiver ran over the napes of their necks. And he maintained the composure of a conqueror in the midst of the heady scents rising from their hair. Between each sentence he continued to take little sips of tea, the perfume of which cooled those other, more pungent scents, in which there was a touch of musk. Baron Hartmann, who had not taken his eyes off him, felt his admiration mounting before Mouret's seductive charm, which reflected such self-possession that he could toy with women like that without being overcome by the intoxicating scents which they exude.

'So woollen things will be worn,' resumed Madame Marty, whose haggard face was lit up by coquettish passion. 'I must go and look.'

Madame Bourdelais, who was keeping a clear head, said in her turn:

'Your remnant sale is on Thursday, isn't it? I shall wait, I've all my little ones to clothe.'

And turning her delicate fair head towards the mistress of the house, she said:

'You still get your dresses from Sauveur, don't you?'

'Oh, yes!' Henriette replied, 'Sauveur's very expensive, but she's the only dressmaker in Paris who knows how to make a bodice . . . And, whatever Monsieur Mouret may say, she has the prettiest designs, designs you don't see anywhere else. I can't bear to see my dress on every woman's back.'

Mouret smiled discreetly at first. Then he intimated that Madame Sauveur bought her material at his shop; no doubt she took certain designs, for which she secured the exclusive rights, direct from the manufacturers; but for black silk goods, for example, she kept an eye open for bargains at the Ladies'

Paradise, and laid in considerable supplies which she later disposed of at two or three times the price.

'So I'm quite sure her buyers will snap up our Paris-Paradise. Why should she go and pay more for this silk at the factory than she would in my shop? Honestly! We're selling it at a loss.'

This dealt the ladies a final blow. The idea of getting goods below cost price aroused in them the ruthlessness of Woman, whose enjoyment as buyer is doubled when she thinks she's robbing the shopkeeper. He knew they were incapable of resisting a real bargain.

'But we sell everything for a song!' he exclaimed gaily, picking up Madame Desforges's fan, which was still lying on the pedestal table behind him. 'Look! Here's this fan . . . How much did you say it cost?'

'Twenty-five francs for the Chantilly, and two hundred for the mount,' said Henriette.

'Well, the Chantilly isn't expensive. But we have the same one for eighteen francs . . . And as for the mount, my dear lady, it's pure theft. I wouldn't dare to sell one like that for more than ninety francs.'

'That's just what I said,' exclaimed Madame Bourdelais.

'Ninety francs!' murmured Madame de Boves. 'One would have to be very poor not to buy one at that price!'

She had picked up the fan again, and was examining it with her daughter Blanche; on her large, regular face, in her big, sleepy eyes, her pent-up, hopeless desire for a whim she would not be able to satisfy was mounting. Then, for a second time, the fan was passed round by the ladies, to the accompaniment of remarks and exclamations. In the mean time Monsieur de Boves and Vallagnosc had left the window. The former came back and took up his former position behind Madame Guibal, his gaze delving into her corsage while he nevertheless maintained his decorous, superior air, while the young man was bending down towards Blanche, trying to think of something agreeable to say.

'It's rather depressing, don't you think, Mademoiselle Blanche, this white frame with black lace?'

'Oh!' she replied gravely, without a blush colouring her puffy cheeks. 'I've seen one in mother-of-pearl with white feathers. It was quite virginal!'

Monsieur de Boves, who had doubtless observed his wife's longing gaze fixed on the fan, finally made his contribution to the conversation:

'They break straight away, those flimsy little things.'

'I know!' Madame Guibal declared, pouting and pretending to be unconcerned. 'I'm tired of having mine re-glued.'

Madame Marty, excited by the conversation, had for some time been feverishly twisting her red leather bag on her lap. She had not yet been able to show her purchases to the others, and was dying, with a kind of sensual urge, to display them. Suddenly she forgot all about her husband, opened her bag, and took out a few metres of narrow lace rolled round a piece of cardboard.

'This is the Valenciennes for my daughter,' she said. 'It's three centimetres wide. Isn't it delightful? One franc ninety centimes.'

The lace passed from hand to hand. The ladies exclaimed in admiration. Mouret declared that he sold little trimmings like that at factory price. But Madame Marty had closed her bag again, as if to hide things in it which could not be shown. However, as the Valenciennes was such a success she could not resist the desire to take out a handkerchief as well.

'There was this handkerchief too . . . Brussels lace, my dear . . . Oh! A real find! Twenty francs!'

From then on, the bag was inexhaustible. As she took out each fresh article she blushed with pleasure, with the modesty of a woman undressing, which made her embarrassment seem quite charming.

There was a scarf in Spanish lace for thirty francs; she had not wanted it, but the assistant had sworn that it was the last one he had and that they were going to go up in price. Next there was a veil in Chantilly; rather dear, fifty francs; if she did not wear it herself she would make something for her daughter with it.

'Lace is so lovely!' she repeated with her nervous laugh. 'Once I'm inside I could buy the whole shop.'

'And this?' Madame de Boves asked her, examining a remnant of guipure.

'That', she replied, 'is for an insertion . . . There are twenty-six metres. It was one franc a metre, you see!'

'Oh!' said Madame Bourdelais, surprised, 'what are you going to do with it, then?'

'I really don't know . . . But it had such a pretty pattern!'

At that moment, as she looked up, she caught sight of her terrified husband opposite her. He had become even paler, his whole person expressing the resigned anguish of a poor man witnessing the decimation of his hard-earned salary. Each fresh piece of lace was for him a disaster, the bitter days of teaching swallowed up, the long journeys through the mud to give private lessons totally engulfed, the endless struggle of his existence resulting in secret poverty, in the hell of a needy household. Faced with his look of growing alarm, she tried to retrieve the handkerchief, the veil, the scarf, moving her feverish hands about, repeating with little embarrassed laughs:

'You'll get me into trouble with my husband . . . I assure you, my dear, I've been very reasonable, for there was a big fichu there at five hundred francs . . . Oh! it was marvellous!'

'Why didn't you buy it?' said Madame Guibal calmly. 'Monsieur Marty is the most generous of men.'

The teacher was forced to admit that his wife was quite free to do as she pleased. But the mention of the big fichu had sent an icy shiver running down his spine; and as Mouret was just at that moment affirming that the new shops were increasing the well-being of middle-class families, he gave him a terrible look, the flash of hatred of a man too timid to murder people.

In any case the ladies had kept hold of the lace. They were becoming intoxicated with it. Pieces were being unwound, passed from one woman to another, drawing them even closer together, linking them with light strands. On their laps they could feel the caress of the miraculously fine material, in which their guilty hands fondly lingered. And they still kept Mouret tightly imprisoned, overwhelming him with further questions. As the light continued to fade, he had to bend forward now and again to examine a stitch or to point out a design, lightly brushing against their hair with his beard as he did so. But in the soft voluptuousness of dusk, surrounded by the warm odour of their shoulders, he still remained their master beneath the rapture he affected. He seemed a woman himself; they felt penetrated and overcome by his delicate understanding of their secret selves, and they forgot their modesty, won over by his seductive charm;

whereas he, brutally triumphant, certain that from that moment onwards he had them at his mercy, appeared like some despotic king of fashion.

'Oh! Monsieur Mouret! Monsieur Mouret!' they stammered in low, rapturous voices in the darkness of the drawing-room.

The dying lights of the sky were fading on the brasswork of the furniture. The laces alone retained a snowy glint on the dark laps of the ladies who surrounded the young man in a blurred group like vague kneeling worshippers. A last gleam of light was shining on the side of the teapot, the short, bright glimmer of a night-light burning in a bedchamber warmed by the perfume of tea. But suddenly the servant came in with two lamps, and the charm was broken. The drawing-room became light and cheerful. Madame Marty was putting the lace back in the depths of her little bag; Madame de Boves was eating another rum baba, while Henriette, who had got up, was talking in a half-whisper with the Baron, in one of the window recesses.

'He's charming,' said the Baron.

'Yes, isn't he?' she exclaimed, with the involuntary cry of a woman in love.

He smiled and looked at her with fatherly indulgence. It was the first time he had felt her conquered to such an extent; and, being above suffering over it himself, he felt only compassion at seeing her in the hands of this handsome young fellow, so loving and yet so cold-blooded. And so, thinking that he should warn her, he murmured jokingly:

'Take care, my dear, or he'll eat you all up.'

A flash of jealousy lit up Henriette's beautiful eyes. Doubtless she guessed that Mouret had simply made use of her in order to make contact with the Baron. She swore to herself she would make him mad with passion for her, for his love, the love of a busy man, had the facile charm of a song scattered to the winds.

'Oh!' she replied, pretending to joke in her turn, 'it's always the lamb that ends up eating the wolf!'

The Baron, greatly intrigued, gave her an encouraging nod. Perhaps she was the woman who would avenge the others?

When Mouret, after reminding Vallagnosc that he wanted to show him his machine at work, came up to say goodbye, the Baron took him aside into a window recess overlooking the darkened garden. At last he was succumbing to Mouret's charm; his confidence had come when he had seen him among the ladies. They talked for a moment in low voices. Then the banker declared:

'Well! I'll look into the matter . . . If your sale on Monday is as successful as you say it will be, then the deal is on.'

They shook hands, and Mouret, looking delighted, took his leave, for he did not enjoy his dinner unless he had first been to have a look at the day's takings at the Ladies' Paradise.

CHAPTER 4

ON that particular Monday, 10 October, a bright, victorious sun pierced through the thick grey clouds which, for a week, had cast a gloom over Paris. Throughout the night there had still been some drizzle, a fine mist that made the streets dirty with its moisture; but at daybreak the pavements had been wiped clean by the brisk gusts which were carrying the clouds away, and the blue sky had the limpid gaiety of springtime.

And so, from eight o'clock the Ladies' Paradise blazed forth in the rays of bright sunshine, in all the glory of its great sale of winter fashions. Flags were waving at the door, woollen goods were flapping in the fresh morning air, enlivening the Place Gaillon with the hubbub of a fairground; and the windows along the two streets developed symphonies with their displays, the brilliant tones of which were further heightened by the clearness of the glass. It was an orgy of colour, the joy of the street bursting out there, a wealth of goods openly displayed, where everyone could go and feast his eyes.

But at that time of day not many people were going in, only a few customers in a hurry, local housewives, women who wished to avoid the afternoon crush. Behind the materials which decked it, the shop seemed to be empty, armed and awaiting action, its floors polished and its counters overflowing with goods. The busy morning crowd scarcely glanced at the shop-windows, and never slackened pace. In the Rue Neuve-Saint-Augustin and the Place Gaillon, where carriages were to take their stand, at nine o'clock there were only two cabs. Only the local inhabitants, especially the small tradesmen, roused by such a display of streamers and plumes, were forming little groups in doorways and at street-corners, gazing up at the shop, and making plenty of sour comments. Their indignation was aroused by the fact that in the Rue de la Michodière, outside the dispatch office, there stood one of the four delivery vans which Mouret had just launched on Paris: they were painted green, picked out with yellow and red, their brilliantly varnished panels flashing gold and purple in the sunlight. The van which was standing there, with its new colour-scheme, the name of the shop emblazoned on each side, and carrying on top a placard advertising the day's sale, finally went off at a trot, pulled by a superb horse, after it had been filled with parcels left over from the day before. Baudu, standing livid on the threshold of the Vieil Elbeuf, watched it as far as the boulevard, where it disappeared, to spread all over the city in a starry radiance the hated name of the Ladies' Paradise.

In the mean time, a few cabs were arriving and lining up. Every time a customer appeared, there was a stir among the page-boys lined up beneath the high porch, dressed in a livery of light green coat and trousers, and yellow and red striped waistcoat. Jouve, the retired captain who worked as a shopwalker, was there too, in frock-coat and white tie, wearing his medal like a sign of respectability and probity, receiving the ladies with an air of solemn politeness, bending over them to point out the various departments. Then they would disappear into the entrance-hall, which had been changed into an oriental hall.

No sooner had they entered than they were greeted with a surprise, a marvel which enchanted them all. It had been Mouret's idea. He had recently been the first to buy in the Levant, on extremely favourable terms, a collection of antique and modern carpets, rare carpets of the sort that until then had only been sold by antique dealers at very high prices; and he was going to flood the market with them; he was letting them go almost at cost price, simply using them as a splendid setting which would attract art connoisseurs to his shop. From the middle of the Place Gaillon passers-by could catch a glimpse of this oriental hall, composed entirely of carpets and door-curtains, which the porters had hung up under his directions. First of all, the ceiling was covered with carpets from Smyrna, their complicated designs standing out on red backgrounds. Then, on all four sides, were hung door-curtains: door-curtains from Kerman and Syria, striped with green, yellow, and vermilion; door-curtains from Diarbekir, of a commoner type, rough to the touch, like shepherds' cloaks; and still more carpets which could be used as hangings, long carpets from Ispahan, Teeran, and Kermanshah, broader carpets from Schoumaka and Madras, a strange blossoming of peonies and palms, imagination running riot in a dream garden. On the floor there were still more carpets;

thick fleeces were strewn there, and in the centre was a carpet
from Agra, an extraordinary specimen with a white background
and a broad border of soft blue, through which ran purplish
embellishments of exquisite design. There were other marvels
displayed everywhere, carpets from Mecca with a velvet reflection, prayer rugs from Daghestan with a symbolic pointed design, carpets from Kurdistan covered with flowers in full bloom;
finally, in a corner, there was a large pile of cheap rugs, from
Geurdis, Kula, and Kirghehir, priced from fifteen francs upwards. This sumptuous pasha's tent was furnished with armchairs and divans made from camel-bags, some ornamented with
multi-coloured lozenges, others with simple roses. Turkey,
Arabia, Persia, the Indies were all there. Palaces had been emptied, mosques and bazaars plundered. Tawny gold was the dominant tone in the worn antique carpets, and their faded tints
retained a sombre warmth, the smelting of some extinguished
furnace, with the beautiful burnt hue of an old master. Visions of
the Orient floated beneath the luxury of this barbarous art, amid
the strong odour which the old wools had retained from lands of
vermin and sun.

At eight o'clock in the morning, when Denise, who was starting work that very Monday, had crossed the oriental hall, she
had stood still in astonishment, unable to recognize the entrance
of the shop, her confusion compounded by the harem scene set
up at the door. A porter had taken her up to the attics and
handed her over to Madame Cabin, who was in charge of the
cleaning and the bedrooms, and who had installed her in No. 7,
where her trunk had already been brought. It was a narrow cell,
with a skylight window opening on to the roof, and furnished
with a small bed, a walnut cupboard, a dressing-table, and two
chairs. Twenty similar rooms led off the convent-like corridor,
which was painted yellow; and, out of the thirty-five girls in the
shop, the twenty who had no home in Paris slept there, while the
other fifteen lived out, some of them with fictitious aunts or
cousins. Denise immediately took off her skimpy woollen dress,
worn thin with brushing and mended on the sleeves, the only
one she had brought from Valognes. Then she put on the uniform of her department, a black silk dress which had been altered
for her and which she found ready on the bed. The dress was still

a little too big, too broad across the shoulders. But she was in such a hurry in her excitement that she paid no attention to the details of her appearance. She had never worn silk before. When she went downstairs again, all dressed up and ill at ease, she looked at the shiny skirt, and the loud rustling of the material embarrassed her.

Downstairs, as she was entering the department, a quarrel broke out. She heard Clara say in a shrill voice:

'I arrived before her, ma'am.'

'It's not true,' Marguerite replied. 'She pushed past me at the door, but I already had one foot inside the salon.'

It was a question of putting their names down on the roster which controlled their turns at selling. The salesgirls wrote their names on a slate in the order of their arrival; and each time they served a customer, they would write their names again at the bottom of the list. In the end Madame Aurélie took Marguerite's side.

'She's always unfair!' Clara muttered furiously.

But Denise's entrance reconciled the girls. They looked at her, then smiled to each other. How could anyone dress like that! The girl went awkwardly to put her name down on the roster, on which she was the last. Meanwhile Madame Aurélie examined her with an anxious pursing of her lips. She could not help saying:

'My dear, two of your size could fit into that dress. It'll have to be taken in . . . In any case, you don't know how to dress yourself. Come here and let me arrange you a bit.'

She led her to one of the tall mirrors which alternated with the solid doors of the cupboards in which the dresses were crammed. The vast room, surrounded by the mirrors and by the carved oak woodwork, and decorated with red moquette bearing a large floral pattern, resembled the commonplace lounge of a hotel with a continual stream of people rushing through it. The young ladies completed the resemblance, dressed as they were in the regulation silk, displaying their salesgirl charms without ever sitting down on the dozen chairs reserved for the customers. Each girl had a long pencil, which seemed plunged into her bosom between the two buttonholes of her bodice, with its point sticking up; and the splash of white of a cash-book could be glimpsed half emerging from a pocket. Several of the girls risked wearing jewellery—rings, brooches, chains—but their greatest coquetry, the luxury with which, in the enforced uniformity of their dress, they struggled to outdo each other, was their bare heads, the profusion of their hair which, if it was insufficient, was augmented by plaits and chignons, combed, curled, and flaunted.

'Pull your belt in,' Madame Aurélie was repeating. 'There, now you haven't got a bulge at the back . . . And your hair, how do you make such a mess of it? It could look superb, if you wanted it to.'

It was, indeed, Denise's only beauty. Ash-blonde in colour, it reached to her ankles; and when she did it up, it got in her way so much that she simply rolled it into a pile and held it in place with the strong teeth of a horn comb. Clara, very annoyed by this hair, tied up so untidily in its untamed grace, pretended to laugh at it. She had made a sign to a salesgirl from the lingerie department, a girl with a broad face and a friendly manner. The two departments, which were adjacent, were always on hostile terms; but these two girls sometimes got together to laugh at people.

'Mademoiselle Cugnot, just look at that mane!' repeated Clara, whom Marguerite was nudging with her elbow while pretending to choke with laughter.

But the girl from the lingerie department was not in a joking mood. She had been watching Denise for a little while, and she remembered what she had suffered herself during the first few months in her department.

'Well, and so what?' she said. 'Not everyone's got a mane like that!'

And she went back to the lingerie department, leaving the other two feeling abashed. Denise, who had heard everything, watched her go with a look of gratitude, while Madame Aurélie gave her a cash-book with her name on it, saying:

'Well, tomorrow you'll look smarter . . . And now, try to pick up the ways of the shop; wait your turn for selling. Today will be very hard; it'll give us a chance to see what you can do.'

The department was still deserted, as very few customers went up to the dress departments at this early hour. The girls, standing straight and still, were saving their strength for the exertions of the afternoon. Denise, intimidated by the thought that they were watching her first efforts, sharpened her pencil for the sake of something to do; then, imitating the others, she stuck it into her bosom, between the two buttonholes. She was trying to summon up all her courage, determined to conquer a position. The day before she had been told that she would start work *au pair*, in other words without a fixed salary; she would have only a percentage and a commission on the sales she made. But she hoped to earn twelve hundred francs in this way, for she knew that good saleswomen could make as much as two thousand when they tried. Her budget was regulated: a hundred francs a month would enable her to pay Pépé's board and lodging and to keep Jean, who was not receiving a penny; she herself would be able to buy a few clothes and some linen. But, in order to reach this considerable sum, she would have to prove herself hard-working and strong, not take the ill will around her to heart, stand up for herself, and seize her share from her companions if necessary. As she was working herself up for the struggle, a tall young man who was passing by the department smiled at her; when she saw that it was Deloche, who had been engaged the day before in the lace department, she returned his smile, happy to rediscover this friendship, and seeing a good omen in his greeting.

At half-past nine a bell rang for the first lunch service. Then a fresh peal summoned people to the second. And still the customers did not come. The assistant buyer, Madame Frédéric, who with the gloomy stiffness of a widow took pleasure in predicting the worst, was swearing curtly that the day was lost; they would not see a soul, they might as well close the cupboards and go home; this prediction darkened the flat face of Marguerite, who was very grasping, whereas Clara, like a runaway horse, was already dreaming of an excursion to the woods at Verrières if the shop were to collapse. As for Madame Aurélie, she was walking about the empty department silent and grave, wearing her Caesar's mask, like a general who bears the responsibility for victory or defeat.

At about eleven o'clock a few ladies appeared. Denise's turn to serve was coming. Just at that moment a customer was pointed out.

'That fat woman from the provinces, you know,' murmured Marguerite.

She was a woman of forty-five who came to Paris from time to time from the depths of some out-of-the-way place. She saved up for months; then no sooner had she stepped out of the train than she would drop in at the Ladies' Paradise and spend it all. She rarely bought anything by post, for she wanted to see the goods, and delighted in touching them, and even went so far as to buy up stocks of needles which, she said, cost the earth in her small town. The whole shop knew her, knew that her name was Boutarel, and that she lived in Albi, without caring any more about either her circumstances or her existence.

'How are you, madam?' graciously asked Madame Aurélie, who had stepped forward. 'And what can we do for you? You will be attended to immediately.'

Then, turning round, she called:

'Young ladies!'

Denise responded, but Clara had already sprung forward. Usually she was lazy about selling, not caring about money as she earned more, and with less effort, outside. But the idea of cheating the newcomer out of a good customer spurred her on.

'Excuse me, it's my turn,' said Denise, indignantly.

With a stern look Madame Aurélie pushed her aside, murmuring:

'There are no turns. I'm the only person who gives orders here. Wait until you know something before you serve our regular customers.'

The girl withdrew; and as tears were welling up in her eyes and she wanted to hide her over-sensitiveness, she turned her back, standing in front of the plate-glass windows and pretending to look out into the street. Were they going to prevent her from selling? Would they all conspire like that to deprive her of important sales? Fear for the future seized her; she felt crushed between all the different interests at play. Yielding to the bitterness of her abandonment, her forehead against the cold glass, she gazed at the Vieil Elbeuf opposite, thinking that she should have begged her uncle to keep her; perhaps he himself regretted his decision, for he had seemed very upset the day before. Now she was quite alone in this huge shop where no one loved her, where she felt hurt and lost; Pépé and Jean, who had never left her side, were living with strangers; it was a cruel separation, and the two big tears she was holding back were making the street dance in a mist.

Meanwhile, the buzz of voices continued behind her.

'This one makes me all bunched up,' Madame Boutarel was saying.

'Madam is mistaken,' Clara was repeating. 'The shoulders fit perfectly . . . Unless madam would rather have a pelisse than a coat.'

Denise gave a start. A hand had been placed on her arm, and Madame Aurélie was talking to her severely.

'What's this! You're not doing anything now, you're just watching the people going by? That won't do at all!'

'But if you won't let me sell, ma'am . . .'

'There's other work for you, Mademoiselle Baudu. Begin at the beginning . . . Do the folding-up.'

In order to satisfy the few customers who had arrived, the cupboards had already had to be turned upside down; and the two long oak tables, on the left and right of the salon, were littered with a jumble of coats, pelisses, cloaks, clothes of every size and in every material. Without replying, Denise set about sorting them, folding them carefully and putting them away again in the cupboards. It was the humblest job for beginners. She did not protest any more, knowing that passive obedience was required of her, biding her time until the buyer would let her sell, as her original intention had seemed to be. She was still folding when Mouret appeared. It was a shock for her; she blushed, and once more felt overcome by her strange fear at the thought that he was going to speak to her. But he did not even see her, he no longer remembered the little girl whom the charming impression of the moment had induced him to support.

'Madame Aurélie!' he called in a curt voice.

He was a little pale, but his eyes were clear and resolute. On going round the departments he had just discovered that they were empty, and the possibility of defeat had suddenly occurred to him, in spite of his obstinate faith in luck. Of course, it was only eleven o'clock; he knew from experience that the crowd

never arrived before the afternoon. But certain symptoms were
worrying him: at other sales there had been some activity from
the morning onwards; furthermore, he could not see any of those
hatless women, local customers, who usually dropped in on him
as neighbours. Like all great captains when joining battle, he had
been overcome by a feeling of superstitious weakness, in spite of
his usual resolute attitude as a man of action. It would not go
well, he was lost, and he could not have said why: he thought he
could read his defeat on the very faces of the ladies who were
passing.

At that moment Madame Boutarel, who always bought something, was leaving, saying:

'No, you haven't got anything I like . . . I'll see, I'll think
about it.'

Mouret watched her go. Then, as Madame Aurélie ran up at
his summons, he took her aside; they exchanged a few rapid
words. She made a gesture that showed her anxiety; she was
obviously replying that the sale was not warming up. For a
moment they remained facing each other, overcome by the kind
of doubt which generals hide from their troops. Then he said out
loud, with a gallant air:

'If you need more staff, take a girl from the work-room
. . . She'd give you some help, after all.'

He continued with his inspection, in despair. Since the morning he had been avoiding Bourdoncle, whose anxious remarks
irritated him. As he was leaving the lingerie department, where
the sale was going even worse, he ran into him and had to put up
with listening to his gloomy thoughts. Then, with a brutality
which even his most senior employees were not spared in his
black moments, he told him flatly to go to the devil.

'Shut up, can't you! Everything's all right . . . I'll end up by
kicking out all the faint-hearted.'

Mouret, standing alone, planted himself beside the hall balustrade. From there he dominated the whole shop, for he had the
mezzanine departments around him, and could look down into
the ground-floor departments. Upstairs, the emptiness seemed
heart-breaking to him: in the lace department an old lady was
having all the boxes ransacked without buying anything; while in
the lingerie department three good-for-nothing girls were sifting

slowly through some ninety-centime collars. Downstairs, under the covered arcades, in the shafts of light coming from the street, he noticed that the customers were becoming more numerous. It was a slow, broken procession, a stroll past the counters; women in jackets were crowding into the haberdashery and hosiery departments; but there was hardly anyone in the household linen or woollen goods departments. The page-boys, in their green uniform with shining brass buttons, their arms dangling, were waiting for customers to arrive. Now and again a shopwalker would pass by with a ceremonious air, very stiff in his white necktie. But what made Mouret's heart ache most of all was the deathly silence of the hall: the light fell on it from above, filtered through a frosted glass roof, into a diffused white dust suspended over the silk department, which seemed to be sleeping amid the chilly silence of a chapel. An assistant's footstep, a few whispered words, the rustle of a skirt, were the only sounds, muffled by the warmth from the heating apparatus. However, carriages were arriving: the sound of the horses suddenly coming to a halt could be heard, followed by the banging of the carriage doors. A distant hubbub was coming from the street—curious onlookers were jostling each other in front of the shop-windows, cabs were drawing up in the Place Gaillon, a crowd seemed to be approaching . . . But Mouret, seeing the idle cashiers leaning back in their chairs behind their cash-desk windows, and observing that the parcel-tables with their boxes of string and reams of blue packing-paper remained bare, was furious with himself for being afraid, and thought he could feel his great machine coming to a standstill and growing cold beneath him.

'I say, Favier,' murmured Hutin, 'look at the governor up there . . . He doesn't look very happy!'

'This is a rotten shop!' Favier replied. 'When you think that I haven't sold a thing yet!'

Both of them, while keeping on the look-out for customers, whispered remarks like this from time to time, without looking at each other. The other salesmen in the department were busy piling up lengths of Paris-Paradise, under Robineau's orders; while Bouthemont, deep in conference with a thin young woman, seemed to be taking an important order in undertones. Around them the silks, on elegant, frail shelves, folded up in long pieces of cream-coloured paper, were piled like strangely shaped pamphlets. Littering the counters were the fancy silks—watered silks, satins, velvets, looking like beds of mown flowers, a whole harvest of delicate and precious materials. It was the most elegant of all the departments, a veritable drawing-room, in which the goods were so ethereal that they seemed to be a kind of luxurious furnishing.

'I must have a hundred francs for Sunday,' Hutin resumed. 'If I don't make an average of twelve francs a day, I'm done for . . . I was counting on this sale.'

'Good Lord! A hundred francs, that's a bit steep,' said Favier. 'I only want fifty or sixty . . . You go in for expensive women, do you?'

'Oh no, old chap. It's just that I did something silly. I made a bet and lost . . . So I've got to stand a dinner for five people, two men and three women . . . What an awful morning this is! I'll offload twenty metres of Paris-Paradise on the first woman who passes!'

They went on talking for a few moments, telling each other what they had done the day before, and what they hoped to do in a week's time. Favier backed horses; Hutin liked boating and music-hall singers. But they were both spurred on by the need for money; they dreamed of nothing but money, they fought for it from Monday to Saturday, and spent it all on Sunday. In the shop it was their sole preoccupation, a constant, pitiless struggle. And there was that cunning Bouthemont, who had just managed to grab hold of the woman sent by Madame Sauveur, that skinny woman he was chatting with! It would be a splendid deal, two or three dozen lengths of material, for the great dressmaker always gave good orders. And a moment earlier Robineau, too, had taken it into his head to do Favier out of a customer!

'Oh! Him! We'll have to get even with him,' resumed Hutin, who took advantage of the slightest thing to stir up the department against the man whose position he coveted. 'The buyer and assistant buyer aren't meant to sell! Word of honour, my dear chap, if ever I become assistant buyer, you'll see how good I'll be to the rest of you!'

And the whole of his little Norman person, fat and jolly, was straining to exude all the good nature he could affect. Favier could not help giving him a sideways look; but he maintained his phlegmatic air, and was content to reply:

'Yes, I know . . . Personally, I'd be delighted.'

Then, seeing a lady approaching, he added under his breath: 'Look out! Here's one for you.'

She was a woman with a blotchy face, in a yellow hat and a red dress. Hutin guessed immediately that she was the sort of woman who would not buy anything. He quickly bent down behind the counter, pretending to do up one of his shoe-laces; hidden from view, he murmured:

'No fear! Let someone else have her . . . Thanks very much! And lose my turn . . . !'.

However, Robineau was calling him.

'Whose turn is it, gentlemen? Monsieur Hutin's? Where's Monsieur Hutin?'

And, as the latter was obviously not replying, it was the salesman who came after him on the roster who served the blotchy lady. She did, indeed, only want some patterns, together with the prices; and she kept the salesman for more than ten minutes, overwhelming him with questions. But Robineau had seen Hutin get up from behind the counter. And so when another customer arrived he interfered with a stern air and stopped the young man as he dashed forward.

'Your turn has gone . . . I called you, and as you were there behind . . .'

'But I didn't hear, sir.'

'That's enough! Put your name down at the bottom . . . Come on, Monsieur Favier, it's your turn.'

Favier, who was really very amused by the whole episode, apologized to his friend with a glance. Hutin, his lips pale, had turned his head away. What infuriated him was that he knew the customer very well; she was a charming blonde who often came to the department and whom the salesmen called among themselves 'the pretty lady', although they knew nothing about her, not even her name. She usually bought a great deal, would have her purchases carried to her carriage, and then would disappear. Tall, elegant, dressed with exquisite taste, she appeared to be very rich and to belong to the highest society.

'Well, how was that tart of yours?' Hutin asked Favier, when the latter came back from the cash desk, where he had accompanied the lady.

'A tart?' Favier replied. 'No, she looks much too lady-like . . . She must be the wife of a stockbroker or a doctor, well, I don't know, something like that.'

'Oh, go on! she's a tart . . . You can't tell nowadays, they all have the airs of refined ladies!'

Favier looked at his cash-book.

'It doesn't matter!' he went on, 'I've stung her for two hundred and ninety-three francs. That means nearly three francs for me.'

Hutin pursed his lips, and vented his spleen on the cash-books: another crazy invention which was cluttering up their pockets! There was a secret rivalry between the two men. Favier, as a rule, pretended to keep in the background, to acknowledge Hutin's superiority, so as to be free to attack him from behind. That was why Hutin was so upset about the three francs which a salesman he considered to be his inferior had pocketed so easily. Really, what a day! If it went on like that he would not earn enough even to buy soda water for his guests. And in the midst of the battle, which was now becoming fiercer, he walked round the counters, his tongue hanging out, wanting his share, even jealous of his superior, who was seeing the skinny young woman off, repeating to her as he did so:

'Very well, it's settled. Tell her I'll do my best to obtain this favour from Monsieur Mouret.'

Mouret had left his post by the hall balustrade some time ago. Suddenly he reappeared at the top of the main staircase which led to the ground floor; from there he still commanded a view of the whole shop. His face had regained its colour, and it seemed larger now that his faith was being reborn at the sight of the crowd which was gradually filling the shop. At last the long-awaited rush had come, the afternoon crush of which he had for a moment despaired in his fever of anxiety; all the assistants were at their posts, and a last bell had just rung to signal the end of the third luncheon service; the disastrous morning, due no doubt to a shower at about nine o'clock, could still be made good, for the blue sky of the morning had regained its victorious gaiety. Now that the mezzanine departments were coming to life, he had to stand back to make way for the women as they went upstairs in little groups to the lingerie and dresses; while behind him, in the lace and shawl departments, he could hear large sums being bandied about. But he was reassured above all by the sight of the ground-floor galleries. There was a crush of people in the haberdashery department; even the household linen and wool departments were overrun; the procession of shoppers was becoming denser, and almost all of them were wearing hats now—there were only a few bonnets of housewives who had arrived late. In the silk hall, under the pale light, ladies had taken off their gloves to feel pieces of Paris-Paradise, while talking in low voices. And he could no longer have any doubt about the sounds arriving from outside, the rattle of cabs, the banging of doors, the growing babble of the crowd. Beneath his feet he felt the machine being set in motion, warming up and coming to life again, from the cash-desks where there was the clink of gold, and the tables where the porters were hurrying to pack up the goods, down to the depths of the basement, where the dispatch department was filling up with the parcels sent down, shaking the whole shop with its subterranean rumbling. In the midst of the mob Jouve was walking about solemnly, on the look-out for thieves.

'Hello! It's you!' said Mouret suddenly, recognizing Paul de Vallagnosc, whom a page-boy had brought to him. 'No, no, you're not disturbing me . . . And, in any case, you may as well follow me around if you want to see everything, because today I'll be totally involved in the sale.'

He still felt anxious. There was no doubt that there were plenty of people, but would the sale be the triumph he had hoped for? Nevertheless, he was laughing with Paul and gaily led him away.

'It seems to be picking up a bit,' said Hutin to Favier. 'But I'm not having any luck, some days are jinxed, honestly! I've just drawn another blank, that bitch didn't buy anything from me.'

With his chin he indicated a woman who was walking off, casting looks of disgust at all the materials. He wouldn't grow fat on his thousand francs a year if he didn't sell anything; usually he made seven or eight francs a day in percentages or commission, which gave him with his regular pay an average of about ten

francs a day. Favier never earned much more than eight; and
here was this animal taking the food out of his mouth, for he had
just sold another dress. A cold-blooded fellow who had never
known how to amuse a customer! It was exasperating!

'The sockers and reelers look as if they're raking it in,' Favier
murmured, referring to the salesmen in the hosiery and haberdashery departments.

But Hutin, who was looking all round the shop, suddenly
asked: 'Do you know Madame Desforges, the governor's
girlfriend? . . . That dark woman over there in the glove department, the one who's having some gloves tried on by Mignot.'

He stopped and then, as if talking to Mignot, and without
taking his eyes off him, he resumed:

'Go on, go on, old man, give her fingers a good squeeze, it
won't do you any good! We know all about your conquests!'

There existed between him and the glove assistant the rivalry
of two good-looking men, both of whom pretended to flirt with
the customers. Neither of them could in fact boast of any real
good fortune; Mignot lived on the myth of a police superintendent's wife who had fallen in love with him, whereas Hutin had
really made the conquest of a trimmer, in his department, who
had got tired of hanging about the shady hotels in the neighbourhood; but they both invented a lot, letting people believe that
they had mysterious adventures, rendezvous with countesses
between purchases.

'You should deal with her yourself,' said Favier in his deadpan
way.

'That's an idea!' exclaimed Hutin. 'If she comes here, I'll get
round her!'

In the glove department a whole row of ladies was seated in
front of the narrow counter covered with green velvet with
nickel-plated corners; the smiling assistants were stacking up in
front of them flat, bright pink boxes, which they were taking out
of the counter itself, like the labelled drawers of a filing cabinet.
Mignot, in particular, was leaning forward with his pretty baby
face, rolling his Rs like a true Parisian, his voice full of tender
inflections. He had already sold Madame Desforges a dozen
pairs of kid gloves, Paradise gloves, the shop's speciality. She
had then asked for three pairs of suede gloves. And she was now

trying on some Saxon gloves, for fear that the size was not right.

'Oh! It's absolutely perfect, madam!' Mignot was repeating. 'Six and three-quarters would be too big for a hand like yours.'

Half lying on the counter, he was holding her hand, taking her fingers one by one and sliding the glove on with a long, practised, and sustained caress; and he was looking at her as if he expected to see from her face that she was swooning with voluptuous joy. But she, her elbow on the edge of the velvet, her wrist raised, gave him her fingers with the same detached air with which she would give her foot to her maid to allow her to button her boots. He was not a man; she used him for such intimate services with the familiar disdain she showed for those in her employ, without even looking at him.

'I'm not hurting you, madam?'

She replied in the negative, with a shake of the head.

The smell of Saxon gloves, that animal smell with a touch of sweetened musk, usually excited her; and she sometimes laughed about it, confessing her liking for this ambiguous perfume, like an animal in rut which has landed in a girl's powder box. But standing at that commonplace counter she did not smell the gloves; they did not provoke any sensual feeling between her and the ordinary salesman simply doing his job.

'Is there anything else you would like to see, madam?'

'Nothing, thank you . . . Would you take that to cash-desk No. 10, for Madame Desforges.'

Being a regular customer, she gave her name at a cash-desk, and had each purchase sent there, so that she wasn't followed there by an assistant. When she had left, Mignot turned towards his neighbour and winked, for he would have had him believe that wonderful things had just taken place.

'It's a pity she can't wear gloves all over!' he murmured crudely.

Meanwhile Madame Desforges was continuing her purchases. She turned to the left, stopping in the linen department to get some dusters; then she walked all round, going as far as the woollens at the end of the gallery.

As she was pleased with her cook, she wanted to make her a present of a dress. The woollen department was overflowing with a dense crowd; all the lower middle-class women were there and were feeling the materials, absorbed in silent calculation; she had to sit down for a moment. The shelves were piled high with thick lengths of material, which the salesmen were taking down one by one, with a sudden pull. They were beginning to get quite confused among the cluttered counters, where the materials were mingling and overflowing. It was a rising tide of neutral tints, of the muted tones of wool, iron greys, yellowish-greys, blue-greys, with here and there a brilliant Scottish tartan, a blood-red background of flannel bursting out. And the white labels on the rolls were like a light shower of white snowflakes, speckling a black December soil.

Behind a pile of poplin Liénard was joking with a tall girl without a hat, a local seamstress sent by her employer to stock up with Merino. He hated these big sale days which made his arms ache, and, since he was largely kept by his father and did not care whether he sold or not, he tried to dodge work, doing just enough to avoid being dismissed.

'You know, Mademoiselle Fanny,' he was saying. 'You're always in a hurry . . . Did the Vicuña go well the other day? I'll come and get my commission from you.'

But the seamstress was making her escape, laughing as she did so, and Liénard found himself facing Madame Desforges; he could not help asking her:

'Can I help you, madam?'

She wanted a dress, inexpensive but hard-wearing. Liénard, with the aim of sparing his arms, which was his sole concern, manœuvred so as to make her take one of the materials already unfolded on the counter. There were cashmeres, serges, Vicuñas; he swore to her that there was nothing better, they never wore out. But none of them seemed to satisfy her. She had glimpsed a bluish serge twill on a shelf, and in the end he reluctantly decided to get it down; but she said it was too coarse. Next it was a Cheviot, some with diagonal stripes, some greys, and every variety of woollen material, which she was curious to touch for sheer pleasure, though she had already decided that she would just buy anything. So the young man was obliged to empty the highest shelves; his shoulders cracked, and the counter had disappeared beneath the silky grain of the cashmeres and poplins, the rough nap of the Cheviots, and the fluffy down of the Vicuñas. Every material and every shade was now on view.

She asked to be shown Grenadine and Chambéry gauze, though she did not have the slightest desire to buy any. Then, when she had had enough, she said:

'Oh well! The first one was the best. It's for my cook . . . Yes, the serge with the little dots, the one at two francs.'

And when Liénard, pale with suppressed anger, had measured it out, she said:

'Will you take it to cash-desk No. 10 . . . For Madame Desforges.'

As she was going away she noticed Madame Marty nearby, accompanied by her daughter Valentine, a tall, lanky girl of fourteen, very uninhibited and already casting the guilty glances of a woman at the goods.

'Ah! It's you, my dear?'

'Yes, dear . . . Quite a crowd, isn't it?'

'Oh! Don't talk to me about it, it's stifling. What a success! Have you seen the oriental hall?'

'Superb! Amazing!'

And, elbowed and jostled by the growing mass of women who had little to spend and were rushing towards the inexpensive woollens, they went into ecstasies over the exhibition of carpets. Then Madame Marty explained that she was looking for some material for a coat; but she had not made up her mind, she wanted to see some woollen quilting.

'But just look at it, mamma,' murmured Valentine, 'it's too common.'

'Come and look at the silks,' said Madame Desforges. 'You must see their famous Paris-Paradise.'

Madame Marty hesitated for a moment. It would be very expensive, and she had faithfully promised her husband that she would be careful! She had been buying for an hour already; quite a pile of articles were following her—a muff and ruching for herself, some stockings for her daughter. In the end she said to the assistant who was showing her the quilting:

'Well, no! I'm going to the silk department . . . There's really nothing here that I want.'

The assistant took the articles and walked ahead of the ladies.

The crowd had reached the silk department too. There was a tremendous crush before the interior display arranged by Hutin, to which Mouret had added the final touches. At the far end of

the hall, around one of the small cast-iron columns which supported the glass roof, material was streaming down like a bubbling sheet of water, falling from above and spreading out on to
the floor. First, pale satins and soft silks were gushing out: royal
satins and renaissance satins, with the pearly shades of spring
water; light silks as transparent as crystal—Nile green, tur-
quoise, blossom pink, Danube blue. Next came the thicker fabrics, the marvellous satins and the duchess silks, in warm shades,
rolling in great waves. And at the bottom, as if in a fountain-
basin, the heavy materials, the damasks, the brocades, the silver
and gold silks, were sleeping on a deep bed of velvets—velvets of
all kinds, black, white, coloured, embossed on a background of
silk or satin, their shimmering flecks forming a still lake in which
reflections of the sky and of the countryside seemed to dance.
Women pale with desire were leaning over as if to look at themselves. Faced with this wild cataract, they all remained standing
there, filled with the secret fear of being caught up in the overflow of all this luxury and with an irresistible desire to throw
themselves into it and be lost.

'So you're here?' said Madame Desforges, on finding Madame
Bourdelais installed in front of a counter.

'Ah! Good-morning!' the latter replied, shaking hands with
the ladies. 'Yes, I've come to have a look.'

'It's wonderful, this display, isn't it? It's like a dream . . . And
the oriental hall, have you seen the oriental hall?'

'Yes, yes, extraordinary!'

But beneath this enthusiasm, which was certainly going
to be the fashionable attitude of the day, Madame Bourdelais
kept her composure as a practical housewife. She was carefully
examining a piece of Paris-Paradise, for she had come
solely to take advantage of the exceptional cheapness of
this silk, if she found it really good value. She was clearly satisfied, for she ordered twenty-five metres, reckoning that it would
easily be enough to make a dress for herself and a coat for her
little girl.

'What! You're going already?' Madame Desforges resumed.
'Come and have a look round with us.'

'No, thank you, they're expecting me at home . . . I didn't
want to risk bringing the children in a crowd like this.'

And she went away preceded by the salesman carrying the twenty-five metres of silk; he conducted her to cash-desk No. 10, where young Albert was losing his head in the midst of all the requests for invoices with which he was besieged. When the salesman could get near him, he called out the sale he had made, after entering it with a pencil on his counterfoil book, and the cashier entered it in the register; then it was counter-checked, and the page torn out of the counterfoil book was stuck on an iron spike near the receipt stamp.

'A hundred and forty francs,' said Albert.

Madame Bourdelais paid and gave her address, for she had come on foot and did not want to be encumbered with a parcel. Joseph was already holding the silk behind the cash-desk and packing it up; and the parcel, thrown into a basket on wheels, was sent down to the dispatch department, where all the goods in the shop now seemed to be swallowed with a noise like a sluice.

Meanwhile, the congestion was becoming so great in the silk department that Madame Desforges and Madame Marty could not find a free assistant at first. They remained standing, mingling with the crowd of ladies who were looking at the materials and feeling them, remaining there for hours without making up their minds. The Paris-Paradise seemed destined for the greatest success of all, for it was attracting growing waves of enthusiasm, that sudden fever which sets a fashion in a single day. The salesmen were all occupied in measuring this silk; the pale light of the unfolded lengths could be seen above the customers' hats, while fingers were moving constantly up and down the oak measuring-sticks hanging from brass rods; the noise of the scissors biting into the material could be heard, without a pause, as fast as it was unpacked, as if there were not enough arms to satisfy the greedy, outstretched hands of the customers.

'It really isn't bad for five francs sixty,' said Madame Desforges, who had succeeded in getting hold of a piece from the edge of a table.

Madame Marty and her daughter Valentine were feeling disillusioned. The newspapers had talked about it so much that they had expected something bigger and more striking. But Bouthemont had just recognized Madame Desforges and, wishing to pay court to this beautiful creature who was reputed

to hold the governor completely in her power, he came up to
her with his rather crude amiability. What! She was not
being served! It was unpardonable! She must be indulgent,
for they really didn't know which way to turn. And he went
to look for some chairs among the surrounding skirts, laughing with his good-natured laugh, which revealed his brutal
love of women, and which Henriette did not, apparently, find
unattractive.

'I say,' murmured Favier as he went to get a box of velvet from
a shelf behind Hutin, 'there's Bouthemont making up to your
special customer.'

Hutin had forgotten Madame Desforges, for he was beside
himself with rage with an old lady who, having kept him for a
quarter of an hour, had just bought a metre of black satin for a
corset. At particularly busy times they took no notice of the
roster; each salesman served customers as they arrived. He was
replying to Madame Boutarel, who was finishing off her afternoon at the Ladies' Paradise, where she had already spent three
hours in the morning, when Favier's warning gave him a start.
Was he going to miss the governor's girlfriend, out of whom he
had sworn to make five francs? That would be the height of bad
luck, for he had not yet made three francs for himself, in spite of
all the skirts cluttering up the place!

Just then Bouthemont was calling out loudly:

'Come on, gentlemen, someone this way!'

Hutin handed Madame Boutarel over to Robineau, who was
not doing anything.

'Here you are, madam, ask the assistant buyer . . . He'll be
able to help you better than I can.'

He rushed off and got the salesman who had accompanied the
ladies from the woollens to hand Madame Marty's articles over
to him. Nervous excitement must have upset his delicate flair
that day. Usually, the first glance told him if a woman would
buy, and how much. Then he would dominate the customer,
hurrying to get rid of her in order to move on to another, forcing
her to make up her mind by persuading her that he knew what
material she wanted better than she did.

'What sort of silk, madam?' he asked in his most courteous
manner.

Madame Desforges had no sooner opened her mouth than he added:

'I know, I've got just what you want.'

When the length of Paris-Paradise had been unfolded on a corner of the counter between piles of other silks, Madame Marty and her daughter drew nearer. Hutin, rather anxious, understood that it was a question of supplying them first of all. Words were being exchanged in hushed tones; Madame Desforges was advising her friend.

'Oh! Absolutely,' she murmured, 'a silk at five francs sixty will never be equal to one at fifteen, or even ten.'

'It's very thin,' Madame Marty was repeating. 'I'm afraid it hasn't got enough body for a coat.'

This remark made the salesman intervene. He had the exaggerated politeness of a man who cannot be mistaken.

'But, madam, flexibility is the main quality of this silk. It doesn't crease . . . It's exactly what you want.'

Impressed by such assurance, the ladies fell silent. They had picked up the material again and were examining it once more when they felt a touch on their shoulders. It was Madame Guibal, who had been walking through the shop at a leisurely pace for at least an hour, feasting her eyes on the piled-up riches, without buying so much as a metre of calico. There was another outburst of chatter.

'What! Is it you!'

'Yes, it's me, a bit knocked about though!'

'Yes, I know. What a crowd, you can't move . . . Did you see the oriental hall?'

'Delightful!'

'What an incredible success . . . Do wait a moment, we can go upstairs together.'

'No, thank you, I've just come down.'

Hutin was waiting, hiding his impatience behind a smile which never left his lips. How much longer were they going to keep him there? Really, women had a nerve; it was just as if they were taking his money out of his pocket. Finally, Madame Guibal took her leave and continued her stroll, going round and round the great display of silks with an air of delight.

'If I were you, I'd buy the coat ready-made,' said Madame Desforges, coming back to the Paris-Paradise. 'It'll cost less.'

'It's true that what with the trimmings and having it made up . . .' murmured Madame Marty. 'And there's more choice too.'

All three ladies had risen to their feet. Madame Desforges turned to Hutin and resumed:

'Would you please take us to the ladieswear department?'

Unaccustomed to defeats of this kind, he was dumbfounded. What! the dark-haired lady wasn't buying anything! His instinct had let him down, then! He abandoned Madame Marty, and concentrated on Henriette, trying his powers as a good salesman on her.

'And you, madam, don't you wish to see our satins and velvets? We have some remarkable bargains.'

'No, thank you, another time,' she replied coolly, not looking at him any more than she had at Mignot.

Hutin had to pick up Madame Marty's things again, and walk ahead of them to show them to the ladieswear department. And he had the additional grief of seeing that Robineau was in the process of selling a large quantity of silk to Madame Boutarel. He certainly had lost his flair, he wouldn't make a penny. Beneath his pleasant, polite manner there was the rage of a man who had been robbed and devoured by others.

'On the first floor, ladies,' he said, without ceasing to smile.

It was no longer easy to get to the staircase. A compact mass of heads was surging through the arcades, spreading out like an overflowing river into the middle of the hall. A real commercial battle was developing; the salesmen were holding the army of women at their mercy, passing them from one to another as if to see who could be quickest. The great afternoon rush-hour had arrived, when the overheated machine led the dance of customers, extracting money from their very flesh. In the silk department especially there was a sense of madness; the Paris-Paradise had attracted such a crowd that for several minutes Hutin could not advance a step; and when Henriette, half-suffocated, looked up, she glimpsed Mouret at the top of the stairs, for he always came back to the same place from where he could watch the victory. She smiled, hoping that he would come down and extricate her. But he did not even recognize her in the crowd; he was still with Vallagnosc, busy showing him the shop, his face radiant with triumph. By now the commotion inside was muffling the sounds from the street; the rumbling of cabs and the banging of doors could no longer be heard; beyond the huge murmur of the sale there remained nothing but a sensation of the vastness of Paris, a city so enormous that it would always provide customers. In the still air, where the stifling central heating brought out the smell of the materials, the hubbub was increasing, made up of all sorts of noises—the continuous trampling of feet, the same phrases repeated a hundred times at the counters, gold clinking on the brass of the cash-desks, besieged by a mass of purses, the baskets on wheels with their loads of parcels falling endlessly into the gaping cellars. In the end everything became intermingled amidst the fine dust; it became impossible to recognize the divisions between the different departments: over there, the haberdashery seemed swamped; further on, in the linen department, a ray of sunlight coming through the window on the Rue Neuve-Saint-Augustin was like a golden arrow in the snow; while, in the glove and woollen departments, a dense mass of hats and hair hid the further reaches of the shop from view. Even the clothes of the crowd could no longer be seen, only head-dresses, decked with feathers and ribbons, were floating on the surface; a few men's hats made black smudges, while the pale complexions of the women, in the general fatigue and heat, were acquiring the transparency of camellias. Finally, thanks to some vigorous elbow-work, Hutin opened up a pathway for the ladies by walking ahead of them. But when she reached the top of the stairs Henriette could not find Mouret, who had just plunged Vallagnosc into the middle of the crowd to complete his bewilderment, and also because he felt the physical need to bathe in his own success. He became breathless with delight as he felt against his limbs a sort of long caress from all his customers.

'To the left, ladies,' said Hutin in a voice which was still courteous in spite of his growing exasperation.

Upstairs it was just as crowded. Even the furniture department, usually the quietest, was being invaded. The shawls, the furs, the underwear departments were teeming with people. As the ladies were going through the lace department, they again

came upon some people they knew. Madame de Boves was there
with her daughter Blanche, both buried in the articles which
Deloche was showing them. Hutin, parcel in hand, once more
had to make a halt.

'Good-afternoon! I was just thinking about you.'

'And I was looking for you. But how can you expect to find
anyone in this crowd?'

'It's magnificent, isn't it?'

'Dazzling, my dear. We can hardly stand up any more.'

'Are you buying anything?'

'Oh! no, we're just looking. It rests us a bit to sit down.'

Madame de Boves, who in fact had nothing but her cab-fare
in her purse, was asking for all sorts of laces to be taken out of
the boxes simply for the pleasure of seeing and touching them.
She had guessed that Deloche was a new salesman, awkward
and slow, who dared not resist the customers' whims; she
was taking advantage of his timid obligingness, and had
already kept him for half an hour, asking all the time for fresh
articles. The counter was overflowing; she was plunging her
hands into the growing cascade of pillow lace, Mechlin lace,
Valenciennes, Chantilly, her fingers trembling with desire, her
face gradually warming with sensual joy; while Blanche, by her
side, possessed by the same passion, was very pale, her flesh soft
and puffy.

Meanwhile, the conversation continued; Hutin, standing
there, awaiting their convenience, could have slapped them.

'I say!' said Madame Marty, 'you're looking at scarves and
veils just like mine.'

It was true; Madame de Boves, tormented by Madame
Marty's lace since the previous Saturday, had not been able to
resist the urge at least to touch the same patterns, as the modest
allowance her husband gave her did not permit her to take any
away. She blushed slightly, and explained that Blanche wanted
to see the Spanish lace scarves. Then she added:

'You're going to the ladieswear department . . . We'll see you
later then. Shall we meet in the oriental hall?'

'All right, in the oriental hall . . . It's superb, isn't it?'

They went into raptures as they separated, amidst the congestion caused by the sale of cheap insertions and small trimmings.

Deloche, happy to have something to do, started emptying the boxes again for Madame de Boves and her daughter. And among the groups crowded along the counters, Jouve the shopwalker was slowly pacing up and down with his military air, flaunting his medal, watching over those fine, precious goods which were so easy to conceal up a sleeve. As he passed behind Madame de Boves he cast a quick glance at her feverish hands, surprised to see her with her arms plunged in such a cascade of lace.

'To the right, ladies,' said Hutin, setting off again.

He was beside himself. As if it wasn't enough to make him miss a sale downstairs! Now they kept him waiting at every turning! His irritation was, above all, full of the resentment felt by the departments selling material against those that sold ready-made goods; they were in continual conflict, fighting over customers, cheating each other out of their percentages and commissions. Those in the silk department, more even than those in woollens, were quite enraged whenever they had to show a lady to the ladieswear department, when she decided to buy a coat after having asked to see taffetas and failles.

'Mademoiselle Vadon!' said Hutin in an angry voice, when he finally reached the counter.

But she passed by without taking any notice, absorbed in a sale she was anxious to finish. The room was full; a stream of people were going through it at one end, entering and leaving by the doors of the lace and lingerie departments, which faced each other, while in the background customers were trying on clothes, arching their backs in front of the mirrors. The red moquette muffled the sound of footsteps, the distant roar from the ground floor was dying away, and there was nothing but a discreet murmur, the warmth of a drawing-room made oppressive by a crowd of women.

'Mademoiselle Prunaire!' cried Hutin.

And as she took no notice either, he added inaudibly between his teeth:

'You old hags!'

He certainly was not fond of them; his legs were aching from climbing the stairs to bring them customers, and he was furious about the earnings he accused them of taking out of his pocket in this way. It was a secret war, in which the girls themselves

participated with as much ferocity as he did; and, in their common fatigue, always on their feet as they were, dead tired, differ-
ences of sex disappeared and nothing remained but opposing
interests inflamed by the fever of business.

'Well, isn't there anyone here?' Hutin asked.

Then he caught sight of Denise. She had been kept busy
unfolding things since the morning, and had only been allowed
to deal with a few doubtful customers to whom she'd been
unable to sell anything. When he recognized her, busy clearing
an enormous pile of clothes off a table, he ran to fetch her.

'Please serve these ladies who are waiting, miss.'

He quickly put Madame Marty's purchases, which he was
tired of carrying about, into her arms. His smile was coming
back, and in it there was the secret malice of the experienced
salesman, who had a shrewd idea of the embarrassment he was
going to cause both the ladies and the girl. The latter, however,
was quite overcome by the prospect of this unexpected sale. For
the second time Hutin had appeared like an unknown friend,
brotherly and affectionate, always waiting in the background to
come and save her. Her eyes shone with gratitude; with a lingering look she watched him go, elbowing his way through the
crowd to get back to his department as quickly as possible.

'I'm looking for a coat,' said Madame Marty.

Denise questioned her. What kind of coat? But the lady did
not know, had no idea; she just wanted to see what models the
shop had. And the girl, already very tired, dazed by the crowd,
lost her head; she had never served anyone but the rare customers who came to Cornaille's, in Valognes; she did not yet know
how many models there were, or where they were kept in the
cupboards. She thus hardly knew what to say to the two friends,
who were getting impatient, when Madame Aurélie caught sight
of Madame Desforges, of whose liaison with Mouret she was no
doubt aware, for she hurried over and asked:

'Are these ladies being looked after?'

'Yes, by that young lady who's looking for something over
there,' Henriette replied. 'But she doesn't seem very well up on
her job, she can't find anything.'

At that, the buyer paralysed Denise completely by walking
over and saying to her in a low voice:

'You can see that you don't know a thing. Just don't interfere, please.'

And she called out:

'Mademoiselle Vadon, coats please!'

She stayed there while Marguerite was showing the ladies the models. The girl affected a crisply polite voice, the disagreeable attitude of a young girl dressed up in silk, used to rubbing shoulders with the smartest people, yet jealous and resentful of them without even realizing it. When she heard Madame Marty say she did not wish to spend more than two hundred francs, she made a grimace of pity. Oh! Madam would spend more than that, it was not possible for madam to find anything decent for two hundred francs! And she threw the common coats on to a counter as if to say: 'You see how cheap they are!' Madame Marty did not even dare to look at them to see if she liked them. She bent forward to whisper in Madame Desforges's ear:

'Don't you prefer being served by men? One feels more at ease.'

Finally Marguerite brought a silk coat trimmed with jet, which she treated with respect. Madame Aurélie called Denise.

'Do something to help, at least. Put this over your shoulders.'

Denise, numbed, despairing of ever succeeding in the shop, had remained motionless, her arms dangling. No doubt she would be given notice, and the children would starve. The tumult of the crowd buzzed in her head, and she felt herself tottering; her muscles were aching from having lifted armfuls of clothes, really hard work which she had never done before. Nevertheless, she had to obey; she had to let Marguerite drape the coat over her, as if on a dummy.

'Stand straight,' said Madame Aurélie.

But almost immediately Denise was forgotten. Mouret had just come in with Vallagnosc and Bourdoncle; he was greeting the ladies, who complimented him on his magnificent display of winter fashions. Inevitably there were exclamations of delight about the oriental hall. Vallagnosc, who was just completing his walk round the counters, showed more surprise than admiration; for, after all, he thought, with the dismissiveness of a pessimist, it was nothing more than a huge collection of calico. As for Bourdoncle, forgetting that he was on the staff, he also congratulated the governor, to make him forget his doubts and anxieties of the morning.

'Yes, yes, it's going quite well, I'm pleased,' repeated Mouret, radiant, replying to Henriette's tender glances with a smile. 'But I mustn't interrupt you, ladies.'

Then all eyes were fixed once more on Denise. She had abandoned herself to Marguerite, who was making her turn round slowly.

'So, what do you think of it?' Madame Marty asked Madame Desforges.

The latter, as supreme arbiter of fashion, made her pronouncement:

'It's not bad, and the cut is original . . . But it doesn't seem to me very elegant round the waist.'

'Oh!' intervened Madame Aurélie, 'you should see it on madam herself. You see, it doesn't look much on this young lady, who isn't exactly well-built . . . Stand up straight, Mademoiselle Baudu, give it its full value.'

They all smiled. Denise had become very pale. She felt ashamed at being treated like a machine which they were freely examining and joking about. Madame Desforges, feeling antipathy to a temperament clearly different from her own, irritated by the girl's gentle face, added maliciously:

'It would certainly look better if the young lady's dress wasn't so loose-fitting.'

And she gave Mouret the mocking look of a Parisian amused by the ridiculous get-up of a girl from the provinces. He felt the amorous caress of this glance, the triumph of a woman proud of her beauty and her art. Therefore, in gratitude for being adored, and in spite of the goodwill he felt towards Denise, whose secret charm had conquered his gallant nature, he felt obliged to laugh at her in his turn.

'And she should have combed her hair,' he murmured.

This was the last straw. The director was condescending to laugh, and all the girls burst into fits of laughter too. Marguerite risked a slight chuckle, like a refined girl controlling herself; Clara had left a customer in order to enjoy the fun at her ease; even the salesgirls from the lingerie department had appeared, attracted by the noise. As for the ladies, they were joking more discreetly, with an air of worldly understanding; Madame Aurélie's imperial profile alone was unmoved, as if the new girl's beautiful, untamed hair and slender, virginal shoulders had somehow brought her well-ordered department into disrepute. Denise had grown even paler, in the midst of all these people making fun of her. She felt violated, defenceless, naked. What had she done, after all, to deserve being attacked like that for her waist being too small and her bun too big? But she was hurt above all by the laughter of Mouret and Madame Desforges, for some instinct had made her aware of their understanding, and some unknown grief was making her heart sink; that lady must be really wicked to attack a poor girl who had said nothing; while he positively made her blood run cold with a fear which froze all her other feelings so that she could not analyse them. Abandoned like an outcast, attacked in her most intimate feelings of feminine modesty, shocked at the unfairness, she choked back the sobs which were rising in her throat.

'You'll make sure that she combs her hair tomorrow, won't you? It's quite unseemly . . . !' the terrible Bourdoncle was repeating to Madame Aurélie. Full of contempt for her small limbs, he had condemned Denise from the moment she arrived.

At last the buyer came and took the coat off Denise's shoulders, saying to her in a low voice:

'Well, Mademoiselle Baudu! That's a good start. Really, if you wanted to show us what you're capable of . . . you couldn't have been sillier.'

Denise, fearing that she might burst into tears, hurried back to the pile of clothes she was sorting out on a counter. There, at any rate, she was lost in the crowd; tiredness prevented her from thinking. But she noticed that the salesgirl from the lingerie department, who had defended her that morning, was standing next to her. She had just witnessed the scene, and murmured in Denise's ear:

'My poor girl, you mustn't be so sensitive. Don't show you're bothered, or it will just encourage them . . . I'm from Chartres. Pauline Cugnot's my name; my parents are millers . . . Well, they'd have eaten me up when I arrived here if I hadn't stood up to them . . . Come on, be brave! Give me your hand; we'll have a nice chat when you feel up to it.'

The hand which was being held out only made Denise feel twice as upset. She shook it furtively, and hastened to carry away a heavy bundle of overcoats, afraid of doing something wrong again and of being scolded if they knew she had a friend.

Madame Aurélie herself had just placed the coat on Madame Marty's shoulders, and everyone was exclaiming: 'Oh! How lovely! It's wonderful!' It immediately began to look as if it had some shape. Madame Desforges declared that it would be impossible to find anything better. There was an exchange of farewells as Mouret took his leave, while Vallagnosc had caught sight of Madame de Boves in the lace department with her daughter, and hastened to offer her his arm. Marguerite, standing at one of the mezzanine cash-desks, was already calling out the various purchases made by Madame Marty, who paid for them and gave orders that the parcel should be taken to her carriage. Madame Desforges had found her own purchases at cash-desk No. 10. Then the ladies met once more in the oriental hall. They were leaving, but not without a final noisy burst of admiration. Even Madame Guibal became enthusiastic.

'Oh! It's delightful! It makes you feel you're actually there!'

'Yes, a real harem, isn't it? And quite cheap!'

'And the Smyrnas! Oh! the Smyrnas! What tones, what delicacy!'

'And that Kurdistan! Just look, a Delacroix!'

The crowd was slowly ebbing away. Peals of bells, at an hour's interval, had already signalled the first two evening meals; the third was about to be served, and in the departments there only remained a few belated customers whose passion for spending had made them forget the time. Outside nothing could be heard but the rattle of the last cabs of Paris, the snore of a replete ogre digesting the linens and cloths, the silks and laces, with which he had been gorged since the morning. Inside, beneath the flaming gas jets which, burning in the dusk, had illuminated the climactic moments of the sale, it was like a battlefield still hot from the massacre of materials. The salesmen, harassed and exhausted, were camping amidst the havoc of their shelves and counters, which looked as if they had been wrecked by the raging blast of a hurricane. The ground-floor galleries were blocked up with an untidy mass of chairs; in the glove department it was necessary to step over a barricade of boxes, piled up round Mignot; in the woollens it was impossible to get through at all, and Liénard was dozing on a sea of materials in which some half-destroyed stacks of cloth were still standing, like ruined houses about to be carried away by an overflowing river; further along, the white linen had snowed all over the ground, and one stumbled against ice-flows of table-napkins and walked on the soft flakes of handkerchiefs. Upstairs in the mezzanine departments the havoc was the same: furs littered the floor, ready-made clothes were heaped up like the greatcoats of disabled soldiers, the lace and underclothes, unfolded, crumpled, thrown about everywhere, gave the impression that an army of women had undressed there haphazardly in a wave of desire; while downstairs, in the depths of the shop, the dispatch department, operating at full stretch, was still disgorging the parcels with which it was bursting, and these were being carried away by the delivery vans in a final movement of the overheated machine. But it was in the silk department that the customers had been at their most voracious. There they had made a clean sweep, and it was quite easy to walk about; the hall was bare, the whole colossal stock of Paris-Paradise had just been torn to pieces and carried away, as if by a swarm of ravenous locusts. In the midst of this emptiness Hutin and Favier, out of breath from the struggle, were turning the pages of their cash-books, calculating their commission. Favier had made fifteen francs, whereas Hutin, who had only managed to make thirteen, had been beaten that day, and was furious at his bad luck. Their eyes were alight with mercenary passion, and around them the whole shop was also making calculations, burning with the same fever, with the brutal gaiety of nights of carnage.

'Well, Bourdoncle!' shouted Mouret, 'are you still worried?'

He had returned to his favourite position, at the top of the mezzanine staircase, by the balustrade; and, surveying the massacre of materials spread out below him, he gave a victorious laugh. His fears of the morning, that moment of unpardonable weakness which nobody would ever know about, had given him an even greater desire for triumph. And so the campaign was finally won, the small tradespeople of the neighbourhood reduced to shreds, Baron Hartmann, with his millions and his building sites, conquered. As he watched the cashiers bent over their ledgers, adding up the long columns of figures, as he listened to the tinkle of the gold falling from their fingers into brass bowls, he could already see the Ladies' Paradise growing beyond all measure, its hall expanding, its arcades being extended as far as the Rue du Dix-Décembre.

'Aren't you convinced now,' he resumed, 'that the shop is too small? We could have sold twice as much.'

Bourdoncle was happy to humble himself; he was delighted in fact at having been wrong. But then they saw a sight which made them serious again: Lhomme, the chief sales cashier, had just collected the individual takings from each cash-desk as he did every evening; after adding them up, he usually wrote out the total amount on a sheet of paper and put it on his spike-file; he would then carry the takings up to the counting-house, in a wallet or bags according to the type of cash. On that particular day gold and silver predominated, and he slowly went upstairs, carrying three enormous bags. As he had lost his right arm, which was amputated at the elbow, he clasped them to his chest with his left arm, holding one of them firmly with his chin to prevent it slipping. His heavy breathing could be heard from afar as he went along, laden down and proud, amid the respectful shop assistants.

'How much, Lhomme?' asked Mouret.

'Eighty thousand, seven hundred and forty-two francs, and ten centimes!'

A laugh of pleasure shook the Ladies' Paradise. News of the figure spread rapidly. It was the highest figure ever attained in one day by a draper's shop.

That evening, when Denise went up to bed, she leaned against the walls of the narrow corridor under the zinc roof. Once in her room and with the door closed, she threw herself on the bed; her feet were hurting her so much. For a long time she stared vacantly at the dressing-table, at the wardrobe, at the whole bare room. This was where she was going to live; and thoughts of her first horrible, endless day welled up in her mind. She would never have the courage to go through it again. Then she noticed that she was dressed in silk; her uniform depressed her, and before unpacking her trunk she had a childish desire to put on her old woollen dress, which had been left on the back of a chair.

But when she was once more dressed in her own poor garment she was overcome with emotion, and the sobs which she had been holding back since the morning suddenly burst forth in a flood of bitter tears. She fell back on the bed again, weeping at the thought of the two children, and she went on weeping, without having the strength to take off her shoes, completely overcome with weariness and sorrow.

CHAPTER 5

THE next day Denise had scarcely been in the department for half an hour when Madame Aurélie said to her in her sharp voice:

'Mademoiselle Baudu, you're wanted in the head office.'

The girl found Mouret alone, sitting in the great office hung with green rep. He had just remembered the 'unkempt girl', as Bourdoncle called her; and, although he was usually reluctant to play the policeman, he had had the idea of sending for her to give her a bit of a jolt, in case she was still looking dowdy like a girl from the provinces. The day before, in spite of the joke he had made, his vanity had been wounded when the smartness of one of his salesgirls had been discussed in front of Madame Desforges. His feelings were confused, a mixture of sympathy and anger.

'Mademoiselle Baudu,' he began, 'we took you on out of consideration for your uncle, and you must not put us to the painful necessity . . .'

But he stopped. Opposite him, on the other side of the desk, Denise was standing erect, serious and pale. Her silk dress was no longer too big, but fitted tightly round her pretty figure, moulding the pure lines of her virgin shoulders; and if her hair, knotted in thick braids, remained untamed, she was at least trying to control it. She had fallen asleep fully clothed, all her tears spent, and when she woke at about four o'clock she had felt ashamed of her attack of nervous sensibility. She had immediately set about taking in her dress, and had spent an hour in front of the narrow mirror, combing her hair, without being able to smooth it down as she would have liked.

'Oh! Thank goodness,' murmured Mouret. 'You look better this morning . . . But there's still that terrible hair!'

He had got up, and went over to her to try and smooth it down with the same familiar gesture as Madame Aurélie when she had tried to arrange it the day before.

'There! Tuck that one behind your ear . . . The bun is too high.'

She said nothing, but let him continue to arrange her hair. In spite of her vow to be brave, when she had reached the office she had been cold all over, certain that she had been sent for to be given notice. And Mouret's obvious kindness did not reassure her; she was still afraid of him, she still felt an uneasiness when close to him, which she explained as a natural anxiety in the presence of a powerful man on whom her fate depended. When he saw how she was trembling as his hands brushed against the nape of her neck, he regretted his gesture of kindness, for the one thing he was afraid of was losing his authority.

'So remember, Mademoiselle Baudu,' he resumed, once more putting the desk between them, 'try to pay attention to your appearance. You're not in Valognes any more; study the girls here in Paris . . . If your uncle's name was enough to allow you into our shop, I would like to believe that you will live up to what you seemed to me to promise. Unfortunately, not everyone here shares my opinion . . . So now you've been warned, haven't you? Don't prove me wrong.'

He was treating her like a child, with more pity than kindness, his curiosity about the feminine sex merely awakened by the disturbing woman he felt developing in this poor, awkward child. And while he was lecturing her, she, having noticed the portrait of Madame Hédouin whose handsome regular face was smiling gravely in its gold frame, felt herself trembling once more, in spite of the encouraging things he was saying to her. It was the dead lady, the one whom the neighbourhood accused him of having killed so that he could found the shop on her life-blood.

Mouret was still talking.

'You can go,' he said at last, and he carried on writing without standing up.

She left, and in the corridor she heaved a deep sigh of relief. From that day on Denise showed great courage. Beneath her attacks of sensitivity her common sense was always at work; the fact of being weak and alone strengthened her resolve, and she carried on cheerfully with the task she had set herself. She made very little fuss, but went straight ahead to her goal ignoring all obstacles; and she did so simply and naturally, for this invincible gentleness was the essence of her nature.

At first she had to learn to cope with the terrible rigours of work in the department. The parcels of clothes made her arms ache so much that, during the first six weeks, she would cry out with pain when she turned over at night, utterly worn out, her shoulders black and blue. But her shoes caused her even more suffering, for they were heavy shoes she had brought from Valognes, lack of money preventing her from replacing them with light boots. She was always on her feet, trotting about from morning to night, scolded if she was caught leaning up against the woodwork for a minute, and her feet, which were like the feet of a little girl, were swollen and felt as though they were being crushed by instruments of torture; her heels were inflamed and throbbed, the soles of her feet were covered with blisters, the skin of which was peeling off and stuck to her stockings. She felt her whole body being worn down, her limbs and organs were strained by the exhaustion of her legs, she had sudden disorders of a feminine nature which were betrayed by the pallor of her skin. And yet, although she was so thin and looked so frail, she kept at it, while many salesgirls were forced to leave the drapery business because they contracted occupational diseases. When she was almost ready to give in, worn out by work which would have made men succumb, she kept going, smiling and erect, because of her obstinate courage and her ability to suffer with good grace.

A further torment was that the whole department was against her. To her physical martyrdom was added the surreptitious persecution of her colleagues. Two months of patience and gentleness had not so far disarmed them. She was the object of wounding remarks and cruel tricks, and constant slights which, in her need for affection, cut her to the quick. They had teased her for a long time about her unfortunate first day; the words 'clogs' and 'gollywog' circulated, girls who failed to make a sale were 'sent to Valognes', in short she was considered the duffer of the counter. Later on, as she quickly became accustomed to the workings of the shop, and proved herself to be a remarkable saleswoman, there was indignant amazement, and from then on the girls conspired never to let her have a good customer. Marguerite and Clara pursued her with instinctive hatred, joining forces in order not to be destroyed by this newcomer whom they really feared in spite of their affectation of disdain. As for Madame Aurélie, she was hurt by the girl's proud reserve, by the fact that she did not hover round her with an air of admiration; she therefore abandoned Denise to the spite of girls she particularly liked, court favourites who were always sucking up to her, busy feeding her with the endless flattery which her strong, authoritarian personality needed to make it blossom out. For a while the assistant buyer, Madame Frédéric, seemed not to enter into the conspiracy, but this must have been an oversight, for she became just as brutal as the others as soon as she realized the difficulties she might get into because of her good manners. Denise was thus completely abandoned, and they were all utterly hostile to the 'unkempt girl', whose life was a perpetual struggle; in spite of her courage it was with the greatest difficulty that she succeeded in keeping her place in the department.

Such was her life now: she had to smile, put on a charming, gracious manner, and wear a silk dress which didn't even belong to her; ill-fed and ill-treated, she suffered agonies of fatigue, in continual fear of being brutally dismissed. Her room was her only refuge, the only place where she would still give way to tears when she'd suffered too much during the day. But a terrible coldness came from the zinc roof when it was covered with December snow; she had to curl up in bed, pile all her clothes on top of her, and cry under the blanket so that her face didn't get chapped from the frost. Mouret no longer spoke to her. When she received one of Bourdoncle's stern looks during business hours she would begin to tremble, for she sensed in him a natural enemy, who wouldn't forgive her the slightest lapse. In the midst of this universal hostility, she was surprised by the strange benevolence of Jouve; if he found her on her own he would smile at her, and try to say something nice; twice he had saved her from being reprimanded, although she'd showed him no gratitude, for she was more troubled than touched by his protection.

One evening, after dinner, while the girls were tidying the cupboards, Joseph came to tell Denise that a young man was asking for her downstairs. She went down, feeling very apprehensive:

'So!' said Clara, 'she's got a young man, has she?'

'He must be desperate . . .' said Marguerite.

Downstairs, at the main door, Denise found her brother Jean. She'd expressly forbidden him to come to the shop like this, as it made a very bad impression. But he seemed so beside himself that she didn't dare scold him; he had no cap and was out of breath from having run all the way from the Faubourg du Temple.

'Have you got ten francs?' he stammered. 'Give me ten francs or I'm done for.'

The young rascal looked so funny, with his flowing blond locks and his handsome girlish face, blurting out his melodramatic phrase, that she would have smiled had it not been for the anguish which this demand for money caused her.

'What do you mean, ten francs?' she murmured. 'What on earth's the matter?'

He blushed and explained that he had met a friend's sister. Denise stopped him, feeling equally embarrassed, not wishing to know any more about it. Twice already he had come running to her for similar loans; but the first time it had only been a question of one franc twenty-five centimes, and the second time one franc fifty. He was always getting involved with women.

'I can't give you ten francs,' she went on. 'I haven't paid for Pépé this month yet, and I've only just got enough for that. I'll hardly have enough left over to buy a pair of boots, which I need very badly . . . You really are unreasonable, Jean. It's too bad of you.'

'Then I'm lost,' he repeated, with a tragic gesture. 'Listen, Sis: she's tall and dark; we went to a café with her brother, and I never thought that the drinks . . . '

She had to interrupt him again, and, as his eyes were filling with tears, she took out her purse and slipped a ten-franc coin into his hand. Immediately he began to laugh.

'I knew you would . . . But I swear I'll never ask you again! I'd have to be an absolute scoundrel to do that.'

And he ran off, kissing her wildly on the cheek. The employees watching from inside the shop seemed quite astonished.

That night Denise slept badly. Since she had started work at the Ladies' Paradise, money had been a bitter worry to her. She was still on probation, without a regular salary; and as the girls in the department prevented her from selling, she could only just manage to pay for Pépé's board and lodging, thanks to the handful of unimportant customers they let her have. It was a time of dire poverty—poverty in a silk dress. Often she had to stay up all night repairing her small stock of clothes, mending her underwear, darning her night-dresses as if they were lace, not to mention her shoes, which she had patched as skilfully as any cobbler could have done. She risked washing things in her basin. Her old woollen dress worried her most of all, for she had no other, and was forced to put it on every evening when she took off the uniform silk dress, and that wore it out terribly; a spot on it gave her a fever, the slightest tear was a catastrophe. And she had nothing for herself, not a penny to help her buy the trifles a woman needs: she had had to wait two weeks to renew her stock of needles and thread. So it was a real disaster when Jean turned up all of a sudden with his stories of love-affairs and wrecked her budget. Each franc he took made a huge hole in it. As for finding ten francs the next day, there was not the slightest hope of that. Until daybreak she had nightmares of Pépé being thrown into the street, while she lifted up the paving stones with her bruised fingers to see if there was any money underneath.

It so happened that the next day she had to smile, to play the part of the well-dressed girl. Some regular customers came into the department, and Madame Aurélie called her several times and used her to show off the new styles of coats. All the time she was stiffly posing in the way prescribed by fashion plates, she was thinking about the forty francs for Pépé's board and lodging which she had promised to pay that evening. She could very well do without the boots for another month; but even if she added those four francs, saved up centime by centime, to the thirty francs she had left, that would only make thirty-four francs; where could she find the six francs needed to complete the sum? Her heart nearly failed her just to think about it.

'You will notice that the shoulders are loose,' Madame Aurélie was saying. 'It's very smart and very comfortable . . . The young lady can fold her arms.'

'Oh yes, easily!' Denise added, keeping up a pleasant manner. 'You hardly feel you've got it on . . . I'm sure madam will be very pleased with it.'

She now blamed herself for having gone to fetch Pépé from Madame Gras's a few Sundays previously in order to take him for a walk in the Champs-Élysées. The poor child went out with her so rarely! But it had meant buying him some gingerbread and a little spade, and then taking him to see Punch and Judy; and in no time she had spent one franc forty-five. Jean clearly didn't give his little brother a thought when he was acting stupidly. Afterwards, it was she who had to find the money.

'Of course, if madam doesn't care for it . . .' the buyer was saying. 'Here, Mademoiselle Baudu! Put this cloak on, so that madam can judge!'

Denise walked round taking mincing steps with the cloak on her shoulders, saying:

'This one is warmer . . . It's this year's fashion.'

Beneath her professional good nature she continued to torture herself, racking her brains trying to think where she could get some money. The other girls, who were rushed off their feet, let her make a big sale; but it was only Tuesday; she had to wait for four days before receiving her week's pay. After dinner she decided to put off her visit to Madame Gras until the next day. She would make an excuse, say that she had been detained; and in the mean time she might perhaps find the six francs.

As Denise avoided spending anything at all, she went to bed early. What could she do in the streets, without a penny, shy as she was, and still frightened by the big city, in which she only knew the streets near the shop? After venturing as far as the Palais-Royal, to get some fresh air, she would hurry back, shut herself in her room, and set about sewing or washing clothes. Along the whole length of the corridor off which the rooms led there was a barrack-like promiscuity; the girls were often very untidy, gossiping over slop buckets and dirty linen, venting their bitterness in continuous bickerings and reconciliations. Moreover, they were forbidden to go upstairs during the daytime; they did not live there, they just slept there at night, going back in the evening at the last minute, and escaping in the morning still only half awake after a rapid wash; and the draught which ceaselessly swept through the corridor, the fatigue of thirteen hours' work which made them drop exhausted into their beds, changed the attics into an inn traversed by a horde of exhausted, ill-tempered travellers. Denise had no friends. Of all the girls only one, Pauline Cugnot, showed her any kindness; but, as the ladieswear and lingerie departments, which were next door to each other, were in open warfare, the friendship between the two salesgirls had been limited so far to occasional words exchanged on the run. Pauline occupied the room on the right of Denise's; but as she disappeared immediately after dinner and did not come back until eleven, Denise only heard her going to bed, and never met her outside working hours.

On that particular night, Denise had resigned herself to playing cobbler again. She was holding her shoes, examining them, wondering how she could make them last until the end of the month. Finally she decided to sew the soles on again with a strong needle, as they were threatening to leave the uppers. In the mean time a collar and a pair of cuffs were soaking in the basin full of soapsuds.

Every evening she heard the same sounds: girls coming in one by one, short whispered conversations, laughter, sometimes a quarrel which they tried to keep quiet. Then the beds creaked, yawns were heard, and deep sleep would descend on the rooms. Her left-hand neighbour often talked in her sleep, which had frightened her at first. Perhaps others, like her, stayed up to mend things, in spite of the rule; but if so they must have taken the same precautions as she did, slowing down her movements and avoiding the slightest noise, for a chilling silence came from the closed doors.

Eleven o'clock had struck ten minutes before when a sound of footsteps made her raise her head. Another girl coming back late! And hearing the door next to hers open, she knew it was Pauline. But she was astonished when the girl quietly re-emerged from her room and knocked on her door.

'Hurry up, it's me.'

Since the girls were forbidden to visit each other in their rooms, Denise unlocked the door quickly in case her neighbour was caught by Madame Cabin, who kept watch to see that the rule was strictly observed.

'Was she there?' she asked, shutting the door again.

'Who? Madame Cabin?' replied Pauline. 'It's not her I'm afraid of . . . As long as I've got a franc to keep her quiet!'

Then she added:

'I've wanted to have a chat with you for a long time. It's impossible downstairs . . . And you looked so miserable at dinner this evening!'

Denise thanked her, and asked her to sit down, touched by her good-natured manner. But she was so confused by this unexpected visit that she was still holding the shoe she was sewing together, and Pauline's eyes fell on it. She shook her head, looked round and noticed the collar and cuffs in the basin.

'You poor thing, I thought as much,' she went on. 'Don't worry! I know what it's like. When I first came here, from Chartres, and my father didn't send me a penny, I washed a good few night-dresses, I can tell you. Yes, yes, my night-dresses even! I had two of them, and one of them was always soaking.'

She had sat down, still out of breath from running. Her broad face, with small bright eyes and a big, kindly mouth, had a certain charm, in spite of her rather coarse features. Suddenly, without any transition, she told Denise all about herself; her childhood spent at the mill, her father's ruin by a lawsuit, her dispatch to Paris to make her fortune with twenty francs in her pocket, how she had started as a salesgirl, first in a shop in the Batignolles district, then at the Ladies' Paradise, how terrible it had been to begin with, all the sufferings and privations she had had to endure; and finally she told about the life she was leading at the moment, how she earned two hundred francs a month, what her pleasures were, how she let her days slip by without heed to the future. Some jewellery—a brooch and a watch-chain—shone on her dark blue cloth dress, drawn in attractively at the waist; beneath her velvet toque, adorned with a big grey feather, she was still smiling.

Denise, shoe in hand, had turned very red. She tried to stammer out an explanation.

'I've been through it all too . . . !' repeated Pauline. 'Look, I'm older than you, I'm twenty-six, though I don't look it . . . Tell me all about your little troubles.'

In the face of this friendship so candidly offered, Denise gave in. In her petticoat, with an old shawl over her shoulders, she sat down next to Pauline, who was still all dressed up, and they launched into a heart-to-heart talk. It was freezing in the room, the cold seemed to seep into it through the bare prison-like walls; but they did not notice that their fingers were numb, they were absorbed in their confidences. Little by little, Denise opened her heart, talked about Jean and Pépé, said how much the question of money tormented her; and this led them both to attack the girls in the ladieswear department. Pauline was thus able to relieve her feelings.

'Oh! How nasty they are! If only they behaved in a reasonable, friendly way you could make over a hundred francs for yourself.'

'Everyone has a grudge against me, and I don't know why,' Denise said, beginning to cry. 'Monsieur Bourdoncle, for example, he's always watching me so that he can catch me doing something wrong, as if I was a bother to him somehow. Old Jouve is the only one . . . '

'What, that awful old shopwalker? Don't you trust him, my dear . . . You want to be careful of men with big noses like that! It's all very well for him to show off his medal; there's a story about something that happened in our department, in the lingerie . . . But what a child you are to take it all to heart! How terrible it is to be so sensitive! You must realize what's happening to you happens to everyone: you're just being given the usual welcome!'

She seized her hands and kissed her, carried away by her kind heart. The money question, however, was more serious. Certainly a poor girl couldn't support her two brothers, pay for the little one's board and lodging and buy treats for the big one's mistresses, out of the few left-over francs picked up from the other girls' cast-off customers; for it was to be feared that she wouldn't be given a salary before business picked up in March.

'Listen, you can't go on living like this much longer . . .' said Pauline. 'If I was you . . .'

But a noise in the corridor silenced her. Perhaps it was Marguerite, who was suspected of prowling about in her night-dress to spy on the others. Pauline, still clasping her friend's hands, looked at her for a moment in silence, listening attentively. Then she began again in a very low voice, with an air of gentle conviction.

'If I was you I'd get someone.'

'What do you mean, get someone?' murmured Denise, not understanding at first.

When she understood what Pauline meant, she took her hands away, quite stupefied. This advice embarrassed her, for it was an idea which had never occurred to her, and she could see no advantage in it.

'Oh! no!' she replied simply.

'In that case,' Pauline continued, 'you'll never manage, I can tell you! The figures just don't add up—forty francs for the little one, five francs every now and then for the big one; and then there's you, you really can't always go about like a pauper, with shoes the girls laugh at; yes, really, your shoes don't help you. Take someone, it would be much better.'

'No,' repeated Denise.

'Well, you're very silly . . . You have to, my dear, and it's so natural! We've all been through it. Take me, I was on probation like you, without a cent. Of course, we get lodged and fed, but we need clothes too, and that means money; you just can't stay shut up in your room counting the flies on the window. You have to let yourself go in the end . . .'

She told Denise about her first lover, a solicitor's clerk she had met during an outing to Meudon. After him, she had taken up with a post office employee. And now, since the autumn, she had been keeping company with a salesman at the Bon Marché, a very nice tall young man, at whose place she spent all her free time. She never had more than one lover at a time, however. She was a decent girl, and became indignant at the mention of the sort of girls who gave themselves to the first young man they met.

'I'm not telling you to misbehave, after all,' she said. 'For example, I wouldn't like to be seen with that Clara of yours, for fear people might accuse me of being as bad as her. But when you live quietly with someone, and have nothing to reproach yourself for . . . Is there anything wicked in that?'

'No,' replied Denise. 'I just don't care for it, that's all.'

There was a fresh silence. They were smiling at each other, both moved by this whispered conversation in the icy little room.

'Besides, you'd have to like someone first,' she went on, her cheeks pink.

Pauline was very surprised, but after a pause she laughed and kissed Denise again, saying: 'But, my dear, people meet and take to each other! You are funny! No one's going to force you . . . Look, would you like Baugé to take us somewhere in the country on Sunday? He'll bring one of his friends.'

'No,' Denise repeated, gently obstinate.

Pauline did not insist any further. Every girl was free to do as she wished. She had said what she had said out of pure kindness of heart, for it made her really sad to see a friend so unhappy. And as it was nearly midnight, she stood up to leave. But before doing so she forced Denise to accept the six francs she needed, begging her not to worry about it, but to repay her when she earned more.

'Now,' she added, 'blow your candle out, so that they can't see which door is opening . . . You can light it again afterwards.'

When the candle was out they shook hands once more; and Pauline slipped out quietly and went back to her room, leaving no sound behind her in the darkness but the rustle of her skirt, as the other little rooms slept on.

Before going to bed Denise wanted to finish mending her shoe and do her washing. The cold was becoming more intense as the night wore on. But she did not feel it; her conversation with Pauline had stirred up her blood. She was not shocked; she felt that people were entitled to arrange their lives as they thought fit when they were alone and free in the world. She had never been a slave to ideas, it was simply her common sense and healthy nature which made her live the clean life she led. Finally, at about one o'clock, she went to bed. No, there was no one she loved, so what would be the point of upsetting her life, spoiling the maternal devotion she had sworn to her two brothers? And yet she did not fall asleep; warm shivers were running up and down her spine, insomnia was making indistinct forms pass before her closed eyes, forms which vanished in the night.

From this time on, Denise took an interest in the love-affairs in her department. Except during the really busy rush-hours, the girls talked about men all the time. Gossip circulated constantly; stories of adventures would keep them amused for a whole week.

Clara was a scandal, for she was kept by three men, so it was said, not to mention the queue of casual lovers she trailed behind her; she only stayed on at the shop (where she worked as little as possible, as she was contemptuous of money she could earn more agreeably elsewhere) in order to cover herself in the eyes of her family; for she lived in perpetual terror of old Monsieur Prunaire, who would threaten to turn up in Paris and give her a good beating with a clog. Marguerite, on the other hand, behaved well, and was not known to have a lover; this caused some surprise, for everyone knew about the trouble she had got into, how she had come to Paris to have a baby in secret; how had she managed to have this child if she was so virtuous? Some said it was just an accident, adding that now she was keeping herself for her cousin in Grenoble. The girls also made fun of Madame Frédéric, saying that she maintained discreet relationships with various important personages; the truth was that they knew nothing about her love-affairs; she would disappear every evening, as stiff as starch and looking as sullen as a widow, seeming to be in a hurry, though no one knew where she was rushing off to. As for Madame Aurélie's passions, the cravings she was alleged to have for submissive young men were certainly an invention; discontented salesgirls made up stories like that for a laugh. Perhaps, in the past, the chief buyer had shown too much maternal affection for one of her son's friends, but she now occupied too responsible a position in the drapery business to allow her to amuse herself in such childish pursuits. Then there was the stampede in the evening, when the girls left, nine out of ten of them having lovers waiting at the door; in the Place Gaillon, all along the Rue de la Michodière and the Rue Neuve-Saint-Augustin, there were whole platoons of men standing motionless, watching out of the corner of their eyes; and, when the girls came out, each one would hold out his arm and lead his girl away, and they would go off, chatting with truly marital equanimity.

But what troubled Denise most was to have discovered Colomban's secret. She could see him at all hours of the day on the other side of the road, in the doorway of the Vieil Elbeuf, always gazing upwards with his eyes fixed on the girls in the ladieswear department. When he felt that she was watching him he would blush and turn his head away, as if afraid that she would betray him to her cousin Geneviève, although the Baudus and their niece had not spoken to each other since the latter had started at the Ladies' Paradise. She had thought at first, on seeing his despairing looks, that he was in love with Marguerite, who was well-behaved and lived in the shop and was therefore not an easy prey. She was flabbergasted when it became clear that the shop assistant's passionate glances were addressed to Clara. He had been like that for months, aflame with passion on the pavement opposite, unable to pluck up the courage to declare himself—and all that for a loose girl who lived in the Rue Louis-le-Grand, whom he could have accosted any evening before she walked off, always on the arm of a different man! Clara herself seemed to have no idea of the conquest she had made. Denise's discovery filled her with a painful emotion. Was love really as stupid as this? This lad, who had real happiness within his reach, was ruining his life, worshipping this good-for-nothing girl as if she were a saint! From that day on, every time she caught sight of Geneviève's pale, sickly face behind the green panes of the Vieil Elbeuf, her heart ached.

In the evenings Denise would day-dream as she watched the girls going off with their lovers. Those who did not sleep at the Ladies' Paradise would disappear until the next day, and when they returned to their departments they brought with them in their skirts the smell of the outside world, all the disquiet of the unknown. Sometimes Denise would respond with a smile to a friendly nod from Pauline, for whom Baugé always waited regularly from half-past eight onwards, standing at the corner near the fountain in the Place Gaillon. She herself was usually the last to leave, and when she had taken a furtive walk, always alone, she would be the first to come in again; then she would either work or go to bed, her head swimming with dreams, full of curiosity about Parisian life, about which she knew nothing. She certainly did not envy the other girls, for she was happy in her solitude, in the unsociable life in which she shut herself away as if in a sanctuary; but her imagination sometimes carried her away, and she tried to guess at things, conjuring up pictures of the pleasures which were always being described in her presence— the cafés, the restaurants, the Sundays spent on the water and in

*guinguettes.** Afterwards she was left spiritually exhausted, filled
with desire mingled with lassitude; she felt as if she was already
tired of these amusements which she had never tasted.

However, there was little time for dangerous day-dreams in
her daily working life. In the shop, worn out as they were by
thirteen hours' work, there was little opportunity to think
about love between salesmen and saleswomen. If the constant
battle for money had not already wiped out the difference
between the sexes, the endless jostle of the crowd, which kept
their minds busy and made their bodies ache, would have
been enough to kill all desire. Very few love-affairs were known
to have taken place in the midst of the hostilities and friend-
ships between men and women, the relentless competition
between departments. They were all nothing but cogs, caught
up in the workings of the machine, surrendering their person-
alities, merely adding their strength to the mighty common
whole of the phalanstery.* It was only outside that they could
resume their individual lives, with the sudden flame of reawakening passions.

However, one day Denise saw Albert Lhomme, the buyer's
son, slipping a note into the hand of a girl in the lingerie department, after walking through the department several times with
an air of indifference. The winter off-season, which lasted from
December to February, was approaching; there were times when
she had nothing to do, hours she spent standing and looking into
the distance, waiting for customers. The salesgirls in the
ladieswear department were especially friendly with the salesmen in the neighbouring lace department, although their enforced intimacy never went beyond jokes exchanged in low
voices. The assistant buyer in the lace department was a bit of a
joker, who used to pester Clara with salacious confidences just
for a laugh, although he really had little interest in her and made
no attempt to meet her outside. And it was like this in all the
departments—the men and women exchanged understanding
glances, remarks which they alone understood, sometimes sly
conversations with their backs half turned and with pensive
looks in order to put the terrifying Bourdoncle off the scent. As
for Deloche, for a long time he contented himself with smiling at
Denise; then, becoming bolder, he murmured a friendly word to

her when he bumped into her. On the day when she had noticed
Madame Aurélie's son giving a note to the girl from the lingerie
department, Deloche, feeling a need to take an interest in her,
and not being able to think of anything to say, was asking her if
she had enjoyed her lunch. He too saw the white smudge of the
letter; he looked at Denise, and they both blushed at this intrigue
set up in front of them.

But, in the midst of these warm breezes which were gradually
awakening the woman in her, Denise still kept her childlike
peace of mind. It was only when she saw Hutin that her heart
beat faster. But that was merely gratitude in her eyes; she
thought that she was simply touched by the young man's politeness. He could not bring a customer to the department without
her becoming quite nervous. Several times, coming back from a
cash-desk, she found herself making a detour, going through the
silk department quite unnecessarily, her heart pounding with
emotion. One afternoon she found Mouret there, and he seemed
to watch her with a smile. He no longer paid any attention to her,
and only said a few words to her from time to time in order to
give her advice about the way she dressed and to joke about her
looking like a tomboy, a little savage whom he would never be
able to turn into a smart girl, in spite of all his experience with
women; he would even laugh about it, he condescended to tease
her, without admitting to himself how much this little salesgirl,
with her funny hair, troubled him. Faced with his silent smile,
Denise trembled as if she had done something wrong. Did he
know why she was going through the silk department, when she
herself could not have explained what made her go out of her
way like that?

Hutin, however, did not seem to notice the girl's grateful
glances at all. The shopgirls were not his type; he affected to
despise them, while at the same time boasting more than ever
about the extraordinary adventures he had with customers: at his
counter a baroness had fallen in love with him at first sight, and
an architect's wife had fallen into his arms one day when he had
gone to her house about an error in measuring some material.
This Norman bragging merely disguised the fact that he picked
up girls in bars and music-halls. Like all the young gentlemen in
the drapery business, he had a mania for spending, and would go

through the whole week in his department struggling like a miser for money, with the sole desire of throwing it away on Sunday at the races, in restaurants and dance-halls. He never saved a penny, never put anything by; his salary was squandered as soon as he drew it, he cared nothing for the future. Favier did not join him in these parties. He and Hutin, so friendly in the shop, would say goodbye to each other at the door and not exchange another word; many of the salesmen, in continual contact while at work, became strangers, ignorant of each other's lives as soon as they set foot in the street. Liénard, however, was a close friend of Hutin's. They both lived in the same hotel, the Hôtel de Smyrne in the Rue Sainte-Anne, a gloomy building inhabited entirely by shop assistants. In the morning they arrived together; then, in the evening, the first to finish tidying up his counter would go and wait for the other at the Café Saint-Roch in the Rue Saint-Roch, a little café in which the shop assistants from the Ladies' Paradise usually congregated, and where they brawled and drank, and played cards in the pipe smoke. They often remained there till almost one in the morning, when the exhausted owner of the establishment threw them out. For the last month they had been spending three evenings a week at a low music-hall in Montmartre; they took their friends there, and were making quite a reputation for Mademoiselle Laure, the singer who worked there and who was Hutin's latest conquest, and whose talents they applauded with such violent bangings of their canes and with such a din that the police had already had to intervene on two occasions.

Thus the winter passed, and at last Denise obtained a fixed salary of three hundred francs. It was high time; her heavy shoes were falling to pieces. In the last month she even avoided going out, for fear of finishing them off at one go.

'My goodness, Mademoiselle Baudu, you do make a noise with your shoes!' Madame Aurélie frequently remarked in an irritated way. 'It's unbearable . . . What's the matter with your feet?'

The day when Denise came down wearing a pair of fabric boots for which she had paid five francs, Marguerite and Clara voiced their surprise under their breath, but loud enough to be heard:

'Look! That unkempt girl has given up her clogs!' said one of them.

'Ah! Well,' said the other, 'that must have been hard for her . . . They were her mother's.'

There was, in fact, a general uprising against Denise. The department had finally discovered her friendship with Pauline, and thought they saw a certain defiance in her liking for a salesgirl from an enemy department. The girls spoke of treason, accusing her of going next door and repeating everything they said. The war between the lingerie and ladieswear departments became more violent than ever; never had it been waged with such passion. The words exchanged were as hard as bullets, and one evening someone even slapped someone else, behind some boxes of chemises. Perhaps this long-standing quarrel had originated because the girls in the lingerie department wore woollen dresses, whereas the girls in the ladieswear department wore silk; in any case, the lingerie girls spoke of their neighbours with the shocked air of respectable girls; and the facts proved them right, the silk seemed to have a noticeable influence on the dissolute behaviour of the ladieswear department girls. Clara was condemned because of her flock of lovers; even Marguerite had, so to speak, had her child thrown in her face; while Madame Frédéric was accused of hidden passions. And all on account of Denise!

'Young ladies, no ugly words, please control yourselves!' Madame Aurélie would say gravely, amidst the angry passions of her little world. 'Show them who you are!'

She preferred to remain neutral. As she confessed one day to Mouret, none of the girls was worth much; there was nothing to choose between them. But she suddenly began to take a passionate interest when she learned from Bourdoncle that he had just caught her son in the basement kissing a girl from the lingerie department, the salesgirl to whom the young man had been passing letters. She was shocked, and immediately accused the lingerie department of having laid a trap for Albert; yes, a plot had been hatched against her; having seen that her department was above reproach, they were trying to disgrace her by ruining a poor innocent child. She only made such a fuss in order to confuse the issue, for she had no illusions about her son; she knew he was capable of anything. At one point the affair nearly became really serious, for Mignot, the glove salesman, became involved; he was a friend of Albert's, and it was rumoured that he gave preferential treatment to the mistresses Albert sent him, hatless girls who spent hours rummaging through the boxes; there was also a story, which was never cleared up, about some suede gloves given to the girl in the lingerie department. In the end the scandal was hushed up out of consideration for Madame Aurélie, whom even Mouret treated with respect. A week later Bourdoncle simply found some pretext for dismissing the salesgirl guilty of having allowed herself to be kissed. The management might turn a blind eye to the terrible goings-on outside, but it would not tolerate the slightest bawdiness inside the shop.

It was Denise who suffered from all this. Madame Aurélie, although she knew perfectly well what was going on, harboured a secret grudge against her; she had seen her laughing with Pauline, and took it as a sign of insolence, concluding that they were gossiping about her son's love-affairs. And so she made the girl even more isolated in the department than she had been before. For some time she had been planning to take the girls to spend a Sunday at Rignolles, near Rambouillet, where she had bought a property with the first hundred thousand francs she had saved; and suddenly she decided to do so: it would be a way of punishing Denise, of openly cold-shouldering her. She was the only one not invited. For two weeks, the department talked of nothing but this excursion; the girls would look at the sky, warm with May sunshine, and were already planning how they would spend every moment of the day, looking forward to all sorts of pleasures, such as donkey-riding, milk, and brown bread. And there would only be women, which made it even more amusing! Madame Aurélie usually killed time on her days off like this, by going for walks with other ladies; for she was so unaccustomed to being at home with her family, and felt so ill at ease, so out of place on the rare evenings when she could dine at home with her husband and son, that she preferred, even on these occasions, to abandon her family and go and dine at a restaurant. Lhomme would go his own way too, delighted to resume his bachelor existence, and Albert, relieved, would go whoring; they were so unused to being at home, and got so much on each other's nerves and so bored with each other on Sundays, that all three seemed to inhabit their flat only fleetingly, as if it was a cheap hotel where one just sleeps at night. As for the excursion to Rambouillet, Madame Aurélie simply declared that propriety prevented Albert from joining them, and that it would be tactful of his father if he refused to come; both men were delighted by this announcement. Meanwhile, the happy day was approaching, the girls could not stop talking about it, discussing the clothes they were preparing, as if they were going on a six months' journey; while Denise, pale and silent at being left out, had to listen to them.

'Don't they make you mad?' Pauline said to her one morning. 'I'd get my own back on them, if I was you! They're having a good time, so I'd have a good time too! Come with us on Sunday; Baugé's taking me to Joinville.'

'No, thanks,' replied Denise, with her calm obstinacy.

'But why not? Are you still afraid someone will take you by force?'

Pauline laughed heartily, and Denise smiled. She knew how things happened: it was on an excursion that all the girls had met their first lovers, friends brought along as if by chance; and that was not what she wanted.

'Come on,' Pauline persisted, 'I swear Baugé won't bring anyone. There'll just be the three of us . . . I certainly won't marry you off if you don't want me to.'

Denise hesitated, tortured by such desire that her cheeks were flushed. Since the other girls had started talking about the country pleasures they were going to have, she had felt stifled, overwhelmed by a longing for the open sky, dreaming of tall grass which would reach to her shoulders, of giant trees with shadows which would flow over her like fresh water. Her child-hood, spent in the lush greenery of the Cotentin,* was reawakening with a yearning for sun and air.

'All right, I'll come,' she said finally.

Everything was arranged. Baugé was to come and fetch the girls at eight o'clock in the Place Gaillon; from there they would go by cab to the station at Vincennes. Denise, whose twenty-five francs a month were swallowed up by the children, had only been able to do up her old black woollen dress by trimming it with check poplin strips; and she had made herself a bonnet-shaped hat, covered with silk and decorated with a blue ribbon. Dressed in this simple way, she looked very young, like a little girl who had grown too quickly; she had the neatness of the poor, and was a little ashamed and embarrassed by the luxuriance of her hair, bursting out from under her simple little hat. Pauline, on the contrary, was flaunting a silk spring dress with violet and white stripes, and a matching toque laden with feathers, and was wearing a necklace, and had rings on her fingers, which gave her the flashy appearance of a rich tradesman's wife. The silk dress was like a Sunday revenge on the woollen dress she was obliged to wear all week in the shop, whereas Denise, who wore her silk uniform from Monday to Saturday, put on her thin, shabby woollen dress again on Sundays.

'There's Baugé,' said Pauline, pointing out a tall young man standing near the fountain.

She introduced her lover, and Denise immediately felt at ease, for he seemed so nice. Baugé, enormous, with the slow strength of an ox at the plough, had a long, Flemish face, in which his vacant eyes laughed with childish puerility. Born in Dunkerque, the younger son of a grocer, he had come to Paris after being virtually turned out by his father and brother, who thought him terribly stupid. Nevertheless, at the Bon Marché he was making three thousand five hundred francs. He was stupid, but very clever when it came to linens. Women thought him nice.

'What about the cab?' asked Pauline.

They had to walk as far as the boulevard. It was already quite warm in the sun; the lovely May morning seemed to be laughing on the paving-stones. There was not a cloud in the sky, and the blue air, as clear as crystal, was full of gaiety.

An involuntary smile played on Denise's half-open lips; she was breathing deeply, and she felt that her chest was emerging from six months' suffocation. At last she no longer felt the stuffy air and the heavy stones of the Ladies' Paradise weighing her down! She had a whole day in the country before her! It was like a new lease of life, infinite joy, into which she was entering with the fresh sensations of a child. However, in the cab she looked away, embarrassed, when Pauline planted a large kiss on her lover's lips.

'Oh, look!' she said, still looking out of the window. 'There's Monsieur Lhomme over there . . . He's walking really fast!'

'He's got his French horn with him,' added Pauline, who had leaned over. 'He's crazy! It almost looks as if he's running to meet some girl.'

Lhomme, his instrument case under his arm, was indeed rushing along past the Gymnase Theatre, his nose in the air, laughing to himself with pleasure at the thought of the treat in store for him. He was going to spend the day at a friend's, a flautist in a small theatre where amateurs played chamber music from breakfast time onwards on Sundays.

'At eight o'clock! He must be keen!' Pauline went on. 'And you know, Madame Aurélie and all her clique must have taken the six twenty-five train to Rambouillet . . . You can bet she and her husband won't meet.'

The two girls talked about the trip to Rambouillet. They didn't want it to rain on the others, because then they would suffer too; but if a cloud could burst over there without the splashes coming as far as Joinville, it would be funny all the same. Then they started on Clara, a hopeless case who didn't know how to spend the money of the men who kept her: didn't she buy three pairs of boots at a time, and throw them away the next day after cutting them with scissors because her feet were covered with lumps? In fact, the girls in the drapery business had no more sense than the men: they squandered everything, never saved a penny, wasting two or three hundred francs a month on clothes and sweets.

'But he's only got one arm!' said Baugé suddenly. 'How does he manage to play the horn?'

He had not taken his eyes off Lhomme. Then Pauline, who sometimes amused herself by playing on his innocence, told him that the cashier held the instrument against a wall; and he quite believed her, thinking it a very ingenious idea. And then when she, filled with remorse, explained to him how Lhomme had adapted a system of pincers to his stump which he then used like a hand, he shook his head, full of suspicion, declaring that they couldn't make him swallow that.

'You really are silly!' she said laughing. 'Never mind, I love you all the same.'

The cab sped on and they arrived at Vincennes station just in time for a train. Baugé paid, but Denise had already declared that she intended to pay her share of the expenses; they would settle up in the evening. They got into the second-class, and found the train full of a gay, noisy throng. At Nogent a wedding party got out amid laughter. Finally, they arrived at Joinville and went straight to the island to order lunch; and they stayed there, on the bank beneath the tall poplars which border the Marne. It was cold in the shade; a sharp breeze was blowing in the sunshine, extending far into the distance, on the other bank, the limpid purity of open country, with its endless folds of cultivated fields. Denise lingered behind Pauline and her lover, who were walking with their arms round each other's waists; she had picked a handful of buttercups, and was watching the water flow past, happy, although her heart sank and she hung her head each time Baugé leaned over to kiss the nape of his sweetheart's neck. Tears came to her eyes. And yet she was not suffering. What gave her this choking feeling, and why did the vast countryside, where she had looked forward to such carefree happiness, fill her with a vague regret she could not explain? Then, at lunch, Pauline's noisy laughter made her feel quite dizzy. The latter, who adored the suburbs with the passion of an actress used to living in gaslight and the stuffy air of crowds, had wanted to lunch in an arbour, in spite of the sharp wind. She was amused by the sudden gusts which made the table-cloth flap; she thought the arbour, which was still bare, was fun, and the freshly painted trellis, with its lozenges silhouetted on the table-cloth. What's more, she devoured her food with the hungry greed of a girl who, badly fed in the shop, gave herself indigestion outside with the things she liked. That was her vice; all her money went on cakes, on indigestible things, on little dishes she would keep on one side for her spare moments. As Denise seemed to have had enough eggs, fried fish, and sautéd chicken, she restrained herself, not daring to order any strawberries, which were still expensive, for fear of making the bill too big.

'Now what are we going to do?' asked Baugé when the coffee was served.

Usually, in the afternoon, he and Pauline went back to Paris for dinner and finished their day at the theatre. But, at Denise's request, they decided that they would stay at Joinville; it would be amusing, and they would have their fill of the country. All the afternoon they wandered about the fields. Once they spoke of a trip in a boat, but abandoned the idea since Baugé rowed too badly. But their wanderings, along paths taken at random, took them back to the banks of the Marne all the same, and they watched with interest the life of the river, the squadrons of skiffs and rowing-boats, and the teams of oarsmen who populated it. The sun was going down, and they were going back towards Joinville, when two skiffs going downstream and racing each other exchanged several volleys of insults, in which the repeated cries of 'pub-crawlers' and 'counter-jumpers' figured prominently.

'I say!' said Pauline, 'it's Monsieur Hutin!'

'Yes,' said Baugé, shading his face with his hand, 'I recognize his mahogany skiff . . . The other one must be manned by a team of students.'

And he explained the old enmity which often set students and shopmen against each other. On hearing Hutin's name, Denise had stopped, and was following the slender craft, looking for the young man among the rowers; but she could only make out the white dresses of two women, one of whom, sitting at the tiller, wore a red hat. Their voices were drowned by the noise of the river.

'Into the water with the pub-crawlers!'

'Into the water with them, into the water with the counter-jumpers!'

In the evening they went back to the restaurant on the island. But it had become too cold outside, and they had to eat in one of the two closed rooms, where the table-cloths were still soaking wet with the dampness of winter. From six o'clock all the tables were occupied, the hikers were hurrying, trying to find a place; and the waiters were bringing more and more chairs and benches, putting plates closer together, cramming people in. It was stifling now; they had to open the windows. Outside the light was fading, and a greenish dusk was falling from the poplars so quickly that the restaurant owner, ill-equipped for these meals under cover, and having no lamps, had to have a candle put on each table. The noise—laughs, calls, the clatter of plates

and dishes—was deafening; the candles were flaring and guttering in the draught from the windows, while moths were fluttering about in the air warmed by the smell of food and cut through
by sudden gusts of icy wind.

'They're really having fun, aren't they?' said Pauline, deep in
a fish stew which she declared quite superb.

She leaned over to add:

'Haven't you noticed Monsieur Albert, over there?'

It was indeed young Lhomme, surrounded by three dubious-
looking women: an old lady in a yellow hat who had the vulgar
appearance of a procuress, and two girls under age, little girls of
about thirteen and fourteen, swaying their hips, and embarrass-
ingly insolent. He was already very drunk, and was banging his
glass on the table and talking of thrashing the waiter if he didn't
bring some liqueurs immediately.

'Oh, well!' Pauline went on, 'what a fine family! The mother at
Rambouillet, the father in Paris, and the son in Joinville
. . . They won't tread on each other's toes!'

Denise, who detested noise, smiled none the less, tasting the
joy of no longer thinking in the midst of all this noise. But
suddenly, in the neighbouring room, there was a burst of voices
which drowned all the others. There were yells, which must have
been followed by blows, for scuffles and the crash of chairs were
heard, a real struggle in which the river cries again rang out:

'Into the water with them, the counter-jumpers!'

'Into the water with them, into the water with them, the
pub-crawlers!'

And when the innkeeper's gruff voice had calmed the battle,
Hutin suddenly appeared. Wearing a red jumper, and a cap
reversed and pushed to the back of his head, he had on his arm
the tall girl in white who had been at the tiller; she, in order to
wear the skiff's colours, had planted a tuft of poppies behind her
ear. A burst of applause greeted their entrance; and he beamed
with pride, throwing out his chest as he swaggered along with a
nautical rolling gait, flaunting a bruise on his cheek caused by a
blow, puffed up with pleasure at being the focus of attention.
Behind them followed the team. They seized possession of one
of the tables, and the din became tremendous.

'It seems,' Baugé explained, after listening to the conversations behind him, 'it seems that the students recognized the

woman with Hutin; she used to live in the neighbourhood, and now sings in a music-hall in Montmartre. And then they came to blows over her . . . Those students never pay their women.'

'In any case,' said Pauline stiffly, 'she's terribly ugly, with her carroty hair . . . Honestly, I don't know where Monsieur Hutin picks them up, but each one's worse than the last.'

Denise had turned pale. She felt an icy cold, as if her heart's blood had drained away drop by drop. Already, on the river bank, at the sight of the speeding skiff, she had felt the first shiver; and now she could no longer have any doubt, this girl was really with Hutin. She felt a lump in her throat; her hands were trembling, and she was no longer eating.

'What's the matter?' her friend asked.

'Nothing,' she stammered, 'it's rather warm in here.'

But Hutin had sat down at a neighbouring table, and when he caught sight of Baugé, whom he knew, he started a conversation in a shrill voice in order to go on holding the attention of the room.

'I say,' he shouted, 'are you still chaste at the Bon Marché?'

'Not as much as all that,' Baugé replied, turning very red.

'Get away! You know they only take virgins, and they've got a confessional permanently attached to the shop for salesmen who look at them . . . A shop where they arrange marriages . . . No thanks!'

The others laughed. Liénard, who was a member of the team, added:

'It isn't like that at the Louvre . . . They've got a midwife attached to the ladieswear department there. It's the truth!'

The gaiety increased. Pauline herself was bursting with laughter, the idea of the midwife seemed so funny. But Baugé was annoyed by the jokes about the innocence of his shop. Suddenly he blurted out:

'But you're not so well off at the Ladies's Paradise! Sacked for the slightest thing, and with a boss who looks as if he picks up the customers!'

Hutin was no longer listening to him, but was launching into a paean of praise for the shop in the Place Clichy. He knew a girl there who was so respectable that the customers didn't dare speak to her for fear of humiliating her. Then, drawing his plate closer, he told how he had made a hundred and fifteen francs that week. Oh! it had been a marvellous week, Favier left behind with fifty-two francs, the whole roster left behind. And it was obvious that he was blowing his money; he would not go to bed until he had got rid of the whole hundred and fifteen francs. Then, as he became tipsy, he attacked Robineau, that fool of an assistant buyer, who pretended to keep aloof to such an extent that he would not even walk with one of his salesmen in the street.

'Shut up,' said Liénard, 'you talk too much, old chap.'

It had become even hotter; the candles were guttering on to the table-cloths stained with wine, and through the open windows, when the noise made by the diners suddenly subsided, a distant, long-drawn-out voice could be heard, the voice of the river and of the tall poplars which were falling asleep in the peaceful night. Baugé had called for the bill on seeing that Denise, quite white, her chin rigid with the tears she was holding back, was feeling no better; but the waiter did not reappear, and she had to go on suffering Hutin's loud talk. Now he was saying that he was smarter than Liénard, because Liénard simply squandered his father's money, whereas he squandered money he had earned, the fruit of his intelligence. At last Baugé paid, and the two women went out.

'There's a girl from the Louvre,' murmured Pauline in the outer room, looking at a tall thin girl putting on her coat.

'You don't know her; you can't tell,' said the young man.

'Of course I can! Look at the way she drapes herself! The midwife's department, obviously! If she heard, she ought to be pleased!'

They were outside. Denise gave a sigh of relief. She had thought she would die in that suffocating heat, in the midst of all that shouting; and she still attributed her faintness to the lack of air. Now she could breathe. A cool breeze was descending from the starry sky. As the two girls were leaving the restaurant garden, a timid voice murmured in the shadows:

'Good evening, ladies.'

It was Deloche. They had not seen him at the back of the outer room, where he had been dining alone, having come from Paris on foot for the sake of the walk. When she recognized his friendly voice Denise, who was feeling weak, yielded automatically to the need for support.

'Monsieur Deloche, come back with us,' she said. 'Give me your arm.'

Pauline and Baugé had already gone on ahead. They were surprised. They had not thought it would happen like this, and certainly not with this boy. However, as they still had an hour before catching the train, they went right to the end of the island, walking along the bank beneath the tall poplars; and from time to time they turned round murmuring:

'Where are they? Ah! There they are . . . It's funny though.'

At first Denise and Deloche remained silent. The noise from the restaurant was slowly dying away, acquiring a musical sweetness in the depths of the night; and they went further in among the cool of the trees, still feverish from that furnace, the candles of which were being extinguished one by one behind the foliage. It was as if a wall of darkness was facing them, a mass of shadow so dense that they could not even make out the pale track of the footpath. However, they went forward quietly, and without fear. Then, as their eyes became accustomed to the dark, to the right they could see the trunks of the poplars, like dark columns supporting the domes of their branches, spattered with stars; while to the left the water shone from time to time like a pewter mirror. The wind was dropping, and they could hear nothing but the flow of the river.

'I'm very pleased I met you,' finally stammered Deloche, who was the first to bring himself to speak. 'You don't know how happy I am that you agreed to walk with me.'

And after a great many embarrassed words, with the darkness helping him, he ventured to say that he loved her. He had been wanting to write to her about it for a long time; and she would never have known it perhaps, but for this lovely night that had come to his assistance, this water singing and these trees covering them with the curtain of their shade. But she did not reply; she continued to walk with her arm in his, with the same air of suffering. He was trying to look into her face when he heard a muffled sob.

'Oh! Good heavens!' he went on, 'you're crying, Mademoiselle, you're crying . . . Have I offended you?'

'No, no,' she murmured.

She was trying to hold back her tears, but she could not. Even at dinner she had thought her heart would burst. And now, in the darkness, she let herself go, her sobs choking her at the thought that if Hutin had been in Deloche's place, saying such tender things to her, she would have been powerless to resist. This confession, which she was at last making to herself, filled her with confusion. A feeling of shame was burning her face as if, beneath these very trees, she had fallen into the arms of that young man who was showing off in the company of tarts.

'I didn't want to offend you,' repeated Deloche, who was almost crying himself.

'No, but listen,' she said, her voice still trembling. 'I'm not at all angry with you. But please never speak to me again like that . . . What you ask is impossible. Oh! You're a nice boy, and I'll be glad to be your friend, but nothing more . . . Your friend, you understand!'

He was trembling. After taking a few steps in silence, he blurted out:

'In other words, you don't love me?'

And since she was trying to spare him the pain of a brutal 'No', he continued in a soft, heart-broken voice:

'In any case, I expected it . . . I've never had any luck, I know I can never be happy. At home they used to beat me. In Paris they've always made fun of me. You see, when you don't know how to steal other people's mistresses, and when you're too clumsy to make as much money as they do, well, the best thing is to go off and die in some corner . . . Don't worry, I won't bother you any more. And as for loving you, you can't prevent me, can you? I'll love you without expecting anything in return, like an animal . . . That's how it is, nothing ever goes right, that's my lot in life.'

In his turn he wept. She tried to console him, and as they were pouring out their hearts to each other, they discovered that they both came from the same part of the world, she from Valognes, he from Briquebec, thirteen kilometres away. This was a new link between them. His father, a penniless bailiff who was always morbidly jealous, used to thrash him, saying he was not his child, exasperated by his long, pale face, and his flaxen hair which, he said, did not come from the family. They went on to talk about the great pastures surrounded by quickset hedges, the over-grown paths which disappeared beneath the elms, the grassy roads like the avenues in a park. Around them the night was growing darker still, though they could distinguish the rushes by the river, the interlaced foliage, black against the twinkling stars; and they began to feel soothed, and forgot their troubles, drawn together in comradeship by their misfortune.

'Well?' Pauline asked Denise brightly, taking her aside when they reached the station.

From her friend's smile and tone of tender curiosity, Denise understood. She turned very red as she replied:

'Of course not, my dear! I told you I didn't want to! He comes from my part of the country. We were talking about Valognes.'

Pauline and Baugé were perplexed, put out in their ideas, not knowing what to think. Deloche left them in the Place de la Bastille; like all the young probationers, he slept in the shop, and had to be back there by eleven o'clock. Not wishing to go back with him, Denise, who had been given a theatre pass, accepted an invitation to accompany Pauline to Baugé's house. In order to be nearer his mistress he had taken a place in the Rue Saint-Roch. They took a cab, and Denise was dumbfounded when, on the way, she learned that her friend was going to spend the night with the young man. There was nothing easier; they only had to give five francs to Madame Cabin; all the girls did it. Baugé did the honours of his room, which was furnished with old Empire furniture, sent him by his father. He got angry when Denise wanted to settle up, and then in the end accepted the fifteen francs sixty she had put on the chest of drawers; but then he wanted to give her a cup of tea, and, after struggling with a kettle and spirit lamp, he was obliged to go downstairs to buy some sugar. Midnight was striking as he was pouring out the tea.

'I must be going,' Denise kept saying.

And Pauline would reply: 'In a minute . . . The theatres don't close so early.'

Denise felt awkward in this bachelor's room. She had seen her friend undress as far as her petticoat and corsets, and she was watching her turn down the bed, opening it, patting the pillows with her bare arms; and these preparations for a night of love-making upset her, and made her feel ashamed, reawakening in her wounded heart the memory of Hutin. Days like this one were certainly not good for her. Finally, at a quarter past midnight, she left them. But she left in embarrassment when, in reply to her innocently wishing them a good night, Pauline thoughtlessly exclaimed:

'Thanks, it *will* be a good night!'

The separate entrance which led to Mouret's flat and to the staff bedrooms was in the Rue Neuve-Saint-Augustin. Madame Cabin would open the door and have a look to check who was coming in. A night-light was burning dimly in the hall, and Denise, standing in its glimmer, hesitated, seized with anxiety, for as she had turned the corner of the street she had seen the door close on the vague shadow of a man. It must have been the governor coming home from a party; and the idea that he was there in the dark, waiting for her perhaps, brought on one of those strange attacks of fear he still caused in her, without any good reason. Someone moved on the first floor; boots squeaked. At that she lost her head entirely; she pushed open a door which led into the shop and which was always left open for the night-watch. She found herself in the printed cotton department.

'My goodness! What shall I do?' she stammered out in her emotion.

It occurred to her that there was another door upstairs leading to the bedrooms, but that would mean going through the whole shop. However, she preferred to take this route, in spite of the darkness which flooded the galleries. Not a gas jet was burning; there were only a few oil-lamps hooked on to the branches of the chandeliers at irregular intervals; and these scattered lights, like yellow spots, their rays lost in the night, resembled the lanterns hung in mines. Huge shadows were floating about; she could hardly distinguish the piles of merchandise, which assumed terrifying shapes of crumbling columns, crouching beasts, lurking thieves. The heavy silence, broken by distant breathing, intensified the darkness even more. However, she found her bearings: the household linen made a long pale streak on her left, like a street of houses turning blue under a summer sky; she wanted to go straight across the hall, but she bumped into some piles of calico and thought it would be safer to go through the hosiery, and then the woollens. When she got there she was alarmed by a noise like thunder, the loud snoring of Joseph, the porter, who was sleeping behind the mourning goods. She ran into the hall, where the glazed roof let in a dim light; it seemed to have grown larger, full of the nocturnal terror which churches have, its drawers immobile, and the outlines of its big measuring sticks forming inverted crosses. Now she was in full flight. In the haberdashery and glove departments she again nearly stepped over some of the duty porters, and she only felt safe when she finally found the staircase. But upstairs, before the ladieswear department, she was seized with terror on catching sight of a lantern, its winking eye walking along: it was a watch patrol, two firemen marking their passage on the dials of the indicators. For a minute she did not understand; she stood watching them making their way from the shawls to the furniture, then on to the underwear, terrified by the strange manœuvres, by the grating of the key, by the iron doors which clanged to with a deafening noise. When they came nearer she took refuge in the depths of the lace department, but the sudden sound of someone calling out made her leave it immediately, and run off to the communicating door. She had recognized Deloche's voice; he slept in his department on a small iron bed which he put up himself every evening. He was not yet asleep but, his eyes still open, was reliving the pleasant hours he had spent that evening.

'What! It's you, Mademoiselle Baudu!' said Mouret, whom Denise found facing her on the staircase, a little pocket candlestick in his hand.

She stammered, and tried to explain that she had just been to fetch something from her department. But he was not at all cross, he was looking at her in his paternal and at the same time inquisitive way.

'You had a theatre pass then, did you?'

'Yes, sir.'

'And did you enjoy yourself? Which theatre did you go to?'

'I went to the country, sir.'

That made him laugh. Then he asked, stressing the words:

'On your own?'

'No, sir, with a girl friend,' she replied, her cheeks burning with shame at the thought which no doubt had occurred to him.

He said no more. But he was still looking at her in her little black dress, her hat trimmed with a single blue ribbon. Would this little savage turn out to be a pretty girl? She smelt sweet from her day in the fresh air, she looked charming with her lovely hair falling over her forehead. And he who for six months had been treating her like a child, sometimes giving her advice, yielding to the ideas of a man of experience, to a malicious desire to find out how a woman might develop and go astray in Paris, was laughing no longer, but was experiencing an indefinable feeling of surprise and fear, mingled with affection. No doubt it was a lover who was making her grow more attractive. At this thought, he felt as if a favourite bird he had been playing with had just pecked him and drawn blood.

'Good-night, sir,' murmured Denise, continuing on her way upstairs without waiting.

He did not answer, but watched her disappear. Then he returned to his own rooms.

CHAPTER 6

WHEN the summer slack season came, there was quite a panic at the Ladies' Paradise. Everyone lived in terror of dismissal, of the mass discharges with which the management cleaned out the shop, now empty of customers during the heat of July and August.

Each morning, during his tour of inspection with Bourdoncle, Mouret would take aside the heads of departments whom he had urged to take on more salesmen than they needed during the winter, so that sales would not suffer, at the risk of having to weed out their staff later on. Now it was a question of reducing costs by turning into the street one-third of the assistants, the weak ones who let themselves be devoured by the strong.

'Come on,' he would say, 'you've got some who are no use to you . . . We can't keep them on so that they can just stand about with nothing to do.'

And if the head of the department hesitated, not knowing whom to sacrifice, he would say:

'You must decide; six salesmen are all you need . . . You can take on more in October, there are enough of them hanging about the streets!'

It was Bourdoncle, in any case, who dealt with executions. He had a terrible way of saying through his thin lips 'Go and collect your wages!'—words which fell like a blow from an axe. He made anything a pretext for getting rid of superfluous staff. He would invent misdeeds, seizing on the slightest act of carelessness. 'You were sitting down, sir: go and collect your wages! You're answering back, I believe: go and collect your wages! Your shoes are not clean: go and collect your wages!' Even the brave trembled at the carnage he left in his wake. Then, as this technique did not work quickly enough, he devised a trap in which, in a few days, he effortlessly garrotted the number of salesmen condemned in advance. From eight o'clock he stood at the entrance door, watch in hand; and if they were three minutes late, the out-of-breath young men were axed by his implacable:

'Go and collect your wages!' The job was done quickly and without fuss.

'You there, you've got an ugly mug!' he even said one day to a poor devil whose crooked nose got on his nerves. 'Go and collect your wages!'

Favoured employees were given a fortnight's holiday without pay, which was a more humane way of cutting costs. In any case, the salesmen accepted their precarious position, for they were forced to do so by necessity and habit. Ever since their arrival in Paris they had roamed about, beginning their apprenticeship in one shop, finishing it in another, getting dismissed or leaving of their own accord on the spur of the moment, as chance and their interests dictated. When the factories lay idle, the workers were deprived of their daily bread; and this took place with the unfeeling motion of a machine—the useless cog was calmly thrown aside, like an iron wheel to which no gratitude is shown for services rendered. So much the worse for those who did not know how to look after themselves!

The departments now talked of nothing else. Each day fresh stories circulated. The names of salesmen who had been dismissed were mentioned in the same way as one counts the dead during epidemics. The shawl and woollen departments suffered especially: seven assistants disappeared from them in a week. Next, a drama convulsed the lingerie department: a customer had felt ill and accused the girl who was serving her of eating garlic; the salesgirl was dismissed on the spot, although, badly fed and always hungry, she had simply been finishing off a store of crusts at the counter. At the slightest complaint from customers the management was merciless; no excuse was accepted, the employee was always wrong, and had to disappear like a defective tool which harmed the smooth working of the business; while his colleagues hung their heads and did not even try to defend him. In the general panic everyone trembled for himself; one day, when Mignot in spite of the rule was leaving with a parcel under his overcoat, he was nearly caught and, for a moment, thought himself in the street; Liénard, whose laziness was legendary, owed it to his father's position in the drapery trade that he was not sacked one afternoon when Bourdoncle found him dozing between two piles of English velvet. But the

Lhommes were especially worried, for they expected every day to hear that their son Albert had been dismissed. There was great dissatisfaction with the way he kept his cash-desk; women often came and distracted him; twice Madame Aurélie was obliged to intercede with the management.

Denise was in such danger, in the midst of the clean sweep which was being made, that she lived in constant fear of a catastrophe. It was in vain that she tried to be brave, struggling with all her cheerfulness and good sense not to give in to her feelings; tears would blind her as soon as she closed the door of her room. She was in despair at the thought of finding herself in the street, on bad terms with her uncle, not knowing where to go, without any savings, and with the two children on her hands. The feelings she had experienced in the first few weeks were stirring again; she felt she was a grain of millet beneath a powerful millstone, and she was utterly forlorn at feeling herself so insignificant in that huge machine, which would crush her with its calm indifference. It was impossible to have any illusions: if one of the salesgirls from the ladieswear department was to be dismissed, she knew it would be her. No doubt, during the trip to Rambouillet the girls had stirred up Madame Aurélie against her, for since then the latter had been treating her with an air of severity which seemed to betray a certain spite. In any case, they had not forgiven her for going to Joinville, which they considered a sign of rebellion, a means of defying the whole department by parading about outside the shop with a girl from a rival counter. Never had Denise suffered so much in the department, and now she had begun to despair of ever winning it over.

'Don't take any notice of them!' Pauline would say. 'They're just stuck up, the silly things!'

But it was precisely their ladylike ways that intimidated Denise. From their daily contact with rich customers, nearly all the salesgirls had acquired airs and graces, and had ended up by forming a vague class floating between the working and middle classes; and often, beneath their dress sense, beneath the manners and phrases they had learned, there was nothing but a false, superficial education, picked up from reading cheap newspapers, from tirades in the theatre, and from all the latest follies of the Paris streets.

'You know, that unkempt girl has got a child!' Clara said one morning as she came into the department.

There was some astonishment, so she went on:

'I saw her yesterday taking the kid for a walk! She must have it stowed away somewhere.' Two days later, on returning from dinner, Marguerite had a fresh piece of news.

'I must tell you, I've just seen her lover . . . A workman, just fancy! Yes, a dirty little workman, with yellow hair, who was watching her through the windows.'

From then on it was an accepted fact: Denise had a lover who was a navvy, and a child whom she was hiding somewhere in the neighbourhood. They bombarded her with nasty innuendoes. When she realized what they meant she became very pale at the monstrosity of their conjectures. It was abominable; she wanted to explain, and stammered:

'But they're my brothers!'

'Oh, her brothers!' said Clara, in a mocking tone.

Madame Aurélie was obliged to intervene.

'Be quiet, young ladies, you'd do better to change these price tickets . . . Mademoiselle Baudu is quite free to misbehave outside the shop. If only she worked while she's here!'

This curt defence was a condemnation. Denise, as flabbergasted as if she had been accused of a crime, tried vainly to explain the facts. They laughed and shrugged their shoulders, and this wounded her to the quick. When the rumour spread, Deloche was so indignant that he talked of boxing the ears of the girls in the ladieswear department; and it was only the fear of compromising her that held him back. Since the evening at Joinville his love for her was submissive, his friendship almost religious, as he showed by gazing at her like a faithful dog. He was anxious that the others should not suspect their friendship, for they would have laughed at them; but that did not prevent him from dreaming of acts of sudden violence, of the avenging blow, if ever anyone should attack her in his presence.

In the end Denise stopped replying to their insults. It was too odious; no one would believe it. When one of the girls ventured to make some fresh allusion, she merely looked at her steadily, with a sad, calm air. In any case, she had other troubles, material anxieties which worried her much more. Jean was still behaving unreasonably, always pestering her for money. Hardly a week passed without her receiving some story from him, four pages long; and when the shop postman brought her these letters written in big, passionate handwriting, she would hasten to hide them in her pocket, for the salesgirls took much pleasure in laughing about them, singing bawdy songs as they did so. Then, having invented a pretext for going to decipher the letters at the other end of the shop, she would be overwhelmed with fear; she felt that poor Jean was lost. She believed all his fibs about extraordinary amorous adventures, and her ignorance of such things made her exaggerate the dangers even more. Sometimes it was forty centimes to save him from a woman's jealousy, at other times five francs or six francs to restore the honour of a poor girl whose father would otherwise kill her. And so, as her salary and commission were insufficient, she had conceived the idea of looking for a little extra work after business hours. She had spoken about it to Robineau, who had continued to show a certain sympathy for her since their first meeting at Vinçard's; and he had found her a little job sewing neckties at twenty-five centimes a dozen. At night, between nine o'clock and one, she could sew six dozen of them, which earned her one franc fifty, from which she had to deduct a candle at twenty centimes. But as this one franc thirty a day kept Jean, she did not complain about the lack of sleep, and would have considered herself very happy had not a catastrophe once more upset her budget. At the end of the second fortnight, when she went to see the woman through whom she obtained the neckties, she found the door closed; the woman had become insolvent, bankrupt, which meant that Denise lost eighteen francs thirty centimes, a considerable sum on which she had been absolutely counting for a week. All her troubles in the department paled before this disaster.

'You look sad,' said Pauline, whom she met in the furniture department. 'Do you need anything?'

But Denise already owed her friend twelve francs. Trying to smile, she replied:

'No, thank you . . . I slept badly, that's all.'

It was the twentieth of July, at the very height of the panic about dismissals. Out of the four hundred employees,

Bourdoncle had already sacked fifty; and there were rumours of fresh executions. However, she gave no thought to the danger of dismissal; she was completely preoccupied by the distress caused by a fresh adventure of Jean's which was even more alarming than the others. That day he needed fifteen francs; that sum alone could save him from the vengeance of a deceived husband. The day before she had received a first letter announcing the drama; then, in rapid succession, two other letters had arrived, and in the last one above all, which she had just finished when Pauline had met her, Jean announced that he would die that evening if she did not give him the fifteen francs. She was racking her brains. She could not take it out of Pépé's board and lodging, which she had paid two days before. All her misfortunes were coming at the same time, for she had hoped to get her eighteen francs thirty centimes back through Robineau, who would perhaps be able to find the necktie dealer; but Robineau, having got a fortnight's holiday, had not returned the night before as expected.

Meanwhile Pauline was still questioning her in a friendly way. When they met like that, in some out-of-the-way department, they would chat for a few minutes, keeping a look-out as they did so. Suddenly Pauline made as if to run off; she had just caught sight of the white tie of a shopwalker who was coming out of the shawl department.

'Oh! it's only old Jouve,' she murmured, relieved. 'I don't know why the old boy laughs like that when he sees us together . . . If I was you I'd be worried; he's much too nice to you. An old humbug whose day's done, a nasty piece of work who still thinks he's talking to his troops.'

Indeed, old Jouve was hated by all the salesmen because his supervision was so strict. More than half the dismissals were the result of his reports. His large red nose—the nose of a rakish ex-captain—became human only in the departments staffed by women.

'Why should I be afraid?' asked Denise.

'Well,' replied Pauline, laughing, 'he may ask you to show some gratitude . . . Several of the girls try to humour him.'

Jouve had moved away, pretending not to see them, and they heard him shouting at a salesman in the lace department who was guilty of looking at a horse which had fallen down in the Rue Neuve-Saint-Augustin.

'By the way', Pauline went on, 'weren't you looking for Monsieur Robineau yesterday? He's back.'

Denise thought she was saved.

'Thanks, I'll go round the other way, through the silk department . . . It can't be helped! They sent me upstairs to the workroom to fetch a dress that had been altered.'

They separated. Denise, with a busy look, as if she was running from cash-desk to cash-desk trying to check up on some error, arrived at the staircase and went down into the hall. It was a quarter to ten, and the bell had just gone for the first meal service. A brilliant sun was warming the glass roof, and in spite of the grey linen blinds the heat was beating down in the still air. Now and then a cool breath rose from the parquet floor which the porters were sprinkling with a thin trickle of water. An atmosphere of somnolence, a summer siesta, reigned in the empty spaces between the counters, which were like chapels filled with sleeping darkness after the last Mass. Salesmen were standing listlessly about; a few customers were going through the galleries, crossing the hall with the tired gait of women tortured by the sun.

As Denise was going downstairs Favier was just measuring out the material for a dress in fine silk with pink spots, for Madame Boutarel, who had arrived in Paris the day before from the south. Since the beginning of the month the provinces had been supplying customers; one saw nothing but dowdy women, yellow shawls, green skirts, a mass influx from the country. The bored shop assistants could not even be bothered to laugh at them. Favier accompanied Madame Boutarel to the haberdashery department, and when he reappeared he said to Hutin:

'Yesterday they were all from Auvergne, today they're all from Provence . . . I'm quite sick of them.'

But Hutin rushed forward; it was his turn, and he had recognized 'the pretty lady', the lovely blonde whom the department described in that way, for they knew nothing about her, not even her name! They all smiled at her; not a week passed without her coming to the Ladies' Paradise, always alone. This time she had with her a little boy of four or five, and this provoked some comment.

'She's married, then?' asked Favier, when Hutin came back from the cash-desk, where he had had thirty metres of duchess satin debited.

'Maybe,' Hutin replied, 'although the kid doesn't prove anything. He might belong to a friend . . . What's certain is that she must have been crying. She looked terribly sad, and her eyes were red!'

A silence ensued. The two salesmen gazed vaguely into the depths of the shop. Then Favier said slowly:

'If she's married, perhaps her husband's been hitting her.'

'Maybe,' Hutin repeated. 'Unless it was a lover who's left her in the lurch.'

And after a fresh silence he added:

'I couldn't care less, anyway!'

At that moment Denise was walking through the silk department, slackening her pace and looking about her, trying to find Robineau. She could not see him, so she went into the household linen gallery, then passed through the silk department a second time. The two salesmen had noticed her stratagem.

'Here's that skinny girl again!' murmured Hutin.

'She's looking for Robineau,' said Favier. 'I don't know what they're up to. Certainly nothing dirty, Robineau isn't like that . . . They say he got her a job sewing neckties . . . What a business, eh?'

Hutin was wondering how he could embarrass Denise. When she passed close by him he stopped her, saying:

'Is it me you're looking for?'

She became very red. Since the evening at Joinville she had not dared read what was in her heart, which was full of confused feelings. She kept seeing him in her mind, with the red-headed girl, and if she still trembled in his presence it was perhaps from uneasiness. Had she ever loved him? Did she love him still? She had no desire to analyse the feelings which caused her such pain.

'No, sir,' she replied, embarrassed.

Seeing that she was embarrassed, Hutin began to make fun of her.

'Do you want us to serve him to you? Favier, please serve Robineau to the young lady.'

She looked at him intently, with the same calm, sad gaze with which she greeted the wounding remarks the girls were always making about her. Oh, how unpleasant he was, attacking her just like the others! And it seemed as if something snapped inside her, as if a last bond was breaking. There was such suffering in her face that Favier, not very soft-hearted by nature, came to her help.

'Monsieur Robineau is in the stock-room,' he said. 'I'm sure he'll be back for lunch . . . You'll find him here this afternoon, if you want to speak to him.'

Denise thanked him, and went upstairs again to the ladieswear department, where Madame Aurélie was waiting for her in cold fury. What! She'd been gone for half an hour! Where had she been? Not in the work-room, to be sure? Denise hung her head, thinking how endless were her misfortunes. If Robineau didn't come back, all was lost. She was planning to go downstairs again, all the same.

In the silk department, Robineau's return had set off quite a revolution. The department had been hoping that he would be so sick of the trouble people constantly made for him that he would not come back; and indeed, at one time, pressed by Vinçard to take over his business, he had almost decided to do so. Hutin's secret campaign, the mine which, for months, he had been digging under the assistant buyer's feet, was finally about to explode. During Robineau's leave, Hutin, as senior salesman, had deputized for him, and had done his best to damage his reputation in the eyes of his superiors, and to install himself in his place by being over-zealous; he discovered and exposed small irregularities, he submitted plans for improvement, he invented new designs. Moreover, everyone in the department, from the newcomer dreaming of becoming a salesman to the senior salesman coveting the manager's job, had only one fixed idea—to dislodge the colleague above them in order to climb a rung of the ladder, to devour him if he became an obstacle; and it was as if this struggle of appetites, this pressure of one against another, was what made the machine run smoothly, stimulating business and igniting the blaze of success which was astonishing Paris.

Behind Hutin, there was Favier, and behind Favier there were
the others, in a queue. The sound of jaws working could be
heard. Robineau was condemned; everyone was already carrying
away a bone. So, when the assistant buyer reappeared, there was
a general grumbling. The question had to be settled, and the
attitude of the salesmen had seemed so menacing to the head of
the department that he had just sent Robineau to the stock-room
to give the management time to come to a decision.

'If they keep him on, we'd all rather leave,' declared Hutin.

This affair was upsetting Bouthemont, whose natural gaiety
was ill-adapted to an internal worry of this sort. It troubled him
to see nothing but sullen faces around him. Nevertheless, he
wanted to be fair.

'Come on, leave him alone, he's not doing you any harm.'

But this provoked an outburst of protests.

'What do you mean, he's not doing us any harm? He's unbearable, always irritable and so stuck-up that he'd walk all over you
without even noticing!'

This was the great grudge the department had against him. As
well as being as nervous as a woman, Robineau was intolerably
stiff and touchy. At least twenty stories were told about him,
from how he had made a poor young fellow ill, to how he had
humiliated customers with his cutting remarks.

'Well, gentlemen,' said Bouthemont, 'I can't take anything
on . . . I've told the management, and I'm going to discuss it
with them a little later!'

The bell was going for the second meal service; the clanging
sound was coming up from the basement, distant and muffled in
the dead air of the shop. Hutin and Favier went downstairs.
From every department salesmen were arriving one by one, in
disorder, hurrying down to the narrow entrance to the kitchen
corridor, a damp passage always lit by gas jets. The crowd
pushed forward without a laugh or a word, surrounded by the
growing noise of crockery and a strong smell of food. At the end
of the corridor, there was a sudden halt at a hatch where a cook,
flanked by piles of plates and armed with forks and spoons which
he was plunging into copper pans, was distributing the helpings.
When he stood aside, beyond his apron-clad stomach the blazing
kitchen could be seen.

'Oh, no!' Hutin muttered, consulting the menu which was written on a blackboard above the hatch. 'Beef with mustard sauce, or skate . . . They never give us any roast meat in this dump! All their stews and fish just don't keep body and soul together . . .'

The fish, moreover, was universally despised, for the pan remained full. Favier, however, took the skate. Behind him Hutin bent down, saying:

'Beef with mustard sauce.'

With a mechanical gesture the cook speared a piece of meat and then poured a spoonful of sauce over it; and Hutin, choking at the hot blast he had received in his face from the hatch, had hardly walked away with his helping when already behind him the words 'Beef with mustard sauce,' 'Beef with mustard sauce,' were being called out like a litany, while the cook continued to spear bits of meat and pour sauce over them with the rapid, rhythmic movement of a well-regulated clock.

'The skate's cold,' declared Favier, whose hand could feel no warmth from the plate.

They were all moving off now, with their arms stretched out, holding their plates straight, afraid of bumping into each other. Ten paces further on was the bar, another hatch with a shining zinc counter on which the servings of wine were set out in small corkless bottles, still damp from rinsing. Everyone received one of these bottles in his empty hand as he passed, and then, heavily laden, would make his way to his table with a serious air, careful not to spill anything.

Hutin was grumbling under his breath.

'What a walk, with all this crockery!'

The table he shared with Favier was at the end of the corridor, in the last dining-room. All the dining-rooms were the same; they had once been cellars thirteen feet by sixteen, and had been plastered with cement and fitted up as refectories, but the damp was coming through the paint, the yellow walls were covered with greenish blotches, and from the narrow ventilation shaft, opening on the street at pavement level, the daylight which fell was livid, with vague shadows of passers-by ceaselessly going through it. In July and December alike it was stifling there in the hot steam, laden with nauseating smells from the neighbouring kitchen.

Hutin went in first. On the table, which was fixed to the wall at one end and covered with oilcloth, there was nothing to indicate the places but glasses and knives and forks. Piles of spare plates stood at each end, while in the middle was a big loaf with a knife stuck in it. Hutin got rid of his bottle and put down his plate; then, after taking his napkin from the bottom of a set of pigeon-holes, the only decoration on the walls, he sat down with a sigh.

'I'm really hungry!' he murmured.

'It's always the same,' said Favier, installing himself on his left. 'When you're starving, there's nothing to eat.'

The table was rapidly filling up. It was laid for twenty-two people. At first there was nothing but the din of knives and forks, the guzzling sound of hearty young men whose stomachs were hollow from thirteen hours' hard work. In the early days the assistants, who had an hour for their meal, had been allowed to go and have their coffee outside; so they would gobble their lunch in twenty minutes, in a hurry to get out into the street. But this stirred them up too much, and they came back inattentive, their minds distracted from their work; so the management had decided that they should no longer go out, but pay an extra fifteen centimes for a cup of coffee if they wanted one. So now they dragged out the meal, not at all anxious to go back to their departments before it was time to do so. Many of them, between huge mouthfuls, were reading a newspaper, folded and propped against their bottle. Others, once they had taken the edge off their appetite, were talking noisily, always coming back to the eternal subjects of the bad food, the money they earned, what they had done the previous Sunday, and what they were going to do the following Sunday.

'I say, what about that Robineau bloke of yours?' a salesman asked Hutin.

All the departments were interested in the silk department's struggle with its assistant buyer. The question was discussed every evening until midnight at the Café Saint-Roch. Hutin, who was busy with his piece of beef, was content to reply:

'Well, he's back.'

Then, suddenly getting angry:

'Damn it all, they've given me donkey! It really is disgusting!'

'Don't complain!' said Favier. 'I was stupid enough to take the skate . . . It's putrid!'

They were all talking at once, complaining and joking. At a corner of the table, against the wall, Deloche was eating in silence. He was cursed with an inordinate appetite which he had never been able to satisfy, and, as he did not earn enough to buy himself any extras, he would cut himself huge slices of bread, and greedily devour the least tempting dishes. As a result, they all made fun of him, shouting:

'Favier, pass your skate to Deloche . . . He likes it like that.'

'And your meat, Hutin: Deloche wants it for pudding.'

The poor lad shrugged his shoulders, and did not even reply. It was not his fault if he was forever hungry. Besides, the others might hate the food, but they were stuffing themselves with it all the same.

But a low whistle silenced them. This signalled the presence of Mouret and Bourdoncle in the corridor. For some time now the complaints of the staff had been such that the management had begun to come down and pretend to judge the quality of the food for itself. Out of the thirty centimes per head per day which they gave to the cook, he had to pay everything— provisions, coal, gas, staff—and they displayed a naïve astonishment when the results were not very good. That very morning each department had chosen a spokesman, and Mignot and Liénard had undertaken to speak for their colleagues. Therefore, in the sudden silence, they strained their ears, listening to the voices coming from the next room, which Mouret and Bourdoncle had just entered. The latter was declaring that the beef was excellent; and Mignot, infuriated by this calm assurance, was repeating: 'Chew it and see'; while Liénard, concentrating on the skate, was saying gently: 'But it stinks, sir!' Then Mouret launched into a cordial little speech: he would do everything for the well-being of his employees, he was a father to them, he would rather eat dry bread himself than see them badly fed.

'I promise I'll look into the matter,' he finally said in conclusion, raising his voice so that he could be heard from one end of the corridor to the other.

The management's inquiry was over; the noise of knives and forks began again. Hutin muttered:

'Yes, if you count on that you can wait until the cows come home . . . ! Oh, they're not stingy with their kind words. If you want promises, you can have as many as you like. But they feed us on old boots, and kick us out like dogs!'

The salesman who had already questioned him repeated:

'You were saying that Robineau . . . ?'

But the clatter of crockery drowned his voice. The assistants changed their plates themselves, and the piles were diminishing at both ends of the table. When a kitchen-help brought in some large tin dishes, Hutin exclaimed:

'Baked rice, this is the end!'

'Let's have a pennyworth of glue!' said Favier, helping himself.

Some liked it, others found it too sticky. Those who were reading remained silent, engrossed in the serial story in their papers, not even knowing what they were eating. They were all mopping their brows, for the small narrow cellar was filling up with reddish steam; while the shadows of the passers-by, like black stripes, were running continuously across the table-cloth.

'Pass Deloche the bread,' shouted a joker.

Everyone would cut himself a slice and then plunge the knife back in the loaf up to the hilt; and the bread was going round the table all the time.

'Who'll swap his dessert for my rice?' asked Hutin.

When he had concluded this deal with a small, thin man, he tried to sell his wine as well; but no one wanted it, they thought it undrinkable.

'As I was saying, Robineau's back,' he went on, in the midst of the general laughter and conversation. 'Oh! It's all getting very serious . . . You know, he leads the salesgirls astray! Yes, he gets neckties for them to sew!'

'Quiet!' murmured Favier. 'They're passing sentence on him!'

And with a glance he pointed out Bouthemont, who was walking between Mouret and Bourdoncle in the corridor; all three were absorbed in an animated, hushed conversation. The dining-room for section-managers and their deputies happened to be just opposite. When Bouthemont had seen Mouret passing by he had got up from the table, having finished, and was telling him about all the trouble in his department, and how difficult he found it. The other two were listening to him, so far refusing to sacrifice Robineau, who was a first-class salesman and had been there since Madame Hédouin's time. But when he came to the story of the neckties, Bourdoncle got angry. The man must be mad to act as a go-between for the salesgirls who wanted extra work. The shop paid them well enough for their time; if they worked at night for themselves it was obvious that they would do less work during the day in the shop; therefore they were robbing it, risking their health, which did not belong to them. The night was made for sleeping; they must all sleep, or they'd be kicked out!

'Things are hotting up,' Hutin remarked.

Each time the three men walked slowly past the dining-room the assistants watched them, and commented on their slightest gestures. It made them forget the baked rice, in which a cashier had just found a trouser button.

'I heard the word "necktie",' said Favier. 'Did you see how Bourdoncle's face suddenly turned pale?'

Mouret shared his colleague's indignation. A salesgirl reduced to working at night seemed to him to be an attack on the very organization of the Paradise. Which of them could be so stupid that she could not support herself on her profits from sales? But when Bouthemont named Denise he softened his tone and found excuses for her. Ah, yes! that poor little thing! She was still wet behind the ears and, so he'd been assured, had dependants to look after. Bourdoncle interrupted him, declaring that she must be dismissed on the spot. They would never do anything with such a plain girl, he'd always said so; he seemed to be satisfying a personal grudge. Mouret became embarrassed and pretended to laugh. Dear me! What a hard man he was! Couldn't they forgive her, for once? They'd call her in and give her a scolding. The long and short of it was that Robineau was really to blame, for, being a senior assistant and knowing the ways of the shop, he should have stopped her from doing it.

'Well! Now the governor is laughing!' said Favier in astonishment, as the group went past the door again.

'Good Lord!' swore Hutin, 'if they persist in saddling us with that Robineau of theirs, we'll give them something to laugh about!'

Bourdoncle looked Mouret straight in the face. Then he simply made a gesture of contempt, as much as to say that he understood at last, and that it was idiotic. Bouthemont had resumed his complaints: the salesmen were threatening to leave, and there were some excellent men amongst them. But what appeared to make a greater impression on these gentlemen was the rumour of Robineau's friendly relations with Gaujean: the latter, it was said, was urging his friend to set up his own business in the neighbourhood, and was offering him the most generous credit in order to make things difficult for the Ladies' Paradise. There was a silence. Ah! So Robineau was dreaming of battle! Mouret had become serious; he pretended to be scornful, and avoided taking a decision, as if the affair was of no importance. They would see, they would speak to him. And he immediately began joking with Bouthemont, whose father had arrived two days earlier from his little shop in Montpellier, and had almost choked with amazement and indignation when he saw the enormous hall where his son reigned. They were still laughing about the old man who, when he had recovered his southern self-possession, had set about disparaging everything, maintaining that the drapery trade would soon be finished.

'Here comes Robineau now,' murmured Bouthemont. 'I sent him to the stock-room to avoid anything unpleasant . . . I'm sorry to insist, but things have got to such a pitch that something's got to be done.'

Robineau, who had come in, greeted them as he made his way to his table.

Mouret simply repeated:

'All right, we'll see about it.'

They left. Hutin and Favier were still waiting for them. When they did not see them reappear, they relieved their feelings. Was the management now going to come down to every meal like that to count how many mouthfuls they had? What fun it would be if they couldn't even eat in peace! The truth of the matter was that they had just seen Robineau come in, and the governor's good humour was making them anxious about the outcome of the struggle they had set in motion. They lowered their voices, trying to think up new ways to annoy Robineau.

'I'm starving!' said Hutin out loud. 'You leave the table even hungrier than when you arrived!'

And yet he had eaten two portions of preserves, his own and the one he had received for his helping of rice. Suddenly he exclaimed:

'Damn it all! I'm going in for an extra helping! Victor, bring me some more preserves!'

The waiter was finishing serving the dessert. Then he brought the coffee, and those who took it gave him their fifteen centimes on the spot. Some of the salesmen had left and were dawdling along the corridor, looking for a dark corner in which to smoke a cigarette. The others remained slouched over the table cluttered up with greasy plates. They were rolling the breadcrumbs into pellets, going over the same stories again and again, in the midst of the smell of burnt fat which they no longer noticed and the sweltering heat which turned their ears red. The walls were oozing with moisture; slow asphyxiation was descending from the mouldy ceiling. Standing against the wall, Deloche, stuffed full of bread, was digesting in silence, looking up at the ventilator; his daily recreation, after lunch, was to watch the feet of the passers-by as they hurried along the pavement—feet cut off at the ankle, heavy shoes, elegant high boots, dainty women's ankle-boots, a continual procession of live feet, without bodies and heads. On rainy days it was very dirty.

'What! Already!' cried Hutin.

A bell was ringing at the end of the corridor; they had to give up their places for the third meal service. The waiters were coming to wash the oilcloth with buckets of tepid water and big sponges. The dining-rooms were slowly emptying, and the salesmen were going back to their departments again, lingering on the stairs. In the kitchen the cook had again taken up his position between the pans of skate, beef, and sauce, armed with his forks and spoons, ready once more to fill the plates with the rhythmic movement of a well-regulated clock.

As Hutin and Favier were lagging behind they saw Denise coming down.

'Monsieur Robineau is back, miss,' Hutin said with mocking politeness.

'He's still having lunch,' Favier added. 'But if it's urgent you can go in.'

Denise carried on without answering or turning round. However, when she passed the dining-room for section-managers and their assistants she could not help glancing in. Robineau was indeed there. She would try to speak to him in the afternoon; and she went on down the corridor to her table, which was at the other end.

The women ate separately, in two rooms reserved for them. Denise went into the first room. It was also an old cellar transformed into a refectory, but it had been fitted up more comfortably. On the oval table in the middle of the room the fifteen places were laid further apart, and the wine was in carafes; a dish of skate and a dish of beef with mustard sauce occupied the two ends of the table. Waiters in white aprons were serving the young ladies, which spared them the trouble of fetching their helpings themselves from the hatch. The management had considered this more seemly.

'So you went all round?' asked Pauline, who was already seated and was cutting herself some bread.

'Yes,' Denise replied, blushing. 'I was accompanying a customer.'

She was lying. Clara nudged the salesgirl sitting next to her. What was the matter with the unkempt girl today? She seemed really strange. She kept getting letters from her lover in rapid succession; then she ran round the shop like a madwoman, pretending to be going on errands to the work-room, where she did not even put in an appearance. There was certainly something going on. Then Clara, eating her skate without distaste, with the indifference of a girl who in the past had been fed on rancid bacon, spoke of a horrible drama which was filling the newspapers.

'Have you read about the man who slit his mistress's throat with a razor?'

'Of course!' remarked a little assistant from the lingerie department, with a gentle, delicate face. 'He found her with another man. Serve her right!'

But Pauline protested. What! Just because you didn't love a man any longer, he had the right to slit your throat! What a mad idea! And breaking off and turning to the waiter, she said:

'Pierre, you know I just can't eat this beef . . . Tell them to do me something else, an omelette, nice and soft, if possible!'

As she always had something sweet in her pocket she took out some chocolate drops and started munching them with her bread while she waited.

'A man like that isn't very funny,' Clara resumed. 'And a lot of men get really jealous! Only the other day there was a workman who threw his wife down a well.'

She did not take her eyes off Denise, and seeing her grow pale she thought she had guessed what was the matter. Obviously, the little prude was terrified of being beaten by her lover, to whom she was probably being unfaithful. It would be funny if he came right into the shop in his pursuit of her, as she seemed to fear. But the conversation was changing, one of the girls was telling them how to take spots out of velvet. Then they talked about a play at the Gaîté, in which some delightful little girls danced better than grown-ups. Pauline, momentarily saddened by the sight of her omelette, which was overdone, brightened up again when she found that it tasted quite nice after all.

'Pass me the wine,' she said to Denise. 'You should order yourself an omelette.'

'Oh! The beef's enough for me,' replied Denise, who, to avoid spending anything, always kept to the food provided by the shop, no matter how repulsive it was.

When the waiter brought the baked rice the girls protested. They had left it the week before, and had hoped it would not appear again. Denise, absent-minded and worried about Jean as a result of Clara's stories, was the only one who ate it; they all watched her with an air of disgust. There was an orgy of extra dishes; they filled themselves up with preserves. In any case, they thought it was quite smart to pay for their food with their own money.

'You know, the gentlemen have complained,' said the delicate-looking girl from the lingerie department, 'and the management has promised . . .'

She was interrupted by a burst of laughter, and their conversation now turned entirely to the management. They all had coffee, except Denise, who could not stand it, so she said. They lingered over their cups, the girls from the lingerie department dressed with lower middle-class simplicity in wool, those from the gown department in silk, their napkins tucked under their chins so as not to get stains on their dresses, like ladies who had come down to eat in the servants' hall with their maids. They had opened the skylight of the ventilator to freshen the stifling, foul-smelling air, but they had to shut it again immediately, for the cab-wheels seemed to be going across the table.

'Shh!' breathed Pauline, 'here's that old fool!'

It was Jouve. He was fond of prowling about towards the end of the mealtime, when the girls were there. In any case, he supervised their dining-rooms. He would come in, eyes smiling, and go round the table; sometimes he would even chat with them, and ask if they had enjoyed their lunch. But, as he both bored them and made them feel uncomfortable, they would all hasten to get away. Although the bell had not yet rung, Clara was the first to disappear; others followed her. Soon only Denise and Pauline remained. The latter, having drunk her coffee, was finishing her chocolate drops.

'Well!' she said as she stood up, 'I'm going to ask a waiter to fetch me some oranges . . . Are you coming?'

'In a minute,' answered Denise, who was nibbling a crust, determined to be the last to leave, so that she could tackle Robineau when she went upstairs again.

However, when she found herself alone with Jouve she felt uneasy, so she left the table. But seeing her go towards the door, he barred her way:

'Mademoiselle Baudu . . .'

He stood before her, smiling with a paternal air. His thick grey moustache and crew-cut hair gave him a respectable military appearance, and he puffed out his chest, on which the red ribbon of his decoration was displayed.

'What is it, Monsieur Jouve?' she asked, reassured.

'I saw you again this morning, talking upstairs, behind the carpets. You know it's against the rules, and if I reported you . . . She's very fond of you, your friend Pauline, isn't she?'

His moustache quivered, his enormous nose, the powerful hooked nose of a man with the appetites of a bull, was aflame.

'What makes you two so fond of each other, eh?'

Denise, not understanding, began to feel uneasy again. He was coming too close, he was speaking right in her face.

'It's true we were talking, Monsieur Jouve,' she stammered. 'But there's no harm in a bit of talking . . . You're very kind to me, and I'm very grateful . . .'

'I ought not to be kind to you,' he said. 'Justice is the only thing I'm interested in . . . But you're so nice that . . .'

He came even closer. Now she was really afraid. Pauline's words came back to her; she remembered the stories that were going round, of salesgirls terrorized by old Jouve and having to buy his goodwill. In the shop he was content with little familiarities, such as gently patting the cheeks of obliging girls with his fat fingers, taking their hands in his and keeping them there as if he had forgotten. It was all very paternal, and he only let the bull loose outside, when they consented to have some bread and butter with him at his place in the Rue des Moineaux.

'Leave me alone,' she murmured, drawing back.

'Come on,' he was saying, 'you're not going to be shy with a friend who's always good to you. Be nice, come and have a cup of tea and a slice of bread and butter this evening. You're very welcome.'

She was struggling now.

'No! No!'

The dining-room was still empty, the waiter had not reappeared. Jouve, keeping his ears open for the sound of footsteps, gave a quick glance round, and, very excited, lost control of himself, went beyond his paternal familiarities, and tried to kiss her on the neck.

'Silly, ungrateful little girl . . . How can you be so silly with hair like that? Come round tonight, just for fun.'

But she was in a panic, terrified and shocked at the approach of this burning face and the feel of its breath. Suddenly she gave him a push which was so strong that he staggered and almost fell on to the table. Fortunately a chair saved him; but the impact knocked over a carafe of wine, bespattering his white tie and soaking his red ribbon. And he stood there, not wiping himself, choking with rage at such brutality. When he wasn't expecting it, wasn't even trying hard, and was simply giving way to his kind nature!

'You'll be sorry for this, I swear, miss!'

Denise had fled. The bell was just ringing; and flustered, still trembling, she forgot about Robineau and went up to her department. She no longer dared to go down again. As the sun fell on the Place Gaillon side of the shop in the afternoon, it was stifling in the rooms on the mezzanine floor in spite of the blinds. A few customers came, bathed the girls in perspiration, and went away without buying anything. The whole department was yawning, watched by Madame Aurélie's big sleepy eyes. Finally, towards three o'clock, seeing the buyer fall asleep, Denise quietly slipped off and resumed her trip round the shop, trying to look busy. In order to put anyone who might be looking off the scent, she did not go straight down to the silk department; first she pretended she had some business in the lace department, went up to Deloche, and asked him something; then, on the ground floor, she went through the cottons, and was just going into the neckties when she stopped short with a start of surprise. Jean was standing in front of her.

'What are you doing here?' she murmured, quite pale.

He was still wearing his overalls and was bare-headed, his fair hair in disorder and his curls falling over his girlish face. Standing before a case full of narrow black ties, he seemed deep in thought.

'What are you doing here?' she repeated.

'What do you think?' he replied, 'I was waiting for you! You forbade me to come. But I came in all the same, though I haven't said a word to anyone. You needn't worry! Pretend you don't know me, if you like.'

Some salesmen were already looking at them with surprise. Jean lowered his voice.

'She wanted to come with me, you know. Yes, she's in the square, by the fountain . . . Give me the fifteen francs quickly, or we're absolutely done for!'

At this, Denise became very agitated. People were grinning, listening to this adventure. As there was a staircase down to the basement at the back of the tie department, she pushed her brother towards it and quickly made him go down it. Once downstairs he went on with his story, embarrassed, inventing his facts, afraid that she would not believe him.

'The money isn't for her. She's too refined . . . and as for her husband, he doesn't care a damn about fifteen francs! He wouldn't give his wife permission for a million . . . a glue manufacturer, did I tell you? They're terribly well off . . . No, it's for a scoundrel, a friend of hers who saw us together; and if I don't give him fifteen francs this evening . . .'

'Be quiet,' murmured Denise. 'Later . . . just carry on walking!'

They had reached the dispatch department. The slack season was sending the vast cellar to sleep, in the pale light from the ventilators. It was cold there, silence was seeping down from the ceiling. Nevertheless, a porter was collecting the few parcels for the Madeleine district* from one of the compartments; and on the big sorting table Campion, the head of the department, was sitting and dangling his legs, staring about him.

Jean started up again:

'The husband, who has a big knife . . .'

'Carry on!' Denise repeated, still pushing him.

They went down one of the narrow corridors, where the gas was kept continually burning. To the right and left, in the depths of dark cellars, the reserve stocks made piles of shadows behind the gates. Finally she stopped in front of one of these wooden screens. Doubtless no one would come; but it was forbidden, and she gave a shudder.

'If that scoundrel says anything,' Jean went on, 'the husband, who has a big knife . . .'

'Where do you think I can find fifteen francs?' Denise burst out in despair. 'Can't you behave sensibly? You're always getting into some silly scrape!'

He beat his chest. In all his romantic inventions, he himself no longer knew what the truth was. He simply dramatized his financial requirements; but behind it there was always some pressing necessity.

'I swear on everything I hold most sacred, that this time it's really true . . . I was holding her like this, and she was kissing me . . .'

She stopped him once more; tortured, at the end of her tether, she lost her temper.

'I don't want to hear about it. Keep your bad behaviour to yourself. It's too disgusting, do you understand? And you pester me every week, I'm killing myself to keep you supplied with money. Yes, I sit up all night for you . . . Not to mention the fact that you're taking the bread out of your brother's mouth.'

Jean stood gaping, his face pale. What! It was disgusting? He did not understand; he had always treated his sister as a friend, and it seemed quite natural to open his heart to her. What choked him above all was to learn that she sat up all night. The idea that he was killing her and taking Pépé's share as well affected him so much that he began to cry.

'You're right, I've been bad,' he exclaimed. 'But it isn't disgusting, really. On the contrary, and that's why I keep on doing it . . . This one, you see, is already twenty. She thought it would be fun because I'm only seventeen . . . Really! I'm furious with myself! I could hit myself!'

He had taken her hands and was kissing them, wetting them with his tears.

'Give me the fifteen francs, it'll be the last time, I swear . . . Or else, no! Don't give me anything, I'd rather die. If the husband murders me it'll be good riddance for you.'

And as she was crying as well, he had a twinge of remorse.

'I say that, but I don't know. Perhaps he doesn't want to kill anyone . . . We'll manage, I promise, Sis. Goodbye, I'm off.'

But a sound of footsteps at the end of the corridor alarmed them. She pulled him over by the stores again, into a dark corner. For a moment they could hear nothing but the hiss of a gas jet near them. Then the footsteps drew nearer; and, craning her neck, she recognized Jouve, who had just entered the corridor, with his stiff military walk. Was he there by chance? Or had some other supervisor, on duty at the door, tipped him off? She was so overwhelmed with fear that she lost her head; and she pushed Jean out of the dark hole where they were hiding, and drove him in front of her, stammering as she did so:

'Get out! Get out!'

They both raced along, hearing old Jouve panting behind them, for he had also started to run. They went back through the dispatch department and arrived at the foot of the stairs whose glazed well-hole led out into the Rue de la Michodière.

'Get out!' repeated Denise. 'Get out! If I can I'll send you the fifteen francs all the same.'

Jean, dazed, scampered away. The shopwalker, who was just reaching the top of the stairs, out of breath, caught sight only of a bit of white overall and some fair curls blowing in the wind. He stood for a moment to catch his breath and to regain his correct bearing. He had a brand new white necktie, which he had taken from the lingerie department, and its knot, which was very wide, was shining like a big snowflake.

'Well, this is nice behaviour, miss,' he said, his lips trembling. 'Yes, it's nice, very nice . . . If you think I'm going to tolerate nice things like that in the basement, you're mistaken.'

And he pursued her with this word while she went upstairs again to the shop, overcome with emotion, unable to think of anything to say in her own defence. She was sorry now that she had run away. Why hadn't she explained everything and introduced Jean as her brother? Again they would all suppose the worst; and no matter how much she might swear that it was untrue, they would not believe her. Once more she forgot Robineau, and went straight back to the department.

Jouve went immediately to the manager's office to report the matter. But the porter on duty told him that the governor was with Monsieur Bourdoncle and Monsieur Robineau; the three of them had been talking for a quarter of an hour. The door was half open; Mouret could be heard gaily asking Robineau if he had had a good holiday; there was not the slightest question of a dismissal—on the contrary, the conversation was about certain measures to be taken in the department.

'Do you want something, Monsieur Jouve?' shouted Mouret. 'Do come in!'

But some instinct forewarned the shopwalker. As Bourdoncle had come out, Jouve preferred to tell him the whole story. They walked slowly through the shawl gallery, side by side, one leaning forward and speaking in a very low voice, the other listening, not a line of his hard face betraying his impressions.

'Very well,' Bourdoncle said at last.

And as they had arrived outside the ladieswear department, he went in. At that moment Madame Aurélie was scolding Denise. Where had she been now? She couldn't say that she had gone up to the work-room this time. Really, these continual disappearances could not be tolerated any longer.

'Madame Aurélie,' called Bourdoncle.

He had decided to force the issue; he did not want to consult Mouret, for fear that he might be weak. The buyer advanced, and once more the story was related in hushed tones. The whole department was waiting, scenting a catastrophe.

Finally Madame Aurélie turned round with a grave air.

'Mademoiselle Baudu . . .'

Her bloated imperial mask had the inexorable immobility of omnipotence.

'Go and collect your wages!'

The terrible sentence rang out very loudly through the department, which was empty of customers. Denise had remained erect and white, holding her breath. Then she stammered:

'Me! Me! But why? What have I done?'

Bourdoncle replied harshly that she knew very well what she had done and would do well not to press for an explanation: and he spoke of the neckties, and said that it would be a fine thing if all the girls went to meet men in the basement.

'But it was my brother!' she cried, with the heartfelt anger of an outraged virgin.

Marguerite and Clara started to laugh, while Madame Frédéric, usually so discreet, shook her head with an air of incredulity. Always saying it was her brother! It really was very silly! Then Denise looked at them all: at Bourdoncle who, from the first day, had not wanted her; at Jouve, who had stayed there to give evidence, and from whom she could expect no justice; and then at the girls, whom she had been unable to soften in spite of nine months of smiling courage, who were happy to push her out at last. What was the point of struggling? Why try to impose herself on them when no one liked her? And she went away without a word, not even casting a last glance at this room where she had struggled for so long.

But, as soon as she was alone by the hall balustrade, her heart was filled with a deeper sense of suffering. No one liked her, and the sudden thought of Mouret had just filled her with resolve. No! she couldn't accept a dismissal like that. Perhaps he would believe that foul story about an assignation with a man down in the cellars. This thought tortured her with shame, with an anguish such as she had never experienced before. She wanted to go and find him; she would explain things to him, simply to let him know the truth; for she was ready to leave once he knew it. And her old fear, the chill which froze her in his presence, suddenly developed into a passionate need to see him and not to leave the shop without swearing to him that she had never belonged to another man.

It was almost five o'clock; the shop was coming slowly to life again in the cool evening air. She hurried off towards Mouret's office. But when she arrived at the door she was once more overwhelmed with a hopeless feeling of sadness. She was tongue-tied; the crushing weight of existence once more fell upon her. He would not believe her, he would laugh like the others; and this fear destroyed her resolve. It was all over; she would be better off alone, out of the way, dead. And so, without even letting Deloche and Pauline know, she went at once to the pay-desk.

'You've got twenty-two days, miss,' said the clerk, 'that makes eighteen francs seventy, to which must be added seven francs percentage and bonus . . . That's right, isn't it?'

'Yes, sir . . . Thank you.'

And Denise was going away with her money when, at last, she met Robineau. He had already heard of her dismissal, and promised to try to find the necktie dealer. He tried to console her in a whisper, but got carried away with anger. What an existence! To be at the continual mercy of a whim! To be thrown out at an hour's notice, without even being able to claim a full month's wages! Denise went upstairs to inform Madame Cabin that she would try to send someone for her trunk that evening. Five o'clock was striking when she found herself on the pavement in the Place Gaillon, dazed in the midst of the cabs and the crowd.

That same evening, as Robineau arrived home, he received a letter from the management informing him in four lines that, for administrative reasons, they were obliged to dispense with his services. He had been in the shop for seven years; that very afternoon he had been talking to those gentlemen; it was a stunning blow. Hutin and Favier were celebrating victory in the silk department as noisily as Marguerite and Clara were exulting in the ladieswear department. Good riddance! A clean sweep makes room for others! Deloche and Pauline, when they met among the crowd in the shop, were the only ones to lament Denise's departure, exchanging bitter words of regret at losing her, for she was so gentle and honest.

'Ah,' said the young man, 'if ever she makes good somewhere else, I wish she'd come back here to show all those good-for-nothings a thing or two!'

It was Bourdoncle who bore the brunt of Mouret's violent reaction to the affair. When the latter heard of Denise's dismissal he became extremely angry. Usually he had very little to do with the staff; but this time he affected to see an encroachment on his power, an attempt to ignore his authority. Was he no longer the master, that they presumed to give orders? Everything must pass through his hands, absolutely everything; and he would crush anyone who resisted him, like a straw. Then, in a nervous torment which he could not conceal, he made certain personal inquiries, and lost his temper again. The poor girl hadn't been lying; it really was her brother; Campion had fully recognized him. So why was she dismissed? He even talked of taking her back.

Meanwhile Bourdoncle, strong in his passive resistance, bent before the storm. He was studying Mouret. Finally, one day when he saw that he was calmer, he ventured to say in a special tone of voice:

'It's better for everyone that she's gone.'

Mouret became embarrassed, his face flushed.

'Well!' he answered, laughing, 'perhaps you're right . . . Let's go down and have a look at the sale. It's picking up; we made nearly a hundred thousand francs yesterday.'

CHAPTER 7

For a moment Denise stood dazed on the pavement in the sunshine, which was still scorching at five o'clock. The July heat was warming the gutters, and Paris was bathed in the chalky summer light with its blinding reflections. The catastrophe had been so sudden, she had been pushed out so roughly, that she kept mechanically turning over the twenty-five francs and seventy centimes in her pocket, wondering where to go and what to do.

A long line of cabs prevented her from leaving the pavement in front of the Ladies' Paradise. When she was able to venture between the wheels, she crossed the Place Gaillon as if she wanted to go down the Rue Louis-le-Grand; then she changed her mind and walked towards the Rue Saint-Roch. But she still had no plan, for she stopped at the corner of the Rue Neuve-des-Petits-Champs which, after looking about her hesitantly, she finally took. When she saw the Passage Choiseul she went down it, found herself in the Rue Monsigny without knowing how she had got there, and ended up again in the Rue Neuve-Saint-Augustin. Her head was swimming, and the thought of her trunk came back to her at the sight of a street-porter; but where could she have it taken to, and why all this trouble when an hour earlier she still had a bed to go to?

Then, looking up at the houses, she began to examine the windows. They displayed a whole series of placards. She saw them confusedly, dazed by her inner turmoil. Was it possible? Suddenly alone, lost in this huge, unknown city, unprotected, penniless! Yet somehow she had to eat and sleep. She passed along the streets, the Rue des Moulins, the Rue Sainte-Anne. She wandered about the neighbourhood, retracing her steps, always coming back to the only spot she knew well. Suddenly she came to a stop, amazed, for she was once more outside the Ladies' Paradise; and, to escape from this obsession, she plunged into the Rue de la Michodière.

Fortunately Baudu was not at his door; the Vieil Elbeuf seemed dead behind its dark windows. She would never have

dared to go to her uncle's, for he affected not to recognize
her any more and, in the misfortune he had predicted for her,
she did not want to be a burden to him. But on the other side of
the street a yellow placard caught her eye: FURNISHED ROOM TO
LET. It was the first notice that did not intimidate her, so poor did
the house appear. Then she recognized it, with its two low
storeys and rust-coloured front, squeezed between the Ladies'
Paradise and what had once been the Hôtel Duvillard.* On the
threshold of the umbrella shop old Bourras, long-haired and
bearded like a prophet, with his spectacles on his nose, was
examining the ivory of a walking-stick knob. He rented the
whole house, and sublet the two upper storeys furnished to help
pay his rent.

'You have a room to let, sir?' asked Denise, obeying an instinctive urge.

He raised his large eyes under bushy eyebrows, surprised to
see her. He knew all the girls at the Ladies' Paradise. And after
looking at her clean little dress and decent appearance, he replied:

'It wouldn't suit you.'

'How much is it, then?' Denise went on.

'Fifteen francs a month.'

She asked to see it. In the narrow shop, seeing that he was still
staring at her with a look of surprise, she told him that she had
left the Paradise and did not wish to be an embarrassment to her
uncle. Finally the old man went to fetch a key hanging in the
room at the back of the shop, a dark room where he did his
cooking and had his bed; beyond it, behind a dusty window-
pane, the greenish light of an inner courtyard, barely two yards
wide, could be seen.

'I'll go first so you won't fall,' said Bourras in the damp
passageway which ran along the side of the shop.

He stumbled against a step and went up, reiterating his warn-
ings to be careful. The banisters were against the wall, and there
was a hole at the corner; sometimes the tenants left their dustbins
on the stairs. Denise, in the total darkness, could distinguish
nothing, but could only feel the chilliness of the old, damp
plaster. On the first floor, however, a small window opening on
to the courtyard enabled her to see vaguely, as if from the bottom

of a stagnant pond, the warped staircase, the walls black with filth, the cracked and peeling doors.

'If only one of these rooms was free!' Bourras said. 'You'd be all right there . . . But they're always occupied by ladies.'

On the second floor the light increased, illuminating the miserable scene with a sickly pallor. A baker's apprentice occupied the first room; and it was the other, at the back, which was vacant. When Bourras had opened the door he had to remain on the landing so that Denise could inspect the room unimpeded. The bed, in the corner by the door, left just enough room for one person to pass. At the end of the room there was a little walnut chest of drawers, a pine table stained black, and two chairs. The lodgers who did any cooking had to kneel down in front of the fireplace, where there was a clay oven.

'Well!' the old man said, 'it's not much, but there's a nice view: you can see the people in the street.'

And, as Denise was looking with surprise at the corner of the ceiling above the bed, where a lady who had made a brief stay there had written her name—'Ernestine'—with the flame of a candle, he added good-naturedly:

'If I did repairs, I'd never be able to make ends meet . . . So, this is all I've got.'

'It'll suit me very well,' declared Denise.

She paid a month's rent in advance, asked for the linen—a pair of sheets and two towels—and made her bed straight away, happy and relieved to know where she would spend the night. An hour later she had sent a street-porter to fetch her trunk, and had settled in.

The first two months were extremely difficult. Being unable to pay for Pépé's board and lodging any longer, she took him to live with her, and he slept on an old armchair lent by Bourras. She needed exactly one franc fifty a day, including the rent, provided that she lived on dry bread so as to give a little meat to the child. For the first fortnight things did not go too badly: she started off with ten francs for the housekeeping, and then she had the good luck to find the woman who had let her have the ties, who paid her the eighteen francs thirty she owed her. But after that she was completely destitute. She applied in vain to various shops, in the Place Clichy, at the Bon Marché, at the

Louvre; the slack season had stopped business everywhere. They told her to try again in the autumn; more than five thousand shop assistants, dismissed like her, were tramping the streets without work. Then she tried to get some odd jobs: but in her ignorance of Paris she did not know where to apply, she accepted ungrateful tasks and sometimes did not even get paid for them. Some evenings she would make Pépé eat alone, just giving him a bowl of soup, telling him that she had already eaten out, and she would go to bed, her head buzzing, fed by nothing but the fever which was making her hands burn. When Jean suddenly turned up in the midst of this poverty he would say he was a scoundrel with such despairing violence that she was obliged to lie to him; often she would still find a way of slipping him a couple of francs to prove that she had a little money left. She never wept in front of the children. On Sundays, when she was able to cook a piece of veal in the fireplace, kneeling on the floor, the narrow room would echo with the heedless laughter of children. Then, when Jean had left and Pépé had fallen asleep, she would spend a dreadful night, racked by anxiety about the following day.

Other fears kept her awake, too. The two ladies on the first floor received visitors very late; and sometimes a man would make a mistake, come upstairs, and bang on her door. As Bourras had quietly told her not to answer, she would bury her head under her pillow to escape from the oaths. Then her neighbour, the baker, started to annoy her; he never returned home until the morning, and he would lie in wait for her when she went to fetch her water; he even made holes in the wall and watched her washing herself, which forced her to hang her clothes along the wall. But she suffered even more from being pestered in the street, from the continual obsession of passers-by. She could not go down to buy a candle in those muddy streets, full of prowlers and the dissolute life-style of the old neighbourhoods, without hearing an eager whistle or a crude remark behind her; and, encouraged by the house's sordid appearance, men followed her right to the end of the dark passageway. Why didn't she have a lover? That surprised people; it seemed ridiculous. She would have to succumb one day. She herself could not have explained how she managed to resist under the threat of hunger, and surrounded by the heady desires which pervaded the air about her.

One evening Denise did not even have any bread for Pépé's soup, when a gentleman wearing a medal started to follow her. Outside the passageway he became brutal, and she, revolted and disgusted, slammed the door in his face. Then, upstairs, she sat down, her hands shaking. The little boy was asleep. What should she say if he woke up and asked for something to eat? And yet she had only to consent and she would no longer be poor, she would have money, dresses, and a fine room. It was easy; they said everyone did it in the end because in Paris a woman could not live on what she earned. But her whole being revolted against it; she felt no indignation against others for giving in, but simply an aversion to anything dirty or senseless. She considered life a matter of logic, good conduct, and courage.

She would often examine her thoughts in this way. An old ballad kept coming back to her, about a sailor's fiancée whose love protected her from the perils of waiting for him. At Valognes she used to hum the sentimental refrain while gazing at the empty street. Was she able to be so brave because she, too, felt love in her heart? She still dreamed uneasily of Hutin. Every day she saw him pass under her window. Now that he was assistant buyer he walked by himself, surrounded by the respect of the ordinary salesmen. He never raised his head, and she thought that it was the young man's vanity that made her suffer, and would watch him without fear of being caught. As soon as she caught sight of Mouret, who also went by every evening, she would begin to tremble, and would quickly hide, her heart pounding. There was no need for him to know where she was living; and then, she was ashamed of the house, and was tormented by the idea of what he thought of her, even though they might never meet again.

In any case, Denise was still living within the orbit of the Ladies' Paradise. A thin wall was all that separated her room from her old department; and, from the early morning, she would relive her days there, sensing the crowd growing with the increasing hum of activity in the shop. The slightest sounds would shake the old hovel clinging to the giant's side; it beat with that enormous pulse. Besides, Denise could not avoid meeting people from time to time. Twice she found herself face to face with Pauline, who, grieved to know that she was so badly off, offered to help her. She had even been obliged to lie to avoid having her friend come to see her and to get out of paying her a visit one Sunday at Baugé's place. But it was more difficult to keep Deloche's hopeless affection at bay; he was always on the look-out for her, was aware of all her troubles, waited for her in doorways; one evening he wanted to lend her thirty francs—his brother's savings, so he said, blushing. And these meetings made her miss the shop all the time, made her take part in the life going on inside it as if she had never left it.

No one ever came up to Denise's room. One afternoon she was surprised to hear a knock on the door. It was Colomban. She stood up to receive him. In great embarrassment, he asked her stammeringly how she was getting on, and talked about the Vieil Elbeuf. Perhaps her uncle Baudu, regretting his hardness, had sent him; for Baudu still did not greet his niece when he saw her, although he could not have been unaware of the poverty in which she was living. But when she asked the shop assistant outright, he seemed even more embarrassed; no, no, it was not his employer who had sent him; and in the end he mentioned Clara, he just wanted to talk about Clara. Little by little he became bolder, and asked for advice, thinking that Denise could further his cause with her former colleague. She vainly tried to discourage him, reproaching him for making Geneviève unhappy just for a heartless trollop. He came back another day, and got into the habit of coming to see her. This was enough to satisfy his timid passion; he would endlessly begin the same conversation, trembling with joy at being with a woman who had been in close contact with Clara. As a result Denise participated more than ever in life at the Ladies' Paradise. Towards the end of September she experienced really dire poverty. Pépé had fallen ill, having caught a heavy cold. He should have been fed on good broth, but she did not even have any bread. One day when, in despair, she was sobbing in one of those fits of depression which make girls take to the streets or throw themselves into the Seine, old Bourras gently knocked at the door. He had brought a loaf and a milk-can full of broth.

'Here, this is for the little boy!' he said in his gruff way. 'Don't cry so loud, it bothers my tenants.'

And as she was thanking him in a fresh bout of tears, he added:

'Be quiet! Come and see me tomorrow. I've got some work for you.'

Since the terrible blow which the Ladies' Paradise had dealt him by creating an umbrella and sunshade department, Bourras no longer employed any staff. In order to reduce costs he did everything himself—cleaning, mending, and sewing. In any case, he had fewer and fewer customers, to such an extent that sometimes he had no work at all; so when he installed Denise in a corner of his shop the next day he had to invent something for her to do. After all, he could not let people die in his house.

'You'll have two francs a day,' he said. 'When you find something better you can leave.'

She was afraid of him, and finished the work so quickly that he did not know what else to give her to do. He had given her some silk to stitch, and some lace to mend. For the first few days she did not dare raise her head, embarrassed to feel him near her, with his old lion's mane and hooked nose, and his piercing eyes under his thick bushy eyebrows. His voice was harsh, his gestures seemed crazy, and the mothers of the neighbourhood would frighten their children by threatening to send for him, as one sends for the police. Yet urchins would never go past his door without shouting some kind of abuse, which he did not even seem to hear. All his maniacal fury was directed against the wretches who were dishonouring his trade by selling cheap goods, trash, goods which, as he would say, even dogs wouldn't want to use.

Denise would tremble when he shouted furiously:

'Art is done for! You can't find a decent handle anywhere. They make sticks, but handles, they're finished! Find me a proper handle, and I'll give you twenty francs!'

He had the pride of an artist; there was not a workman in Paris capable of making a handle like his, both light and strong. Above all he carved the knobs with delightful inventiveness, always finding fresh subjects, flowers, fruit, animals, heads, executed in a lifelike but distinctive style. A penknife was all he needed, and he could be seen for whole days at a stretch, his spectacles on the end of his nose, carving pieces of boxwood or ebony.

'A load of ignoramuses,' he would say, 'satisfied with sticking silk on whalebone! They buy their handles by the gross, ready-made . . . And they can sell however many they like! Art's done for, that's for sure!'

After a while Denise lost her misgivings. He had wanted Pépé to come down and play in the shop, for he adored children. When the little boy was crawling about on all fours there was no room to turn round, she in her corner doing some mending, and Bourras by the window carving with his penknife. Each day now brought the same tasks and the same conversation. As he worked he would always come back to the Ladies' Paradise; he was never tired of explaining the stage his terrible duel with it had reached. He had been in that house since 1845, and he had a thirty years' lease at a rent of eighteen hundred francs a year; as he made a thousand francs out of his four furnished rooms, he only paid eight hundred for the shop. It was not much, he had no expenses, he could hold out for a long time yet. To listen to him, there was no doubt of his victory; he would certainly devour the monster.

Suddenly he would break off.

'Have they got any dogs' heads like this?'

And he would blink behind his glasses the better to judge the mastiff's head he was carving with its lips drawn back and its fangs showing in a lifelike growl. Pépé, full of admiration for the dog, would raise himself up to look at it, putting his two little arms on the old man's knees.

'As long as I can make both ends meet, I don't care about anything else,' Bourras would resume, delicately shaping the tongue with the point of his knife. 'Those scoundrels have killed my profits; but, if I'm not making anything these days, I'm not losing anything so far, or at least very little. You see, I'd rather die here than give in.'

He would brandish his knife, and his white hair would blow about in a gust of anger.

'Yes,' Denise would venture to say gently, without looking up from her mending. 'But if they made you a reasonable offer, it would be wiser to accept.'

At that his fierce obstinacy would flare up.

'Never! Even if they held a knife to my throat, I'd still say no, by God! I've got ten years' lease left, they won't get the shop before then, even if I have to starve between four bare walls . . . Twice already they've been here, trying to get round me. They offered me twelve thousand francs for the business and eighteen thousand for the lease, thirty thousand altogether . . . I wouldn't sell, not for fifty thousand! I've got them, I want to see them lick the dust in front of me!'

'Thirty thousand francs, that's not bad,' Denise would resume. 'You could go and set up shop somewhere else . . . And what if they bought the house?'

Bourras, who was putting the finishing touches to his mastiff's tongue, would seem absorbed in his task for a moment, a childish smile spread vaguely over his snowy face, like God the Father. Then he would start off again.

'The house is absolutely safe! They were talking of buying it last year, and offered eighty thousand francs, double what it's worth today. But the landlord, a retired fruiterer, a scoundrel like them, wanted to blackmail them. And in any case they don't trust me; they know I'd be even less likely to give in . . . No! No! Here I am, here I stay! The Emperor with all his cannon wouldn't be able to get me out!'

Denise never dared say another word. She went on sewing, while between two notches with his knife the old man would continue to mutter broken phrases: this was just the beginning, later on they'd see amazing things happen, he'd got plans which would sweep away their umbrella department; and in his obstinacy was the muttered rebellion of the small individual manufacturer against the invasion of cheap goods sold by the big stores.

Pépé, meanwhile, had finally succeeded in climbing on to Bourras's lap. He was stretching his hands out impatiently towards the mastiff's head.

'Give me, sir.'

'In a minute, dear,' the old man would reply in a voice that suddenly became tender. 'He hasn't got any eyes, I must make his eyes now.'

And while he was working on one of the eyes, he would continue talking to Denise.

'Can you hear them? What a roar they make, next door! That's what exasperates me most of all! Having them on top of you all the time like that, with that damned steam-engine sound.'

It made his little table vibrate, he said. The whole shop was shaken by it; he would spend his afternoons without a single customer, being jarred by the vibration of the crowd packed into the Ladies' Paradise. He was constantly harping on this subject. They'd had another good day, he would say, there was a din on the other side of the wall, the silk department must have made ten thousand francs; or else he was really pleased because the wall had remained silent, a shower of rain had killed the takings. The slightest sounds, the merest whispers would thus provide him with endless occasions for comment.

'There! Someone slipped! Oh! If only they'd all fall and break their necks! And that, my dear, is some ladies quarrelling. So much the better! So much the better! Can you hear the parcels going down into the basement, eh? It's disgusting!'

It was pointless for Denise to argue with him about it, for he would bitterly remind her of the shameful manner in which she had been dismissed. Then she would have to describe for the hundredth time her life in the ladieswear department, the hardships she had endured at the beginning, the small, unhealthy bedrooms, the bad food, the endless battle between the salesmen; and thus, from morning till evening, the two of them would talk of nothing but the shop, drinking it in all the time in the very air they breathed.

'Give me, sir,' Pépé was eagerly repeating, still holding out his hands.

The mastiff's head was finished; Bourras was holding it at a distance and then examining it closely with boisterous pleasure.

'Look out, he's going to bite you . . . There you are, play with it, and try not to break it.'

Then, once more overtaken by his obsession, he would shake his fist at the wall.

'You can push as hard as you like to make the house fall down . . . But you won't have it, even if you take over the whole street!'

Now Denise always had something to eat. She felt extremely grateful to the old shopkeeper, whose kind heart she could sense beneath his violent eccentricities. She had a strong desire, however, to find work elsewhere, for she saw him inventing little jobs, and realized that since his business was collapsing he did not need any staff, and that he employed her out of pure charity. Six months had passed, and the winter slack season had just started again. She was losing hope of finding a job before March when, one evening in January, Deloche, who was watching out for her in a doorway, gave her some advice. Why didn't she go and apply at Robineau's, for perhaps they needed staff there?

In September Robineau had made up his mind to buy Vinçard's business, although he feared that this might endanger his wife's sixty thousand francs. He had paid forty thousand francs for the silk shop, and he was trying to establish his own business with the other twenty thousand. It wasn't much, but he had the support of Gaujean, who had undertaken to give him long-term credit. Since his break with the Ladies' Paradise Gaujean had been longing to create competition for the colossus; he believed that victory would be certain if several specialized shops where customers could find a very varied choice of goods could be created in the neighbourhood. It was only the rich manufacturers in Lyons, like Dumonteil, who could meet the requirements of the big shops; they were content to keep their looms busy for them, while looking to make profits by selling to less important shops. But Gaujean was far from having Dumonteil's capacity in business. For many years a simple commission-agent, he had only had his own looms for five or six years, and he still had a lot of work done by home-workers, whom he provided with raw materials and paid so much per metre. In fact, it was this system which, by increasing his manufacturing costs, prevented him from competing with Dumonteil for the supply of the Paris-Paradise. He was resentful of this, and saw in Robineau an instrument for a decisive battle against the cheap drapery stores, which he accused of ruining French manufacturers.

When Denise called she found Madame Robineau alone. The daughter of a foreman platelayer in the Department of Highways, she was totally ignorant about business matters, and still had the charming awkwardness of a girl brought up in a convent in Blois. She was very dark, and very pretty, with a gentle, cheerful manner which gave her great charm. Moreover, she adored her husband, and lived only for this love. Denise was about to leave her name when Robineau came in and engaged her on the spot, as one of his two salesgirls had left him the day before to go to the Ladies' Paradise.

'They don't leave us a single good worker,' he said. 'But with you there's no need to worry; you're like me, you can't be very fond of them . . . Come tomorrow.'

That evening Denise hardly knew how to tell Bourras that she was leaving him, and in fact he did say she was ungrateful and lost his temper; then, when she defended herself with tears in her eyes, giving him to understand that she had not been taken in by his acts of charity, he became quite emotional as well, stammering that he had plenty of work, that she was abandoning him just when he was going to bring out an umbrella of his own invention.

'What about Pépé?' he asked.

The child was Denise's great worry. She did not dare take him back to Madame Gras, and at the same time could not leave him alone in her room, shut up all day.

'Look, I'll keep him,' the old man went on. 'He's all right in my shop, the little fellow . . . We'll do the cooking together!'

Then, as she refused, afraid of being a nuisance to him, he said:

'Good heavens! You do distrust me . . . I'm not going to eat him, you know!'

Denise was happier at Robineau's. He paid her very little, sixty francs a month, and gave her nothing but her meals, no commission on sales, just as in the old-fashioned shops. But she was treated with great kindness, especially by Madame Robineau, who was always smiling behind the counter. He himself, nervous and worried, was sometimes rather abrupt. Within a month Denise was one of the family, as was the other salesgirl, a silent, consumptive little woman. The Robineaus no longer stood on ceremony with the girls, but talked business during meals in the room at the back of the shop, which opened on to a big courtyard. And it was there, one evening, that it was decided to start a campaign against the Ladies' Paradise.

Gaujean had come to dinner. As soon as the joint, a homely leg of mutton, was served, he had broached the question in the toneless voice, thickened by the Rhône mists, of a man from Lyons.

'It's becoming intolerable,' he repeated. 'They go to Dumonteil's, reserve the exclusive rights of a design, and carry off three hundred lengths straight away, while insisting on a rebate of fifty centimes a metre; and, as they pay with ready cash, they also get the eighteen per cent discount . . . Often Dumonteil doesn't even make twenty centimes. He works to keep his looms busy, because if they're not used they die . . . So how can you expect us, with our more limited equipment and especially with our home-workers, to keep up the struggle?'

Robineau, pensive, was forgetting to eat.

'Three hundred lengths!' he murmured. 'It makes me really nervous when I take twelve, and with ninety days to pay . . . They can price it at a franc or two francs cheaper than us; I've worked out that their list prices are at least fifteen per cent lower compared to ours . . . That's what's killing small businesses.'

He was in a mood of despondency. His wife, worried, was looking at him tenderly. Business was quite beyond her; she was bewildered by all those figures, and could not understand why people took such trouble when it was so easy to be happy and love each other. However, it was enough for her that her husband wished to conquer; she became as impassioned as he was, and would have been willing to die at her counter.

'But why don't all the manufacturers come to an agreement between themselves?' Robineau went on violently. 'They could lay down the law then, instead of having to submit to it.'

Gaujean, who had asked for another slice of mutton, was slowly munching.

'Ah! Why, why . . . ?' The looms must be kept going, as I said. When there are weavers everywhere, in the Gard, in the Isère,* you can't stop work for a day without huge losses . . . And people like me who sometimes employ home-workers with ten or fifteen looms are better able to control production from the point of view of stock, whereas the big manufacturers are always obliged to get rid of their stock as quickly as they can . . . That's why they go down on their knees to the big shops. I know three or four who are always quarrelling over them, and who would rather lose money than fail to get the orders. They make up for it with the small shops like yours. Yes, if the big shops keep them going, they make their profits out of you . . . God knows how the crisis will end!'

'It's odious!' concluded Robineau, who felt better after this cry of rage.

Denise was listening in silence. With her instinctive love of logic and life, she was secretly on the side of the big shops. They had fallen silent, and were eating some bottled French beans; finally she ventured to say in a cheerful tone:

'Anyway, the public doesn't complain!'

Madame Robineau could not suppress a chuckle, which displeased her husband and Gaujean. Of course the customers were satisfied since, after all, it was the customers who profited from the reduction in prices. But everyone had to live; where would they be if, under the pretext of general well-being, the consumer was fattened at the expense of the producer? An argument started. While pretending to joke, Denise produced sound arguments: the middlemen—factory agents, representatives, commission-agents—were disappearing, and this was an important factor in reducing prices; besides, the manufacturers could no longer exist without the big shops, for as soon as one of them lost their custom, bankruptcy became inevitable; in short, it was a natural development of business, it was impossible to stop things going the way they ought to, when everyone was working for it, whether they liked it or not.

'So you're on the side of the people who kicked you out into the street?' asked Gaujean.

Denise became very red. She was surprised herself at the enthusiasm with which she was defending them. What could there be in her heart to inflame her with such passion?

'Good heavens, no!' she answered. 'Perhaps I'm wrong, you know more about it . . . I'm just saying what I think. Prices, instead of being fixed by about fifty shops as they used to be, are fixed nowadays by four or five, which have lowered them, thanks to the power of their capital and the number of their customers . . . So much the better for the public, that's all!'

Robineau managed to keep his temper. He had become very serious, and was looking at the table-cloth. He had often felt the new way of business in the air, this development Denise was talking about; and he sometimes wondered, in his clear-sighted moments, why he should want to resist such a powerful current, which would carry all before it. Madame Robineau herself, seeing her husband so thoughtful, gave a look of approval at Denise, who had fallen silent again.

'Look,' Gaujean resumed, 'to cut the argument short, all that is just theory . . . Let's talk about what concerns us.'

After the cheese, the maid brought in some preserves and some pears. He helped himself to the preserves, and ate them by the spoonful, with the unconscious greed of a fat man who was fond of sweet things.

'What you must do is beat their Paris-Paradise, which was their great success this year . . . I've made an arrangement with some of my colleagues in Lyons, and I'm going to make you an exceptional offer, a black silk, a faille, which you'll be able to sell at five francs fifty . . . They sell theirs at five francs sixty, don't they? Very well! Yours will be ten centimes cheaper, and that will be enough to get the better of them.'

Robineau's eyes had lit up again. His nerves were always in such turmoil that he would often jump from fear to hope like that.

'Have you got a sample?' he asked.

When Gaujean had taken a little square of silk from his wallet, he became quite ecstatic, and exclaimed:

'But it's even finer than the Paris-Paradise! In any case it makes a better effect, the texture's stronger . . . You're right, we must have a go. I want them at my feet this time, or I give up!'

Madame Robineau, sharing this enthusiasm, declared the silk superb. Even Denise thought they would succeed. Thus the end of the dinner was very boisterous. They were talking in loud voices; it seemed as if the Ladies' Paradise was at its last gasp. Gaujean, who was finishing off the jar of preserves, explained what enormous sacrifices he and his colleagues would have to make to supply a material of that kind so cheaply; but they were ready to ruin themselves over it, for they had sworn to kill the big shops. As the coffee was brought in the gaiety was increased even further by the arrival of Vinçard. He had been passing, and had called in to see how his successor was getting on.

'Splendid!' he exclaimed, feeling the silk. 'You'll beat them, I'm absolutely sure of it! You should be very grateful to me, eh? Didn't I tell you this place was a gold-mine?'

He himself had just taken a restaurant at Vincennes. It was an old dream he had secretly cherished while he was struggling in the silk business, terrified that he would not be able to sell his business before the crash came, and swearing that he would put what little money he had into a business that would enable him to rob people in comfort. The idea of a restaurant had come to him after a cousin's wedding; stomachs were always good business, for he had been made to pay ten francs for some washing-up water with a few noodles swimming about in it. In the presence of the Robineaus, his joy at having saddled them with a bad business he had been desperate to rid himself of made his face, with its round eyes and big, honest mouth, seem even broader; it positively beamed with health.

'And how are your pains?' Madame Robineau asked kindly.

'What? My pains?' he murmured in surprise.

'Yes, those rheumatic pains you suffered from so badly when you were here.'

He remembered and blushed slightly.

'Oh! I've still got them . . . However, the country air, you know . . . Never mind, you got a real bargain. If it hadn't been for my rheumatism I'd have retired within ten years with an income of ten thousand francs . . . That's for sure.'

A fortnight later the struggle between Robineau and the Ladies' Paradise began. It immediately became celebrated, and for a time the whole Parisian market was taken up with it. Robineau, using his opponent's own weapons, had put advertisements in the newspapers. And he also took great pains over his display, heaping up huge piles of the famous silk in his windows, announcing it with big white placards on which the price of five francs fifty stood out in giant figures. It was this figure that caused a revolution amongst the ladies—ten centimes cheaper than at the Ladies' Paradise, and the silk seemed stronger! From the very first day there was a stream of customers: Madame Marty, under the pretext of showing how economical she was, bought a dress she did not need; Madame Bourdelais thought the material was lovely, but said she would rather wait, sensing no doubt what was going to happen. And in fact the following week Mouret boldly reduced the price of the Paris-Paradise by twenty centimes, offering it at five francs forty; he had had a lively discussion with Bourdoncle and the other managers before convincing them that they had to take up the challenge, and accept losing on the purchase price; those twenty centimes meant a dead loss, for the silk was already being sold at cost price. It was a severe blow for Robineau; he had not thought that his rival would lower his prices, for such suicidal competitions, such loss-leading sales, were then unknown; and the stream of customers, responding to the lower prices, had immediately flowed back to the Rue Neuve-Saint-Augustin, while the shop in the Rue Neuve-des-Petits-Champs gradually emptied. Gaujean rushed up from Lyons, there were anxious confabulations, and in the end a heroic decision was taken: the price of the silk would be reduced; they would sell it at five francs thirty, a price below which no one in their senses would go. The next day Mouret priced his material at five francs twenty. And, from then on, they all went mad. Robineau replied with five francs fifteen, where-upon Mouret changed his price tickets to five francs ten. They were now fighting with only five centimes, and lost considerable sums each time they made this gift to the public. The customers laughed, delighted with this duel, excited by the terrible blows the two shops were giving each other in order to please them. Finally, Mouret ventured as low as five francs; his staff paled in terror before such defiance of fortune. Robineau, utterly beaten, out of breath, also stopped at five francs, not having the courage to go any lower. They remained entrenched, face to face, with the wreckage of their goods around them.

But if honour was saved on both sides, for Robineau the situation was becoming critical. The Ladies' Paradise had loans and enough customers to enable it to break even; whereas he, with no one but Gaujean to support him, and unable to recoup his losses with other wares, remained at a low ebb, and every day slipped a little further down the slope towards bankruptcy. He was dying from his own rashness, in spite of the many customers he had gained as a result of the ups and downs of the struggle. One of his secret torments was to see those customers slowly leaving him to go back to the Ladies' Paradise, after all the money he had lost and the efforts he had made to win them over.

One day he lost all patience. A customer, Madame de Boves, had come to look at his coats, for he had added a ladieswear department to the silks which were his speciality. She could not make up her mind, and was complaining about the quality of the materials. Finally she said:

'Their Paris-Paradise is much stronger.'

Robineau restrained himself, and assured her with his salesman's politeness that she was mistaken; and he was all the more respectful because he was afraid that his anger might get the better of him.

'Just look at the silk this cloak is made of!' she resumed.

'It looks just like a spider's web . . . You may say what you like, Monsieur, their silk at five francs is like leather compared with this.'

He did not say any more, his face crimson and his lips tightly closed. It so happened that he had had the ingenious idea of buying the silk for his ready-made clothes from his rival. This meant that it was Mouret who was losing on the material, not him. He simply cut off the selvedge.

'Really, you think the Paris-Paradise is thicker?' he murmured. 'Oh, a hundred times thicker!' said Madame de Boves. 'There's no comparison.'

The unfairness of his customer, running down his goods in this way, was making his blood boil. And, as she was still turning the cloak round with a distasteful air, a little bit of the blue and silver selvedge which had escaped the scissors showed under the lining. Whereupon he could no longer contain himself, and owned up, not caring now what she might think.

'Well, madam, this silk *is* Paris-Paradise. I bought it myself! Yes, look at the selvedge!'

Madame de Boves went away very annoyed. The story spread very quickly, and many of Robineau's customers promptly left him. And in the midst of his downfall, when fear for the future seized him, he worried only for his wife, who had been brought up in happy security, and was incapable of living in poverty. What would happen to her if a catastrophe were to throw them into the street with piles of debts? It was his fault, he should never have touched her sixty thousand francs. She had to console him. Hadn't the money been as much his as hers? He loved her, she did not want anything else, she gave him everything, her heart, her life. In the room at the back of the shop they could be heard kissing. Little by little their affairs became more stable; every month their losses increased relatively slowly, which postponed the fatal issue. Stubborn hope kept them going; they still proclaimed the imminent collapse of the Ladies' Paradise.

'Pooh!' he would say, 'we're still young, aren't we? The future is ours!'

'In any case, what does it matter, as long as you did what you wanted to do?' she would say. 'As long as you're happy, I'm happy, darling.'

Seeing how much they loved each other, Denise herself began to feel quite fond of them. She was afraid that the crash was inevitable, but she no longer dared to interfere. It was now that she finally understood the power of the new business methods, and became full of enthusiasm for this force which was transforming Paris. Her ideas were becoming more mature, and the grace of a woman was emerging from the timid child who had arrived from Valognes. Besides, in spite of her tiredness and lack of money, her life was fairly pleasant. Having spent the whole day on her feet, she had to hurry home to look after Pépé whom old Bourras, fortunately, insisted on feeding; and she had other things to do as well, a shirt to wash, a blouse to mend, not to mention the noise the little boy made, which gave her splitting headaches. She never went to bed before midnight. Sunday was the day when she did all the heavy work: she cleaned her room, and tidied herself up, so busy that it was often five o'clock before she had time to comb her hair. However, she was sensible enough to go out sometimes, taking the child with her for a long walk in the direction of Neuilly; and, once there, they would have a treat and drink a cup of milk at a dairyman's, who allowed them to sit down in his yard. Jean disdained these outings; he would turn up now and again on weekday evenings, then would disappear, saying he had other visits to make; he no longer asked for money, but he would arrive looking so dejected that his sister, who worried about him, always had a five-franc piece put aside for him. This was her extravagance.

'Five francs!' Jean would exclaim each time. 'I say! You are too good to me! It just so happens that the stationer's wife . . .'

'Shut up,' Denise would say. 'I don't want to know.'

But he would think she was accusing him of boasting.

'But I tell you she's a stationer's wife . . . Oh! really gorgeous!'

Three months went by. Spring was coming round again. Denise refused to go to Joinville again with Pauline and Baugé. She met them sometimes in the Rue Saint-Roch, when she was leaving Robineau's. One evening Pauline confided to her that she was perhaps going to marry her lover—it was she who couldn't make up her mind; they didn't like married salesgirls at the Ladies' Paradise. This idea of marriage surprised Denise, and she did not dare to advise her friend. One day Colomban stopped her near the fountain to talk to her about Clara, and just at that moment the latter crossed the square; Denise had to make her escape, for he was begging her to ask her former colleague if she would like to marry him. What was the matter with them all? Why did they torment themselves like this? She considered herself very lucky not to be in love with anyone.

'Have you heard the news?' the umbrella dealer said to her one evening as she came in.

'No, Monsieur Bourras.'

'Well! The scoundrels have bought the Hôtel Duvillard . . . I'm surrounded!'

He was waving his long arms about in a fit of rage which was making his white mane stand on end.

'It's all very fishy, and impossible to understand!' he resumed. 'It seems that the *hôtel* belonged to the Crédit Immobilier, and its chairman, Baron Hartmann, has just sold it to that devil Mouret . . . Now they've got me on the right, on the left, and behind—just like I'm holding the knob of this stick in my fist!'

It was true; the sale was due to have been concluded the day before. It had seemed as if Bourras's little house, squeezed in between the Ladies' Paradise and the Hôtel Duvillard, hanging on there like a swallow's nest in a crack in the wall, would certainly be crushed on the day the shop invaded the Hôtel

Duvillard; and this day had come; the colossus was encircling the feeble obstacle, surrounding it with stacks of goods, threatening to swallow it up, to absorb it by the sheer force of its gigantic suction. Bourras could feel the pressure which was making his shop crack. He thought he could see the place shrinking; the terrible machine was roaring so loudly now that he was afraid of being swallowed up himself, of being sucked through the wall with his umbrellas and walking-sticks.

'Can you hear them?' he shouted. 'It's as if they were eating the walls! And everywhere, in my cellar, in my loft, there's the same noise, of saws cutting into plaster . . . Never mind! Perhaps after all they won't be able to flatten me out like a sheet of paper. I'll stay, even if they make my roof cave in and the rain falls on my bed in bucketfuls!'

It was now that Mouret made fresh proposals to Bourras: the figure was increased—they would buy his business and the lease for fifty thousand francs. This offer redoubled the old man's fury and he refused it with insults. How these scoundrels must be robbing people to pay fifty thousand francs for something which wasn't worth ten thousand! And he defended his shop as a decent girl defends her virtue, in the name of honour, out of self-respect.

For about a fortnight Denise saw that Bourras was preoccupied. He moved around feverishly, measuring the walls of his house, looking at it from the middle of the street with the air of an architect. Then, one morning, some workmen arrived. The decisive battle had begun; he had had the rash idea of beating the Ladies' Paradise at its own game by making certain concessions to modern luxury. Customers who reproached him for his dark shop would certainly come back again when they saw it bright and new. First of all, the cracks were filled in and the front was distempered; next, the woodwork in the shop-window was painted light green; he even carried this magnificence so far as to gild the signboard. Three thousand francs, which Bourras had been keeping in reserve as a last resource, were swallowed up in this way. The neighbourhood, what is more, was in uproar; people came to gaze at him losing his head amid these riches, unable to pick up his old ways again. Bewildered, his long beard and white hair wilder than ever, he no longer seemed at home in this gleaming new setting, against this pastel background. Passers-by on the opposite side of the street watched him in astonishment as he waved his arms about and carved his handles. He was in a state of fever, afraid of making things dirty, sinking ever deeper into this luxury business, of which he understood nothing.

Meanwhile, like Robineau, Bourras had launched his campaign against the Ladies' Paradise. He had just put his new invention on the market, the frilled umbrella, which later on was to become popular. The Paradise, however, immediately improved the invention. Then the struggle over prices began. He had a model at one franc ninety-five, in zanelle, with a steel frame, which, according to the label, would last for ever. But he hoped above all to beat his rival with his handles, handles of bamboo, of dogwood, of olive wood, of myrtle, of rattan, every imaginable kind of handle. The Paradise, being less artistic, paid more attention to the materials, boasting of its alpacas and mohairs, its serges and taffetas. And it was victorious. The old man repeated in despair that art was done for, that he was reduced to carving handles for pleasure, with no hope of selling them.

'It's my fault!' he cried to Denise. 'I should never have got trash like that at one franc ninety-five . . . That's where new ideas get you. I wanted to follow those robbers' example; so much the better if I've ruined myself because of it!'

July was very hot, and Denise suffered greatly in her little room under the tiles. Therefore, when she left the shop she would fetch Pépé from Bourras and, instead of going up to her room straight away, she would go to the Tuileries Gardens for a breath of fresh air until the gates were closed. One evening, as she was walking towards the chestnut trees, she stopped short: she thought she recognized Hutin, a few steps away and walking straight towards her. Then her heart beat violently: it was Mouret, who had dined on the Left Bank and was hurrying along on foot to Madame Desforges's house. Denise's sudden attempt to avoid him caught his attention. Night was falling, but he recognized her all the same.

'Is it you, Mademoiselle Baudu?'

She did not reply, astonished that he had deigned to stop. With a smile, he hid his embarrassment beneath an air of kindly patronage.

'So you're still in Paris?'

'Yes, sir,' she said at last.

She was slowly backing away, trying to say goodbye and continue her walk. But he turned and followed her under the dark shadows of the tall chestnut trees. The air was getting cooler; in the distance children were laughing and bowling hoops.

'That's your brother, isn't it?' he went on, looking at Pépé.

The little boy, intimidated by the unusual presence of a gentleman with them, was walking solemnly by his sister's side, holding her hand.

'Yes, sir,' she replied once more.

She blushed, thinking of the dreadful stories which Marguerite and Clara had invented. No doubt Mouret understood why she was blushing, for he quickly added:

'Listen, Mademoiselle Baudu, I owe you an apology . . . Yes, I would have liked to tell you before how much I regretted the mistake that was made. You were too lightly accused of misbehaviour . . . Well, the harm's been done; I just wanted to tell you that everyone in the shop now knows of your love for your brothers . . .'

He went on, with a respectful politeness to which the salesgirls in the Ladies' Paradise were not at all accustomed. Denise's embarrassment had increased; but her heart was filled with joy. So he knew that she had not given herself to anyone! They both remained silent; he stayed close beside her, adjusting his gait to the child's small steps; and the distant sounds of Paris were dying away under the dark shadows of the spreading chestnut trees.

'There is only one thing I can offer you, Mademoiselle Baudu,' he resumed. 'Naturally, if you would like to come back to us . . .'

She interrupted him, refusing with feverish haste.

'I can't, sir . . . Thank you all the same, but I've found another situation.'

He knew, for he had been told that she was at Robineau's. And calmly, on a footing of equality which was charming, he talked to her about Robineau, giving him his due: a very intelligent young man, but too highly strung. He would certainly come to grief; Gaujean had burdened him with too big an affair, which would be the end of them both. Denise, won over by this familiarity, began to confide in him more, making it clear that in their battle with the small tradespeople she was on the side of the big shops; she became excited, quoted examples, showed that she knew all about the question, and was even full of bold new ideas. He listened to her with surprise and delight and turned towards her, trying to distinguish her features in the growing dark. She seemed to be just the same still, with her simple dress and gentle face; but this modest simplicity gave off a penetrating perfume, and he felt its power. No doubt this little girl had grown accustomed to the air of Paris; she was becoming a woman, and she was disturbing, with her sensible manner and her beautiful hair heavy with passion.

'Since you're on our side,' he said, laughing, 'why do you stay with our opponents? I think someone told me that you lodge with that man Bourras.'

'He's a very worthy man,' she murmured.

'No, not at all, he's a silly old fool, a madman who'll force me to ruin him, though I'd be happy to get rid of him by paying him a fortune! Besides, his house isn't the right place for you; it has a bad reputation, he lets to certain women . . .'

But he felt that Denise was embarrassed, and hastened to add:

'One can be decent wherever one lives, and there's even more merit in being so when one isn't well off.'

They took a few more steps in silence. Pépé, with the attentive air of a precocious child, seemed to be listening to them. From time to time he looked up at his sister, whose burning hand, shaken by slight quivers, surprised him.

'I know!' Mouret went on gaily, 'will you be my ambassador? I had intended to increase my offer tomorrow, to propose eighty thousand francs to Bourras . . . You speak to him about it first; tell him he's cutting his own throat. Perhaps he'll listen to you, because he's fond of you, and you'll be doing him a real service.'

'All right!' Denise replied, smiling back at him. 'I'll give him the message, but I doubt if I'll succeed.'

They fell silent again. They had nothing more to say to each other. For a moment he tried to talk about her uncle Baudu; but seeing how ill at ease she was, he had to stop. They carried on walking side by side, and they finally came out near the Rue de Rivoli in an avenue where it was still light. Leaving the darkness of the trees was like a sudden awakening. He understood that he could not detain her any longer.

'Good-night, Mademoiselle Baudu.'

'Good-night, sir.'

But he did not go away. Raising his eyes, he had just caught sight of Madame Desforges's lighted windows in front of him at the corner of the Rue d'Alger, where she was waiting for him. And looking at Denise again, he could now see her clearly in the pale dusk: she was really quite skinny compared to Henriette. Why was it that she stirred his heart like this? It was a stupid whim.

'Here's a little boy who's getting tired,' he resumed, just for something to say. 'And you will remember, won't you, that our shop is always open to you. You've only to knock, and I'll give you all the compensation possible . . . Good-night.'

'Good-night, sir.'

When Mouret had left her, Denise went back under the chest-nut trees, into the dark shadows. For a long time she walked aimlessly between the enormous trunks, her face burning, her head buzzing with confused ideas. Pépé, still hanging on to her hand, was stretching his short legs to keep up with her. She had forgotten him. Finally he said:

'You're going too fast, Sis.'

At this she sat down on a bench; and, as he was tired, Pépé fell asleep across her lap. She held him, pressing him to her virginal bosom, her eyes far away in the distance. And when, an hour later, they walked slowly back to the Rue de la Michodière, she was again wearing the calm expression of a sensible girl.

'Hell!' Bourras shouted to her as soon as he saw her. 'It's happened . . . That scoundrel Mouret has just bought my house.'

He was beside himself, thrashing about by himself in the middle of his shop, making such wild gestures that he was in danger of breaking the windows.

'Oh! The scoundrel! The fruiterer wrote to tell me. And d'you know how much he's sold it for, my house? A hundred and fifty thousand francs, four times its value! He's another thief! Just imagine, he used my decorations as a pretext; yes, he made the most of the fact that the house has just been done up like new . . . When are they going to stop making a fool of me?'

The thought that his money, spent on distemper and paint, had brought the fruiterer a profit exasperated him. And now Mouret would be his landlord: he would have to pay him! It was in his house, in the house of his detested rival, that he would be living from now on! Such a thought raised his fury to an even higher pitch.

'I knew I could hear them digging through the wall . . . Now they're here, it's as if they're eating out of my plate!'

And he slammed his fist on the counter, shaking the whole shop, making the umbrellas and parasols dance.

Denise, feeling dazed, had not been able to get a word in. She stood there motionless, waiting for his rage to subside, while Pépé, who was very tired, fell asleep on a chair. Finally, when Bourras calmed down a little, she resolved to give him Mouret's message; no doubt the old man was angry, but the very excess of his anger and the impossible position in which he found himself might bring about a sudden acceptance.

'I've just met someone,' she began. 'Yes, someone from the Paradise, and very well informed . . . It seems that tomorrow they're going to offer you eighty thousand francs . . .'

He interrupted her with a terrible roar:

'Eighty thousand francs! Eighty thousand francs! Not for a million, now!'

She wanted to reason with him. But the shop-door opened, and she suddenly drew back, pale and mute. It was her uncle Baudu, with his sallow face looking aged. Bourras seized his neighbour by the buttonholes, and shouted into his face without letting him say a word:

'D'you know what they've had the nerve to offer me? Eighty thousand francs! They've stooped to that, the sharks! They think I'll sell myself like a prostitute . . . Ah! They've bought the house and they think they've got me! Well, that's it, they won't get it! I might have given in perhaps, but now that it belongs to them, just let them try to get it!'

'So it's true?' said Baudu in his slow voice. 'I was told it was, and I came over to find out.'

'Eighty thousand francs!' Bourras was repeating. 'Why not a hundred thousand? It's all that money which makes me so angry. Do they think they'll make me do such a foul thing, with their money? They won't get it, by God! Never, never, d'you hear?'

Denise broke her silence to say in her calm way:

'They'll get it in nine years' time, when your lease expires.'

And, despite the presence of her uncle, she begged the old man to accept. The struggle was becoming impossible; he was fighting against a superior force, he was mad to refuse the fortune they were offering. But he still refused. In nine years' time, he truly hoped he would be dead, so as not to see them take over.

'D'you hear that, Monsieur Baudu?' he resumed. 'Your niece is on their side, it's her they've told to corrupt me . . . She's on the side of those scoundrels, my word of honour!'

Her uncle, until then, had appeared not to notice Denise. He was tossing his head with the surly movement he affected on the doorstep of his shop every time she passed. But he slowly turned round and looked at her. His thick lips were trembling.

'Yes, I know,' he answered in a low voice.

He carried on looking at her. Denise, moved to the point of tears, found him much changed by grief. He was overwhelmed with secret remorse at not having helped her, and was perhaps thinking of the life of poverty she had just been through. Then the sight of Pépé asleep on the chair, in the middle of all the noise of the discussion, seemed to soften his heart.

'Denise,' he said simply, 'come tomorrow with the little one and have some soup with us. My wife and Geneviève asked me to invite you if I saw you.'

She blushed deeply and kissed him. And as he was leaving, Bourras, pleased about this reconciliation, shouted after him:

'She just needs a good talking to, she isn't a bad girl . . . As far as I'm concerned, the house can fall down; they'll find me in the rubble.'

'Our houses are already falling down, neighbour,' said Baudu with a gloomy air. 'And we'll all be buried in them.'

CHAPTER 8

MEANWHILE, the whole neighbourhood was talking about the great thoroughfare which was going to be opened up from the new Opéra* to the Bourse, and which was to be called the Rue du Dix-Décembre. The expropriation notices had been served, and two gangs of demolition workers were already attacking the site at both ends, one pulling down the old mansions in the Rue Louis-le-Grand, the other knocking down the flimsy walls of the old Vaudeville; and, as the pickaxes could be heard getting closer to each other, the Rue de Choiseul and the Rue de la Michodière got very excited about their condemned houses. Before a fortnight was out the breach would make a great gash through them, full of noise and sunshine.

But the neighbourhood was even more agitated by the building work going on at the Ladies' Paradise. There was talk of considerable extensions, of gigantic shops occupying the three frontages of the Rue de la Michodière, the Rue Neuve-Saint-Augustin, and the Rue Monsigny.* Mouret, it was said, had made a deal with Baron Hartmann, the chairman of the Crédit Immobilier, and was to occupy the whole block, except the future frontage on the Rue du Dix-Décembre where the Baron wanted to build a rival to the Grand Hotel. Everywhere the Paradise was buying up leases, shops were closing, tenants were moving out; and, in the empty buildings, an army of workmen was starting on the alterations, beneath clouds of plaster. In the midst of the upheaval, old Bourras's narrow hovel was the only one that remained standing and intact, obstinately hanging on between the high walls swarming with bricklayers.

When, the next day, Denise went with Pépé to her uncle Baudu's, the street was blocked up by a line of tip-carts which were unloading bricks outside what had once been the Hôtel Duvillard. Baudu was standing at his shop-door, looking on with a gloomy air. It seemed as if the Vieil Elbeuf was shrinking as the Ladies' Paradise expanded. Denise thought the window-panes looked blacker, crushed even more beneath the low mezzanine floor with its round, prison-like bay windows; the damp had further discoloured the old green signboard; the whole front of the house, livid and somehow shrunken, was oozing with anguish.

'Ah, there you are,' said Baudu. 'Be careful! They'll run you over!' Inside the shop Denise felt the same sense of sadness. It now seemed even gloomier, more overcome by the somnolence of ruin; empty corners formed dark cavities, dust was invading the counters and cash-desks, while a smell of cellars and saltpetre was coming from the bales of cloth, which were no longer moved around. At the cash-desk Madame Baudu and Geneviève stood mute and motionless, as if in some lonely spot where no one ever came to disturb them. The mother was hemming dusters. The daughter, her hands resting on her knees, was gazing into space.

'Good-evening, Aunt,' said Denise. 'I'm so happy to see you again, and if I hurt your feelings, please forgive me.'

Madame Baudu, deeply moved, kissed her.

'My dear,' she replied, 'if that was all that bothered me, you'd find me much more cheerful!'

'Good evening, Cousin,' Denise went on, kissing Geneviève on the cheeks.

The latter seemed to wake up with a start. She returned her kisses, but could find nothing to say. Then the two women picked up Pépé, who was holding out his little arms. The reconciliation was complete.

'Well! It's six o'clock, let's have dinner,' said Baudu. 'Why didn't you bring Jean?'

'Well, he was supposed to be coming,' murmured Denise, embarrassed. 'I saw him this morning, and he faithfully promised me . . . Oh! You mustn't wait for him, his employer must have kept him late.'

She suspected some extraordinary adventure, and wanted to make excuses for him in advance.

'Then let's sit down,' her uncle said.

Then, turning towards the dark back of the shop, he called: 'Colomban, you can have your dinner at the same time as us. No one will come.'

Denise had not noticed the shop assistant. Her aunt explained that they had had to dismiss the other salesman and the girl. Business was becoming so bad that they only needed Colomban;

and even he spent hours doing nothing, apathetic, dropping off to sleep with his eyes open.

In the dining-room the gas was burning, although they were still enjoying the long days of summer. Denise shivered slightly as she went in, her shoulders chilled by the coldness given off by the walls. Once more she saw the round table, the places laid on the oilcloth, the window getting its air and light from the depths of the stinking alley of the little yard. And these things, like the shop, seemed to her to have become gloomier than ever, and to be shedding tears.

'Father,' said Geneviève, embarrassed for Denise, 'shall I close the window? It doesn't smell very nice.'

He could smell nothing, and seemed surprised.

'Close the window if you want,' he answered finally, 'but we won't get any air if you do.'

And indeed it became quite stifling. The dinner was a family affair, very simple. After the soup, as soon as the maid had served the boiled beef, Baudu inevitably began to talk about the people opposite. At first he was very tolerant, and allowed his niece to have a different opinion.

'Of course, you're quite free to stick up for those hulking great shops . . . Everyone to his own taste, my dear . . . Since you didn't mind too much being kicked out in that awful way, you must have good reasons for liking them; and if you went back there, you know, I wouldn't hold it against you. Isn't that so? No one here would hold it against you.'

'Oh, no!' murmured Madame Baudu.

Denise calmly stated her view, giving the same reasons as she had at Robineau's: the logical development of business, the needs of modern times, the magnitude of these new creations, and finally the increasing well-being of the public. Baudu, with his round eyes and thick mouth, was listening with a visible mental effort. Then, when she had finished, he shook his head.

'It's all illusion. Business is business, you can't get away from it . . . Oh! They're successful, I grant you that, but that's all. For a long time I thought they'd crash; yes, that's what I expected, I was waiting patiently for it to happen, you remember? Well, no! It seems that nowadays it's thieves who make fortunes, while honest folk are starving to death . . . That's what we've come to, and I've got to bow to the facts. And I'm bowing, by God! I'm bowing!'

His repressed rage was gradually rising. Suddenly he brandished his fork and said:

'But the Vieil Elbeuf will never make any concessions . . . I told Bourras, you know: "Neighbour, you're coming to terms with those charlatans, that crude paint of yours is a disgrace."'

'Eat your dinner,' Madame Baudu interrupted, worried at seeing him so worked up.

'Wait a minute, I want my niece to know my motto. Listen, my girl: I'm like this jug, I don't budge. They're successful—so much the worse for them! As for me, I protest—that's all!'

The maid brought in a piece of roast veal. He carved it with trembling hands; he no longer had his sure judgement, the authority with which he had weighed the helpings. The consciousness of his defeat had deprived him of the self-assurance he used to have as a respected employer. Pépé thought his uncle was getting angry, and they had to pacify him by giving him his dessert, some biscuits near his plate, straight away. Then his uncle, lowering his voice, tried to talk about something else. For a moment he discussed the demolition work, approving of the Rue du Dix-Décembre, the opening up of which would certainly increase business in the neighbourhood. But that again brought him back to the Ladies' Paradise; everything brought him back to it, it was a morbid obsession. They were covered in plaster, and business had stopped now that the builders' carts were blocking the road. In any case, its sheer size would soon make it look ridiculous; the customers would get lost, they might just as well take over the Halles.* And in spite of his wife's imploring looks, and in spite of himself, he went on from the rebuilding to discuss the shop's turnover. Wasn't it inconceivable? In less than four years they had increased it fivefold; their annual takings, formerly eight million, were approaching the figure of forty million according to the last stock-taking. It was madness, it was unheard of, and it was pointless to struggle against it any longer. They were getting bigger all the time, they now had a thousand employees, they were proclaiming that they had twenty-eight departments. It was this figure of twenty-eight departments that enraged him more than anything. No doubt they had split some of them into two, but others were completely new: a furniture department for example, and a fancy-goods department. What an idea! Fancy goods! Really, those people had no pride, they'd end up selling fish. While pretending to respect Denise's opinions, Baudu was trying to win her over.

'Frankly, you can't defend them. Can you see me adding a saucepan department to my drapery business? You'd say I was mad . . . At least admit that you have no respect for them.'

Denise merely smiled, embarrassed, realizing how useless sound reasoning was. He went on:

'So, you're on their side. We won't talk about it any more, there's no point in letting them make us fall out again. It would be too much to see them coming between me and my family! Go back to them if you want, but please don't let me hear anything more about them!'

A silence fell. His former violence was subsiding into feverish resignation. As it was stifling in the narrow room, heated by the gas burner, the maid had to open the windows again; and the damp stench from the yard wafted over the table. Some sautéed potatoes had appeared. They helped themselves slowly, without a word.

'Look at those two,' Baudu resumed, pointing to Geneviève and Colomban with his knife. 'Ask them if they like it, your Ladies' Paradise!'

Side by side, in the accustomed place where they had been meeting twice a day for the past twelve years, Colomban and Geneviève were eating with restraint. They had not said a word. Colomban, exaggerating the stolid good nature of his face, seemed to be hiding, behind his drooping eyelids, the inner fire which was consuming him; whereas Geneviève, her head drooping even more under the weight of her hair, seemed to be giving way to despair, as if stricken by some secret suffering.

'Last year was disastrous,' Baudu was explaining. 'Their marriage just had to be postponed . . . Ask them, just for fun, what they think of your friends.'

Denise, to satisfy him, questioned the young people.

'I can't be very fond of them,' Geneviève replied. 'But don't worry, not everyone hates them.'

She was looking at Colomban, who was rolling a pellet of

bread with an absorbed air. When he felt the girl's eyes upon him, he launched into a series of violent exclamations:

'It's a rotten shop! They're scoundrels, every one of them! In fact, it's a real blot on the neighbourhood!'

'Can you hear what he's saying, can you hear what he's saying?' shouted Baudu, delighted. 'That's one person they'll never get! Believe me, you're the last, my boy, there won't be any more like you!'

But Geneviève, with her grave, suffering look, did not take her eyes off Colomban. She was penetrating to his very heart, and he, feeling uncomfortable, became even more abusive. Facing them, Madame Baudu, anxious and silent, was looking from one to the other as if she had foreseen that a fresh misfortune was about to overtake them. For some time her daughter's sadness had been alarming her; she felt that she was dying.

'There's no one looking after the shop,' she said at last, getting up from the table, wishing to put an end to the scene. 'Have a look, Colomban, I thought I heard someone.'

They had finished, and stood up. Baudu and Colomban went to talk to a commercial traveller who had come to take orders. Madame Baudu took Pépé off to show him some pictures. The maid had quickly cleared the table, and Denise stood lost in thought near the window, gazing at the little yard, when, turning round, she saw that Geneviève was still sitting at her place, staring at the oilcloth, still damp from the sponge with which it had been wiped.

'Is something the matter?' Denise asked her.

The girl did not answer, but carried on studying a crack in the oilcloth, as if totally preoccupied by her thoughts. Then she raised her head painfully, and looked at the sympathetic face which was leaning towards her. The others had gone, then? What was she doing sitting on this chair? Suddenly she was choked with sobs; her head fell forward on to the table again. She was weeping, soaking her sleeve with tears.

'Oh, dear! What's the matter?' exclaimed Denise in dismay. 'Shall I call someone?'

Geneviève had nervously seized her by the arm. She held on to it, stammering:

'No, no, no, stay . . . Oh! Don't let Mamma know! With you I don't mind, but the others . . . not the others! I just can't help it,

I swear to you . . . It was when I saw I was all alone . . . Wait a minute, I'm better, I'm not crying any more.'

But fresh waves of tears overwhelmed her, shaking her frail body with great shudders. It seemed as if her piled up black hair was weighing down on her neck. As she rolled her feverish head on her folded arms, a hairpin came undone and her hair fell down over her neck, burying it beneath its dark folds. Meanwhile, for fear of attracting attention, Denise was trying to comfort her without making any noise. She unfastened her dress, and was heart-broken to see how thin and sickly she was; the poor girl had the hollow chest of a child, the nothingness of a virgin wasted by anaemia. Denise picked up her hair by the handful, that superb hair which seemed to be absorbing her life; then she tied it up firmly, in order to free her and give her some air.

'Thank you, you are kind,' Geneviève said. 'Oh! I'm not fat, am I? I used to be fatter, and it's all gone . . . Do up my dress again, Mamma might see my shoulders. I hide them as much as I can . . . Oh goodness! I'm not well, I'm not well.'

However, the crisis was subsiding. She sat there on her chair, exhausted, staring fixedly at her cousin. After a pause, she asked:

'Tell me the truth, does he love her?'

Denise felt her cheeks going red. She understood perfectly well that Geneviève was referring to Colomban and Clara. But she pretended to be surprised.

'Who do you mean, dear?'

Geneviève shook her head with an incredulous air.

'Please don't lie to me. Do me the favour of telling me for certain, at least . . . You must know, I feel you do. Yes, you used to know that woman, and I've seen Colomban following you, whispering to you. He was giving you messages for her, wasn't he? Oh, for pity's sake, tell me the truth, I swear to you it'll do me good.'

Never had Denise been in such a dilemma. Faced with this child who never said a word and yet guessed everything, she lowered her eyes. However, she found sufficient strength to go on deceiving her.

'But it's you he loves!'

At that Geneviève made a gesture of despair.

'All right, you don't want to tell me . . . It doesn't make any difference, in any case. I've seen them. He's always going outside to look at her. And she, up there, laughs like anything . . . Of course they meet outside.'

'No, they don't, I swear to you!' cried Denise, forgetting herself, carried away by the desire to give her at least that consolation.

The girl took a deep breath, and smiled feebly. Then, with the weak voice of a convalescent, she said:

'I'd love a glass of water . . . I'm sorry to bother you. Over there, in the sideboard.'

When she had taken the jug, she emptied a big glass with one gulp. With one hand she held Denise at a distance, for the latter was afraid that she might do herself some harm.

'No, no, leave me, I'm always thirsty . . . At night I always get up to drink.'

There was another silence. Then she went on quietly:

'If only you knew—for ten years I've been accustomed to the idea of this marriage. When I was still wearing short dresses Colomban was already destined for me . . . And then, I can't remember any more how it all happened. From always living together, staying shut up with each other here without ever having any fun together, I must have ended up thinking he was my husband before he actually was. I didn't know if I loved him, I was his wife, that's all . . . And now he wants to go off with someone else! Oh, God! It's breaking my heart! You see, I've never felt pain like this before. I feel it in my chest and in my head, and then it spreads all over. It's killing me!'

Her eyes were filled with tears again. Denise, whose own eyes were growing moist with pity, asked her:

'Does my aunt suspect anything?'

'Yes, Mamma does suspect something, I think . . . As for Papa, he's too worried, he doesn't know the pain he's causing me by postponing the marriage . . . Mamma's questioned me several times. She's very worried to see me wasting away. She's never been strong herself, she's often said to me: "You poor thing, I didn't make you very strong." Besides, in these shops, one doesn't grow much. But she must think I'm really getting too thin . . . Look at my arms, that's not normal, is it?'

With a trembling hand she had picked up the jug again. Her cousin wanted to stop her drinking.

'No, I'm too thirsty, let me have some water!'

They could hear Baudu raising his voice. Then, yielding to an impulse of her heart, Denise knelt down and put her arms round Geneviève in a sisterly way. She kissed her, swearing to her that everything would be all right, that she would marry Colomban, that she would get well and would be happy. Quickly, she stood up again. Her uncle was calling her.

'Come on, Jean's here.'

It was indeed Jean. He had just arrived for dinner, and seemed agitated. When he was told that it was striking eight, he looked amazed. It couldn't be; he had only just left his employer's. They teased him about this—no doubt he had come by way of the Bois de Vincennes!* But as soon as he could get near his sister he whispered to her:

'It's a little laundress who was taking back her washing . . . I've got a hired cab outside. Give me five francs.'

He went out for a minute and then came back to have dinner, for Madame Baudu absolutely refused to let him go away again without at least having some soup. Geneviève had reappeared, as silent and unobtrusive as ever. Colomban was half asleep behind a counter. The evening passed, slowly and sadly, enlivened only by Baudu's footsteps as he walked up and down the empty shop. A single gas jet was burning; the dark shadows were falling from the ceiling in great shovelfuls, like black earth into a grave.

Months passed. Denise would call in nearly every day to cheer up Geneviève for a moment. But the melancholy in the Baudu house was increasing. The building work going on opposite was constant torture, and seemed to heighten their misfortune. Even when they had an hour of hope, some unexpected joy, the din of a cart full of bricks, or a stone-cutter's saw, or simply the shout of a bricklayer, was enough to spoil it immediately. It shook the whole neighbourhood, in fact. From behind the wooden fence which skirted and blocked off the three streets, there came a whir of feverish activity. Although the architect was making use of the existing buildings, he was opening them up on all sides in order to convert them; and in the middle, in the gap made by the backyards, he was building a central gallery as vast as a church, which was to lead out into the Rue Neuve-Saint-Augustin through a grand entrance in the centre of the façade. They had at first had great difficulty in building the basements, for they had come across drain seepage, and also some loose earth full of human bones. Next, the sinking of the well had caused tremendous anxiety in the neighbouring houses: a well a hundred metres deep, which was to provide five hundred litres a minute. The walls were now up to the first floor, and scaffolding and wooden towers enclosed the whole island; there was an incessant noise from the creaking of windlasses pulling up blocks of stone, the sudden unloading of metal plates, the clamour of the army of workmen, accompanied by the noise of pickaxes and hammers. But what deafened people above all was the jarring noise of machinery; everything worked by steam, and the air was rent with piercing whistles; while at the slightest breath of wind a cloud of plaster would fly up and descend on the neighbouring roofs like a fall of snow. The Baudus, in despair, watched this relentless dust penetrating everywhere, getting through the most closely fitting woodwork, soiling the materials in the shop, even infiltrating their beds; and the idea that they were forced to breathe it in, that they would end up dying of it, was poisoning their existence.

Moreover, the situation was to become even worse. In September the architect, afraid of not being ready in time, decided that the work should go on throughout the night. Powerful electric lamps were installed, and the general uproar became continuous; gangs succeeded each other, hammers never stopped, machines whistled endlessly, the din which never diminished seemed to lift and scatter the plaster. Now the exasperated Baudus even had to forgo their sleep; they were shaken in their bed, the noises turned into nightmares as soon as exhaustion overcame them. Then, if they got up barefoot to calm their fever, and went and lifted the curtain, they were terrified by the vision of the Ladies' Paradise blazing away in the darkness, like a colossal forge, forging their ruin. In the middle of the half-built walls, pitted with empty windows, electric lamps were casting broad blue rays of blinding intensity. It would strike two o'clock in the morning, then three, then four o'clock. In its troubled sleep the neighbourhood saw the site enlarged by this lunar brightness, grown colossal and fantastic, crawling with black shadows and noisy workmen, whose silhouettes gesticulated against the garish white of the new walls.

As uncle Baudu had foretold, the small tradespeople of the neighbouring streets were receiving yet another terrible blow. Each time the Ladies' Paradise created new departments, there was fresh ruin among the shopkeepers round about. The disaster was spreading; even the oldest shops could be heard cracking. Mademoiselle Tatin of the underwear shop in the Passage Choiseul had just been declared bankrupt; Quinette, the glove-maker, could hardly hold out for another six months; the Vanpouilles, the furriers, were obliged to sublet part of their premises; and if Bédoré the hosier and his sister were still holding out in the Rue Gaillon, it was obviously because they were living on what they had saved up in the past. Now fresh cases of ruin were about to be added to those long since foreseen: the fancy-goods department was threatening Deslignières, a fat, red-faced man who owned a trinket shop in the Rue Saint-Roch, while the furniture department was hitting Piot and Rivoire, whose shops slept in the shadow of the Passage Sainte-Anne. It was even feared that the trinket dealer might have apoplexy for, having seen the Paradise advertise purses at a thirty per cent reduction, he was in a constant state of fury. The furniture dealers, who were calmer, pretended to joke about these counter-jumpers who were now trying to sell tables and cupboards; but customers were already leaving them—the success of the rival department promised to be tremendous. It was no good; they had no choice but to bow their heads in resignation; after them others would be swept away, and there was no longer any reason why all the remaining businesses should not be driven from their counters, one after another. One day the roof of the Paradise would cover the whole neighbourhood.

Nowadays, morning and evening, when the thousand employees were going in and leaving, they stretched out in such a long queue in the Place Gaillon that people would stop to look at them, as they would at a passing regiment. They blocked up the pavements for ten minutes; and the shopkeepers standing at their doors would think of their sole assistant whom they already had trouble feeding. The big shop's last stock-taking, when the turnover had been forty million, had also revolutionized the neighbourhood. The figure had spread from house to house, amidst cries of surprise and rage. Forty million! It was unimaginable! Doubtless with their heavy trade expenses and their system of low prices the net profit was at most four per cent. But a profit of sixteen hundred thousand francs was still a pretty good sum; one could be content with four per cent when one operated on such a scale. It was said that Mouret's starting capital of five hundred thousand francs, increased every year by the total profits, a capital which by now must have become four million, had thus passed ten times over the counters in the form of goods. Robineau, when he made this calculation before Denise, after dinner, was overcome for a moment, his eyes fixed on his empty plate: she was right, it was this incessant renewal of capital that constituted the invincible strength of the new way of business. Bourras alone, as proud and stupid as a monument, still denied the facts, and refused to understand. They were just a pack of thieves, and nothing more! A bunch of liars! Charlatans, who would be fished out of the river one fine morning!

The Baudus, however, in spite of their wish not to make any changes in the ways of the Vieil Elbeuf, were still trying to compete. The customers no longer came to them, so they did all they could to go to the customers by using agents. There was at that time in the Place de Paris an agent who had connections with all the great tailors, and who was the salvation of small shops selling cloth and flannel when he chose to represent them. Naturally there was a lot of competition to get him; he was becoming an important personality; and Baudu, having haggled with him over his fee, had the misfortune of seeing him come to an agreement with the Matignons in the Rue Croix-des-Petits-Champs. Two other agents robbed him in quick succession; a third, who was honest, did nothing to help him. They were dying a slow death: there were no shocks, just a continuous slowing-down of business as customers disappeared one after another. Eventually it became difficult to pay the bills. Until then, they had been living on their savings; from now on they began to accumulate debts. In December, Baudu, terrified by the number of his promissory notes, resigned himself to the cruellest of sacrifices: he sold his country house at Rambouillet, the house which cost so much money in continual repairs, and for which the tenants had not even paid the rent when he decided to get rid of it. This sale killed the only dream of his life, and his heart bled for it as for the loss of a loved one. And he had to accept seventy thousand francs for a property which had cost him more than two hundred thousand. He was lucky, indeed, to find the Lhommes, his neighbours, whose desire to add to their property made them decide to buy it. The seventy thousand francs would keep the shop going for a little while longer. In spite of all the set-backs, the idea of a fight was reviving: if they were careful, they might still be able to win through.

On the Sunday on which the Lhommes paid the money, they consented to dine at the Vieil Elbeuf. Madame Aurélie arrived first, but they had to wait for the cashier, who arrived late and agitated as a result of having spent the whole after-noon making music; as for young Albert, he accepted the invitation, but did not put in an appearance. It was, moreover, a rather painful evening. The Baudus, living without any air in the depths of their narrow dining-room, suffered from the sud-den gust of wind brought into it by the Lhommes, with their scattered family and their taste for the free life. Geneviève, offended by Madame Aurélie's imperial manner, did not open her mouth; whereas Colomban looked at her with admiration, thrilled at the thought that she reigned over Clara.

That evening, when Madame Baudu was already in bed, Baudu, before joining her, walked about the room for a long time. It was a mild night, thawing and damp. Outside, in spite of the tightly closed windows and drawn curtains, the roar of the machines on the building site opposite could be heard.

'Do you know what I'm thinking about, Elizabeth?' he said finally. 'Well, although those Lhommes are making a lot of money, I'd rather be in my shoes than in theirs . . . They're successful, it's true. She told us, didn't she, that she's made nearly twenty thousand francs this year, and that enabled her to take my poor house from me. It doesn't matter! I've lost my house, but at least I don't go playing music in one direction while you go gadding about in the other . . . No, you know, they can't be happy.'

He was still grieving over his sacrifice, and still felt a grudge against them for having bought his dream from him. When he came near the bed, he leaned over his wife, gesticulating; then, returning to the window, he was silent for a moment, listening to the din from the building site. Then he started making his old accusations again, his despairing complaints about modern times: such things had never been seen before; shop assistants were now earning more than shopkeepers, cashiers were buying up their employers' estates! As a result, everything was breaking up, the family no longer existed, people lived in hotels instead of supping decently at home. Finally, he ended by prophesying that before long young Albert would swallow up the estate at Rambouillet with his actresses.

Madame Baudu listened to him, her head flat on the pillow, so pale that her face was the same colour as the sheets.

'They've paid you,' she finally said softly.

At this Baudu fell silent. He walked up and down for a few seconds, his eyes on the ground. Then he resumed:

'They've paid me, it's true; and, after all, their money's as good as anyone else's . . . It would be funny if we got the shop on its feet again with *that* money. Oh! If only I wasn't so old and tired!'

A long silence ensued. The draper was absorbed by vague plans. Suddenly, looking at the ceiling and without moving her head, his wife spoke:

'Have you noticed your daughter lately?'

'No,' he replied.

'Well. she rather worries me . . . She's growing pale; she seems to be pining away.'

Standing by the bed, he was full of surprise.

'Really? But why? If she's ill she should say so. We must send for the doctor tomorrow.'

Madame Baudu still remained motionless. After a good minute she simply declared in her thoughtful way:

'This marriage with Colomban—I think it would be better to get it over with.'

He looked at her, then started to walk up and down again. Certain things were coming back to him. Could his daughter really be falling ill on account of the shop assistant? Did she love him so much that she couldn't wait? This was yet another misfortune! It upset him, especially as he himself had definite ideas about the marriage. He would never have wanted it to take place under present circumstances. However, anxiety was softening him.

'Very well,' he said finally, 'I'll speak to Colomban.'

And without saying another word he continued to walk up and down. Soon his wife's eyes closed, and she looked quite white as she slept, as if she were dead. But he still kept on walking about. Before getting into bed he parted the curtains and glanced out; on the other side of the street the gaping windows of the old Hôtel Duvillard formed holes through which he could see the building site, where workmen were moving about in the glare of the electric lamps.

The following morning Baudu led Colomban to the end of a narrow part of the shop on the mezzanine floor. He had decided the day before what he would say.

'My boy,' he began. 'You know that I've sold my house at Rambouillet. That's going to enable us to make a special effort . . . But first of all I'd like to have a little talk with you.'

The young man, who seemed very nervous about the interview, waited awkwardly. His small eyes were blinking in his broad face, and he stood there with his mouth open, which was always a sign that he was deeply disturbed.

'Listen,' the draper resumed. 'When old Hauchecorne handed the Vieil Elbeuf over to me, the shop was prosperous; he himself had received it in good condition from old Finet . . . You know my ideas; I'd think it wrong if I passed this family trust on to my children in a depleted state; and that's why I've always put off your marriage to Geneviève. Yes, I was stubborn, I hoped to bring back our former prosperity. I wanted to hand you the books and say: "Look! In the year I joined we sold so much cloth, and this year, the year I retire, we've sold ten or twenty thousand francs' worth more of it . . ." In short, it was a vow I'd made to myself, you see, the very natural desire to prove to myself that the shop had not gone downhill while it was in my hands. Otherwise I'd feel that I was robbing you.'

His voice was choking with emotion. He blew his nose in order to pull himself together, and asked:

'Why don't you say something?'

But Colomban had nothing to say. He shook his head, and waited, more and more worried, thinking he had guessed what his employer was getting at. It was marriage without further delay. How could he refuse? He would never have the strength to do so. And what about the other girl, the one he dreamed of at night, his flesh scorched by such burning passion that he would throw himself on the floor, quite naked, afraid it would kill him!

'At the moment,' Baudu continued, 'we've got some money which might save us. The situation's becoming worse every day, but perhaps if we make a supreme effort . . . Well, I wanted to warn you. We're going to stake everything. If we're beaten, well, that'll be the end of us . . . But I'm afraid, my boy, that this means that your marriage will have to be postponed again, for I don't want to throw you two into the fight all on your own. That would be too cowardly, wouldn't it?'

Colomban, relieved, had sat down on some pieces of duffel. His legs were still shaking. He was afraid that he might show his joy, and held his head down, while rapping his fingers on his knees.

'Why don't you say something?' Baudu repeated.

No, he did not say anything, he could think of nothing to say. So the draper went on slowly:

'I was sure that this would grieve you . . . Pull yourself together a bit, don't be crushed like that . . . Above all, try to understand my position. How can I tie a stone like that round your neck? Instead of leaving you a good business, I might perhaps leave you a bankruptcy. No, only scoundrels play tricks like that . . . Of course, I just want you to be happy, but no one will ever make me go against my conscience.'

He went on for a long time, struggling with contradictory phrases, like a man who would have liked to be understood without saying anything and finds himself forced to explain everything. As he had promised his daughter and the shop to Colomban, strict probity obliged him to hand them both over in good condition, without defects or debts. But he was tired; he felt that the burden was too heavy for him, and his faltering voice betrayed a note of supplication. The words became even more confused on his lips; he was waiting for Colomban to burst out with something, to utter a heartfelt cry; but it never came.

'Of course I know,' he murmured, 'old people lack fire . . . With young people things light up. They're full of fire, it's natural . . . But, no, no, I can't do it, really I can't! If I handed it over to you now, you'd blame me for it later on!'

He finally stopped, trembling; and, as the young man was still hanging his head, after a painful silence he asked him for the third time:

'Why don't you say something?'

At last, without looking at him, Colomban replied:

'There's nothing to say . . . You're the master, you're wiser than the rest of us. Since you insist, we'll wait, we'll try to be sensible.'

That was all Colomban had to say. Baudu was still hoping that he would throw himself into his arms, crying, 'Father, you should rest, it's our turn to fight; give us the shop as it is, so that we can perform the miracle of saving it!' Then he looked at him, and was overcome with shame; he secretly accused himself of having wanted to dupe his children. The shopkeeper's mania for honesty was aroused in him; it was this cautious young man who was right, for there are no feelings in business, there are only figures.

'Give me a kiss, my boy,' he said in conclusion. 'It's settled then, we won't talk about the marriage for another year. We must think about serious things first.'

That evening in their bedroom, when Madame Baudu questioned her husband as to the results of his conversation with Colomban, he had regained his obstinate determination to fight personally to the bitter end. He praised Colomban to the skies: a reliable lad, steadfast in his ideas and, what's more, brought up according to sound principles, incapable, for example, of joking with the customers like those young dandies at the Paradise. No, he was honest, he was one of the family, he didn't gamble on the sales as if they were shares on the Stock Exchange.

'Well, when will the wedding be?' asked Madame Baudu.

'Later,' he replied. 'When I'm in a position to keep my promises.'

She made no movement, but simply remarked:

'It'll be the death of her.'

Roused to anger, Baudu controlled himself. It would be the death of him if they continually upset him like that! Was it his fault? He loved his daughter, he talked of laying down his life for her; but he couldn't make the shop do well when it refused to do so. Geneviève should be sensible and wait patiently until they had a better balance sheet. Damn it all! Colomban was going to stay there, no one would steal him!

'It's incredible!' he went on repeating. 'Such a well-brought-up girl!'

Madame Baudu said no more. No doubt she had guessed the agonies of jealousy Geneviève was suffering; but she did not dare confide them to her husband. A strange feminine modesty had always prevented her from broaching certain delicate, intimate subjects with him. When he saw that she remained silent, he directed his anger against the people opposite, shaking his fists in the air at the building site where, that night, iron girders were being installed with great blows from a hammer.

Denise had decided to go back to the Ladies' Paradise. She could see that the Robineaus, forced to cut down their staff, did not know how to give her notice. The only way they could keep going was by doing everything themselves; Gaujean, persisting in his feud with the Paradise, kept extending their credit, and even promised to find funds for them; but they were starting to get frightened, and they wanted to make an attempt at economy and order. For a fortnight Denise felt that they were ill at ease with her; and she was forced to take the initiative and say that she had a job elsewhere. It was a relief; Madame Robineau, deeply moved, kissed her, swearing that she would always miss her. Then when, in reply to a question, the girl answered that she was going back to Mouret's shop, Robineau turned pale.

'You're right,' he shouted violently.

It was not so easy to break the news to old Bourras. Nevertheless, Denise had to give him notice, and she dreaded it, for she remained deeply grateful to him. Bourras, just at this time, was in a constant state of anger, for he was now totally surrounded by the hubbub of the neighbouring building site. The builders' carts blocked the way to his shop; pickaxes beat against his walls;

everything in his house, all the umbrellas and walking-sticks, danced to the noise of hammers. It seemed as if the hovel, obstinately remaining in the midst of all this demolition work, was going to give way. But what was worst of all was that the architect, in order to connect the shop's existing departments with those which were being installed in the old Hôtel Duvillard, had had the idea of digging a passage underneath the little house which separated them. This house belonged to Mouret & Co. Ltd., and as the lease stipulated that the tenant had to agree to any repair work that might be carried out, one fine morning some workmen turned up. At this, Bourras nearly had a stroke. Wasn't it enough to constrict him on all sides, left, right, and centre, without grabbing him by the feet as well and eating the earth from under him? He had chased the workmen away, and was taking the matter to court. Repair work, agreed! But this was a question of making improvements. It was thought in the neighbourhood that he would win the case, but no one was certain. At any rate, it threatened to be a long one, and people were taking a passionate interest in this interminable duel.

On the day when Denise finally resolved to give him notice, it so happened that Bourras was just returning from his lawyer.

'Would you believe it!' he exclaimed. 'They're saying now that the house is unsound; they're trying to make out that the foundations need repairing. Really! They've shaken it up so much with their damned machines. It's not surprising if it's breaking up!'

Then, when the girl had announced to him that she was leaving, that she was going back to the Paradise with a salary of a thousand francs, he was so shaken that he could only raise his old, trembling hands in the air. Emotion had made him sink into a chair.

'You! You too!' he stammered. 'Well, I'm the only one now, I'm the only one left!'

After a silence he asked:

'What about the boy?'

'He'll go back to Madame Gras,' Denise replied. 'She was very fond of him.'

They fell silent again. She would have preferred him to be furious, swearing, banging his fists; the sight of the old man speechless and crushed made her heart bleed. But he gradually recovered, and started shouting again.

'A thousand francs, you don't turn that sort of money down . . . You'll all go. Go on then, leave me on my own. Yes, on my own, do you hear? There's one person who'll never give in . . . And tell them I'll win my case, even if I have to put my last shirt on it!'

Denise was not leaving Robineau until the end of the month. She had seen Mouret again, and everything was settled. One evening she was just going to go up to her room when Deloche, who was standing under an archway on the look-out for her, stopped her as she walked past. He was very happy; he had just heard the great news, the whole shop was talking about it, he said. And he gaily related to her the gossip of the counters.

'You know, the girls in the ladieswear department are full of it!'

Then, breaking off, he said:

'By the way, you remember Clara Prunaire . . . Well! It seems that the governor has . . . D'you follow me?'

He had become quite red. Denise, very pale, exclaimed:

'Monsieur Mouret!'

'Strange taste, isn't it?' he went on. 'A woman who looks like a horse . . . That little thing from the lingerie department whom he had twice last year was at least nice. Anyway, it's his business.'

Back in her room, Denise began to feel faint. It was no doubt because she had climbed the stairs too quickly. Leaning on the window-sill, she had a sudden vision of Valognes, of the empty street with its mossy paving stones which she used to see from her room as a child; and she was filled with desire to live there again, to take refuge in the oblivion and peace of the country. Paris irritated her; she hated the Ladies' Paradise, she couldn't think why she had agreed to go back there. She was sure to suffer there again; she was already suffering from some nameless malaise since hearing Deloche's stories. And suddenly, for no reason, a flood of tears forced her to leave the window. She cried for a long time before finding a little courage with which to go on living.

The next day, at lunch-time, Robineau sent her on an errand, and as she was passing by the Vieil Elbeuf and saw that

Colomban was alone in the shop, she pushed open the door. The Baudus were having lunch; the sound of knives and forks could be heard at the far end of the little hall.

'You can come in,' said the shop assistant, 'they're having lunch.'

But she motioned to him to be silent and drew him into a corner. Lowering her voice, she said:

'It's you I want to talk to . . . Haven't you any heart? Can't you see that Geneviève loves you, and that it's killing her?'

She was shaking all over; the previous night's fever had taken possession of her again. Startled and amazed at this sudden attack, he could think of nothing to say.

'Don't you understand?' she went on. 'Geneviève knows that you love someone else. She told me so, she sobbed like a child . . . Oh! the poor girl! She doesn't weigh much now, I can tell you! You should see how thin her arms are! It's enough to make you cry . . . You can't leave her to die like that!'

Finally, completely overwhelmed, he spoke.

'But she isn't ill, you're exaggerating . . . I can't see it myself . . . Besides, it's her father who's putting off the wedding.'

Denise sharply pointed out that this was a lie. She had sensed that the slightest insistence on the part of the young man would have persuaded her uncle. As to Colomban's surprise, it was not feigned: he had really never noticed that Geneviève was slowly dying. It was a very unpleasant discovery for him. As long as he had remained unaware of it, he had not had very much to reproach himself with.

'And who for?' Denise went on. 'For someone who just isn't worth it! Don't you know what sort of person you're in love with? I didn't want to hurt your feelings before, I've often avoided answering your endless questions . . . Well, she goes with everybody, she couldn't care less about you, you'll never have her; or perhaps you'll have her like all the others, once, in passing.'

He listened to her, very pale; and at each sentence she threw in his face through clenched teeth, his lips trembled slightly. She was giving way to a rage of which she had been unaware, and had become cruel.

'Anyway,' she said with a final cry, 'she's with Monsieur Mouret, if you want to know!'

Her voice was choking, and she had become paler than he was. They looked at each other.

Then he stammered:

'I love her.'

Denise felt ashamed. Why was she talking to the boy in this way, and why had she got so excited? She remained mute; the simple reply he had just given resounded in her heart like the distant sound of bells and deafened her. 'I love her, I love her,' the words continued to re-echo. He was right, he couldn't marry anyone else.

As she turned round she saw Geneviève on the threshold.

'Be quiet!' she said quickly.

But it was too late, Geneviève must have heard. All the blood had left her face. Just at that moment a customer opened the door—it was Madame Bourdelais, one of the last faithful customers of the Vieil Elbeuf, where she found hard-wearing articles; Madame de Boves had followed the fashion and gone over to the Paradise long ago, and even Madame Marty, completely conquered by the seductive displays opposite, did not come any more. Geneviève was forced to step forward to say in her flat voice:

'What does madam require?'

Madame Bourdelais wanted to see some flannel. Colomban took down a roll from the shelf, Geneviève showed her the material; and so both of them, their hands cold, found themselves brought together behind the counter. Meanwhile Baudu came out last from the little dining-room, following his wife, who had gone to sit down at the cash-desk. At first he did not interfere in the sale; he had smiled at Denise, and remained standing, looking at Madame Bourdelais.

'That's not pretty enough,' she was saying. 'Show me what you have that's stronger.'

Colomban took down another roll. There was a silence. Madame Bourdelais examined the material.

'And how much is it?'

'Six francs, madam,' Geneviève replied.

The customer made a gesture of surprise. 'Six francs! But they've got the same thing opposite at five francs!'

A shadow passed over Baudu's face. He could not help intervening, very politely. No doubt madam had made a mistake; the material should have been sold at six francs fifty, it was impossible to sell it at five francs. She must be thinking of some other material.

'No, no,' she repeated, with the obstinacy of a middle-class woman who prided herself on being an expert.

'It's the same material. It may even be a little thicker.'

The argument became quite heated. Baudu, his face becoming bilious, made an effort to continue smiling. His resentment against the Ladies' Paradise was bursting within him.

'Really,' said Madame Bourdelais in the end. 'You'll have to treat me better than that, or I shall go across the road, like the others.'

At that he lost his head and, shaking with pent-up rage, shouted:

'Very well! Go across the road then!'

She stood up, deeply offended, and left without looking back, saying:

'That's just what I'm going to do, sir.'

They were dumbfounded. The governor's violence had startled them all. He himself was still frightened and trembling at what he had just said. The phrase had slipped out against his will, in an outburst of long pent-up resentment. And the Baudus now stood there, motionless, their arms sagging, watching Madame Bourdelais as she crossed the street. She seemed to them to be carrying away their fortune. When she went through the high doorway of the Paradise, at her leisurely pace, when they saw her disappear in the crowd, they felt as if something had been wrenched from them.

'There goes another one they're taking away from us!' murmured the draper.

Then, turning towards Denise, of whose re-engagement he was aware, he said:

'You too, they've taken you back . . . Well, I don't blame you for it. Since they've got the money, they've got the power.'

Just at that moment, Denise, still hoping that Geneviève had not been able to overhear Colomban, was whispering in her ear:

'He loves you. Cheer up!'

But, in a very low, heart-broken voice, the girl replied:

'Why lie to me? Look! He can't help it, he's always looking over there . . . I know full well that they've stolen him from me, just as they've robbed us of everything else.'

She sat down on the seat at the cashier's desk, beside her mother. The latter had no doubt guessed the fresh blow her daughter had received, for her eyes travelled anxiously from her to Colomban, and then back to the Paradise again. It was true, it was stealing everything from them: from the father, his money; from the mother, her dying child; from the daughter, a husband for whom she had waited ten years. Faced with this doomed family, Denise, whose heart was flooded with compassion, felt for a moment that she was perhaps wicked to go back. Wasn't she once more going to assist the machine which was crushing the poor? But it was as if she was being swept along by some invisible force; she felt that she was not doing wrong.

'Bah!' Baudu resumed, in an attempt to give himself more courage, 'we shan't die of it! If we lose one customer, we'll find two more from somewhere else . . . Listen, Denise: I've got seventy thousand francs here, and they're going to give that Mouret of yours some sleepless nights . . . Come on, everybody! Don't look as if you were at a funeral!'

But he could not cheer them up, and he himself relapsed into black despair; there they all stood, staring at the monster, attracted by it, obsessed by it, utterly preoccupied by their misfortune. The work was almost finished; the scaffolding had been taken away from the front of the building, and a whole section of the colossal edifice was now visible, with its white walls and large, light windows. Along the pavement, which was at last open to traffic again, eight vans were lined up and were being loaded one after the other by porters outside the dispatch office. In a ray of sunlight which ran along the street, the green door panels, picked out in yellow and red, were sparkling like mirrors, sending blinding reflections into the furthest depths of the Vieil Elbeuf. The drivers, dressed in black and with a dignified bearing, were holding in the horses, superb teams, tossing their silver bits as they waited. Each time a van was loaded, there was a resounding rumble on the paving stones, which made the small neighbouring shops shake.

And then, faced with this triumphal procession which they had to suffer twice a day, the Baudus' hearts finally broke. The father's spirits sank as he wondered where this continual stream of goods could be going; while the mother, made ill by her daughter's suffering, went on looking without seeing, her eyes drowned with great tears.

CHAPTER 9

ON Monday, 14 March, the Ladies' Paradise inaugurated its new building with a grand display of summer fashions, which was to last for three days. Outside, a bitter wind was blowing, and the passers-by, surprised by this return of winter, were hurrying along, buttoning up their overcoats. Meanwhile, the small shops in the neighbourhood were in a ferment of excitement; and the pale faces of the small tradesmen could be seen pressed against their windows, busy counting the first carriages which were drawing up outside the new main entrance in the Rue Neuve-Saint-Augustin. This entrance, as high and deep as the porch of a church, surmounted by a group representing Industry and Commerce shaking hands in the midst of an array of symbolic emblems, was sheltered by a vast awning whose fresh gilding seemed to light up the pavements with a flash of sunlight. To the right and left stretched the shop-fronts, still blindingly white, going round the corners into the Rue Monsigny and the Rue de la Michodière, occupying the whole block except on the side of the Rue du Dix-Décembre, where the Crédit Immobilier was going to build. When the small tradespeople raised their heads they saw, along the whole length of this barracks-like extension, great piles of goods visible through the plate-glass windows which, from the ground floor to the second floor, opened up the shop to the public gaze. This enormous block, this colossal bazaar, blotted out their sky, and seemed to them to have something to do with the cold which was making them shiver behind their icy counters.

Meanwhile, from six o'clock onwards, Mouret was there, giving his final orders. In the centre, on a straight line from the main entrance, a wide gallery ran from one end of the shop to the other, flanked on the right and left by two narrower galleries, the Monsigny Gallery and the Michodière Gallery. The courtyards had been glazed in and transformed into halls; and iron staircases rose from the ground floor, while iron bridges had been thrown across from one end to the other on both floors. The architect, who happened to be intelligent, a young man in love with modernity, had only used stone for the basements and the corner pillars, and then had used iron for the rest of the framework, with columns supporting the assemblage of beams and girders. The counter-arches of the flooring and the internal partitions were of brick. Space had been gained everywhere, light and air entered freely, and the public circulated with ease beneath the bold curves of the wide-spaced trusses. It was the cathedral of modern business, strong and yet light, built for vast crowds of customers. In the central gallery on the ground floor, after the bargains near the door, came the tie, glove, and silk departments; the Monsigny Gallery was occupied by the household linen and the printed cotton goods, the Michodière Gallery by the haber-dashery, hosiery, cloth, and woollen departments. Then, on the first floor, there were the ready-made clothes, lingerie, shawls, lace, and other new departments, while the bedding, carpets, and furnishing materials, all the bulky goods and those which were difficult to handle, had been relegated to the second floor. By this time there were thirty-nine departments and eighteen hundred employees, of whom two hundred were women. A whole world was springing up amidst the life echoing beneath the high metal naves.*

Mouret's sole passion was the conquest of Woman. He wanted her to be queen in his shop; he had built this temple for her in order to hold her at his mercy. His tactics were to intoxicate her with amorous attentions, to trade on her desires, and to exploit her excitement. He racked his brains night and day for new ideas. Already, to spare delicate ladies the trouble of climbing the stairs, he had installed two lifts lined with velvet. In addition, he had just opened a buffet, where fruit cordials and biscuits were served free of charge, and a reading-room, a colossal gallery decorated with excessive luxury, in which he even ventured to hold picture exhibitions.* But his most inspired idea, which he deployed with women devoid of coquetry, was that of conquer-ing the mother through the child; he exploited every kind of force, speculated on every kind of feeling, created departments for little boys and girls, stopped the mothers as they were walk-ing past by offering pictures and balloons to their babies. Pre-senting a balloon as a free gift to each customer who bought something was a stroke of genius; they were red balloons, made of fine indiarubber and with the name of the shop written on them in big letters; when held on the end of a string they travelled through the air, parading a living advertisement through the streets!

Mouret's greatest source of power was publicity. He spent as much as three hundred thousand francs a year on catalogues, advertisements, and posters. For his sale of summer fashions he had sent out two hundred thousand catalogues, of which fifty thousand, translated into every language, were sent abroad. He now had them illustrated with drawings, and even enclosed samples with them, glued on to the pages. His displays appeared everywhere. The Ladies' Paradise was staring the whole world in the face, invading walls, newspapers, and even the curtains of theatres. He declared that Woman was helpless against advertisements; in the end she inevitably went to see what all the noise was about. And he set even more cunning snares for her, analysing her like a great moralist. For example, he had discovered that she could not resist a bargain, that she bought things without needing them if she thought she was getting them cheaply; and on this observation he based his system of price reductions, progressively lowering the prices of unsold items, preferring to sell them at a loss, faithful to the principle of the rapid turnover of stocks. Then, penetrating even further into women's hearts, he had recently conceived of 'returns', a masterpiece of Jesuitical seduction. 'Take it all the same, madam: you can return the article to us if you find you don't like it.' And a woman who was resisting was thus given a final excuse, the possibility of going back on an act of folly; her conscience satisfied, she would buy it. Returns and price reductions were now part of the standard methods of the new business.

But it was in the interior arrangement of the shops that Mouret revealed himself to be an unrivalled master. He laid it down as a law that not a corner of the Ladies' Paradise was to remain deserted; everywhere he insisted upon noise, crowds, life; for life, he would say, attracts life, gives birth and multiplies. He put this law into practice in a whole variety of ways. First of all, there should be a crush at the entrance; it should seem to people in the street that there was a riot in the shop; and he obtained this crush by placing bargains at the entrance, shelves and baskets overflowing with articles at very low prices, so that working-class people began to congregate there, barring the threshold, and giving the impression that the shop was bursting with customers, when often it was only half full. Then, all through the galleries, he had the art of hiding the departments in which business was slack—the shawl department in summer and the cotton materials in winter, for example; he would surround them with active departments, drowning them with blaring noise. It was he alone who had thought of putting the carpet and furniture departments on the second floor, for in those departments customers were rarer, and their presence on the ground floor would have created cold, empty gaps. If he could have found a way of making the street run right through his shop, he would have done so.

Just now Mouret was undergoing one of his fits of inspiration. On Saturday evening, as he was casting a last glance over the preparations for Monday's big sale, which they had been working on for a month, he had suddenly realized that the way he had arranged the departments was stupid. It was, however, an absolutely logical arrangement—materials on one side, manufactured goods on the other, an intelligent system which should enable the customers to find their own way about. He had dreamed of this system while he was still working in the muddle of Madame Hédouin's little shop; and now, on the day when he was putting it into effect, he felt his faith in it shaken. Suddenly he had shouted that he wanted it all changed. This meant moving half the shop, and they had forty-eight hours to do it in. The staff, bewildered and working at full stretch, had had to spend two nights and the whole of Sunday in the midst of an appalling mess. Even on Monday morning, an hour before the opening, the goods were not yet in place. The governor was surely losing his mind; no one could understand it, and there was general consternation.

'Come on! Let's hurry!' Mouret shouted, with the calm assurance born of his genius. 'Here are some more suits I want taken upstairs . . . And are the Japanese things installed on the central landing? . . . One last effort, lads, and you'll see what a sale we're going to have!'

Bourdoncle, too, had been there since dawn. He understood no better than the others, and was watching the governor most anxiously. He hadn't dared to question him, knowing how he responded in such moments of crisis. All the same, he decided to risk it, and asked gently:

'Was it really necessary to turn everything upside-down like that, on the eve of our exhibition?'

At first Mouret shrugged his shoulders without replying. Then, since Bourdoncle insisted, he burst out:

'So that the customers should all huddle together in the same corner, perhaps? An excellent geometrical idea I had when I thought of that! I'd never have forgiven myself . . . Can't you see that I'd have localized the crowd? A woman would have come in, gone straight to where she wanted, passed from the petticoat department to the dress department, from the dresses to the coats, and then left, without even having got a bit lost! Not one of them would really have seen our shop!'

'But,' Bourdoncle pointed out, 'now that you've mixed everything up and thrown everything all over the place, the staff will wear their legs out taking customers from department to department.'

Mouret made a gesture of supreme contempt.

'I don't care a damn! They're young; it'll make them grow. So much the better if they walk about! They'll look more numerous, they'll swell the crowd. As long as there's a crush, all will be well!'

He was laughing, and deigned to explain his idea, lowering his voice:

'Listen, Bourdoncle, this is what will happen . . . First, this continual circulation of customers scatters them all over the place, multiplies them, and makes them lose their heads; secondly, as they have to be conducted from one end of the shop to the other—for example, if they want a lining after having bought a dress—these journeys in every direction triple, as they see it, the size of the shop; thirdly, they're forced to go through departments where they'd never have set foot, temptations present themselves as they pass, and they succumb; fourthly . . .'

Bourdoncle was now laughing with him. At this Mouret, delighted, stopped in order to shout to the porters:

'That's very good, lads! A quick sweep, and it'll look splendid!'

But, turning round, he caught sight of Denise. He and Bourdoncle were opposite the ladieswear department, which he had just split in two by having the dresses and costumes taken up to the second floor, at the other end of the shop. Denise, the first to come down, was wide-eyed with astonishment at the new arrangements.

'What's this,' she murmured; 'are we moving?'

This surprise seemed to amuse Mouret, who adored these theatrical effects. Denise had been back at the Paradise since the beginning of February, and she had been agreeably surprised to find the staff polite, almost respectful. Madame Aurélie especially was very kind; Marguerite and Clara seemed resigned; even old Jouve was obsequious in a rather embarrassed way, as if he wanted to wipe out the unpleasant memory of the past. It sufficed that Mouret had said a few words; everyone was whispering, watching her as they did so. In the midst of this universal friendliness, the only things which hurt her were Deloche's curious sadness, and Pauline's inexplicable smiles.

Meanwhile, Mouret was still looking at her with delight:

'What is it you're looking for, Mademoiselle Baudu?' he asked at last.

Denise had not noticed him. She blushed slightly. Since her return he had taken an interest in her, and this touched her very much. Without her knowing why, Pauline had given her a full account of the governor's affair with Clara: where he saw her, what he paid her; and she often returned to the subject, even adding that he had another mistress, that Madame Desforges who was well known to everyone in the shop. These stories upset Denise, and in his presence she was again filled with all the fears she had had in the past, an uneasiness in which her gratitude struggled against her anger.

'It's all this moving around,' she murmured.

Then Mouret came closer and said in a lower voice:

'This evening, after the sale, will you come and see me in my office? I want to speak to you.'

Quite agitated, she nodded without saying a word, and went into the department where the other salesgirls were arriving. But Bourdoncle had overheard Mouret, and was watching him with a smile. He even ventured to say, when they were alone:

'That girl again! Be careful, it'll end up by getting serious!'

Mouret sharply defended himself, hiding his emotion beneath an air of casual superiority.

'Don't worry, it's just fun! The woman who can catch me isn't yet born, my dear chap!'

As the shop was opening at last, he rushed off to give a final glance at the various departments. Bourdoncle shook his head. That girl Denise, so simple and gentle, was beginning to worry him. He had defeated her once already by brutally dismissing her. But here she was again, and he was treating her now as a serious enemy, saying nothing, but once more biding his time.

He caught up with Mouret, who was downstairs in the Saint-Augustin Hall opposite the entrance, shouting:

'Didn't you hear what I said? I said that the blue parasols were to be put round the edge . . . I want all that redone, and be quick about it!'

He was deaf to all arguments, and a team of porters had to rearrange the display of parasols. Seeing the customers arriving, he even had the doors closed for a moment, declaring that he would rather not open at all than leave the blue parasols in the centre. It ruined his composition. Those with a reputation as window-dressers, Hutin, Mignot, and several others, came to have a look, craning their necks; but they pretended not to understand what he was trying to do, for they belonged to a different school.

Finally the doors were opened again, and the crowd streamed in. From the beginning, even before the shop was full, there was such a crush in the entrance hall that the police had to be called in to keep people moving along on the pavement. Mouret's calculations had been right: all the housewives, a serried band of shopkeepers' and workmen's wives, were assaulting the bargains and remnants, which were displayed right into the street. Outstretched hands were continually feeling the materials hanging at the entrance, a calico at thirty-five centimes, a wool and cotton grey material at forty-five centimes, and above all an Orleans cloth at thirty-eight centimes which was playing havoc with the poorer purses. There was much elbowing, a feverish scrimmage round the racks and baskets in which piles of goods at reduced prices—lace at ten centimes, ribbons at twenty-five centimes, garters at fifteen, gloves, petticoats, ties, cotton socks and stockings—were collapsing and disappearing, as if devoured by the voracious crowd. In spite of the cold weather, the assistants who were selling to the crowd on the pavement could not serve fast enough. A fat woman screamed. Two little girls nearly suffocated.

The crush increased as the morning wore on. Towards one o'clock queues were being formed, and the street was barricaded as if there were a riot. Just at that moment, as Madame de Boves and her daughter Blanche were standing hesitantly on the opposite pavement, they were approached by Madame Marty, who was likewise accompanied by her daughter Valentine.

'What a crowd, eh?' said Madame de Boves. 'They're killing each other inside. I shouldn't have come; I was in bed, but I got up for a breath of fresh air.'

'It's the same with me', the other declared, 'I promised my husband to go and see his sister in Montmartre. Then, as I was passing, I remembered I needed a piece of braid; I might as well buy it here as anywhere else, don't you think? Oh! I shan't spend a penny! I don't need anything, anyway.'

However, they had not taken their eyes off the door, caught up and carried away by the strength of the crowd.

'No, no, I'm not going in, I'm frightened,' murmured Madame de Boves. 'Let's go, Blanche, or we'll be crushed to death.'

But her voice was faltering, and she was gradually giving way to the desire to follow everyone else inside; her fear was melting away in the irresistible lure of the crush. Madame Marty had also given way. She was repeating:

'Hold my dress, Valentine . . . My goodness! I've never seen anything like this. You're just carried along. What's it going to be like inside!'

Caught in the current, the ladies were no longer able to turn back. As rivers draw together the stray waters of a valley, so it seemed that the stream of customers, flowing through the en-

trance hall, was drinking in the passers-by from the street, sucking in the population from the four corners of Paris. They were
advancing very slowly, jammed so tightly that they could hardly
breathe, held upright by shoulders and stomachs, whose flabby
warmth they could feel; and their satisfied desire revelled in this
painful approach, which inflamed their curiosity even more.
There was a pell-mell of ladies dressed in silk, tradesmen's wives
in shabby dresses, hatless girls, all of them excited and carried
away by the same passion. A few men, swamped by all these
ample bosoms, were casting anxious glances around them. A
nurse, in the thick of the crowd, was holding her baby high in the
air, and it was laughing with delight. Only one of them, a skinny
woman, lost her temper, shouting out abuse, and accusing a
woman next to her of digging her elbows into her.

'I think I might lose my petticoat in this crowd,' Madame de
Boves was repeating.

Silent, her face still fresh from the air outside, Madame Marty
was craning her neck above the heads to see, before the others,
the depths of the shop stretching into the distance. The pupils of
her grey eyes were as small as those of a cat coming in out of the
daylight; and she had the fresh complexion and clear gaze of
someone who had just woken up.

'Ah! At last!' she said, letting out a sigh.

The ladies had just extricated themselves. They were in the
Saint-Augustin Hall, and were most surprised to find it almost
empty. But a feeling of well-being was stealing over them; they
felt they were entering spring after leaving the winter of the
street. Whereas outside the icy wind of sleet storms was blowing,
in the galleries of the Paradise the warm summer months had
already arrived, with the light materials, the flowery brilliance of
soft shades, and the rustic gaiety of summer dresses and parasols.

'Just look!' cried Madame de Boves, brought to a standstill
and gazing upwards.

It was the display of parasols. Wide open and rounded like
shields, they covered the hall from the glazed ceiling to the
varnished oak mouldings. They formed festoons round the arcades of the upper storeys; they hung down in garlands along
the pillars; they ran in close lines along the balustrades of the
galleries, and even on the banisters of the staircases; symmetric-

ally arranged everywhere, speckling the walls with red, green, and yellow, they seemed like great Venetian lanterns, lit for some colossal entertainment. In the corners there were complicated patterns, stars made of parasols at ninety-five centimes, and their light shades—pale blue, creamy white, soft pink—were burning with the gentleness of a night-light; while above, huge Japanese sunshades covered with golden cranes flying across a purple sky were blazing with glints of fire.

Madame Marty tried to think of a phrase to express her delight, and could only exclaim:

'It's enchanting!'

Then, trying to find her way, she said:

'Now, let's see, the braid is in the haberdashery . . . I'll just buy my braid, and then I'll be off.'

'I'll come with you,' said Madame de Boves. 'We'll just walk through the shop, and nothing more, won't we, Blanche?'

But the ladies had hardly stepped away from the door before they were lost. They turned to the left; and, as the haberdashery had been moved, they found themselves surrounded by ruches, then by head-dresses. It was very warm under the covered galleries; the heat was that of a hothouse, moist and close, laden with the insipid smell of the materials; it muffled the trampling feet of the crowd. Then they went back to the entrance, where a stream of people on their way out was beginning to form, an interminable procession of women and children, above whom there floated a cloud of red balloons. Forty thousand balloons had been prepared; there were boys specially detailed to distribute them. To see the customers who were leaving, one would have thought that in the air above them there was a flight of enormous soap bubbles, on the end of invisible strings, reflecting the fire of the sunshades. The whole shop was lit up by them.

'What a crowd,' declared Madame de Boves. 'You don't know where you are any more.'

However, the ladies could not stay in the eddy by the doorway, right in the crush of the entrance and exit. Fortunately, Jouve came to their assistance. He was standing in the entrance hall, solemn-looking and attentive, staring at every woman who passed. Specially charged with responsibility for internal security, he was on the look-out for thieves, and in particular would follow pregnant women, when the feverish look in their eyes made him suspicious.

'The haberdashery, ladies?' he said obligingly. 'Turn to the left, look, over there, behind the hosiery.'

Madame de Boves thanked him. But Madame Marty, on turning round, had found that her daughter Valentine was no longer with her. She was beginning to be alarmed when she caught sight of her, already in the distance at the end of the Saint-Augustin Hall, deeply absorbed in front of an auction table, on which there were piles of women's scarves at ninety-five centimes. Mouret employed the auctioneering method of selling goods, by which customers were caught and robbed of their money as they passed; for he used any kind of advertisement, laughing at the discretion of some of his colleagues, who thought that the goods should speak for themselves. Special salesmen, idle Parisians with the gift of the gab, got rid of considerable quantities of small, trashy articles in this way.

'Oh! Mamma!' murmured Valentine. 'Just look at these scarves. They've got an embroidered bird on the corner.'

The salesman was going through his patter, swearing that the scarf was all silk, that the manufacturer had gone bankrupt, and that they would never come across such a bargain again.

'Ninety-five centimes, can it be true?' said Madame Marty, captivated like her daughter. 'Well, I could take two of them, that won't ruin us!'

Madame de Boves remained disdainful. She detested this type of selling; a salesman who called out to her put her to flight. Madame Marty was surprised; she did not understand this nervous horror of the salesman's patter, for her temperament was quite different; she was one of those women who are happy to be taken by force, to bathe in the caress of a public proposition, and have the pleasure of feeling everything with their hands, wasting their time in useless words.

'Now,' she resumed, 'let's hurry and get my braid . . . I don't even want to see anything else.'

However, as she was going through the silk scarves and glove departments, her will weakened once more. There, in the diffused light, stood a bright, gaily coloured display which made a delightful effect. The counters, symmetrically arranged, looked like flower-beds, transforming the hall into a formal garden, smiling with a range of soft flower tones. Spread out on the wooden counter, falling from overflowing shelves, and in boxes which had been torn open, a harvest of silk scarves displayed the brilliant red of geraniums, the milky white of petunias, the golden yellow of chrysanthemums, the sky blue of verbena; and higher up, entwined on brass stems, there was another mass of blossom—fichus strewn about, ribbons unrolled, a dazzling strand extending and twisting up round the pillars, and multiplying in the mirrors. But what most attracted the crowd was a Swiss chalet in the glove department, made entirely of gloves: it was Mignot's masterpiece, and had taken two days to arrange. First of all, black gloves formed the ground floor; then came straw-coloured, greyish-green, and burgundy gloves, forming part of the decoration, bordering the windows, sketching in the balconies, replacing tiles.

'What does madam require?' asked Mignot, seeing Madame Marty rooted in front of the chalet. 'Here are some suede gloves at one franc seventy-five, the finest quality . . .'

He was an extremely persistent salesman, calling out to passing customers from the far end of his counter, pestering them with his politeness. As she shook her head in refusal, he went on:

'Tyrolean gloves at one franc twenty-five . . . Children's gloves from Turin, embroidered gloves in all colours . . .'

'No, thank you, I don't want anything,' Madame Marty declared.

But, feeling that her voice was softening, he attacked her even more vigorously by holding the embroidered gloves in front of her; she was helpless to resist, and bought a pair. Then, as Madame de Boves was watching her with a smile, she blushed.

'I am a child, aren't I? If I don't hurry up and get my braid and leave, I'm lost!'

Unfortunately, there was such a crush in the haberdashery department that she could not get served. They had both been waiting for ten minutes and were beginning to get annoyed, when an encounter with Madame Bourdelais and her three children took up their attention. Madame Bourdelais explained, with the calm manner of a pretty but practical woman, that she had wanted to show the shop to the children. Madeleine was ten,

Edmond eight, and Lucien four. They were laughing with delight; it was a cheap outing they had been promised for a long time.

'I'm going to buy a red parasol, they're such fun,' said Madame Marty suddenly, stamping with impatience at waiting there doing nothing.

She chose one at fourteen francs fifty. Madame Bourdelais, who watched the purchase with a look of disapproval, said to her in a friendly way:

'You shouldn't be in such a hurry. In a month's time you could have got it for ten francs . . . They won't catch me like that!'

And she explained the theory of good housekeeping she had developed. As the shops were lowering their prices, one only had to wait. She did not want to be exploited by them; it was she who took advantage of their real bargains. There was even a touch of malice in her battle with the shops; she boasted that she had never let them make a penny's profit.

'Well,' she ended by saying, 'I've promised to show my little ones some pictures, upstairs in the lounge . . . Come up with me, you've got plenty of time.'

At that the braid was forgotten; Madame Marty gave in at once, whereas Madame de Boves refused, preferring to walk round the ground floor first. In any case, the ladies hoped that they would meet again upstairs. Madame Bourdelais was looking for a staircase when she caught sight of one of the lifts; and she pushed the children into it, to make the outing complete. Madame Marty and Valentine also entered the narrow cage, in which people were squeezed tightly together; but the mirrors, the velvet seats, and the decorated brass door took up their attention to such an extent that they arrived on the first floor without even having felt the gentle gliding of the machine. In any case, another treat was awaiting them, as soon as they went into the lace gallery. As they passed the buffet, Madame Bourdelais did not neglect to gorge her little family on fruit cordial. The room was square, with a large marble counter; at either end silver-plated fountains flowed with a thin trickle of water; behind, on small shelves, rows of bottles were lined up. Three waiters were continually wiping and filling glasses. To control the thirsty customers it had been necessary to form a queue, as at theatre doors, by erecting a barrier covered with velvet. There was a tremendous crush. Some people, losing all shame before the free refreshments, were making themselves ill.

'Well! Where are they?' exclaimed Madame Bourdelais when she had extricated herself from the crowd, after wiping the children's faces with her handkerchief.

Then she caught sight of Madame Marty and Valentine at the end of another gallery, a long way off. They were both still buying, drowned beneath an overflow of petticoats. It was hopeless; mother and daughter disappeared, swept away by a fever of spending.

When she finally arrived in the reading- and writing-room, Madame Bourdelais installed Madeleine, Edmond, and Lucien at the large table; then she helped herself to some photograph albums from a bookcase and took them over to them. The dome of the long room was laden with gilding; at either end monumental fireplaces faced each other; mediocre pictures, very ornately framed, covered the walls; and, between the pillars, in front of each of the arched bays opening on to the shop, were tall green plants in majolica pots. A crowd of silent people surrounded the table, which was littered with magazines and newspapers, and furnished with stationery and ink-pots. Ladies were removing their gloves, and writing letters on paper stamped with the name of the shop, which they crossed out with a stroke of the pen. A few men, lolling back in the armchairs, were reading newspapers. But many people were simply doing nothing: husbands waiting for wives who were wandering freely through the departments, young ladies discreetly looking out for their lovers, elderly parents deposited there as if in a cloakroom, to be picked up again when it was time to leave. This crowd, comfortably seated, was resting, glancing through the open bays into the depths of the galleries and halls, from which the distant murmur could be heard above the scratching of pens and the rustling of newspapers.

'What! You're here!' said Madame Bourdelais. 'I didn't recognize you.'

Near the children, a lady was half hidden behind the pages of a magazine. It was Madame Guibal. She seemed annoyed by the encounter. But she recovered immediately, and said that she had come upstairs to sit down for a while in order to escape the crush. And when Madame Bourdelais asked her if she had come to make some purchases, she replied in her languid way, hiding behind her eyelids the ruthless egoism of her gaze:

'Oh, no! On the contrary, I've come to return something. Yes, some door-curtains I'm not satisfied with . . . but there are so many people that I'm waiting until I can get near the department.'

She carried on talking, saying how convenient the 'return' system was; previously, she never used to buy anything, whereas now she occasionally yielded to temptation. In fact, she returned four articles out of five, and was beginning to be known in all the departments for the strange dealings which were suspected to lie behind the constant dissatisfaction which made her bring articles back one by one, after having kept them for several days. While she was speaking, she did not take her eyes off the doors of the reading-room; and she seemed relieved when Madame Bourdelais rejoined her children so as to explain the photographs to them. Almost at the same moment Monsieur de Boves and Paul de Vallagnosc came in. The Count, who was pretending to show the young man round the new parts of the shop, exchanged a quick glance with her; then she buried herself in her magazine again, as if she had not noticed him.

'Hello, Paul!' exclaimed a voice from behind the gentlemen.

It was Mouret, who was walking round in order to keep an eye on the various departments. They shook hands, and he asked at once:

'Has Madame de Boves done us the honour of coming?'

'I'm afraid not,' the Count replied, 'and she's terribly sorry. She's not well . . . But it's nothing serious.'

Suddenly he pretended to catch sight of Madame Guibal. He made his escape and went up to her, holding his hat in his hand; the other two were content to greet her from a distance. She, too, pretended to be surprised. Paul had given a smile; he understood, at last, and he told Mouret in a low voice how he had met the Count in the Rue Richelieu and how the latter, having tried to shake him off, had in the end dragged him off to the Paradise under the pretext that one simply had to see it. For a year the lady had been extracting from the Count all the money and pleasure she could, never writing to him, but meeting him in public places, in churches, museums, or shops, to arrange further, private meetings.

'I think they meet in a different hotel room each time,' the young man murmured. 'Not long ago, when he was on a tour of inspection, he wrote to his wife every other day from Blois, Libourne, and Tarbes;* and yet I'm positive I saw him going into a family boarding-house near the Batignolles . . .* Just look at him! Isn't he handsome, standing there in front of her with all the decorum of a true official! That's the old France for you, my friend, the old France!'

'What about your marriage?' asked Mouret.

Without taking his eyes off the Count, Paul replied that they were still waiting for his aunt to die. Then, with a triumphant air, he said:

'There, did you see? He bent down, and slipped her an address. There, she's taking it, with her most virtuous expression: she's a terrible woman, that dainty redhead is, with her unconcerned air . . . Well, there are some fine goings-on in your shop!'

'Oh!' said Mouret smiling, 'these ladies aren't in my shop, they're at home here!'

He went on to joke about it. Love, like swallows, brought luck to houses. Of course he knew all about the tarts who had their beat along the counters, and the ladies who accidentally met a friend there; but if they did not buy anything, they at least swelled the numbers; they warmed up the shop. While he was talking, he led his old schoolfellow along and made him stand on the threshold of the room, facing the great central gallery, its successive halls stretching out below them. Behind them, the reading-room retained its atmosphere of meditation, disturbed only by the scratching of pens and the rustling of newspapers. An old gentleman had fallen asleep over the *Moniteur*. Monsieur de Boves was studying the pictures, with the obvious intention of losing his future son-in-law in the crowd. And, alone in the midst of the calm, Madame Bourdelais was amusing her children in a loud voice, as if in conquered territory.

'You see, they're at home here,' repeated Mouret with a grand gesture towards the crowds of women with which the departments were almost bursting.

Just then Madame Desforges, who had nearly lost her coat in the crowd, at last came in and walked through the first hall. When she reached the main gallery, she looked up. It was like the concourse of a station, surrounded by the balustrades of the two upper storeys, intersected by hanging staircases, and with suspension bridges built across it. The iron staircases, with double spirals, opened out in bold curves, multiplying the landings; the iron bridges, thrown across the void, ran straight along, very high up; and beneath the pale light from the windows all this metal formed a delicate piece of architecture, a complicated lacework through which the daylight passed, the modern realization of a dream-palace, of a Babel-like accumulation of storeys in which halls opened out, offering glimpses of other storeys and other halls without end. In fact, iron was dominant everywhere; the young architect had had the honesty and courage not to disguise it under a coating of whitewash imitating stone or wood. Down below, so as not to outshine the merchandise, the decoration was sober, with large sections in one colour, in a neutral tint; then, as the metal framework ascended, the capitals of the columns became richer, the rivets formed rosettes, the corbels and brackets were loaded with sculpture; finally, at the top, there was a brilliant burst of green and red paint, in the midst of a wealth of gold, cascades of gold, a whole crop of gold, right up to the windows, the panes of which were enamelled and inlaid in gold. Under the covered galleries, the exposed brickwork of the counter-arches was also enamelled in bright colours. Mosaics and ceramics formed part of the decorations, brightening up the friezes, lighting up with their fresh tones the austerity of the whole; while the staircases, their banisters covered with red velvet, were decorated with a strip of carved, polished iron, which shone like a piece of steel armour.

Although she had already visited the new building, Madame Desforges stopped, struck by the tempestuous life which, that day, was animating the immense nave. Downstairs, all round her, the eddy of the crowd continued endlessly, its dual stream of entry and exit making itself felt as far as the silk department; the crowd was still very mixed, though the afternoon was adding a greater number of ladies to the shopkeepers and housewives; there were many women in mourning, wearing long veils; and the inevitable contingent of wet-nurses, shielding their babies with their arms. This sea of multi-coloured hats, of bare heads, both fair and dark, was flowing from one end of the gallery to the other, looking blurred and faded against the stunning brilliance of the materials. Wherever she looked Madame Desforges could see nothing but large price tickets with huge figures on them, garish spots standing out against the bright prints, the glossy silks, and the sombre woollens. Heads were half cut off from sight by piles of ribbons; a wall of flannel stood out like a promontory; on all sides the mirrors made the departments recede further into the distance, reflecting the displays together with patches of the public—faces in reverse, bits of shoulders and arms—while to the left and right sides galleries opened up further vistas, the snowy drifts of household linen, the dappled depths of the hosiery—lost in the distance, illuminated by a ray of light from some bay window, and where the crowd had become nothing but specks of human dust. Then, when Madame Desforges looked up, she saw, along the staircases, on the suspension bridges, round the balustrades of each storey, an unbroken, murmuring stream of people ascending, a whole multitude of people in the air, travelling through the fretwork of the enormous metal frame, silhouetted in black against the diffused light of the enamelled windows. Great gilded chandeliers hung from the ceiling; an awning of rugs, embroidered silks, and materials worked with gold was hanging down, draping the balustrades with brilliant banners; from one end to the other there were flights of lace, quivering muslin, triumphal wreaths of silk, apotheoses of half-dressed dummies; and above all this confusion, at the very top, the bedding department, as if suspended in the air, displayed little iron bedsteads with their mattresses, hung with white curtains, like a dormitory of schoolgirls sleeping in the midst of the trampling customers, who became rarer as the departments rose higher.

'Does madam require some cheap garters?' said a salesman to Madame Desforges, seeing her standing there. 'All silk, one franc forty-five.'

She did not deign to reply. Around her the salesmen were yelping, becoming more and more animated. She wanted, however, to know where she was. Albert Lhomme's cash-desk was on her left; he knew her by sight and, completely unhurried in the midst of the stream of invoices with which he was besieged, he took the liberty of giving her a pleasant smile; behind him, Joseph was struggling with the string-box, unable to parcel up the articles fast enough. Then she realized where she was; the silk department must be ahead of her. But it took her ten minutes to get there, for the crowd was growing all the time. Above her the red balloons at the end of their invisible strings had become even more numerous; they were piling up into crimson clouds, moving gently towards the doors, continuing to pour out into Paris; and when they were held by very small children with the string wound tightly round their little hands, she had to bend her head down beneath the flight of balloons.

'What! It's very bold of you to come here, madam,' exclaimed Bouthemont gaily, as soon as he caught sight of Madame Desforges.

The manager of the silk department, who had been taken to her house by Mouret himself, now called on her occasionally for tea. She thought him common, but very pleasant, with a fine full-blooded temperament which she found surprising and amusing. What is more, two days earlier he had told her straight out about Mouret's affair with Clara, without thinking, with the stupidity of a crude lad who loves a good laugh; and, stung with jealousy, hiding her wounded feelings under an air of disdain, she had come to seek out this girl, for he had simply said it was a young lady from the ladieswear department, refusing to name her.

'Can we help you in any way?' he resumed.

'Of course, otherwise I wouldn't have come . . . Do you have any silk for a matinée jacket?'

She hoped to extract the name of the girl from him, for she had been seized with an urge to see her. He immediately summoned Favier; and he started to chat with her again while waiting for the salesman, who was just finishing serving a customer, the 'pretty lady' as it happened, that beautiful blonde woman whom the whole department occasionally talked about, without knowing anything about her life or even her name. This time the pretty lady was in deep mourning. Ah, whom had she lost, her husband or her father? Certainly not her father, or she would have looked sadder. So she was not a tart then, she had a real husband. Unless, of course, she was in mourning for her mother? For a few minutes, despite the pressure of work, the department exchanged these various conjectures.

'Hurry up! It's intolerable!' shouted Hutin to Favier, who was coming back from escorting his customer to the cash-desk. 'When that lady's here you take ages . . . As if she cared for you!'

'I bet she couldn't care as little for me as I care for her,' replied the irritated salesman.

But Hutin threatened to report him to the management if he did not show more respect for the customers. He had become insufferable, peevishly severe, ever since the department had banded together to get him Robineau's place. In fact, he was so unbearable, after all the promises of good comradeship with which he had previously curried favour with his colleagues, that they now secretly supported Favier against him.

'Now then, don't answer back,' Hutin went on severely. 'Monsieur Bouthemont's asking for some foulard, the palest designs.'

In the middle of the department an exhibition of summer silks was illuminating the hall with the brilliancy of dawn, like the rising of a star amidst the most delicate shades of daylight—pale pink, soft yellow, clear blue, a shimmering scarf of all the colours of the rainbow. There were foulards as fine as a cloud, surahs lighter than the down blown from trees, satiny Peking fabrics as soft as the skin of a Chinese virgin. And there were also pongees from Japan, tussores and corahs from India, not to mention light French silks—fine stripes, tiny checks, floral patterns, every design imaginable—which conjured up visions of ladies in fur-belows walking on May mornings beneath great trees in a park.

'I'll take this one, the Louis XIV design with the bouquets of roses,' said Madame Desforges at last.

While Favier was measuring it, she made a last attempt to get some information out of Bouthemont, who had remained near her.

'I'm going up to the ladieswear department to look at the travel coats . . . Is she fair, the girl you were telling me about?'

The section-manager, who was becoming alarmed by her insistence, merely smiled. But, just at that moment, Denise happened to pass by. She had just handed over to Liénard, in the merinos, Madame Boutarel, the provincial lady who came to Paris twice a year to throw away at the Paradise the money she scraped together out of her housekeeping. And as Favier had already taken Madame Desforges's foulard, Hutin, thinking to annoy him, stopped the girl as she went by.

'There's no need, this young lady will be very pleased to accompany madam.'

Denise, confused, naturally consented to take charge of the parcel and the invoice. She could not meet this young man face to face without feeling ashamed, as if he reminded her of some past indiscretion. Yet the sin had only been in her dreams.

'Tell me,' Madame Desforges asked Bouthemont in a very low voice, 'isn't this the girl who was so clumsy? He's taken her back then? So she must be the heroine of the adventure!'

'Perhaps,' replied the section-manager, still smiling and determined not to tell the truth.

Then, preceded by Denise, Madame Desforges slowly ascended the staircase. She had to stop every two or three seconds to avoid being carried away by the stream of people coming down. In the living vibration of the whole shop, the iron supports were perceptibly moving underfoot, as if trembling at the breath of the crowd. On each step, fixed to the floor, was a dummy displaying a motionless garment, a suit, or an overcoat, or a dressing-gown; they looked like a double row of soldiers lined up for some triumphal procession, and each one had a little wooden handle, like the handle of a dagger, stuck in the red flannel, which seemed to be bleeding where the neck had been severed.

Madame Desforges was at last reaching the first floor when a particularly violent surge of the crowd forced her to stop for a moment. The ground-floor departments, and the scattered crowd of customers she had just gone through, were now spread out below her. A fresh spectacle greeted her, an ocean of heads foreshortened, hiding the bodices beneath them, swarming with ant-like activity. The white price tickets had become nothing but thin lines, the piles of ribbon were crushed, the headland of flannel was a narrow wall cutting across the gallery; whilst the carpets and embroidered silks which decked the balustrades hung at her feet like processional banners attached to the rood-screen of a church. In the distance she could pick out the corners of the side-galleries, just as, from the eaves of a steeple, one can pick out the corners of neighbouring streets from the black spots of passers-by as they move about. But what surprised her most, exhausted as she was and her eyes blinded by the brilliant mixture of colours, was when she closed her eyelids: she found herself even more conscious of the crowd because of the muffled sound of a rising tide it was making, and the human warmth it gave off. A fine dust was rising from the floor, laden with the odour of Woman, the odour of her underlinen and the nape of her neck, of her skirts and her hair, a penetrating, all-pervading odour which seemed to be the incense of this temple dedicated to the worship of her body.

Mouret, still standing outside the reading-room with Vallagnosc, was breathing in this odour, intoxicating himself with it, repeating:

'They're at home. I know some women who pass the whole day here, eating cakes and writing their letters. It only remains for me to put them to bed.'

This joke made Paul smile; in the boredom born of his pessimism, he still considered the crowd utterly stupid to get so excited about a few new clothes. Every time he came to see his old school-friend he would go away almost annoyed, to see him so full of life in the midst of his following of coquettes. Wouldn't one of them, empty-headed and empty-hearted as they were, teach him the stupidity and uselessness of existence? On that particular day, Octave seemed to be losing his splendid poise; he who usually breathed fire into his customers with the calm grace of someone operating a machine, seemed to have been swept up in the wave of passion which was gradually consuming the shop. Since he had seen Denise and Madame Desforges coming up the main staircase, he had been talking more loudly, gesticulating in spite of himself; and, though he pretended not to turn his head round towards them, he was nevertheless becoming more and more animated as he felt them approaching. He was getting red in the face; his eyes had something of the bewildered rapture which flickered in the end in the eyes of the customers.

'You must be robbed of huge amounts,' murmured Vallagnosc, who thought the crowd had a criminal look about it.

Mouret threw his arms out. 'My dear chap, you can't imagine how much.'

And excitedly, delighted to have something to talk about, he gave him all sorts of details and related various cases, dividing the thieves into categories. First, there were the professional thieves; these women did the least harm, for the police knew almost all of them. Then came the kleptomaniacs, who stole from a perverse desire, a new kind of neurosis which had been scientifically classified by a mental specialist who saw it as a symptom of the acute temptation exercised by the big shops.* Finally, there were pregnant women, who specialized in stealing particular items: thus, for example, the police superintendent had discovered in the home of one of them two hundred and forty-eight pairs of pink gloves, stolen from every shop in Paris.

'So that's why the women here have such an odd look in their eye!' Vallagnosc murmured. 'I've been watching them, with their greedy, guilty looks, like mad creatures . . . A fine school for honesty!'

'I know!' Mouret replied. 'Although we make them at home here, we can't let them take away the merchandise under their coats . . . And very respectable people, too. Last week we had a chemist's sister and a judge's wife. We're trying to hush it up.'

He broke off in order to point out Jouve, who at that precise moment was shadowing a pregnant woman downstairs in the ribbon department. This woman, whose enormous belly was suffering a great deal from the pushing of the crowd, was accompanied by a woman friend whose business it was, no doubt, to defend her against the rougher knocks; each time she stopped in a department Jouve did not take his eyes off her, while her friend near her rummaged at leisure in the depths of the display boxes.

'Oh! He'll nab her,' Mouret went on. 'He knows all their tricks.'

But his voice trembled; his laugh was forced. Denise and Henriette, for whom he had been on the look-out all the time, were at last passing behind him, having had great difficulty in freeing themselves from the crowd. He turned round, and greeted his customer with the discreet greeting of a friend who does not want to compromise a woman by stopping her in the middle of a crowd of people. But she, on the alert, noticed immediately the glance with which he had first enveloped Denise. This girl must definitely be the rival whom she'd had the curiosity to come and see.

In the ladieswear department the salesgirls were losing their heads. Two girls were ill, and Madame Frédéric, the assistant buyer, had calmly given notice the day before, had gone to the pay-desk to have her account made up, and had dropped the Paradise from one minute to the next, just as the Paradise itself regularly dropped its employees. Since the morning, in the feverish activity of the sale, they had talked of nothing but this incident. Clara, kept on in the department because of Mouret's whim, thought it was wonderful; Marguerite was describing Bourdoncle's exasperation; while Madame Aurélie, who was very annoyed by it, declared that Madame Frédéric might at least have warned her, for no one could have imagined such deceit. Although Madame Frédéric had never confided in anyone, she was nevertheless suspected of having left the drapery business to marry the owner of some public baths not far from the Halles.

'Madam requires a travel coat?' Denise asked Madame Desforges, after offering her a chair.

'Yes,' the latter replied curtly, determined to be rude.

The department's new decorations were of an austere richness: tall cupboards of carved oak, mirrors filling the whole width of the wall-panels, a red carpet which deadened the continual footsteps of customers. While Denise was fetching the travel coats Madame Desforges, looking round her, caught sight of herself in a mirror; and she sat there contemplating herself. Was she growing old then, if he was unfaithful to her with the first girl who passed by? The mirror reflected the whole department, with its endless commotion; but she saw nothing but her own pale face, she did not hear Clara behind her telling Marguerite about one of Madame Frédéric's little mystifications, how she used to take a roundabout way, morning and evening, going through the Passage Choiseul, to create the impression that she lived, perhaps, on the Left Bank.

'Here are our latest models,' said Denise. 'We have them in several colours.'

She laid out four or five coats. Madame Desforges looked at them with an air of disdain; and, as each one was shown her, she became more difficult. Why all those gathers, which made the garment look skimpy? And this one, with square shoulders, looked as if it was cut out with an axe! It's all very well to travel, but one didn't want to look like a sentry-box.

'Show me something else, young lady.'

Denise unfolded the garments and folded them up again without allowing herself to show the slightest sign of irritation. And it was precisely her serene patience which made Madame Desforges more and more exasperated. She kept glancing at the mirror opposite her. Now that she could see herself in it next to Denise, she began to make comparisons. Was it possible for anyone to prefer this insignificant creature to her? She remembered now, this was the creature she had seen before, when she had first started work, and had seemed so hopeless and awkward, like a peasant girl who had just arrived from her village. Of course, nowadays, she did hold herself better, looking prim and proper in her silk dress. But how insignificant she was, how commonplace!

'I'll fetch some other model to show madam,' Denise said calmly.

When she came back the scene started all over again. This time it was the materials which were too heavy, and were no good at all. Madame Desforges kept turning round and raising her voice, trying to attract Madame Aurélie's attention in the hope that she would get the girl into trouble. But Denise, since her return, had little by little conquered the department; she felt at home there now, and the buyer even acknowledged that she had qualities rare in a salesgirl—stubborn gentleness and smiling conviction. And so Madame Aurélie gave a slight shrug of her shoulders, taking care not to interfere.

'If madam would be kind enough to point out the type of thing she requires . . .' Denise asked once more with her polite insistence, which nothing could discourage.

'But you haven't got a thing!' cried Madame Desforges.

She broke off, surprised to feel a hand on her shoulder. It was Madame Marty, who was being propelled through the shop by her attack of spending. Since buying the scarves, the embroidered gloves, and the red parasol, her purchases had swollen to such an extent that the last salesman had just decided to put her parcels down on a chair, for they were breaking his arms; and he walked in front of her, pulling behind him the chair, on which petticoats, table-napkins, curtains, a lamp and three door-mats were piled up.

'Hello there!' she said, 'are you buying a travel coat?'

'Oh! Good heavens, no,' replied Madame Desforges. 'They're awful!'

But Madame Marty had just noticed a striped coat which she rather liked. Her daughter Valentine was already examining it. So Denise, in order to get rid of the article, which was a model from the preceding year, called Marguerite; she, after a glance from her companion, described it as an exceptional bargain. When she had sworn that it had twice been reduced in price, that from a hundred and fifty francs it had been reduced to a hundred and thirty, and that it was now priced at a hundred and ten, Madame Marty was powerless to resist the temptation of such cheapness. She bought it, and the salesman who was accompanying her abandoned the chair and the whole bundle of invoices, which were still attached to the goods.

Meanwhile, behind the ladies' backs, in the midst of the jostlings of the sales, the gossip of the department about Madame Frédéric still went on.

'Really? Was she going with someone?' asked a little salesgirl who was new to the department.

'The man from the baths, of course!' replied Clara. 'You've got to watch those widows who seem so quiet.'

Then, while Marguerite was making out the bill for the coat, Madame Marty looked round; and, indicating Clara with a slight flutter of her eyelids, she said in a very low voice to Madame Desforges:

'You know, she's Monsieur Mouret's whim of the moment.'

The other, surprised, looked at Clara, then her eyes travelled back to Denise as she replied:

'Oh no, it isn't the tall girl, it's the little one!'

And, as Madame Marty did not dare to insist, Madame Desforges added in a louder voice, full of a lady's contempt for chambermaids:

'The small girl and the tall one as well, perhaps, all those who are willing!'

Denise had heard them. She looked up with her large, innocent eyes at the lady who was thus wounding her, and whom she did not know. No doubt it was the lady they had told her about, the friend whom her employer used to visit outside. In the look they exchanged Denise had such sad dignity, such candid innocence, that Henriette felt quite embarrassed.

'As you haven't got anything decent to show me,' she said sharply, 'would you please conduct me to the dresses and suits.'

'Oh!' said Madame Marty, 'I'll come with you . . . I wanted to look at a suit for Valentine.'

Marguerite took the chair by its back and dragged it along by its back legs, which were gradually getting worn out by its being carted about in this way. Denise had only to carry the few metres of foulard which Madame Desforges had bought. It was quite a journey, now that the suits and dresses were on the second floor, at the other end of the shop.

So the great trek through the crowded galleries began. Marguerite walked at the head of the procession, pulling the chair along like a little cart, slowly opening up a path for herself. As soon as she reached the lingerie department, Madame Desforges began to complain: they were ridiculous, these bazaars where you had to walk two miles to lay your hand on the slightest thing! Madame Marty, too, was saying that she was about to drop; and yet she was deriving great enjoyment from her tiredness, the slow exhaustion of her energies, in the midst of the inexhaustible display of merchandise. Mouret's genius held her completely in its grip. As she passed through each department she could not help stopping. She made a first halt at the trousseaux, tempted by some chemises which Pauline sold to her, whereupon Marguerite got rid of the chair, which Pauline had to take over. Madame Desforges could have carried on walking, and thus liberated Denise more quickly; but she seemed happy to feel the girl standing behind her, motionless and patient, while she too lingered, giving her friend advice. In the baby-linen department the ladies went into ecstasies, without buying anything. Then Madame Marty's weakness came over her again; she succumbed successively to a black satin corset, some fur cuffs which had been marked down because of the season, and some Russian lace which was often used at that time for trimming table-linen. All this was piling up on the chair; the parcels were mounting, making the wood creak; and the salesmen who succeeded each other harnessed themselves to it with increasing difficulty as the load became heavier.

'This way, madam,' Denise said without complaint after each halt.

'But it's absurd!' exclaimed Madame Desforges. 'We'll never get there. Why didn't they put the dresses and suits near the ladieswear department? What a mess!'

Madame Marty, whose eyes were dilating, intoxicated as she was by this parade of wondrous things dancing before her eyes, repeated under her breath:

'Oh, dear! What will my husband say? You're right, there's no system in this shop. You lose your way, and do all sorts of silly things.'

On the great central landing the chair could hardly get through. Mouret had cluttered up the landing with a great display of fancy goods—cups with gilded zinc mounts, workbaskets, and trashy liqueur cabinets—because he felt that people were able to move about there too easily, that there was no crush there. He had also authorized one of his salesmen to display there, on a small table, Chinese and Japanese curiosities, a few trinkets at low prices, which the customers were eagerly snatching up. It was an unexpected success, and he was already thinking of extending this type of trade. While two porters were carrying the chair up to the second floor, Madame Marty bought six ivory buttons, some silk mice, and an enamelled match-case.

On the second floor the journey started again. Denise, who had been showing customers round in this way since the morning, was ready to drop with exhaustion; but she continued to be correct, amiable, and polite. She had to wait for the ladies once again at the furnishing fabrics, where a ravishing cretonne had caught Madame Marty's eye. Then, in the furniture depart-

ment, it was a work-table that took her fancy. Her hands
were trembling, and she laughingly begged Madame Desforges
to prevent her from spending any more, when a meeting
with Madame Guibal gave her an excuse. It was in the carpet
department; Madame Guibal had at last come upstairs to
return a whole purchase of oriental door-curtains which she
had made five days earlier! She stood talking to the salesman,
a brawny young fellow with arms like a wrestler, who,
from morning till night, moved loads which were enough to
kill an ox. Naturally, he was full of consternation at this
'return', which robbed him of his percentage. Therefore he
was trying to make his customer feel embarrassed; he suspected
some shady goings-on. No doubt she had given a ball, and the
door-curtains had been taken from the Paradise, and now returned, to avoid hiring them from a carpet dealer; he knew that
this sort of thing was sometimes done by the thrifty middle
classes. Madam must have some reason for returning them; if it
was the designs or the colours which did not suit madam, he
would show her something else—there was an extremely wide
choice. To all these insinuations Madame Guibal replied calmly,
with regal assurance, that she did not like the door-curtains any
more, without deigning to give an explanation. She refused to
see any others, and he had to give in, for the salesmen had orders
to take back goods, even when they noticed that they had been
used.

As the three ladies were walking off together, and
Madame Marty, whose conscience was still troubling her,
was again coming back to the work-table she did not need
at all, Madame Guibal said to her in her calm voice:

'Well! You can return it . . . Didn't you just see? It's so
easy . . . Anyhow, let them send it to your house. You can put it
in your drawing-room, and look at it; then, when you're tired of
it, bring it back.'

'That's a good idea!' exclaimed Madame Marty. 'If my husband gets too angry, I'll return the whole lot.'

This was for her the supreme excuse; she no longer counted
the cost but went on buying with the secret desire of keeping
everything, for she was not the kind of woman who returns
things.

At last they arrived at the dresses and suits. But, as Denise was about to hand over to the salesgirls the foulard purchased by Madame Desforges, the latter seemed to change her mind, and declared that she would definitely take one of the travel coats, the light grey one; and Denise had to wait obligingly in order to take her back to the ladieswear department. She was quite aware that what lay behind the capricious behaviour of this imperious customer was a desire to treat her like a servant; but she had sworn to herself that she would stick to her job, and maintained her calm manner in spite of her pounding heart and her rebellious pride. Madame Desforges bought nothing in the dress and suit department.

'Oh, Mamma!' said Valentine, 'that little suit there, if it fits me . . .'

In a low voice Madame Guibal was explaining her tactics to Madame Marty. When she saw a dress she liked in a shop, she would have it sent to her; she would copy the pattern, and then return it. And Madame Marty bought the suit for her daughter, murmuring:

'That's a good idea! You're most practical, my dear!'

They had had to abandon the chair. It had simply been left in the furniture department, beside the work-table. The weight was becoming too much for it, and the back legs were threatening to break; and it was decided that all the purchases should be centralized at one cash-desk, and from there sent down to the dispatch service.

Then the ladies, still accompanied by Denise, wandered around. They revisited all the departments. They seemed to take up all the space on the staircases and in the galleries. Every moment a fresh encounter held them up. Thus, they bumped into Madame Bourdelais and her three children again, near the reading-room. The children were loaded with parcels; Madeleine had a dress for herself, Edmond was carrying a collection of small shoes, while the youngest, Lucien, was wearing a new peaked cap.

'You too!' said Madame Desforges laughingly to her old school-friend.

'Don't talk to me about it!' exclaimed Madame Bourdelais. 'I'm furious. They get at you through your children now! You know, it isn't as if I spend a lot on myself! But how can I say "no" to these little ones who want everything? I came to show them round, and now I'm plundering the whole shop!'

Mouret, who was still there with Vallagnosc and Monsieur de Boves, was listening to her with a smile. She caught sight of him and complained to him gaily, but with a certain amount of real irritation, about the traps laid for mothers; the idea that she had just succumbed to the fevers aroused by advertising made her indignant; and he, still smiling, bowed, enjoying his triumph. Monsieur de Boves had manœuvred so as to get nearer to Madame Guibal, whom he finally followed, trying for a second time to lose Vallagnosc; but the latter, tired of the crowd, hastened to rejoin the Count. Once more Denise had stopped to wait for the ladies. She was standing with her back to them, and Mouret was pretending not to see her. From that moment on Madame Desforges, with the delicate flair of a jealous woman, no longer had any doubts. While he was complimenting her and walking a few steps at her side, like a gallant host, she was deep in thought, asking herself how she might convict him of his treachery.

Meanwhile, Monsieur de Boves and Vallagnosc, who were walking ahead with Madame Guibal, were arriving at the lace department. It was a luxurious room near the ladieswear department, lined with show-cases whose carved oak drawers had folding flaps. Spirals of white lace twined around the pillars, which were covered with red velvet; from one end of the room to the other were threaded lengths of guipure lace; while on the counters there were avalanches of big cards round which were wound Valenciennes, Malines, and needle-point lace. At the far end of the room two ladies were sitting before a transparency of mauve silk on to which Deloche was throwing some Chantilly; and they looked on in silence, unable to make up their minds.

'I say!' said Vallagnosc, in great surprise, 'you said Madame de Boves wasn't well . . . But there she is, standing over there with Mademoiselle Blanche.'

The Count could not help giving a start, casting a sideways glance at Madame Guibal as he did so.

'Good heavens! So she is!' he said.

It was very warm. The customers, who were suffocating, were pale-faced and shiny-eyed. It seemed as if all the seductions of the shop had been leading up to this supreme temptation, that this was the hidden alcove where the customers were doomed to fall, the place of perdition where even the strongest succumbed. Hands were being plunged into the overflowing piles of lace, quivering with excitement from touching them.

'It looks as if these ladies are ruining you,' resumed Vallagnosc, amused by the encounter.

Monsieur de Boves made the gesture of a husband all the more sure of his wife's common sense because he did not give her a penny. The Countess, having tramped through all the departments with her daughter without buying anything, had just ended up in the lace department in a rage of unsatisfied desire. Totally exhausted, she was leaning up against a counter. She was rummaging in the heap of lace; her hands were growing limp, and her shoulders appeared hot with fever. Then suddenly, as her daughter turned her head away and the salesman was walking off, she tried to slip a piece of Alençon under her coat. But she gave a start and dropped it, on hearing Vallagnosc's voice saying gaily:

'We've caught you, madam!'

For several seconds she remained speechless and extremely pale. Then she explained that, as she was feeling much better, she'd wanted to get a breath of air. When she at last noticed that her husband was with Madame Guibal, she completely recovered herself, and looked at them in such a dignified way that Madame Guibal felt obliged to say:

'I was with Madame Desforges; these gentlemen ran into us.'

Just then the other ladies arrived. Mouret had accompanied them, and he detained them a moment longer in order to point out Jouve, who was still shadowing the pregnant woman and her friend. It was very odd; one couldn't imagine the number of thieves that were arrested in the lace department. Madame de Boves, who was listening to him, could see herself—forty-five years old, well off, her husband in an important position—with a policeman on either side of her; and yet she felt no remorse, she was only thinking that she should have slipped the lace up her sleeve. In the mean time, Jouve had just made up his mind to apprehend the pregnant woman, having given up hope of catching her red-handed, but suspecting her of having filled her pockets with such sleight of hand that it had escaped him. But

when he had taken her aside and searched her, to his embarrassment he found nothing, not even a scarf or a button. The friend
had disappeared. Suddenly he understood: the pregnant woman
was a blind; it was the friend who did the stealing.

The story amused the ladies. Mouret, a little annoyed, merely
said:

'Old Jouve's been had this time . . . But he'll have his
revenge.'

'Oh!' replied Vallagnosc, 'I don't think he's up to it . . . In any
case, why do you display so much merchandise? It serves you
right if you're robbed. You shouldn't tempt poor defenceless
women like that.'

This was the last word, and in the mounting fever of the shop
it struck the jarring note of the day. The ladies were separating,
going through the crowded departments for the last time. It was
four o'clock, and the rays of the setting sun were entering obliquely through the wide bays at the front of the shop, lighting
up from the side the glazed roofs of the halls; in this fiery
brightness, the thick dust, raised from the morning onwards by
the trampling of the crowd, was floating upwards, like a golden
vapour. A sheet of fire was running through the great central
gallery, making the staircases, the suspension bridges, and the
hanging iron lacework stand out against a background of flames.
The mosaics and the ceramics of the friezes were sparkling, the
greens and reds of the paintwork were lit up by the fires from the
gold so lavishly applied. It was as if the displays, the palaces of
gloves and ties, the clusters of ribbons and lace, the tall piles of
woollens and calicoes, the variegated flower-beds blossoming
with light silks and foulards, were now burning in live embers.
The mirrors were resplendent. The display of sunshades, curved
like shields, was throwing off metallic glints. In the distance,
beyond some long shadows, there were faraway, dazzling departments, teeming with a mob gilded by the sunshine.

In this final hour, in the midst of the overheated air, the
women reigned supreme. They had taken the shop by storm,
camping in it as in conquered territory, like an invading horde
which had settled among the devastation of the goods. The
salesmen, deafened and exhausted, had become their slaves,
whom they treated with sovereign tyranny. Fat women were

pushing their way through the crowd. Thinner ones were standing their ground, becoming quite aggressive. All of them, their heads held high and their gestures offhanded, were at home there; they showed no civility to each other, but were making use of the shop to such an extent that they were even carrying away the dust from the walls. Madame Bourdelais, wanting to get back some of the money she had spent, had once again taken her three children to the buffet; the customers were now hurling themselves at it in fits of greed, and even the mothers were gorging themselves on Malaga; since the opening eighty litres of fruit juice and seventy bottles of wine had been drunk. After having bought her travel coat Madame Desforges had been presented with some pictures at the cash-desk; and she went away wondering how she could get Denise into her house and humiliate her in front of Mouret himself, so that she could watch their faces and confirm her suspicions. Finally, just as Monsieur de Boves was successfully losing himself in the crowd and disappearing with Madame Guibal, Madame de Boves, followed by Blanche and Vallagnosc, had had the whim to ask for a red balloon, although she had not bought anything. It was always like that; she would not go home empty-handed, she would win the friendship of her caretaker's little girl with it. At the distribution counter they were starting on their fortieth thousand: forty thousand red balloons had taken flight in the hot air of the shop, a whole cloud of red balloons which were now floating from one end of Paris to the other, carrying up to heaven the name of the Ladies' Paradise!

Five o'clock struck. Of all the ladies, Madame Marty and her daughter were the only ones to remain, in the final paroxysms of the sale. She could not tear herself away, dead tired though she was; she was held there by an attraction so strong that she kept retracing her steps needlessly, wandering through the departments with insatiable curiosity. It was the hour during which the mob, already excited by the advertisements, got completely out of hand. The sixty thousand francs spent on announcements in the newspapers, the ten thousand posters on walls, and the two hundred thousand catalogues which had been sent out had emptied the women's purses and left their nerves suffering from the shock of their intoxication; they were still shaken by all Mouret's devices: the reduced prices, the system of 'returns', his constantly renewed attentions. Madame Marty was lingering by the auction tables, amid the hoarse cries of the salesmen, the clinking of gold from the cash-desks, and the rumble of parcels falling into the basements; once more she walked across the ground floor, through the household linen, the silk, the gloves, and the woollens. Then she went upstairs, again abandoning herself to the metallic vibration of the hanging staircases and suspension bridges, returning to the ladieswear, to the underwear, to the laces, even going as far as the second floor, to the heights of the bedding and furniture departments; and everywhere the salesmen, Hutin and Favier, Mignot and Liénard, Deloche, Pauline, and Denise, their legs nearly dropping off, were making a last effort, snatching victories out of the final fever of the customers. This fever had been gradually growing since the morning, like the intoxication exuded by the materials which were being handled. The crowd was ablaze under the fire of the five o'clock sun. By now Madame Marty had the animated, nervous face of a child that has drunk undiluted wine. She had come into the shop with her eyes clear and her skin fresh from the cold of the street and her sight and complexion had gradually become scorched by the spectacle of all that luxury, of those violent colours, the continual succession of which inflamed her passion. When she finally left, after saying that she would pay at home, terrified by the size of her bill, her features were drawn and she had the dilated eyes of a sick woman. She had to fight her way through the crowd at the door; people were killing each other for the bargains there. Then, outside on the pavement, when she had found her daughter, whom she had lost, the fresh air made her shiver, and she stood there frightened, unhinged by the neurosis caused by big shops.

That evening, as Denise was returning from dinner, a porter called out to her.

'You're wanted at the director's office, miss.'

She had forgotten the order Mouret had given her in the morning to go to his office after the sale. He was standing waiting for her. As she went in she did not push the door to, and it remained open.

'We're very pleased with you, Mademoiselle Baudu,' he said,

'and we thought we'd give you proof of our satisfaction . . . You know about the shameful way Madame Frédéric left us. From tomorrow you will take her place as assistant buyer.'

Denise listened to him in surprise, unable to move. She murmured in a shaking voice:

'But, sir, there are salesgirls who've been in the department much longer than I have.'

'What does that matter?' he went on. 'You're the most capable and the most reliable. It's very natural that I should choose you . . . Aren't you pleased?'

She blushed. She felt a delicious sensation of happiness and embarrassment in which her initial fear was dissolving. Why had she thought first of all of the assumptions with which this unhoped-for favour would be greeted? And she remained confused, in spite of her surge of gratitude. He was smiling and looking at her, in her simple silk dress, without a single piece of jewellery, with no other extravagance than her regal head of blonde hair. She had become more refined; her skin was fairer, her manner softer and more serious. The skinny insignificance she had had in the past was developing into a charm which was discreet, yet penetrating.

'You're very kind, sir,' she stammered. 'I don't know how to express . . .'

But she was cut short. Framed in the doorway stood Lhomme. With his sound hand he was holding a big leather wallet, and with his mutilated arm he was pressing an enormous portfolio to his chest; behind him, his son Albert was carrying a load of bags which were making his arms break.

'Five hundred and eighty-seven thousand, two hundred and ten francs thirty centimes!' exclaimed the cashier, whose flabby, worn face seemed lit up with a ray of sunshine, reflected by such a sum.

It was the takings for the day, the largest the Paradise had ever had. Far away, in the depths of the shop through which Lhomme had just slowly walked with the heavy gait of an overloaded ox, could be heard the uproar, the stir of surprise and joy which these giant takings left in their wake.

'It's magnificent!' said Mouret, delighted. 'My dear Lhomme, put it down there, and have a rest, for you look quite done in. I'll have the money taken to the counting-house . . . Yes, yes, put it all on my desk. I want to see it piled up.'

He was like a child in his happiness. The cashier and his son unloaded themselves. The wallet gave out the clear ring of gold, streams of silver and copper came from two of the bursting sacks, while corners of bank notes were sticking out from the portfolio. One end of the large desk was entirely covered; it was like the crumbling of a fortune which had taken ten hours to collect.

When Lhomme and Albert had retired, mopping their brows, Mouret remained motionless for a moment, lost in thought, his eyes on the money. Then he looked up and caught sight of Denise, who had stepped back. He began to smile again; he made her come forward, and ended by saying that he would give her as much as she could take in one handful; and behind his joke there was a kind of love-bargain.

'Take some from the wallet! I bet you can't take more than a thousand francs, your hand is so small!'

But she drew back again. So he was in love with her? Suddenly she understood; she felt the growing flame of desire with which he had been surrounding her ever since her return to the ladieswear department. What overwhelmed her even more was feeling her own heart beating as if it would burst. Why did he offend her with all that money, when she was brimming over with gratitude and he could have rendered her helpless with one friendly word? He was coming closer to her, still joking, when, to his great annoyance, Bourdoncle appeared under the pretext of giving him the entry figure, the enormous figure of seventy thousand customers who had visited the Paradise that day. She quickly took her leave, after thanking him once again.

CHAPTER 10

On the first Sunday in August stock-taking took place, and it had to be finished by the evening. All the employees were at their posts early in the morning as if it was a weekday, and the task had begun behind closed doors, in the shop now empty of customers.

Denise had not come down at eight o'clock, with the other salesgirls. She had been confined to her room since the preceding Thursday with a sprained ankle, which she had acquired when going up to the work-rooms; she was now much better, but, as Madame Aurélie was pampering her, she was not hurrying, and sat putting her shoe on with difficulty, resolved to put in an appearance in the department all the same. The girls' rooms were now on the fifth floor of the new buildings, along the Rue Monsigny; there were sixty of them on either side of a corridor, and they were more comfortable, though still furnished with the iron bedstead, large wardrobe, and little walnut dressing-table. As the girls' situation improved, so their personal habits became cleaner and more refined; they developed a taste for expensive soap and dainty underwear, and there was a natural upward movement towards the middle class; but coarse words and banging doors could still be heard as they dashed in and out morning and evening, as if in a cheap hotel. In any case Denise, being assistant buyer, had one of the biggest rooms, with two dormer windows overlooking the street. Now that she was better off she allowed herself little luxuries—a red eiderdown covered with lace, a small carpet in front of the wardrobe, two blue glass vases on the dressing-table in which some roses were wilting.

When she got her shoes on she tried to walk round the room. She had to hold on to the furniture, for she was still lame. But she would soon improve. All the same, she had been right to decline uncle Baudu's invitation to dinner that evening, and to ask her aunt to take out Pépé, whom she had again sent to lodge with Madame Gras. Jean, who had come to see her the day before, was also dining with his uncle. She was still gingerly trying to walk, having resolved that she would go to bed early so as to rest her leg, when Madame Cabin, the housekeeper, knocked on the door and, with an air of mystery, gave her a letter.

When the door was closed again Denise, astonished by the woman's discreet smile, opened the letter. She dropped on to a chair; the letter was from Mouret, and in it he said he was happy to hear that she was better, and invited her to come down that evening to dine with him, as she could not go out. The tone of the note, at once familiar and paternal, was in no way offensive; but it was impossible for her to mistake its meaning; the Paradise was well aware of the true significance of these invitations, which had become legendary. Clara had dined with him, others too, all the girls who had caught their employer's eye. After the dinner, so wags among the salesmen used to say, came the dessert. And the girl's pale cheeks were gradually flooded with colour.

The letter slipped on to her lap and, her heart pounding, Denise remained with her eyes fixed on the blinding light from one of the windows. In this very room, during hours of insomnia, she had been forced to make a confession to herself: if she still trembled when he passed, she knew now that it was not from fear; and her uneasiness in the past, her former dread, could have been nothing but her frightened ignorance of love, the confusion caused by feelings which were beginning to dawn in her childish shyness. She did not reason with herself; she simply felt that she had always loved him, ever since the first moment when she had stood trembling and stammering before him. She had loved him when she had feared him as a pitiless master, she had loved him when her bewildered heart, giving way to a need for affection, had unconsciously dreamed of Hutin. Perhaps she might have given herself to another, but never had she loved anyone but this man, whose mere glance terrified her. Her past experiences were coming back, unfolding before her in the light from the window—the hardships she had suffered at the beginning, the walk which had been so pleasant beneath the shady trees in the Tuileries, and lastly his desire, which had been brushing against her ever since her return to the shop. The letter slipped on to the floor; Denise still gazed at the window, dazzled by the glare of the sun.

Suddenly there was a knock on the door, and she hastened to pick up the letter and hide it in her pocket. It was Pauline who, having found a pretext to escape from her department, had come to have a chat with her.

'Are you better, my dear? We never see each other these days.'

But as it was forbidden to go upstairs to their rooms and, above all, for two girls to shut themselves up there together, Denise took her to the end of the corridor where there was a common-room—a present from Mouret to the girls, who could chat or work there until eleven o'clock. The room, decorated in white and gold, had the commonplace bareness of a hotel room, and was furnished with a piano, a pedestal table in the centre, and armchairs and sofas protected with white covers. However, after a few evenings spent together there in the first flush of its novelty, the salesgirls could no longer meet there without immediately starting to quarrel with each other. They had yet to be educated to it; the little phalansterian city lacked harmony. Meanwhile there was hardly anyone there in the evening but the assistant buyer from the corset department, Miss Powell, who would strum Chopin discordantly on the piano and whose envied talent succeeded in putting the others to flight.

'You see, my foot's better,' said Denise. 'I was coming down.'

'Good heavens!' exclaimed Pauline. 'What enthusiasm! I'd stay and take it easy if I had an excuse!'

They were both sitting on a sofa. Pauline's attitude had changed since her friend had become assistant buyer in the ladieswear department. Mingled with her good-natured heartiness there was now a shade of respect, of surprise that the salesgirl who had been such a skinny little thing in the past was now on the road to success. However, Denise was very fond of her and, of the two hundred women now employed in the shop who were endlessly rushing about in it, she confided only in her.

'What's the matter?' Pauline asked sharply, when she noticed Denise's agitation.

'Oh, nothing,' she assured her, with an embarrassed smile.

'Oh yes, there is something the matter . . . Don't you trust me now, if you won't tell me your troubles any more?'

At that Denise, her breast heaving with emotion and unable to regain her composure, gave way. She held out the letter to her friend, stammering:

'Look! He's just written to me!'

When they were together they had never spoken openly of Mouret. But their very silence was like a confession of their secret preoccupations. Pauline knew everything. After having read the letter she clasped Denise to her, and putting her arm round her waist murmured gently:

'My dear, if you want me to be frank, I thought it had happened already . . . Don't be shocked, I assure you the whole shop must think the same as me. After all, he promoted you to assistant buyer so quickly, and then he's always after you, it's so obvious!'

She gave her a big kiss on the cheek, and then asked her:

'You'll go tonight, of course?'

Denise looked at her without replying. Then suddenly she burst into sobs, her head resting on her friend's shoulder. Pauline was taken by surprise.

'Come on, calm down. There's nothing in all this to upset you like that.'

'No, no, leave me alone,' stammered Denise. 'If you knew how upset I am! Since I got that letter I haven't known what to do with myself . . . Let me cry, it makes me feel better.'

Feeling sorry for her, though not understanding, Pauline tried to console her. First of all, he was no longer seeing Clara. They did say that he visited a lady outside the shop, but that was not proved. Then she explained that one couldn't be jealous of a man in his position. He had too much money; he was the master, after all.

Denise listened to her; and if she had not been aware of her love before, she could no longer have any doubts about it after the pain she felt in her heart at the name of Clara and the allusion to Madame Desforges. She could hear Clara's disagreeable voice, she could see Madame Desforges once more as, with the contempt of a rich woman, she had made her follow her round the shop.

'So you'd go, would you?' she asked.

Without a moment's hesitation, Pauline exclaimed:

'Of course, how could one do otherwise?'

Then she reflected, and added:

'Not now, but in the past, because now I'm going to marry Baugé, and it wouldn't be right.'

Indeed Baugé, who had recently left the Bon Marché for the Ladies' Paradise, was going to marry her towards the middle of the month. Bourdoncle did not care much for married couples; however, they had obtained permission, and they even hoped to have a fortnight's leave.

'You see,' declared Denise, 'when a man loves you, he marries you . . . Baugé's marrying you.'

Pauline laughed heartily.

'But, my dear, it's not the same thing. Baugé's marrying me because he's Baugé. He's my equal, it's quite straightforward . . . Whereas Monsieur Mouret! D'you think Monsieur Mouret could marry one of his salesgirls?'

'Oh no! Oh no!' cried Denise, shocked by the absurdity of the question. 'And that's why he shouldn't have written to me.'

This reasoning completed Pauline's astonishment. Her broad face, with her small, gentle eyes, was assuming a look of motherly commiseration. Then she stood up, opened the piano, and gently played 'Le Roi Dagobert'* with one finger, no doubt in order to brighten up the situation. Sounds from the streets, the distant chant of a man selling green peas, were drifting up to the bare common-room, which the white chair-covers seemed to make even emptier. Denise was leaning back on a sofa, her head against the woodwork, shaken by a fresh bout of sobs, which she stifled in her handkerchief.

'Again!' resumed Pauline, turning round. 'You really aren't being reasonable . . . Why did you bring me in here? We'd have done better to stay in your room.'

She knelt down in front of her, and began lecturing to her again. How many girls would have liked to be in her place! Besides, if the idea did not appeal to her, it was very simple: she only had to say no, without taking it to heart so much. But she ought to think it over before risking her job with a refusal which would be quite inexplicable, considering that she had no other commitments. Was it really so terrible? And the lecture was ending with some gaily whispered jokes, when the sound of footsteps came from the corridor.

Pauline ran to the door and peeped out.

'Shh! It's Madame Aurélie!' she murmured. 'I'm off . . . And you, wipe your eyes. You don't want her to know.'

When Denise was alone she stood up and forced back her tears; and, her hands still trembling for fear of being caught like that, she closed the piano which her friend had left open. But she heard Madame Aurélie knock at the door of her room, and left the common-room.

'What's this! You're up!' exclaimed the buyer. 'That's very silly of you, my dear child; I was just coming up to see how you were, and to tell you we don't need you downstairs.'

Denise assured her that she was better, and that it would do her good to do some work, for it would take her mind off things.

'I won't get too tired, madam. If you give me a chair to sit on, I'll do the accounts.'

They both went downstairs. Madame Aurélie, full of attentions, insisted that she should lean on her shoulder. She must have noticed that her eyes were red, for she was studying her surreptitiously. No doubt there was little she did not know.

Denise had won an unexpected victory: she had at last conquered the department. After having struggled in the past for nearly ten months, subjected to the tortures of a drudge, without exhausting the ill will of her fellow workers, she had now overcome them in just a few weeks, and found them docile and respectful towards her. Madame Aurélie's sudden affection had been of great assistance to her in the ungrateful task of softening their hearts; it was whispered that the buyer would oblige Mouret by rendering him certain services of a delicate nature; and she had taken Denise under her wing with such enthusiasm that the girl must, indeed, have been specially commended to her. But Denise, too, had used all the charm she had in order to disarm her enemies. The task was all the more difficult because she had to make them forget her appointment as assistant buyer. The girls complained vociferously about what they saw as an injustice, accusing her of having won the job over dessert with the governor; they even added various salacious details. Yet, in spite of their hostility, the title of assistant buyer had an effect on them, and Denise came to assume an authority which astonished and pacified even the most rebellious among them. Soon she found flatterers among the newcomers, and her gentleness and modesty completed the conquest. Marguerite came over to her side. Only Clara carried on being hostile, and would still venture to use the insulting reference to her 'unkempt' appearance, which no longer amused anyone. She had taken advantage of Mouret's brief infatuation with her to avoid work, for she had a lazy, gossipy nature; and although he had tired of her very quickly, she had not even made any recriminations, for her amorous life was so confused that she was incapable of jealousy, and was content merely to have obtained the advantage of having her idleness tolerated. However, she considered that Denise had robbed her of Madame Frédéric's job. She would never have accepted it because of the stress it involved; but she was annoyed by this lack of courtesy, for she had the same claim to it as Denise, and a prior claim too.

'Look! Here comes the young mother!' she murmured when she saw Madame Aurélie leading Denise in on her arm.

Marguerite shrugged her shoulders, saying:

'If you think that's funny . . .'

Nine o'clock was striking. Outside, a blazing blue sky was warming the streets; cabs were travelling along towards the stations; the whole population, dressed in its Sunday best, was streaming out towards the woods and suburbs. Inside the shop, which was flooded with sunshine from the big open bay windows, the staff, completely shut in, had just begun the stock-taking. The door knobs had been removed, and people on the pavement were stopping to look through the windows, surprised to see the shop closed when there was such extraordinary activity going on inside. From one end of the galleries to the other, from the top floor to the basement, there was an endless scurrying of employees, their arms in the air, parcels flying above their heads; and all this was taking place in a storm of shouting, figures being called out, confusion growing and exploding in a tremendous din. Each of the thirty-nine departments was carrying out its task on its own, without taking any notice of the adjacent departments. In any case, they had hardly started to tackle the shelves; there were so far only a few lengths of material on the ground. The machine would have to get up more steam if they were to finish that evening.

'Why did you come down?' Marguerite went on kindly, speaking to Denise. 'You'll only make your foot worse, and there are enough of us to do the work.'

'That's what I told her,' declared Madame Aurélie. 'But she insisted on coming down to help us.'

Work was interrupted as all the girls flocked round Denise. They complimented her, listening with exclamations to the story of her sprained ankle. In the end Madame Aurélie made her sit down at a table; it was agreed that she would merely enter the goods as they were called out. In any case, on the stock-taking Sunday, every employee who was capable of holding a pen was commandeered: the shopwalkers, the cashiers, the bookkeepers, even the porters; the various departments shared these one-day assistants between them, in order to get the job done as quickly as possible. Thus, Denise found herself installed near Lhomme the cashier and Joseph the porter, who were both bent over large sheets of paper.

'Five coats, cloth, fur trimming, size three, at two hundred and forty!' Marguerite was shouting. 'Four ditto, size one, at two hundred and twenty!'

The work began again. Behind Marguerite three salesgirls were emptying the cupboards, sorting the goods, giving them to her in bundles; and, when she had called them out, she threw them on to the tables, where they gradually piled up in enormous heaps. Lhomme wrote down the articles, while Joseph compiled another list as a cross-check. In the mean time Madame Aurélie herself, helped by three other salesgirls, counted the silk garments, which Denise entered on a sheet of paper. Clara was charged with looking after the heaps, with arranging them and piling them up so that they took up as little room as possible. But her mind was not on her job, and some piles were already falling down.

'I say,' she asked a little salesgirl who had joined the shop that winter, 'are they going to give you a rise? Did you know that they're going to give the assistant buyer two thousand francs, which means that, with the commission, she'll be earning almost seven thousand.'

The little salesgirl, while continuing to pass some cloaks down, replied that if they did not put her salary up to eight hundred francs she would leave. The rises were always given on the day after the stock-taking; it was also the time of the year when, the turnover for the year being known, the heads of departments received their commission on the increase in this figure compared with the preceding year. Therefore, in spite of the uproar and bustle of the job in hand, impassioned gossip went on everywhere. Between calling out two articles they talked of nothing but money. There was a rumour that Madame Aurélie would get over twenty-five thousand francs; such a huge sum made the girls very excited. Marguerite, the best salesgirl after Denise, had made four thousand five hundred francs, of which fifteen hundred was her salary, and about three thousand her percentage; whereas Clara had not made two thousand five hundred altogether.

'I couldn't care about those rises of theirs!' Clara went on, still talking to the little salesgirl. 'If Papa was dead, I'd drop the lot of them! But what gets my goat is to see that skinny little thing earning seven thousand francs. Don't you agree?'

Madame Aurélie sharply interrupted the conversation. Turning round majestically, she said:

'Be quiet, young ladies! Upon my word, we can't hear ourselves speak!'

Then she started shouting again:

'Seven cloaks, old style, Sicilian silk, size one, a hundred and twenty! Three pelisses, surah, size two, a hundred and fifty! Have you got that down, Mademoiselle Baudu?'

'Yes, ma'am.'

Clara was forced to turn her attention to the armfuls of clothes piled up on the tables. She pushed them together to make more room. But she soon left them again to reply to a salesman who was looking for her. It was the glover, Mignot, who had escaped from his department. He whispered a request for twenty francs; he already owed her thirty, which he had borrowed the day after the races, after losing his week's salary on a horse; this time he had already squandered the commission he had been paid the day before, and had not got fifty centimes left for his Sunday. Clara had only ten francs on her, which she lent him with fairly good grace. Then they chatted, talking of how a party of six of them had gone to a restaurant in Bougival, and how the women had paid their share: it was better like that, everyone felt at ease. Then Mignot, wanting his twenty francs, went and bent down to Lhomme's ear. The latter, who suddenly stopped writing, seemed greatly troubled. However, he did not dare refuse, and was looking for a ten-franc piece in his purse when Madame Aurélie, surprised at no longer hearing the voice of Marguerite, who had had to break off, noticed Mignot and understood at once. She brusquely sent him back to his department, for she did not want people coming to distract her girls! The truth of the matter was that the young man made her very nervous, for he was a great friend of her son Albert, and his accomplice in the shady pranks which she was terrified would get him one day. Therefore, when Mignot had taken the ten francs and made off, she could not help saying to her husband:

'Really! How could you let yourself be taken advantage of like that!'

'But, my dear, I really couldn't refuse the lad . . .'

She shut him up with a shrug of her great shoulders. Then, as the salesgirls were slyly grinning at this family argument, she carried on severely:

'Come on, Mademoiselle Vadon, don't let's fall asleep!'

'Twenty overcoats, double cashmere, size four, eighteen francs fifty!' Marguerite cried out in her sing-song voice.

Lhomme, his head bowed, had resumed writing. Little by little his salary had been raised to nine thousand francs; but he remained humble towards Madame Aurélie, who earned nearly three times as much as that for the family.

For a little while the work went ahead. Figures flew about, parcels of clothes rained thick and fast on to the table. But Clara had thought of another amusement: she was teasing Joseph the porter about the crush he was supposed to have on a young lady who worked in the sample department. This girl, already twenty-eight years old, thin and pale, was a protégée of Madame Desforges, who had tried to make Mouret take her on as a salesgirl by telling him a touching story: she was an orphan, the last of the Fontenailles, an old aristocratic family from Poitou.* She had been dragged to Paris by a drunken father, and had remained virtuous in spite of her misfortune; but her education had unfortunately been too rudimentary for her to become a teacher or to give piano lessons. Usually Mouret became quite angry when people recommended poor society girls to him; there was no one, he would say, more inefficient, more unbearable,

more insincere than a creature like that; and in any case you
could not suddenly become a salesgirl, you had to serve an
apprenticeship, it was a complex and difficult profession. However, he took Madame Desforges's protégée, but put her in the
sample department, just as he had obliged some friends by
finding jobs for two countesses and a baroness in the publicity
department, where they folded envelopes and wrappers.
Mademoiselle de Fontenailles earned three francs a day, which
just enabled her to live in a little room in the Rue d'Argenteuil.
Joseph, who had a soft heart under his dour soldier's manner,
had been touched on seeing her so sad-looking and poorly
dressed. He did not admit it, but he would blush when the girls
from the ladieswear department teased him; the sample department was in a nearby room, and they had often noticed him
hanging about outside the door.

'Joseph's easily distracted,' Clara murmured. 'His head keeps
turning towards the lingerie.'

Mademoiselle de Fontenailles had been conscripted to help
with the stock-taking at the trousseau counter. As the lad was, in
fact, continually casting glances at the counter, the salesgirls
began to laugh. He became very confused and buried his nose in
his papers; while Marguerite, in order to smother the flood of
mirth which was tickling her throat, began to shout even louder:

'Fourteen jackets, English cloth, size two, fifteen francs.'

For once the voice of Madame Aurélie, who was in the process
of calling out the cloaks, was drowned. With an offended air and
majestic deliberation she said:

'A little quieter, Mademoiselle Vadon. We're not at the
market . . . And you're all very silly to amuse yourselves in this
childish way when our time is so precious.'

Just then, as Clara was no longer watching the piles of clothes,
a catastrophe occurred. Some coats tumbled down and all the
other piles on the tables were pulled after them and fell down one
after another. The carpet was littered with them.

'There, what did I say!' cried the buyer, beside herself.
'Do take a little care, Mademoiselle Prunaire; this is becoming
intolerable!'

But a tremor had suddenly run round the room: Mouret and
Bourdoncle had just appeared, making their tour of inspection.

Voices started calling out again, pens scratched, while Clara hastened to pick up the clothes. The director did not interrupt the work. He stood there for a few minutes, silent and smiling; his face was happy and triumphant, as it always was on stock-taking days, and his lips alone betrayed a nervous quiver. When he caught sight of Denise he almost made a gesture of astonishment. So she had come down? His eyes met Madame Aurélie's. Then, after a short hesitation, he walked away and went into the trousseau department.

Meanwhile Denise, distracted by the slight murmur, had raised her head. Having recognized Mouret, she had simply bent over her papers again. A feeling of calm had stolen over her since she had begun writing in this mechanical way to the rhythmic sound of the articles being called out. She always gave way to her sensitive nature's initial flood of feeling like that: tears would choke her, uncontrollable emotion doubled her suffering; then she would come to her senses again, and she would regain her splendid, calm courage, and her gentle but inexorable strength of will. Now, her eyes clear and her face pale, she was totally calm, absorbed in her work, resolved to ignore her heart and follow only her head.

Ten o'clock struck, and in the frenetic activity of the departments the din of the stock-taking grew even louder. And, despite the endless shouting on all sides, the same news was circulating with surprising rapidity: every salesman knew already that Mouret had written that morning to invite Denise to dinner. It was Pauline who had broken the news. As she had gone downstairs again, still shaken, she had met Deloche in the lace department; and, without noticing that Liénard was talking to the young man, she had got the news off her chest.

'It's happened, you know . . . She's just got the letter. He's invited her for this evening.'

Deloche had turned very pale. He had understood, for he often questioned Pauline, and they both talked every day about their common friend, about Mouret's soft spot for her, about the famous invitation which would bring the whole thing to a head. And she would scold him for secretly loving Denise, for it would never result in anything, and would shrug her shoulders when he expressed his approval of the girl's resistance to the governor.

'Her foot's better; she's coming down,' she continued. 'Don't make such a long face . . . This invitation is a piece of good luck for her.'

And she hurried back to her department.

'Ah! I see,' murmured Liénard, who had overheard. 'It's about the young lady with the sprained ankle . . . Well! You were right to be in a hurry to defend her in the café last night!'

And he, too, disappeared; but by the time he got back to the woollens he had already told the story of the letter to four or five salesmen. In less than ten minutes it was all round the shop.

Liénard's last remark referred to a scene which had taken place the day before at the Café Saint-Roch. These days he and Deloche were never apart. Deloche had taken Hutin's room at the Hôtel de Smyrne when the latter, promoted to assistant buyer, had moved into a little three-roomed flat; and the two shop assistants came to the Paradise together in the morning and waited for each other in the evening in order to go home together. Their rooms, which were adjacent, looked out over the same dark courtyard—a narrow hole, the smells from which poisoned the hotel. They got on well together, despite their different characters—the one squandering without a qualm the money he drew from his father, the other penniless, obsessed by ideas of economy—they did, however, have one thing in common: their lack of skill as salesmen, which left them both vegetating at their counters, without increases in salary. After work they spent most of their time at the Café Saint-Roch. Empty during the day, at about half-past eight this café would fill up with a great crowd of shop assistants, the crowd let out into the street through the big doorway in the Place Gaillon. From then on, there was a deafening noise of dominoes, laughter, and shrill voices, bursting out in the midst of the thick pipe smoke. Beer and coffee flowed. Seated in the left-hand corner Liénard would ask for the most expensive drinks, while Deloche made do with a glass of beer which he took four hours to consume. It was here that he had heard Favier, at a neighbouring table, saying abominable things about Denise, how she had 'caught' the governor by pulling up her skirts every time she went up a staircase in front of him. He had had to control himself in order not to hit him. Then, as Favier had continued, saying that the girl went downstairs every night to meet her lover, Deloche, beside himself with rage, had called him a liar.

'What a swine! He's lying, he's lying, d'you hear?'

And in his agitation he let out confessions in a stammering voice, pouring out his heart.

'I know her, I know it isn't true . . . She's never been fond of any man except one: yes, Monsieur Hutin, and as he didn't notice it he can't even boast of having touched her with his little finger.'

An account of this quarrel, exaggerated and distorted, was already amusing the whole shop, when the story of Mouret's letter went the rounds. It so happened that Liénard confided the news first of all to a silk salesman. In the silk department stock-taking was in full spate. Favier and two assistants, perched on stools, were emptying the shelves, passing the lengths of material to Hutin who, standing in the middle of a table, was calling out the figures after looking at the labels; then he would throw the lengths of material on to the floor, where they gradually piled up, rising like a spring tide. Other employees were writing; Albert Lhomme was helping them, his face blotchy from having spent the whole night in a low dance-hall at La Chapelle. A flood of sunshine was falling from the glazed roof of the hall, through which could be seen the blazing blue of the sky.

'Draw those blinds!' shouted Bouthemont, who was very busy supervising the job. 'That sun's unbearable!'

Favier, who was stretching up to reach a piece of material, grumbled under his breath:

'How can they shut people up on such a superb day! There's no danger of it raining on a stock-taking day! And they keep us under lock and key like galley-slaves while the whole of Paris is out walking!'

He passed the material to Hutin. The measurement was written on the label, and each time a piece was sold the quantity was deducted from it, which made the work much simpler. The assistant buyer shouted:

'Fancy silk, small checks, twenty-one metres, six francs fifty!'

And the silk was added to the pile on the floor. Then he resumed a conversation he had already begun by saying to Favier:

'So he wanted to fight you?'

'Yes! I was quietly drinking my beer . . . There was no point in his saying that I was lying! She's just had a letter from the governor inviting her to dinner . . . The whole shop is talking about it.'

'What! I thought it had happened ages ago!'

Favier handed him another piece of material.

'I know, I was absolutely sure. It looked as if they'd been together for ages.'

'Ditto, twenty-five metres!' shouted Hutin.

The dull thud of the material could be heard as he added in a lower voice:

'You know what a loose life she led in that old fool Bourras's house.'

Now the whole department was laughing about it without, however, interrupting the work. They were murmuring the girl's name to themselves; backs were heaving with amusement, and there was a licking of lips at this juicy bit of gossip. Even Bouthemont, who took great delight in any sort of vulgarity, could not refrain from letting out a joke, the bad taste of which filled him with pleasure. Albert, who had woken up, swore that he had seen Denise between two soldiers at the Gros-Caillou.*
At that moment Mignot was coming downstairs with the twenty francs he had just borrowed; he stopped, slipped ten francs into Albert's hand, and arranged where they should meet that evening: the spree they had been planning, which had been held up for lack of money, was possible after all, in spite of the smallness of the sum. 'Handsome' Mignot, when he learned of the letter, made such a crude remark that Bouthemont felt obliged to intervene:

'That's enough now, gentlemen. It's not our business . . . Come along now, Monsieur Hutin.'

'Fancy silk, small check, thirty-two metres, six francs fifty!' the latter shouted.

Pens were moving again, parcels were falling regularly, and the tide of materials was still rising, as if the waters of a river had been poured into it. The names of the fancy silks were called out ceaselessly. Favier remarked under his breath that the stock was going to be really impressive: the management would be so pleased—that idiot Bouthemont might be the best buyer in Paris, but as a salesman he was totally inept! Hutin smiled in delight, approving with a friendly glance; for, although he himself had introduced Bouthemont into the Ladies' Paradise in order to get Robineau out, he was now undermining him in his turn with the firm intention of taking his place. It was the same type of warfare as before—treacherous insinuations slipped into the ears of the directors, excessive zeal in order to push himself forward, a whole campaign waged with suave cunning. Meanwhile Favier, towards whom Hutin was now showing renewed condescension, was furtively watching him, with a bilious expression, as if he had worked out how many mouthfuls the stocky little man would be, looking as if he was waiting until his comrade had devoured Bouthemont in order to devour him in his turn. He hoped to have the job of assistant buyer if Hutin were to become head of the department. Then they would see. Both of them, consumed by the fever which was raging from one end of the shop to the other, were talking of the probable increases in salary, without ceasing to call out the stock of fancy silks as they did so: they expected Bouthemont to get his thirty thousand francs that year; Favier estimated his salary and percentage at five thousand five hundred. Each season that the turnover of the department increased, the salesmen in it rose in rank and doubled their pay, like officers during a campaign.

'Now then, haven't you finished those light silks yet?' said Bouthemont suddenly, with an irritated air. 'What a dreadful spring it's been, nothing but rain! People haven't bought anything but black silks!'

His fat, jovial face darkened; he was watching the pile on the ground spreading, while Hutin was repeating even louder than before, in a ringing, almost triumphant voice:

'Fancy silk, small check, twenty-eight metres, six francs fifty!'

There was still another shelf-full. Favier, his arms aching, had slowed down. As he handed the last lengths of material to Hutin he resumed in a low voice:

'Oh, I was forgetting . . . Did you know that the assistant buyer from the ladieswear department used to be really keen on you?'

The young man seemed very surprised.

'What! How so?'

'Yes, that fool Deloche told us the secret . . . I remember how she used to make eyes at you.'

Since he had become assistant buyer Hutin had dropped music-hall singers and gone in for schoolteachers. In reality very flattered, he replied with an air of scorn:

'I like them better upholstered, my dear fellow, and then I don't go out with just anyone, as the governor does.'

He broke off and shouted:

'White poult, thirty-five metres, eight francs seventy-five!'

'Ah! At last!' murmured Bouthemont, relieved.

But a bell rang, for the second meal service to which Favier always went. He got down from the stool and another salesman took his place; he had to step over the huge pile of material on the floor, which had grown even bigger. Similar piles were littered about in all the departments; the shelves, boxes, and cupboards were being gradually emptied, while the goods were overflowing on every side, under foot, between the tables, in a continual rising movement. In the linen department could be heard the dull sound of piles of calico falling on to the floor; in the haberdashery there was a light clattering of boxes; and distant rumblings were coming from the furniture department. All sorts of voices could be heard at the same time, shrill voices and thick voices; figures were whistling through the air; the immense nave was resounding with a rattling roar, the roar of forests in January, when the wind whistles in the branches.

Favier got clear at last and went upstairs to the dining-room. Since the extensions had been made to the Ladies' Paradise, the refectories had been moved to the fourth floor of the new buildings. As he was hurrying along he caught up with Deloche and Liénard, who had gone up ahead of him, so he fell back to walk with Mignot, who was following him.

'Damn!' he said in the kitchen corridor, staring at the blackboard on which the menu was inscribed. 'You can see it's stock-taking. What a treat! Chicken or rehashed mutton, and artichokes with salad oil! Their mutton won't be very popular!'

Mignot sniggered, murmuring:

'Everybody's mad about chicken, then?'

Meanwhile Deloche and Liénard had taken their helpings and moved on. Then Favier, leaning through the hatch, said in a loud voice:

'Chicken.'

But he had to wait; one of the waiters who was carving had just cut his finger, and this was causing some confusion. Favier remained in front of the hatch, looking into the kitchen. It had giant appliances—a central range on which two rails fixed to the ceiling carried, by means of a system of pulleys and chains, the colossal cooking-pots, which four men could not have lifted. Several cooks, standing out in their white aprons against the dark red of the cast iron, mounted on iron ladders and armed with skimmers on the end of long sticks, were supervising the hot-pot for the evening. Against the wall were grills big enough to roast martyrs on, saucepans in which a whole sheep could be cooked, a monumental plate-warmer, and a marble basin filled with a continual trickle of water. To the left could be seen a scullery with stone sinks that seemed like swimming-pools; while on the other side, to the right, there was a larder where red meat could be seen hanging on steel hooks. A potato-peeling machine was working away, tick-tocking like a mill. Two little carts, full of washed salad, were passing, pulled along by some kitchen-helps who were going to put them in the cool, under a fountain.

'Chicken,' repeated Favier, getting impatient.

Then, turning round, he added softly:

'One of them's cut himself . . . It's disgusting, it's running on to the food!'

Mignot wanted to see. A whole queue of shop assistants had formed and was getting longer; there was a lot of laughing and pushing. The two young men, their heads in the hatch, were exchanging remarks about this phalansterian kitchen, in which even the smallest utensils, even the skewers and larding-needles, seemed gigantic. Two thousand lunches and two thousand dinners had to be served there, and the number of employees was increasing every week. It was a great chasm which, each day, swallowed up sixteen hectolitres of potatoes, a hundred and twenty pounds of butter, and six hundred kilos of meat; and at each meal three casks had to be tapped; almost seven hundred litres of wine flowed over the counter of the bar.

'Ah! At last!' muttered Favier, when the cook on duty re-appeared with a pan from which he speared a leg for him.

'Chicken,' said Mignot behind him.

Holding their plates, they both went into the dining-room, having taken their wine at the bar; while behind them the word 'chicken' was called out endlessly, and the cook's fork made a rapid, rhythmic little sound as he picked up each piece.

The shop assistants' dining-room was now an immense hall in which five hundred could be accommodated with ease for each of the three meal services. The places were laid on long mahogany tables arranged in parallel lines across the room; at either end of the hall similar tables were set apart for shopwalkers and heads of departments; and in the middle there was a counter where extra dishes were served. Large windows on the right and left illumi-nated this great gallery with a white light; the ceiling, in spite of being almost fourteen feet high, seemed low, crushed by the enormous development of the other dimensions. On the walls, painted a pale yellow, shelves for the table-napkins were the sole ornaments. Beyond this first dining-room came that of the porters and coachmen, where the meals were served irregularly, when their work permitted.

'What! You've got a leg as well, Mignot!' said Favier, as he took his place at one of the tables opposite his companion.

Other shop assistants sat down around them. There was no table-cloth; the plates made a cracked sound on the bare ma-hogany, and everyone was complaining noisily in this corner of the room.

'These birds are all legs!' remarked Mignot.

Those who had bits of carcass were annoyed. However, the food had greatly improved since the new alterations. Mouret no longer dealt with a contractor for a fixed sum; he now ran the kitchen himself, and had made it an organized service like one of his departments, with a cook, under-cooks, and an inspector; and if he spent more as a result, he got more work out of his better-fed staff—a calculation based on practical humanitarianism which had for a long time dismayed Bourdoncle.

'Mine's pretty tender all the same,' Mignot resumed. 'Pass the bread!'

The big loaf was going round, and after cutting himself a slice he stuck the knife back into the crust. Some latecomers hurried in one after another; ferocious appetites, sharpened by the morning's work, were raging all down the long tables, from one end of the dining-room to the other. There was a growing clatter of forks, the sound of bottles being emptied, the clink of glasses being put down too hard, the grinding sound of five hundred powerful jaws energetically munching. Words, which were rare, were stifled in mouths full of food.

Meanwhile Deloche, seated between Baugé and Liénard, found himself nearly opposite Favier, only a few places away. Each had cast a spiteful glance at the other. Their neighbours, who knew about their quarrel of the day before, were whispering. They had laughed at Deloche's bad luck; he was always starving and, as if by some cruel fatality, always chanced on the worst bits at the table. This time he had arrived with a chicken neck and some bits of carcass. Without saying a word he let them carry on joking, swallowing great mouthfuls of bread and picking at the neck with the infinite skill of a lad who held meat in respect.

'Why don't you complain?' Baugé said to him.

But he shrugged his shoulders. What was the point? It never worked. When he did complain, it got even worse.

'You know, the cotton-reelers have got their own club now,' remarked Mignot suddenly. 'Yes, really, the Reel Club . . . They meet in a wine-merchant's place in the Rue Saint-Honoré; they hire a room there on Saturdays.'

He was talking of the haberdashery salesmen. At that, the whole table began to joke. Between two mouthfuls, their voices clogged with food, each one made some remark, added a detail; it was only the most determined readers who remained silent, absorbed, their noses buried in their newspapers. Everyone was agreed: every year shop assistants were bettering themselves. About half of them could now speak German or English. It was no longer smart to go and live it up at Bullier,* to do the rounds of the music-halls in order to whistle derisively at the ugly singers. No, about twenty of them would get together now and found a club.

'Have they got a piano like the linen dealers?' asked Liénard.

'Has the Reel Club got a piano? I should jolly well think so!' exclaimed Mignot. 'And they play on it, and they sing! There's even one of them, that little fellow Bavoux, who recites poetry.'

Their mirth was redoubled, and they made fun of Bavoux; however, beneath their laughter there was great respect. They talked about a play at the Vaudeville, in which a draper's assistant played an unpleasant part; several of them expressed their annoyance at this, while others were worrying about when they would be able to get away that evening, for they had been invited to parties given by bourgeois families. From every corner of the immense hall similar conversations were going on, in the midst of the growing clatter of crockery. In order to get rid of the smell of food and the hot steam which was rising from the five hundred plates, they had opened the windows, and the lowered blinds were burning hot in the fierce August sun. Blasts of hot air were coming from the street, and golden reflections were making the ceiling yellow, bathing the sweating men in a reddish light as they ate.

'How can they shut people up on a Sunday like this!' Favier repeated.

This remark brought them back to the subject of the stock-taking. It was a superb year. And they went on to talk about salaries, rises, the eternal subject, the great questions which always stirred them. It was always the same on the days when they had chicken, wild excitement would break out; the noise would finally become unbearable. When the waiters brought the artichokes they could no longer hear themselves speak. The inspector on duty had orders to be tolerant.

'By the way,' Favier exclaimed. 'Have you heard the news?'

But his voice was drowned. Mignot was asking:

'Who doesn't like artichokes? I'll swop my dessert for an artichoke.'

No one replied. Everyone liked artichokes. This lunch would go down as a good one, for they had seen that there were peaches for dessert.

'He's invited her to dinner, old man,' Favier was saying to his right-hand neighbour, concluding the story. 'What! You didn't know?'

The whole table knew, and they were tired of talking about it all morning. The same old jokes passed from mouth to mouth. Deloche was trembling; in the end he fixed his eye on Favier, who was insistently repeating:

'If he hasn't had her, he will do . . . and he won't be the first to have her. Oh no, he won't be the first!'

He, too, was looking at Deloche. He added provocatively:

'Those who like them bony can have her for five francs.'

Suddenly, he ducked his head. Deloche, yielding to an irresistible urge, had just thrown his last glass of wine into Favier's face, stammering:

'Take that! You dirty liar, I should have done it yesterday!'

This caused quite a scene. Favier's neighbours had been spattered with a few drops, while he only had his hair slightly wet; the wine, thrown too hard, had fallen on the other side of the table. But the others were annoyed. She must be his mistress, if he defended her like that! What a ruffian! He deserved a good hiding to teach him some manners. They lowered their voices, however, for they spotted an inspector approaching, and there was no point in involving the management in the quarrel. Favier was content to say:

'If he'd got me you'd really have seen something!'

It ended in jeers. When Deloche, still trembling, wanted to have a drink to hide his embarrassment and mechanically seized his empty glass, there was a burst of laughter. He put his glass down again awkwardly, and began sucking the artichoke leaves which he had already eaten.

'Pass the carafe to Deloche,' said Mignot calmly, 'he's thirsty.'

The laughter increased. The young men were taking clean plates from the piles which were standing at intervals on the table: the waiters were taking round the dessert, baskets full of peaches. And they all clutched their sides with laughter when Mignot added:

'Everyone to his own taste. Deloche has wine with his peaches.'

The latter remained motionless. His head bowed, as if deaf, he seemed not to hear the jokes; he was feeling hopeless regret for what he had just done. They were right, what business was it of his to defend her? Now they would say all sorts of terrible things; he could have kicked himself for having compromised her like that, when he had wanted to prove her innocent. It was his usual luck; it would have been better if he had died on the spot, for he could not even give way to the instincts of his heart without doing something stupid. Tears came to his eyes. Wasn't it his fault, too, that the shop was talking about the letter the governor had written? He could hear them all sniggering and making crude comments about the invitation, which had been confided only to Liénard, and he blamed himself: he should not have allowed Pauline to mention it in front of a third person; he held himself responsible for the indiscretion which had been committed.

'Why did you tell everyone about it?' he murmured finally, in a sorrowful voice. 'That was very bad.'

'Me!' replied Liénard. 'But I only told one or two people, and told them to keep it secret . . . You never know how things get out.'

When Deloche finally drank a glass of water, the whole table burst out laughing again. The meal was finishing, and they were lolling back in their chairs, waiting for the bell, shouting to each other with a lack of restraint brought on by the meal. Few extras had been asked for at the big central counter, especially as it was the shop which was paying for the coffee. Cups were steaming, perspiring faces were shining under the haze of fumes floating like clouds of blue cigarette smoke. In the windows the blinds were hanging down motionless, without flapping at all. One of them rolled up again, and the sunshine flooded across the hall, lighting up the ceiling. The hubbub of voices was beating against the walls with such force that at first the sound of the bell was heard only by those sitting at the tables near the door. They got up, and the stampede as they left filled the corridors for a long time.

Deloche, however, lagged behind to escape the malicious jokes which were still being made. Even Baugé went out ahead of him; and Baugé was usually the last to leave the dining-room, for he would go a roundabout way and meet Pauline as she was going into the women's dining-hall: they had agreed on this scheme as the only way they could see each other for a minute during working hours. But this time, just as they were kissing each other full on the lips in a corner of the corridor, they were surprised by Denise, who was also going up to lunch. She was walking with difficulty, because of her foot.

'Oh, my dear!' stammered Pauline, very red, 'you won't say anything, will you?'

Baugé, with his huge limbs and giant build, was trembling like a little boy. He murmured:

'You know, they'd very probably throw us out . . . Our marriage may have been announced, but those monsters don't allow you to kiss!'

Denise, quite upset, pretended that she had not seen them. And Baugé was making his escape when Deloche, who was going the longest way round, appeared in his turn. He tried to apologize, stammering out phrases which Denise did not at first understand. Then, as he was reproaching Pauline for having spoken in front of Liénard, and as Pauline became embarrassed, Denise finally understood the words people had been whispering behind her back all morning. So it was the story of the letter which was going round! Once more the shiver which this letter had given her ran down her spine; she felt she was being undressed by all those men.

'I didn't know,' Pauline was repeating. 'In any case, there's nothing bad about it . . . Let them talk, they're all jealous, of course!'

'My dear,' said Denise in the end, in her sensible way. 'I'm not cross with you at all . . . You've only said the truth. I've received a letter, and it's up to me to answer it.'

Deloche went away heart-broken, for he had understood that Denise was accepting the situation and would keep the appointment that evening. When the two salesgirls had lunched, in a small dining-room next to the big one, where the women were served more comfortably, Pauline had to help Denise downstairs, as her foot was getting tired.

Downstairs, in the bustle of the afternoon, the stock-taking was proceeding more vigorously than ever. The time had come for the supreme effort, when, faced with the lack of progress made in the morning, everything was done to finish by the evening. The voices became even louder; nothing could be seen but waving arms, still emptying shelves, throwing down the merchandise; and it was no longer possible to walk about, for the rising tide of bales and piles of goods on the floor was now as high as the counters. A sea of heads, brandished fists, and flying limbs seemed to extend to the further reaches of the departments, like the distant confusion of a riot. It was the final fever, the machine at breaking point; while in front of the plate-glass windows all round the closed shop there were still occasional passers-by, pale with the stifling boredom of Sunday. On the pavement in the Rue Neuve-Saint-Augustin, three tall, bare-headed girls with a sluttish look about them had taken their stand, their faces brazenly pressed against the windows, trying to make out what sort of mess was being cooked up inside.

When Denise returned to the ladieswear department Madame Aurélie left Marguerite to finish calling out the garments. The checking still had to be done and, requiring quiet in which to do it, she retired into the pattern-room, taking Denise with her.

'Come with me, we'll compare the two lists . . . Then you can add up the totals.'

But, as she wanted to leave the door open in order to keep an eye on the girls, the din came in and they could hardly hear each other, even at the far end of the room. It was a vast, square room, furnished only with chairs and three long tables. In one corner stood great mechanical cutters for making the patterns. Whole lengths of material went through them; in one year more than sixty thousand francs' worth of material was sent out, cut up into strips. From morning to night the cutters sliced up silk, wool, and linen with the sound of a scythe. Then the pattern-books had to be put together, either glued or sewn. And there was also, between the two windows, a little printing-press for the labels.

'Not so loud, please!' cried Madame Aurélie from time to time, unable to hear Denise reading out the articles.

When the checking of the first lists was finished, she left the girl seated at one of the tables, absorbed in her adding up. Then she reappeared almost immediately and installed Mademoiselle de Fontenailles there, for the trousseau department no longer needed her and had handed her over. It would save time if she helped with the adding up. But the appearance of the Marchioness, as Clara mischievously called her, had stirred up the department. They were laughing, and teasing Joseph; ferocious words were coming through the door.

'Don't move, you're not in my way at all,' said Denise, seized with pity. 'Here, my inkstand will do, we can both use it.'

Mademoiselle de Fontenailles, stupefied by her downfall, could not even find a word of gratitude. She looked as if she drank; her thin body had a livid hue, and only her hands, white and slender, still bore witness to her distinguished ancestry.

The laughter suddenly stopped, and they could hear the work resuming its regular hum. It was Mouret, once again making a tour of the departments. He stopped and looked for Denise, surprised at not seeing her. He made a sign to Madame Aurélie; and they both moved to one side, and talked in low voices for a moment. He must have been questioning her. With a glance she indicated the pattern-room; then appeared to be giving him a report. No doubt she was relating that the girl had been crying that morning.

'Splendid!' Mouret said out loud, drawing nearer. 'Show me the lists.'

'This way, sir,' the buyer replied. 'We ran away from the noise.'

He followed her into the neighbouring room. Clara was not taken in by this manœuvre: she murmured that they might as well go and fetch a bed straight away. But Marguerite was throwing the garments to her more quickly in order to keep her busy and stop her talking. Wasn't the assistant buyer a good sort? Her affairs did not concern anyone else. The department was becoming an accomplice; the salesgirls were becoming more and more excited; the backs of Lhomme and Joseph were swelling out, as if becoming soundproof. And Jouve, having noticed Madame Aurélie's tactics from afar, came to walk up and down outside the door of the sample room, with the regular step of a sentry on guard, awaiting his superior's convenience.

'Give Monsieur Mouret the lists,' said the buyer as she went in.

Denise gave them to him, then remained looking up at him. She had given a slight start, but had controlled herself, and she remained splendidly composed, her cheeks pale. For a moment Mouret appeared to be absorbed in the list of articles, without glancing at the girl. Silence reigned. Then Madame Aurélie went up to Mademoiselle de Fontenailles, who had not even looked round, and, seemingly dissatisfied with her adding-up, she said to her in a low voice:

'Go and help with the parcels . . . You're not used to figures.'

Mademoiselle de Fontenailles stood up, and went back to the department, where she was greeted by a lot of whispering. Joseph, under the mocking eyes of the girls, was writing all crooked. Clara, delighted to have an assistant, was very rough with her all the same because of the hatred she felt for all women in the shop. How idiotic it was, when one was a marchioness, to yield to the love of an ordinary working man! And she envied her that love.

'Very good, very good!' Mouret was repeating, still pretending to read.

Madame Aurélie, meanwhile, did not know how to withdraw decently in her turn. She walked up and down, and went to look at the mechanical cutters, furious that her husband had not invented a pretext for calling her; but he was never any good for serious things, he would have died of thirst beside a pond. It was Marguerite, finally, who had the wit to come and ask her about something.

'I'll come and see,' replied the buyer.

And, her dignity safeguarded now that she had an excuse in the eyes of the girls who were watching her, she left Mouret and Denise alone, walking out of the room with a majestic air, her profile so lofty that the salesgirls did not even dare to smile.

Mouret had slowly replaced the lists on the table. He stood looking at the girl, who remained seated, pen in hand. She did not look away; she had only become paler.

'You'll come tonight?' he asked in a low voice.

'No, sir,' she replied. 'I can't. My brothers are going to be at my uncle's, and I've promised to dine with them.'

'But what about your foot? You still can't walk properly!'

'Oh! I can easily get as far as that; I've been feeling much better since this morning!'

Faced with this calm refusal, he had become pale in his turn. His lips betrayed a nervous quiver. Nevertheless, he controlled himself, and with the air of a kindly employer simply taking an interest in one of his salesgirls, he resumed:

'Come now, if I invite you . . . You know how highly I think of you.'

Denise maintained her respectful attitude.

'I'm very touched by your kindness to me, sir, and I thank you for the invitation. But I must repeat that it's impossible, my brothers are expecting me this evening.'

She was obstinately refusing to understand. The door had remained open, and she could feel the whole shop urging her on. Pauline had, in a friendly way, called her a silly ass, and the others would laugh at her if she refused the invitation. Madame Aurélie, who had left the room, Marguerite, whose raised voice she could hear, Lhomme, whose motionless and discreet back she could see—they all desired her fall, they were all throwing her at their employer. And the distant hum of the stock-taking, the millions of goods being called out on all sides, being turned over in armfuls, was like a hot wind carrying the breath of passion towards her.

There was a silence. At times the noise drowned Mouret's words, accompanying them with the formidable din of a king's fortune won in battle.

'Well, when will you come?' he asked again. 'Tomorrow?'

This simple question upset Denise. For a moment she lost her composure and stammered:

'I don't know . . . I can't . . .'

He smiled; he tried to take her hand, which she drew back.

'What are you afraid of?'

But she quickly raised her head, looked him straight in the face, and said, smiling in her gentle, honest way:

'I'm not afraid of anything, sir . . . One only does as one wants, doesn't one? I just don't want to, that's all!'

As she stopped speaking she was surprised to hear a creak. She turned round and saw the door slowly closing. Jouve had taken it upon himself to close it. Doors formed part of his duties; none were supposed to remain open. Then he returned gravely to his sentry post. No one seemed to notice the door being closed in this simple way. Only Clara let out a crude word in the ear of Mademoiselle de Fontenailles, who remained pale and expressionless.

Meanwhile, Denise had stood up. Mouret was saying to her in a low and trembling voice:

'Listen, I love you . . . You've known it for a long time; don't play the cruel game with me of pretending not to know . . . And don't be afraid of anything. I've wanted to call you into my office scores of times. We'd have been alone, I'd only have had to bolt the door. But I didn't want to; you can see how I'm talking to you, anyone can come in here . . . I love you, Denise.'

She stood there, her face white, still looking him straight in the face.

'Tell me, why do you refuse? Don't you have any needs? Your brothers are a heavy responsibility. Anything you ask, anything you require . . .'

With a word, she cut him short:

'Thank you, I'm now earning more than I need.'

'But it's freedom I'm offering you, a life of pleasure and luxury . . . I'll set you up with a home of your own; I'll make sure that you're well off.'

'No, thank you, I'd be bored doing nothing . . . I was earning my own living before I was ten years old.'

He made a frantic gesture. She was the first one not to yield. He had only to stoop to get the others; they all waited on his whim like obedient servants; but she was saying no, without even giving him a reasonable excuse. His desire, controlled for so long, exacerbated by her resistance, was becoming stronger than ever. Perhaps he was not offering her enough? He doubled his offers, becoming more and more insistent.

'No, no, thank you,' she replied each time, without weakening.

Then a cry from the heart escaped him:

'Can't you see that I'm suffering? Yes, it's stupid, I'm suffering like a child!'

Tears came to his eyes. A fresh silence reigned. Behind the closed door the muffled hum of the stock-taking could still be heard. It was like a dying sound of triumph, a discreet accompaniment to the master's defeat.

'But if I wanted . . .' he said in a passionate voice, seizing her hands.

She let him hold them; her eyes grew dim, all her strength was ebbing away. She felt the warmth of the man's hot hands, filling her with a delicious sense of weakness. Goodness! How she loved him, and what delight if she had flung her arms round his neck and leaned on his breast!

'I want you to come, I want you to come,' he was repeating, beside himself. 'I'll expect you tonight, or I'll take steps . . .'

He was becoming brutal. She uttered a faint cry, and the pain she felt at her wrists restored her courage. With a jerk, she freed herself. Then, standing erect and seeming taller because of her defencelessness, she said:

'No, let me go . . . I'm not a Clara, to be dropped the next day. Besides, you love someone else, yes, that lady who comes here . . . Stay with her. I don't share people's affections.'

He was struck dumb with surprise. What was she saying and what did she want, then? Never had the girls he picked up in the departments worried themselves about being loved. He should have laughed about it, but this attitude of gentle pride completed the confusion in his heart.

'Please open the door, sir,' she went on. 'It's not proper that we should be together like this.'

Mouret obeyed and, his temples throbbing, not knowing how to hide his anguish, he called Madame Aurélie back again, and lost his temper about the stock of cloaks, saying that the prices would have to be lowered, and continue to be lowered until the last one was sold. It was the rule of the shop, they got rid of everything each year; they sold goods at a sixty per cent loss rather than keep an old model or shop-soiled material. As it happened Bourdoncle, looking for the director, had been waiting for him; he had been stopped outside the closed door by Jouve, who had whispered a few words in his ear with a serious air. He was growing impatient without, however, having the courage to interrupt the tête-à-tête. Was it possible? On such a day too, and with that puny creature! When the door finally opened, Bourdoncle spoke of the fancy silks, of which the left-over stock was going to be enormous. It was a relief for Mouret to be able to shout as much as he liked. What was Bouthemont thinking of ?

He went off, declaring that he would not tolerate that a buyer should be so lacking in flair that he committed the folly of stocking more goods than sales allowed.

'What's the matter with him?' murmured Madame Aurélie, very upset by his reproaches.

The girls looked at each other in surprise. At six o'clock the stock-taking was finished. The sun was still shining, a pale summer sun, the golden reflection of which was coming through the hall windows. In the heavy air of the streets tired families were already coming back from the suburbs, loaded with bunches of flowers and dragging their children along. One by one, the departments had fallen silent. Nothing could be heard in the galleries but the belated shouts of a few salesmen emptying a last shelf. Then these voices too became silent, and all that remained of the day's hubbub was a mighty chill which hung over the huge piles of merchandise. The shelves, cupboards, boxes, and cases were empty: not a metre of material, not a single object had remained in its place. The huge shop now displayed nothing but its empty framework, its wooden counters and shelves completely bare, as on the day they had been installed. This bareness was the visible proof of the complete and accurate returns of the stock-taking. And on the ground was piled up sixteen million francs' worth of goods, a rising sea which had, in the end, submerged the tables and counters. The salesmen, plunged in it up to their shoulders, were beginning to put each article back. It was hoped that they would finish by ten o'clock.

When Madame Aurélie, who went to the first dinner service, came back from the dining-room, she announced the turnover figure for the year, a figure which had just been worked out by adding up those of the various departments. The total was eighty million, ten million more than the preceding year. The only actual loss was on the fancy silks.

'If Monsieur Mouret isn't satisfied, I don't know what he wants,' added the buyer. 'Look! He's over there, at the top of the main staircase, looking furious.'

The girls went to look. He was standing alone, scowling down at the millions scattered at his feet.

'Would you be good enough to let me go to my room, ma'am?' Denise came to ask at that moment. 'I'm no longer any use because of my leg, and as I've got to dine at my uncle's with my brothers . . .'

They were astonished. She had not succumbed, then? Madame Aurélie hesitated, and seemed on the verge of forbidding her to go out, her voice curt and displeased; while Clara, quite incredulous, shrugged her shoulders: it was probably quite simple, he didn't want her any more! When Pauline learned of this ending to the story, she was standing with Deloche in the babywear department. The young man's sudden joy made her furious: a lot of good it did him, didn't it? He was pleased, was he, that his friend was silly enough to turn her back on making a fortune? Bourdoncle, who did not dare to go and disturb Mouret in his terrible isolation, was walking about amid the noise, feeling downcast himself, and full of misgivings.

Meanwhile, Denise went downstairs. As she arrived at the bottom of the small left-hand staircase, leaning on the banisters, she came upon a group of sniggering salesmen. Her name was pronounced, and she felt that they were still talking about her encounter with Mouret. They had not seen her.

'Not at all—it's all put on!' Favier was saying. 'She's utterly vicious . . . Yes, I know someone she wanted to take by force.'

And he kept looking at Hutin who, in order to preserve his dignity as assistant buyer, was standing a few paces away, without taking part in the jokes. But he was so flattered by the envious way in which the others were looking at him that he deigned to murmur:

'She really was a nuisance, that girl!'

Denise, cut to the quick, clung to the banisters. They must have seen her, for they all scattered amid laughter. He was right; she blamed herself for her ignorance in the past, when she used to dream about him. But how cowardly he was, and how she despised him now! She was deeply disturbed: it was strange that a moment ago she had found the strength to repulse a man whom she adored, whereas in the past she had felt such weakness in the presence of that wretched boy, whose love she had only dreamed about! Her reason and her courage were foundering in these contradictions of her nature, which she could not fully understand.

She hurried through the hall. Then, as a commissionaire was opening the door which had been closed since the morning, instinct made her raise her head, and she caught sight of Mouret. He was still at the top of the staircase, on the big central landing overlooking the gallery. But he had forgotten the stock-taking; he did not see his empire, the shop bursting with riches. Everything had disappeared—the resounding victories of yesterday, the colossal fortune of tomorrow. With a look of despair he was watching Denise, and when she had gone through the door there was nothing left, and the shop was plunged into darkness.

CHAPTER 11

THAT day Bouthemont was the first to arrive at Madame Desforges's house at four o'clock for tea. She was still alone, in her large Louis XVI drawing-room, the brass and brocades of which shone with a bright gaiety; when he entered she stood up with an air of impatience:

'Well?'

'Well!' replied the young man, 'when I told him that I'd certainly call on you, he promised me he'd come.'

'And you gave him to understand that I'm expecting the Baron today?'

'Of course . . . That's what seemed to make him decide to come.'

They were referring to Mouret. The year before, he had suddenly taken such a liking to Bouthemont that he had allowed him to share his private pleasures; and he had even introduced him into Henriette's house, glad to have an obliging person at hand to enliven somewhat a liaison of which he was beginning to tire. Thus, the buyer from the silk department had finally become the confidant both of his employer and of the pretty widow: he ran small errands for them, talked about one of them to the other, and sometimes patched up their quarrels. Henriette, in her fits of jealousy, allowed herself a degree of familiarity with him that he found surprising and embarrassing, for she would lose all the discretion she possessed, as a woman of the world using all her skill to keep up appearances.

She exclaimed violently:

'You should have brought him with you. Then I'd have been sure.'

'But how?' he said, with a good-natured laugh. 'It's not my fault if he escapes all the time nowadays . . . Oh! but he's very fond of me all the same. Without him, I'd be in trouble in the shop.'

Indeed, since the last stock-taking, his position at the Ladies' Paradise was precarious. In spite of his excuses that the wet weather was to blame, he was not forgiven his considerable stocks of fancy silks; and as Hutin was making the most of the affair by undermining his reputation with his superiors with a fresh burst of crafty energy, he could feel the ground crumbling beneath his feet. Mouret had condemned him, tired, no doubt, of having a witness who was now preventing him from breaking off his liaison and bored with profitless familiarity with him. But, following his usual tactics, he was pushing Bourdoncle to the fore; it was Bourdoncle and the other directors who were demanding Bouthemont's dismissal at every board meeting; whereas Mouret, according to his own account, was holding out against them—so he said—stoutly defending his friend at the risk of creating great difficulties for himself.

'Well, I shall wait,' Madame Desforges went on. 'You know that girl is coming at five . . . I want to see them face to face. I must discover their secret.'

She described her plan, repeating in her excitement how she had asked Madame Aurélie to send Denise to her to look at a coat which fitted badly. Once she had the girl there in her room, she would easily find some way of calling Mouret; and then she would take action.

Bouthemont, sitting opposite her, watched her with his handsome laughing eyes, trying hard to look serious. This gay young fellow with his ink-black beard, whose hot Gascon blood tinged his face with crimson, was thinking that society women were not much good, and that they certainly let out a lot of secrets once they opened their hearts. His friends' mistresses, who were shopgirls, certainly never made such detailed confessions.

'Come now,' he ventured to say at last, 'why should it matter so much? I swear to you that there's absolutely nothing between them.'

'That's just it!' she exclaimed, 'he loves her . . . I don't care about the others, they're just pick-ups, they only last a day!'

She spoke of Clara with contempt. She had heard that Mouret, after Denise's refusal, had fallen back on that big redhead with a face like a horse; no doubt it was a calculated move, for he kept her in the department, loading her with presents in order to draw attention to her. In any case, for almost three months now he had been leading a tremendous life of pleasure, scattering money with an extravagance which was causing a great deal of comment: he had bought a house for some chorus girl and, at the same time, was being milked by two or three other tarts, who seemed to be competing with each other in expensive, idiotic whims.

'It's that creature's fault,' Henriette was repeating. 'I feel he's ruining himself with the others because she's spurning him . . . In any case, I don't care about his money! I'd have loved him more if he'd been poor. You've become our friend, and you know how much I love him.'

She stopped, choking, on the verge of bursting into tears; and, with a gesture of abandon, she held out both hands to him. It was true, she adored Mouret for his youth and his triumphs; never had a man possessed her so completely, thrilling both her body and her pride; but, at the thought of losing him, she could also hear the knell of forty sounding, and she was wondering with terror how to fill the place of this great love.

'But I'll have my revenge,' she murmured. 'I'll have my revenge if he behaves badly!'

Bouthemont was still holding her hands. She was still beautiful, but she would be a nuisance as a mistress, and she wasn't really his type. Yet it was worth considering; it might be worth risking the problems it could involve.

'Why don't you set up on your own?' she said suddenly, withdrawing her hands.

He was taken aback. Then he replied:

'But it would require a lot of capital . . . I kept thinking about it last year. I'm sure there are still enough customers in Paris for one or two more big shops; but the district would have to be chosen very carefully. The Bon Marché has got the Left Bank; the Louvre is in the middle; at the Paradise we monopolize the rich districts of the west. That leaves the north, where a rival to the Place Clichy could be created. And I'd discovered a superb site, near the Opéra . . .'

'Well?'

He began to laugh heartily.

'Just imagine, I was stupid enough to speak to my father about it . . . Yes, I was naïve enough to ask him to find shareholders in Toulouse.'

He told her gaily about the old man's rage and how, in his little country shop, he was bitterly opposed to the big Parisian stores. Old Bouthemont, infuriated by the thirty thousand francs his son earned, had replied that he'd rather give his money and that of his friends to charity than contribute a penny to one of those shops which were nothing more than the brothels of business.

'Besides,' the young man concluded, 'it would require millions.'

'And if you could find them?' said Madame Desforges simply.

He looked at her, suddenly serious. Was it just the phrase of a jealous woman? But without giving him time to question her, she added:

'Well, you know what an interest I take in you . . . We'll talk about it again.'

The bell in the hall had sounded. She stood up, and with an instinctive movement he drew his chair away, as if they were already liable to be caught unawares. Silence reigned in the drawing-room; with its pretty hangings and its profusion of green plants it looked rather like a miniature wood between the two windows. She stood waiting, listening with strained attention.

'Here he is,' she murmured.

The servant announced:

'Monsieur Mouret, Monsieur de Vallagnosc.'

She could not help making a gesture of anger. Why didn't he come alone? He must have gone to fetch his friend, fearing a possible tête-à-tête. Then she gave a smile, and held out her hand to the two men.

'I see you so rarely these days! And that goes for you, too, Monsieur de Vallagnosc.'

Her figure was her despair; she squeezed herself into black silk dresses to conceal the fact that she was putting on weight. But her face was still pretty, with her dark hair, and she had not lost the delicacy of her features. Mouret, sweeping his eyes over her, was able to say to her familiarly:

'There's no need to ask how you are . . . You're as fresh as a daisy.'

'Oh! I'm too well,' she replied. 'In any case, I might have been dead; you wouldn't have known anything about it.'

She was examining him too, and thought he looked very nervous and tired, with puffy eyes and a livid complexion.

'Well!' she resumed in a tone which she tried to make agreeable, 'I'm not going to return your flattery. You don't look at all well this evening.'

'Overwork!' said Vallagnosc.

Mouret made a vague gesture, without replying. He had just noticed Bouthemont, and nodded to him in a friendly way. During the time when they had been on intimate terms he used to carry Bouthemont off from the department at the busiest time of the afternoon, and take him to Henriette's. But times had changed, and he said to him in a low voice:

'You left very early . . . You know, they saw you leaving and they're furious, in the shop.'

He was talking of Bourdoncle and the other directors as if he was not the master.

'Oh!' murmured Bouthemont nervously.

'Yes, I want to talk to you . . . Wait for me; we'll leave together.'

Meanwhile Henriette had sat down again; and while she was listening to Vallagnosc, who was telling her that Madame de Boves would probably be coming to see her, she did not take her eyes off Mouret. He had lapsed into silence again; he was gazing at the furniture and seemed to be looking for something on the ceiling. Then, as she laughingly complained that she no longer had anyone but men at her tea parties, he so far forgot himself as to let slip the phrase:

'I thought I'd find Baron Hartmann here.'

Henriette had turned pale. Doubtless she knew that he came to her house only in order to meet the Baron; but he might have refrained from throwing his indifference in her face like that. Just then the door opened, and the servant stood before her. When she questioned him with a movement of her head, he leaned down and said to her in a whisper:

'It's about that coat. Madam told me to let her know . . . The young lady is here.'

Then she raised her voice to make herself heard and, releasing all the sufferings of jealousy in a few sharply contemptuous words, she said:

'Let her wait!'

'Shall I show her into madam's dressing-room?'

'No, no, let her stay in the hall!'

When the servant had gone out, she calmly resumed her conversation with Vallagnosc. Mouret, who had relapsed into his lassitude, had half heard what she had said, without really taking it in. Bouthemont, preoccupied by the affair, was lost in thought. But almost immediately the door opened again, and two ladies were shown in.

'Just fancy!' said Madame Marty, 'I was getting out of the carriage when I saw Madame de Boves coming through the arcade.'

'Yes,' the latter explained, 'it's a nice day, and my doctor is always telling me I should walk . . .'

Then, after everyone had shaken hands, she asked Henriette:

'So you're engaging a new housemaid?'

'No,' she replied, surprised. 'Why?'

'Well, I've just seen a girl in the hall who . . .'

Henriette interrupted her, laughing.

'It's funny, isn't it? Shopgirls all look like housemaids . . . Yes, it's a girl who's come to alter a coat.'

Mouret looked at her intently, suspicion crossing his mind. She went on talking with forced gaiety, explaining how she had bought the coat ready-made at the Ladies' Paradise the week before.

'What!' said Madame Marty, 'don't you get your clothes from Sauveur any more?'

'Yes, my dear, I do, but I wanted to make an experiment. I was quite pleased with the first thing I bought at the Paradise, a travel coat . . . But this time it wasn't at all a success. You may say what you like, you just can't dress well in those big shops of yours. I don't mind saying it in front of Monsieur Mouret . . . You'll never be able to dress a woman who has any sense of style.'

Mouret did not defend his shop; still looking at her, he was trying to reassure himself, telling himself that she would never dare to do such a thing. It was Bouthemont who had to defend the Paradise.

'If all the society women who buy their clothes from us were to boast about it,' he retorted gaily, 'you'd be very surprised at the customers we have . . . Order a garment from us made-to-measure, and it'll be as good as one of Sauveur's, and it'll cost you half the price. And it's only because it's less expensive that it seems less good.'

'So the coat's not a success?' Madame de Boves went on. 'Now I recognize the girl . . . It's rather dark in the hall.'

'Yes,' added Madame Marty, 'I was trying to think where I'd seen that face . . . Well, go on, my dear, don't stand on ceremony with us.'

Henriette made a gesture of disdainful unconcern.

'Oh, later on, there's no hurry.'

The ladies went on with their discussion about clothes from the big department stores. Then Madame de Boves spoke of her husband who, she said, had just left on a tour of inspection to visit the stud farm at Saint-Lô, and Henriette was telling them how the day before Madame Guibal had been called away to the Franche-Comté because of an aunt's illness. She was not expecting Madame Bourdelais that day either, for at the end of each month the latter shut herself up with a seamstress in order to go through her children's clothes. Meanwhile, Madame Marty seemed troubled by some secret anxiety. Monsieur Marty's job at the Lycée Bonaparte was in jeopardy as a result of some lessons the poor man had been giving in some shady establishments which were doing quite a trade in matriculation diplomas; he was frenziedly raising money where he could, in order to meet the orgies of spending which were ruining his home; and after she'd seen him weeping one evening in fear of dismissal, she had had the idea of using her friend Henriette's influence with an undersecretary she knew at the Ministry of Education. Finally Henriette set her mind at rest with a few words. In any case, Monsieur Marty was going to come himself to discover his fate and to thank her.

'You don't look well, Monsieur Mouret,' Madame de Boves observed.

'Overwork!' Vallagnosc repeated, in his ironical, phlegmatic way.

Mouret quickly stood up, sorry at having forgotten himself in this way. He took his usual place in the midst of the ladies, regaining all his charm. He was now occupied with the winter fashions, and he spoke of a large consignment of lace; Madame de Boves asked him about the price of Alençon point: she felt inclined to buy some. She was now reduced to saving the one franc fifty it cost for a cab, and would arrive home ill from having stopped to look at the shop-windows. Wearing a coat which was already two years old, in her imagination she would drape over her regal shoulders all the expensive materials she saw; it was like tearing her flesh off when she awoke and found herself dressed in her patched-up dresses, without hope of ever satisfying her passion.

'Baron Hartmann,' the servant announced.

Henriette noticed how warmly Mouret shook the newcomer's hand.

The latter greeted the ladies and glanced at the young man with the subtle expression which sometimes lit up his coarse Alsatian face.

'Always talking about clothes!' he murmured with a smile.

Then, being a friend of Madame Desforges, he ventured to add:

'There's a very charming girl in the hall . . . Who is she?'

'Oh! No one,' replied Madame Desforges in her unpleasant voice. 'Just a shopgirl waiting to see me.'

The door remained half open, as the servant was serving the tea. He was going out and coming back again, putting the china service, then plates of sandwiches and biscuits, on the pedestal table. In the vast drawing-room, a bright light, softened by the green plants, illuminated the brasswork, bathing the silk of the furniture in a warm glow, and each time the door opened a dim corner of the hall, lit only by frosted glass windows, could be seen. There, in the dark, a sombre form could be discerned, motionless and patient. Denise had remained standing: there was a leather-covered seat, but pride prevented her from sitting on it. She was conscious of the insult. She had been there for half an hour, without a movement, without a word; those ladies and the Baron had stared at her in passing; she could now hear scraps of conversation from the drawing-room, and she was hurt by the indifference of all that pleasant luxury; but still she did not move. Suddenly, through the half-open door, she recognized Mouret. He had guessed at last that it was she who was waiting.

'Is it one of your salesgirls?' Baron Hartmann asked.

Mouret had succeeded in hiding his great agitation. But his emotion made his voice shake.

'I'm sure it is, but I don't know which.'

'It's the little fair-haired one from the ladieswear department,' Madame Marty quickly interjected. 'The one who's assistant buyer, I believe.'

Henriette looked at Mouret in her turn.

'Ah!' he said, simply.

And he tried to turn the conversation towards the festivities that had been organized in honour of the King of Prussia,* who had arrived in Paris the day before. But the Baron mischievously went back to the subject of the girls who worked in the big stores. He was pretending that he wanted information, and was asking questions: What sort of background did they have? Were their morals really as bad as people said? This sparked off quite a discussion.

'Really,' he repeated, 'you think they're decent girls?'

Mouret defended their virtue with a conviction that made Vallagnosc laugh. Then Bouthemont intervened, in order to save his master. My goodness! There were all sorts, hussies as well as decent girls. What is more, their moral standard was rising. In the past they had had nothing but the dregs of the trade, poor, distracted girls who just drifted into the drapery business; whereas nowadays families in the Rue de Sèvres, for example, were definitely bringing up their little girls for the Bon Marché. In short, when they wanted to behave properly, they could; for unlike the working girls of the Paris streets, they were not obliged to pay for their board and lodging: they were lodged and fed, and their existence was assured, though doubtless it was a very hard existence. The worst thing of all was their neutral, ill-defined position, somewhere between shopkeepers and ladies. Plunged into the midst of luxury, often without any previous education, they formed an anonymous class apart. All their troubles and vices sprang from that.

'I certainly don't know any creatures so disagreeable,' said Madame de Boves. 'One could slap them sometimes.'

The ladies vented their spite. They devoured each other at the counters: woman ate woman there, in a bitter rivalry of money

and beauty. The salesgirls were jealous of well-dressed customers, ladies whose style they tried to imitate; and poorly dressed
customers, lower middle-class women, felt even more sourly
jealous of the salesgirls, the girls dressed in silk whom they
wanted to treat like servants each time they made a purchase
costing a few pence.

'Well, in any case,' Henriette concluded, 'the poor wretches
are all for sale, like their goods!'

Mouret had the strength to smile. The Baron was studying
him, touched by his remarkable self-control. Therefore he
changed the conversation by mentioning again the festivities in
honour of the King of Prussia: they were superb, the whole
business world of Paris would profit from them. Henriette remained silent, and seemed lost in her thoughts; she was divided
between her desire to go on forgetting Denise in the hall, and her
fear that Mouret, now forewarned, might leave. In the end she
got up from her chair.

'Will you excuse me?'

'Of course, my dear!' said Madame Marty. 'Look! I'll do the
honours of your house!'

She stood up, took the teapot and filled the cups. Henriettte
turned towards Baron Hartmann, saying:

'You'll stay a few minutes longer, won't you?'

'Yes, I want to talk to Monsieur Mouret. We're going to
invade your small drawing-room.'

Then she went out, and her black silk dress rustled against the
door like a snake disappearing into the undergrowth.

The Baron immediately manœuvred so as to lead Mouret
away, abandoning the ladies to Bouthemont and Vallagnosc.
Standing by the window of the other drawing-room, they
chatted in low voices, discussing a whole new scheme. For a long
time Mouret had been cherishing the dream of realizing his old
plan—the invasion of the entire block by the Ladies's Paradise,
from the Rue Monsigny to the Rue de la Michodière, and from
the Rue Neuve-Saint-Augustin to the Rue du Dix-Décembre. In
this enormous block there was still a vast frontage on the Rue
du Dix-Décembre which he did not own; and this was enough
to spoil his triumph: he was tortured by the desire to complete
his conquest by erecting a monumental façade there, as an

apotheosis. As long as the main entrance remained in the Rue Neuve-Saint-Augustin, in a dark street of old Paris, his work would be incomplete; it would lack logic. He wanted to flaunt it before the new Paris, on one of those recently built avenues where, in full sunlight, all the figures of the modern crowd passed by; he could see it towering above everything, imposing itself as the giant palace of commerce, casting a bigger shadow over the city than the old Louvre did. But, so far, he had come up against the obstinacy of the Crédit Immobilier, which was still clinging to its original idea of using the frontage site to build a rival to the Grand Hotel. The plans were ready; they were only waiting for the Rue du Dix-Décembre to be opened up in order to dig the foundations. Mouret, making a final effort, had at last almost succeeded in winning over Baron Hartmann.

'Well!' the latter began, 'we had a meeting yesterday, and I came here, thinking I'd see you, to tell you what happened . . . They still won't agree.'

The young man allowed himself a gesture of irritation.

'That's very unreasonable of them . . . What did they say?'

'They said what I said to you myself, and what I'm still inclined to think . . . Your façade is only a decoration; the new buildings would only increase the shop area by a tenth, and that means throwing away huge sums on a mere advertisement.'

At this Mouret burst out:

'An advertisement! An advertisement! This one will be in stone, and it'll outlast us all. Can't you see that it would increase our business tenfold! We'd get our money back in two years. What does it matter, what you call this lost ground, if it creates enormous interest! You'll see the crowds we'll have when our customers are no longer crammed into the Rue Neuve-Saint-Augustin, and can simply charge down a street wide enough for six carriages to travel abreast quite easily.'

'No doubt,' resumed the Baron, laughing. 'But, I must repeat, you're a poet in your own way. These gentlemen think it would be dangerous to expand your business any more. They want to be prudent on your behalf.'

'What! Prudence? I don't understand . . . Don't the figures speak for themselves, don't they show the constant increase in our sales? In the beginning, with a capital of five hundred thousand francs, I had a turnover of two million. The capital was used four times over. Then it became four million, turned over ten times, and produced forty million. Finally, after successive increases, I've just ascertained from the last stock-taking that the turnover has now reached a total of eighty million; and the capital, which has increased very little, for it's only six million, has therefore passed over our counters in the form of goods more than twelve times.'*

He was raising his voice, tapping the fingers of his right hand on his left palm, knocking off millions as if he was cracking nuts. The Baron interrupted him.

'I know, I know . . . But surely you don't expect to go on expanding like that?'

'Why not?' said Mouret naïvely. 'There's no reason why it should stop. The capital can be turned over fifteen times; I've been predicting it for a long time. In certain departments it'll be turned over twenty-five and thirty times . . . and after that, well, after that we'll find some way to use it even more.'

'So you'll end up drinking the money of Paris as you'd drink a glass of water?'

'Of course. Doesn't Paris belong to women, and don't the women belong to us?'

The Baron placed his hands on Mouret's shoulders and looked at him in a fatherly way.

'Look! You're a good chap, and I'm very fond of you . . . You really are very charming. We're going to discuss the idea seriously and I hope I'll be able to make them see reason. Up till now we've nothing but praise for you. The Stock Exchange is amazed at your dividends. You're probably right, it's better to put even more money into your business than to risk competition with the Grand Hotel, which would be dangerous.'

Mouret's excitement subsided, and he thanked the Baron, but without his usual enthusiasm; the latter saw him turn his eyes towards the door of the neighbouring room, once more seized by the secret anxiety he was trying to hide. Meanwhile Vallagnosc, seeing that they were no longer talking business, had approached them. He stood close to them, listening to the Baron, who was murmuring with the knowing air of one who had had many amorous adventures:

'I say, I believe they're having their revenge, aren't they?'

'Who do you mean?' asked Mouret, embarrassed.

'Why, the women . . . They're tired of being in your power, now you're in theirs, my friend: fair exchange!'

He was joking, for he was well aware of the young man's spectacular love-affairs. The mansion bought for the chorus girl and the enormous sums squandered on girls picked up in the private rooms of restaurants amused him as if they were an excuse for the follies he had himself committed in the past. His long experience was revelling in it.

'Really, I don't understand,' Mouret repeated.

'Oh! You understand very well. They always have the last word . . . That's why I used to think: it's impossible, he's just boasting, he's not as clever as that! And now you see what's happened! You can take everything you can from women, exploit them as you would a coal-mine, but afterwards they'll exploit you and make you cough up! Take care, for they'll extract more blood and money from you than you'll have sucked from them.'

He was laughing even more, and Vallagnosc, near him, was sniggering too, without saying a word.

'Ah, well! You've got to try everything once,' Mouret confessed finally, pretending to be amused too. 'It's stupid to have money if you don't spend it.'

'I couldn't agree more,' the Baron went on. 'You enjoy yourself, my dear fellow. I'm not one to preach to you, nor to worry about the large investments we've entrusted to you. One must sow one's wild oats, one has a clearer head afterwards . . . In any case, it's not so bad to ruin yourself when you're able to rebuild your fortune again . . . But even if money isn't everything, there are other ways of suffering . . .'

He stopped, and his laugh became sad; old sorrows were flitting through his ironical scepticism. He had followed the duel between Henriette and Mouret with the curiosity of one who was still fascinated by other people's amorous battles, and he now sensed that the crisis had come; he guessed the drama, for he had heard stories about this girl Denise, whom he had seen in the hall.

'Oh! As for suffering, that's not my style,' said Mouret in a tone of bravado. 'It's quite enough to have to pay.'

The Baron looked at him for a few seconds in silence. Without wishing to be insistent, he added slowly:

'Don't make yourself out to be worse than you are . . . You'll lose something more than your money in that game. You'll lose part of yourself, my friend.'

He broke off, once more joking, in order to ask:

'It sometimes happens, doesn't it, Monsieur de Vallagnosc?'

'So they say, Baron,' the latter declared simply.

Just at that moment, the door opened. Mouret, who was about to reply, gave a slight start. The three men turned round. It was Madame Desforges, looking very gay; she merely put her head round the door, calling urgently:

'Monsieur Mouret! Monsieur Mouret!'

Then, when she caught sight of them, she said:

'Oh! Gentlemen, will you let me take Monsieur Mouret away for a minute? The least he can do is to give me the benefit of his knowledge, because he's sold me an awful coat! The girl is an absolute idiot, she doesn't know a thing . . . Come on, I'm waiting for you.'

He hesitated, torn, recoiling from the scene which he could foresee. But he had to obey. The Baron said to him in his paternal yet mocking way:

'Go on, go on, my dear fellow. Madam wants you.'

Mouret followed her out. The door swung to again, and he thought he could hear Vallagnosc's laughter, muffled by the hangings. His courage was exhausted. Ever since Henriette had left the drawing-room and he had known Denise to be in jealous hands at the other end of the apartment, he had been feeling a growing anxiety, nervous pangs which made him keep his ears open as if there was a distant sound of weeping which made him wince with pain. What could the woman devise in order to torture her? All his love, this love which still astonished him, went out to the girl like a support and a consolation. Never had he loved anyone like this, never had he found such powerful charm in suffering. Since he led such a busy life, the loves he had had—including Henriette herself, who was so subtle and pretty that his possession of her flattered his pride—had been merely an agreeable pastime, sometimes a calculated one, in which he looked only for profitable pleasure. He would leave his mistresses' houses calm, and would go home to bed happy in his bachelor freedom, without a regret or a worry on his mind; whereas now his heart was beating with anguish, his life was no longer his own, and he had ceased to enjoy the oblivion of sleep in his huge solitary bed. He thought of Denise all the time. Even at this moment only she existed for him, and while he was following the other woman in fear of some distressing scene, he was thinking that he was glad to be there to protect her.

First of all they passed through the bedroom, which was silent and empty. Then Madame Desforges, pushing open a door, went into the dressing-room, and Mouret followed her. It was a fairly spacious room, hung with red silk, furnished with a marble dressing-table and a three-door wardrobe with broad looking-glasses on each door. As the window overlooked the courtyard, it was already dark there; and two gas burners had been lighted, their nickel-plated brackets extending on the right and left of the wardrobe.

'So,' said Henriette, 'perhaps we'll get somewhere now.'

On entering, Mouret had found Denise standing erect in the middle of the bright light. She was very pale, modestly dressed in a cashmere jacket and a black hat; and she was holding over one arm the coat which had been bought at the Paradise. When she saw the young man her hands shook slightly.

'I want this gentleman to give his opinion,' Henriette resumed. 'Help me, girl.'

Denise, drawing nearer, had to help her into the coat again. When she had tried it on the first time she had put pins in the shoulders, which did not fit properly. Henriette turned round to look at herself in the looking-glass.

'It's impossible, isn't it? Tell me exactly what you think.'

'You're quite right, it doesn't fit,' said Mouret to cut the matter short. 'It's very simple, the young lady will take your measurements and we'll make you another one.'

'No, I want this one, I need it immediately,' she said emphatically. 'But it's too tight across my chest, and too loose between the shoulders.'

Then, in a harsh voice, she added:

'You won't make it fit any better by just looking at me, girl! . . . Come on, do something about it. It's your job.'

Denise, without saying a word, began putting in pins once again. It took a long time: she had to go from one shoulder to the other; she even had to bend down, almost to kneel for a moment to pull down the front of the coat. Madame Desforges, standing over her and passively accepting all the trouble she was taking, had the hard expression of a mistress difficult to please. Happy at having reduced the girl to this servant's task, she gave her a series of curt orders, watching for the slightest betrayal of emotion on Mouret's face.

'Put a pin here. No, not there, here, near the sleeve. Can't you understand? No, not like that, you've made it all baggy again . . . Be careful, now you're pricking me!'

Twice more Mouret tried vainly to intervene in order to bring this scene to a close. His heart was pounding at his love's humiliation; and he loved Denise more than ever, filled with tenderness at the dignified silence she maintained. Although her hand was trembling a little at being treated like that in his presence, she accepted the demands of her position with the proud resignation of a courageous girl. When Madame Desforges saw that they were not going to give themselves away, she tried another approach; she kept smiling at Mouret, treating him openly as her lover. And so, as Denise had run out of pins, she said:

'Darling, could you look in the ivory box on the dressing-table . . . ? Really, it's empty? Be a dear and go and look on the mantelpiece in the bedroom, then: you know, in the corner, next to the looking-glass.'

She was showing that he was at home there, that he had slept there and knew where the brushes and combs were kept. When he brought her a handful of pins she took them one by one, and forced him to stand close to her, while she looked at him and talked to him in a low voice.

'I'm not hunchbacked, am I?' Put your hand there, feel my shoulders, just for fun! Am I built like that?'

Denise had looked up slowly, even paler than before, and in silence had carried on sticking in the pins. Mouret could only see her thick fair hair twisted on the slender nape of her neck; but, from the slight tremor which was stirring it, he felt he could see the pain on her face. Now she would spurn him; she would send him back to this woman who did not even hide her liaison with him in front of strangers. He felt ready to do something brutal; he could have beaten Henriette. How could he make her be quiet? How could he tell Denise that he adored her, that she alone existed for him at this moment, that he was sacrificing for her all his old loves of a day? A prostitute would not have taken the ambiguous liberties this lady was taking. He withdrew his hand and repeated:

'You're wrong to persist, madam, since I myself consider that this garment's defective.'

One of the gas burners was hissing; and in the stifling, moist air of the room nothing could be heard but this hot hissing sound. The wardrobe mirrors reflected broad patches of bright light on to the red silk hangings, on which the shadows of the two women were dancing. A flask of verbena which had been left with its stopper out was giving off a vague smell of fading flowers.

'There, madam, that's all I can do,' said Denise at last, as she stood up.

She felt that she could bear it no more. Twice, as if blinded, her eyes clouded over and she had dug a pin into her hand. Had he taken part in this plot? Had he made her come to avenge himself for her refusal, by showing that there were other women who loved him? This thought made her blood run cold; she could not remember ever having had to summon up so much courage, even during the terrible moments in her existence when she had been starving. It was nothing to be humiliated like that, compared to seeing him practically in the arms of another woman as if she had not been there!

Henriette was studying herself in front of the looking-glass. Once more she started to speak sharply to Denise:

'It's absurd, girl. It's worse than it was before . . . Look how tight it is across the bust. I look like a wet-nurse.'

At that Denise, her patience exhausted, said something unfortunate:

'Madam is a little plump . . . And unfortunately we can't make madam any slimmer.'

'Plump, plump,' repeated Henriette, who was turning pale in her turn. 'Now you're becoming insolent, my dear girl . . . You must learn not to make remarks like that!'

They stood staring at each other, face to face, trembling. The lady and the shopgirl had ceased to exist. They were simply two women made equal by their rivalry. The one had violently pulled off the coat and thrown it on a chair, while the other tossed on to the dressing-table the few pins which remained in her hand.

'What surprises me,' Henriette went on, 'is that Monsieur Mouret tolerates such insolence . . . I thought, sir, that you were more particular about your staff.'

Denise had recovered her courageous composure. She replied gently:

'If Monsieur Mouret keeps me, it's because he has nothing to reproach me with . . . But I'm prepared to apologise to you, if he insists.'

Mouret was listening, paralysed by this quarrel, unable to find a word to put a stop to it. He had a horror of such scenes between women, the asperity of which offended his constant desire that everything should be graceful. Henriette wanted to force him to say something in condemnation of Denise; and, as he remained silent, still hesitating, she threw a final insult at him:

'What a sorry state of affairs, sir, that I should have to put up with insolence from your mistresses in my own home! A tart you picked up out of the gutter!'

Two big tears fell from Denise's eyes. She had been holding them back for a long time; but the whole of her being was smarting from the insult. When he saw her weeping like that without answering back, in silent, despairing dignity, Mouret no longer hesitated; his heart went out to her with immense tenderness. He took her hands and stammered:

'Leave now, my dear, forget all about this house.'

Henriette, full of amazement, choking with anger, stood watching them.

'Wait,' he continued, folding the coat up himself, 'take this garment with you. Madam can buy another one somewhere else . . . And don't cry any more, please. You know what a high opinion I have of you.'

He accompanied her to the door, which he closed after her. She had not said a word; but a pink flush had risen to her cheeks, while her eyes were moist with fresh tears, this time of delicious sweetness.

Henriette, choking, had taken out her handkerchief and was crushing it to her lips. All her plans had been reversed; she herself had been caught in the trap she had laid. She was upset at having gone too far, tortured by jealousy. To be left for a creature like that! And to be treated like that in front of her! Her pride was suffering more than her love.

'So it's that girl you love?' she said painfully when they were alone.

Mouret did not reply at once; he was walking up and down between the window and the door, trying to control his violent emotion. At last he stood still and, very politely, in a voice he was trying to make cold, he said simply:

'Yes, madam.'

The gas burner was still hissing in the stifling atmosphere of the dressing-room. Dancing shadows were no longer passing across the reflections in the mirrors; the room seemed bare and had taken on an oppressive sadness. Suddenly Henriette threw herself on to a chair, twisting her handkerchief between her feverish fingers and repeating between her sobs:

'Oh God! How miserable I am!'

He stood looking at her for a few seconds. Then he calmly walked away. Left alone, she continued to weep amidst the silence, with the pins strewn over the dressing-table and floor in front of her.

When Mouret went back into the small drawing-room, he found no one there but Vallagnosc, for the Baron had gone back to the ladies. As he was still feeling very shaken, he sat down at the end of the room on a sofa; and his friend, seeing how pale he looked, charitably came and stood in front of him to hide him from prying glances. At first they looked at each other without saying a word. Then Vallagnosc, who seemed inwardly amused by Mouret's agitation, finally asked in his bantering voice:

'Enjoying yourself?'

Mouret did not seem to understand at first. But when he remembered their former conversations about the empty stupidity and the pointless torture of life, he replied:

'Of course; I've never lived so intensely . . . Ah! Don't laugh, old man, the moments when you seem to die of suffering are the briefest of all!'

He lowered his voice and, with tears in his eyes, he went on gaily:

'Yes, you know all about it, don't you? They've just been pulling my heart to pieces, the two of them. But it's still all right, you know, the wounds they make are almost as good as caresses . . . I'm totally worn out; but it doesn't matter, you'd never believe how much I love life! Oh! I'll have her in the end, that little girl who keeps saying no . . .'

Vallagnosc said simply:

'And then?'

'Then? But I'll have her, simply! Isn't that enough? If you think you're clever just because you refuse to be silly and to suffer, you're making a big mistake! You're just gullible, that's all! Try wanting a woman and getting her in the end; in one minute that makes up for all the unhappiness.'

But Vallagnosc was giving full rein to his pessimism. What was the point of working so hard, since money could not buy everything? If it had been him, on the day he realized that his millions could not even buy the woman he desired he would have shut up shop and given up work for ever. Listening to him, Mouret became serious. Then he responded quite violently, affirming his belief in the omnipotence of his will.

'I want her, and I'll get her! And if she escapes me, you'll see what a place I'll build to cure myself. It'll be quite superb! You don't understand this language, old fellow: otherwise you'd know that action contains its own reward. To act, to create, to fight against facts, to overcome them or be overcome by them—the whole of human health and happiness is made up of that!'

'That's an easy way to forget your sorrows,' murmured the other.

'Well, I'd rather forget my sorrows . . . If we've got to die I'd rather die of passion than die of boredom!'

They both laughed, for their conversation reminded them of their old arguments at school. Then Vallagnosc, in a lifeless voice, rehearsed his views on how platitudinous everything was, taking great pleasure in doing so, boasting almost about the inertia and emptiness of his existence. Yes, the next day he would be bored at the Ministry, as he had been bored the day before. In three years his salary had gone up by six hundred francs; he was now getting three thousand six hundred, not even enough to allow him to buy decent cigars; it was getting worse all the time, and if he didn't kill himself it was simply from laziness, to save himself the trouble. When Mouret mentioned his marriage with Mademoiselle de Boves, he replied that, in spite of his aunt's determination not to die, it was going ahead all the same; at any rate, so he thought, the parents had agreed to it, and he pretended not to have any will of his own. What was the point of wanting something or not wanting it, since things never turned out as one desired? He quoted as an example his future father-in-law, who'd been sure he'd found in Madame Guibal an indolent blonde, the caprice of an hour, and who was now forced along by her with a whip, like an old horse being ridden to death. While people thought he was busy inspecting the stud-farms at Saint-Lô, she was finishing him off in a little house he had rented at Versailles.

'He's happier than you are,' said Mouret, getting up.

'Of course he is!' declared Vallagnosc. 'Perhaps it's only doing wrong that's rather fun.'

Mouret had recovered. He wanted to escape, but did not wish his departure to look like flight. Therefore, resolved to have a cup of tea, he went back into the large drawing-room with his friend, both of them joking as they did so. Baron Hartmann asked him if the coat was all right now, and Mouret, quite unperturbed, replied that as far as he was concerned he had given it up as a bad job. At that, there were cries of surprise. While Madame Marty hastened to pour him his tea, Madame de Boves accused the shops of always having clothes that were too tight. In the end he managed to sit down next to Bouthemont, who was still there. They were immediately forgotten by the ladies, and in reply to the anxious questions of Bouthemont, who wanted to know his fate, he did not wait until they were outside in the street, but told him at once that the members of the board had decided to dispense with his services. Between each sentence he took a sip of tea, protesting how sorry he was as he did so. Oh! There had been a quarrel from which he had scarcely recovered, for he had left the room beside himself with rage. But what could he do? He couldn't break with those gentlemen just over a question of staff. Bouthemont, very pale, was obliged to thank him once more.

'What a terrible coat it must be,' said Madame Marty. 'Henriette's still out there.'

Indeed, her prolonged absence was beginning to make everyone feel embarrassed. But, at that very moment, Madame Desforges reappeared.

'So you're giving it up as a bad job too?' cried Madame de Boves gaily.

'How do you mean?'

'Monsieur Mouret told us you couldn't do anything with it.'

Henriette displayed the greatest surprise.

'Monsieur Mouret was joking. The coat will be perfectly all right.' She was all smiles, and seemed very calm. Doubtless she had bathed her eyelids, for they were quite fresh, without a trace of redness. Although the whole of her being was still quivering and bleeding, she found the strength to hide her torment beneath the mask of her society charm. She offered some sandwiches to Vallagnosc with her customary laugh. Only the Baron, who knew her well, noticed the slight contraction of her lips and the melancholy fire which she had not been able to extinguish in the depths of her eyes. He could picture the whole scene.

'Dear me! Everyone to his own taste,' said Madame de Boves, as she too accepted a sandwich. 'I know some women who wouldn't buy a ribbon anywhere but at the Louvre. Others swear only by the Bon Marché . . . It's a question of temperament, no doubt.'

'The Bon Marché is terribly provincial,' murmured Madame Marty, 'and one gets so jostled at the Louvre!'

The ladies had resumed their discussion about the big stores. Mouret had to give his opinion; he came back into their midst, pretending to be impartial. The Bon Marché was an excellent shop, reliable and respectable; but the Louvre certainly had a better class of customers.

'In short, you prefer the Ladies' Paradise,' said the Baron, smiling.

'Yes,' Mouret replied calmly. 'In our shop, we like the customers.'

All the women present were of his opinion. That was how it really was; at the Paradise it was as if they were at a private party; when they were there, they felt constantly courted with flattery and showered with adoration which entranced even the most virtuous. The shop's enormous success came from the seductive way it paid court to them.

'By the way,' asked Henriette, wishing to appear very detached, 'what about my protégée; what are you doing with her, Monsieur Mouret? You know, Mademoiselle de Fontenailles.'

And turning towards Madame Marty, she said:

'A marchioness, my dear, a poor girl who's found herself in rather difficult straits.'

'Oh,' said Mouret, 'she earns three francs a day sewing pattern-books together, and I think I'm going to marry her off to one of my porters.'

'Shame! What a horrible idea!' exclaimed Madame de Boves.

He looked at her, then carried on in his calm voice:

'But why, madam? Isn't it better for her to marry an honest, hard-working porter than run the risk of being picked up in the street by some good-for-nothing?'

Vallagnosc jokingly tried to interrupt.

'Don't encourage him, madam. He'll tell you that all the old families of France should start selling calico.'

'Well,' Mouret declared, 'for many of them it would at least be an honourable end.'

In the end they all laughed; the paradox seemed too outrageous. Mouret, however, continued to sing the praises of what he called the aristocracy of labour. A slight blush had coloured the cheeks of Madame de Boves, who was maddened by the various ploys she was reduced to by her poverty; whereas Madame Marty, on the contrary, stricken with remorse at the thought of her poor husband, was full of approval. Just then the servant announced the teacher, who had come to take her home.

His thin, shiny frock-coat made him seem gaunter than ever, dried up by his hard work. When he had thanked Madame Desforges for having spoken of him to the Minister, he gave Mouret the nervous glance of a man confronted with the disease which is killing him. He was totally confused when he heard the latter ask him:

'Isn't it true, sir, that work can achieve everything?'

'Work and economy,' he replied, his whole body giving a slight shudder. 'You must add economy, sir.'

Bouthemont, meanwhile, had remained motionless in his armchair.

Mouret's words were still ringing in his ears. Finally he got up, and went to tell Henriette in an undertone:

'You know, he's given me notice. In a very nice way, of course . . . But I'll be damned if I don't make him regret it! I've just thought of a name for my shop: Aux Quatre Saisons, and I'll take up my position near the Opéra!'

She looked at him and her eyes darkened.

'Count on me, I'm with you. Wait a moment.'

She drew Baron Hartmann into a window-recess. Without beating about the bush, she commended Bouthemont to him, as a young fellow who, in his turn, was going to revolutionize Paris by setting up in business on his own. When she spoke of financial backing for her new protégé, the Baron, although he was no longer surprised at anything, could not suppress a gesture of dismay. This was the fourth young man of genius she had commended to him, and he was beginning to feel ridiculous. He did not refuse outright, for the idea of creating competition for the Ladies' Paradise quite appealed to him; he had already, in banking, had the idea of creating competition for himself in order to discourage others. Besides, the idea amused him. He promised to look into it.

'We must talk about it this evening,' Henriette came back to whisper in Bouthemont's ear. 'At about nine o'clock, don't forget . . . The Baron's on our side.'

At that moment the vast room was filled with voices. Mouret, still standing in the midst of the ladies, had regained his composure: he was gaily defending himself from the charge of ruining them with his clothes, offering to prove with figures that he was enabling them to save thirty per cent on their purchases. Baron Hartmann was looking at him, once more overcome with the fraternal admiration of one who had himself been quite a womanizer in the past. So the duel was over; Henriette was beaten; she certainly would not be the woman who would come to avenge the others. And he thought he saw once more the modest profile of the girl he had glimpsed when passing through the hall. There she was, patiently waiting, alone, formidable in her gentleness.

CHAPTER 12

On 25 September work began on the new façade of the Ladies' Paradise. Baron Hartmann, true to his promise, had carried the day at the previous general meeting of the Crédit Immobilier. Mouret was at last within reach of realizing his dream: this façade, which was about to arise in the Rue du Dix-Décembre, seemed to represent the full blossoming of his fortune. He wanted therefore to celebrate the laying of the foundation stone. He made a ceremony out of it, distributed bonuses to his salesmen, and gave them game and champagne for dinner. People noticed his happy mood on the building site, and his victorious gesture as he cemented the stone with a stroke of the trowel.* For weeks he had been worried, troubled by nervous anxiety which he did not always succeed in hiding; and his triumph brought distraction and a respite to his unhappiness. Throughout the afternoon he seemed to have rediscovered the high spirits of a man in the best of health. But, from dinner onwards, when he went through the canteen to drink a glass of champagne with his staff, he looked feverish again, smiling painfully, his features drawn with the pain which was gnawing at him and which he would not acknowledge.

The next day, in the ladieswear department, Clara Prunaire did her best to be disagreeable to Denise. She had noticed Colomban's bashful love for her, and took it into her head to make fun of the Baudus. She said loudly to Marguerite, who was sharpening her pencil while waiting for customers:

'You know my sweetheart opposite . . . It really distresses me to see him in that dark shop which no one ever goes into.'

'He's not so badly off,' Marguerite replied. 'He's going to marry his employer's daughter.'

'Really?' Clara replied. 'It would be fun to steal him, then! I'll do it for a laugh, just wait and see!'

She went on in the same vein, delighted to feel that Denise was shocked. The latter forgave her everything else, but the thought of her dying cousin Geneviève being finished off by cruelty of that sort made her beside herself with rage. Just then a customer appeared, and, as Madame Aurélie had gone down to the basement, Denise took charge of the department and called Clara over.

'Mademoiselle Prunaire, you ought to see to this lady instead of standing there chatting.'

'I wasn't chatting.'

'Please be quiet and see to madam immediately.'

Clara gave in, beaten. When Denise showed her authority like that, without raising her voice, no one could stand up to her. By her very gentleness she had won absolute authority for herself. For a moment she walked in silence among the girls, who had become very serious. Marguerite had gone back to sharpening her pencil, the lead of which was continually breaking. She was the only one who still approved of the assistant buyer not giving in to Mouret and, shaking her head, declared that, if people had any idea of the trouble caused by such folly, they would prefer to behave themselves.

'Are we getting angry?' said a voice behind Denise.

It was Pauline, who was passing through the department. She had witnessed the scene, and spoke in a low voice, smiling as she did so.

'I have to,' Denise replied in the same tone. 'I can't manage those girls otherwise.'

Pauline shrugged her shoulders.

'Get away with you, you could be queen over us all whenever you wanted.'

She still could not understand her friend's refusal. At the end of August she had married Baugé, a silly thing to do, as she would say cheerfully. The awful Bourdoncle now treated her as a hopeless case, a woman lost to business. She lived in dread that one fine day they would be sent away to love each other elsewhere, for the members of the board had decreed that love was deplorable, and fatal to business. So great was her terror that when she met Baugé in one of the galleries she would pretend not to know him. She had just had a fright—old Jouve had nearly caught her talking to her husband behind a pile of dusters.

'Look! He's followed me,' she added, quickly describing the incident to Denise. 'Just look at him smelling me out with his big nose!'

Jouve, dressed very correctly in a white tie, and his nose on the scent of any misdemeanour he could find, was just coming out of the lace department. But when he saw Denise, he drew himself up to his full height and passed by with a kindly air.

'Saved!' murmured Pauline. 'My dear, it was because of you that he didn't say anything . . . I say, if I got into trouble, would you put a word in for me? Yes, yes, don't look so surprised, everybody knows that a word from you could revolutionize the shop.'

She hurried back to her department. Denise had blushed, upset by these friendly remarks. It was true, however. The flattery with which she was surrounded gave her a vague idea of her power. When Madame Aurélie came upstairs again and found the department peaceful and busy under the assistant buyer's supervision, she gave her a friendly smile. She was even dropping Mouret himself; every day her friendliness was increasing towards the person who could, one fine day, aspire to her position as buyer. The reign of Denise was beginning.

Bourdoncle alone was unyielding. The secret war he continued to wage against the girl was based on a natural antipathy. He detested her for her gentleness and charm. He fought her, too, as a baneful influence which would endanger the shop if Mouret succumbed. His master's business faculties must surely founder, he thought, in the midst of such idiotic love: what had been won through women would be lost through this woman. All women left him cold; he treated them with the disdain of a man without passion, whose profession it was to live on them, and who, seeing them at such close quarters in the pursuit of his trade, had lost his last illusions. Instead of intoxicating him, the odour of seventy thousand female customers gave him appalling headaches: as soon as he got home, he would beat his mistresses. And what worried him above all about this little salesgirl, who had gradually become so formidable, was the fact that he did not believe in her disinterestedness, nor in the sincerity of her refusals. As far as he was concerned, she was playing a part, and an extremely artful one; for, if she had succumbed on the first day, Mouret would doubtless have forgotten her on the next; whereas, by refusing, she had whetted his desire, driven him mad, made him capable of any kind of folly. The most experienced woman of the world, the slyest prostitute, would have acted no differently from this innocent girl. Thus Bourdoncle had only to see her, with her clear eyes, her gentle face, and all her simple ways, to be seized now with real fear, as if faced by a vampire in disguise, the dark enigma of woman, death disguised as a virgin. How could he foil the tactics of this false *ingénue*? He no longer thought of anything except how to see through her stratagems, in the hope of revealing them to the world. She was sure to make some mistake; he would surprise her with one of her lovers, she would be thrown out again, and the shop would at last resume its smooth running like a well-made machine.

'Keep your eyes peeled, Monsieur Jouve,' Bourdoncle would repeat to the shopwalker. 'I'll reward you personally.'

But Jouve went about his task with little enthusiasm, for he knew something about women, and was thinking of taking the side of this child who might become the sovereign mistress of the future. Even if he no longer dared touch her, he considered her infernally pretty. His colonel had killed himself for a kid like that with an innocent face, refined and modest, a single glance from whom played havoc with men's hearts.

'I am, I am,' he would reply. 'But I can't discover a thing, I really can't!'

Yet there were stories circulating; there was an undercurrent of foul gossip beneath the flattery and respect which Denise could feel rising around her. Now the whole shop was recounting how Hutin had been her lover; no one dared claim that the relationship still continued, but they were suspected of seeing each other from time to time. And Deloche slept with her, too: they were always meeting in dark corners, and talking together for hours. It was a real scandal!

'So, you've got nothing on the buyer in the silk department, nothing on the young man in the lace department?' Bourdoncle would repeat.

'No, sir, nothing so far,' the inspector would reply.

It was with Deloche above all that Bourdoncle reckoned on catching Denise. One morning he himself had caught sight of them laughing together in the basement. In the mean time, he treated the girl as one power treats another, for he no longer looked down his nose at her, sensing that she was sufficiently powerful to overthrow him, in spite of his ten years' service, if he should lose the game.

'Keep your eye on the young man in the lace department,' he would conclude each time. 'They're always together. If you catch them, call me, and I'll deal with the rest.'

Mouret, meanwhile, was living in a state of agony. How could that child torture him to such an extent? He could still see her arriving at the Paradise with her clogs, her thin black dress, and her timid look. She had stumbled over her words; everyone had laughed at her; he himself had thought her ugly at first. Ugly! And now with a glance she could have made him go down on his knees; he saw her surrounded with radiance! Then, she had been the lowest of the low in the shop, rebuffed, teased, treated by him like a strange animal. For months he had wanted to see how a girl develops, he had amused himself with this experiment, without understanding that in doing so he was risking his heart. Little by little she had grown, becoming formidable. Perhaps he had loved her from the very first minute, even when he thought he felt only pity. Yet it had only been on the evening of their walk beneath the chestnut trees in the Tuileries that he had felt he belonged to her. His life had started at that moment; he could still hear the laughter of a group of little girls, the distant trickle of a fountain, while in the shade she walked beside him in silence. From then on he was lost; his fever had increased hour by hour, his life-blood, his whole being was given over to her. A child like that—could it be true? Nowadays when she passed by the slight wind from her dress seemed to him so strong that it made him reel.

For a long time he had struggled against it, and sometimes it still made him furious; he wanted to break free from this idiotic obsession. What was it about her that enslaved him in this way? Hadn't he seen her in clogs? Hadn't she been taken on almost out of charity? If it had even been one of those superb creatures who excite the crowd! But that little girl, that nobody! She had, in short, one of those blank faces about which there is nothing to be said. She was probably not even very intelligent, for he could remember what a bad start she had made as a salesgirl. Then, after each bout of anger, he would be repossessed by his passion, as if filled with superstitious fear at having insulted his idol. She possessed all the good to be found in women—courage, gaiety, simplicity—and her gentleness exuded charm with the penetrating subtlety of perfume. One could ignore her, elbow her aside as if she was like any other girl; but soon the charm would begin to take effect with a slow but invincible force; if she deigned to smile, one was hers for life. Then the whole of her pale face—her periwinkle eyes, her cheeks and her chin full of dimples—would smile; while her heavy blonde hair seemed to light up too, with a regal, all-conquering beauty. He acknowledged himself vanquished; she was as intelligent as she was beautiful, her intelligence came from all that was best in her. Whereas the other salesgirls in his shop had only a smattering of education, the peeling varnish of girls who have come down in the world, she, without any false elegance, retained the charm and savour of her origins. Behind her narrow forehead, the pure lines of which were signs of a strong will and a love of order, the most liberal commercial ideas were being formed by her experience. He was on the point of begging her to forgive him for blaspheming in his moments of rebellion.

But why did she refuse so obstinately to yield? Twenty times he had implored her, increasing his offers, offering money, a great deal of money. Then, thinking that she must be very ambitious, he had promised to make her buyer as soon as a department became vacant. And still she refused! It amazed him, and the struggle inflamed his desire. The whole thing seemed impossible to him: she would capitulate in the end, for he had always considered a woman's virtue as a relative thing. He no longer had any other objective; everything else disappeared in his desire to have her in his house at last, to take her on his knee, kissing her on the lips; and, at this vision, his heart would pound, and he would find himself trembling, distressed at his powerlessness.

From then on his days passed in the same painful obsession. The image of Denise rose with him in the morning. He had dreamed of her during the night; she followed him to the big desk in his office where, from nine till ten, he signed bills and money orders—a task he performed mechanically, without ceasing to feel that she was there, still saying no in her composed way. Then at ten o'clock there was the board meeting, a real cabinet meeting, which gathered together the twelve people with a financial interest in the shop, and at which he had to preside: questions of internal organization were discussed, purchases were inspected, displays were decided; and she was still there, he could hear her soft voice amidst the figures, he could see her bright smile through the most complicated financial discussions. After the board meeting she still accompanied him, she made the daily inspection of the departments with him, and in the afternoon she came back with him to his office and stood near his chair from two to four, when he saw a whole crowd of people— manufacturers from all over France, important business men, bankers, inventors: a continuous coming and going of money and brains, a crazy dance of millions of francs, rapid interviews at which the biggest deals on the Paris market were hatched. If he forgot her for a moment while deciding on the ruin or the prosperity of an industry, a twinge in his heart would remind him that she was still standing there; his voice would die away, and he would ask himself what was the point of this great fortune if she would not yield. Finally, when five o'clock struck, he had to sign the mail, and his hand again began to work mechanically, while she would rise up more dominating than ever, taking him over completely so that she alone might possess him during the solitary, passionate hours of the night. And the following day was the same day all over again, another of those days which were so busy, so full of immense labour, and which the slender shadow of a girl could sear with anguish.

But it was during his daily tour of inspection of the shop that he felt his misery most. To have built this gigantic machine, to reign over so many people, and to be in agonies of suffering because a little girl rejected him! He despised himself; he was pursued by the fever and shame of his affliction. On some days he felt disgusted with his own power, feeling nothing but nausea as he went from one end of the galleries to the other. At other times he would have liked to extend his empire, to make it so vast that she might perhaps yield out of sheer admiration and fear.

First of all, downstairs in the basement, he would stop by the chute. It was still in the Rue Neuve-Saint-Augustin; but it had had to be enlarged, and was now as wide as a river-bed along which a continual flow of goods rolled with the resounding noise of a flood tide; there were deliveries from every part of the world, queues of wagons from all the railway stations of Paris ceaselessly unloading boxes and bales which, flowing underground, were swallowed by the insatiable shop. He watched this torrent falling into his shop; he reflected that he was one of the masters of public wealth, that he held the fate of the French textile industry in his hands, and yet he could not buy a kiss from one of his salesgirls.

Then he moved on to the receiving department, which now occupied that part of the basement which ran along the Rue Monsigny. Twenty tables were laid out there, in the pale light from the ventilators; an army of assistants was bustling about, emptying the boxes, checking the goods, and marking the prices on them, while the roar of the nearby chute continued unabated, drowning their voices. Section-managers would stop him; he had to resolve disputes, confirm orders. The depths of the cellar were filling up with the delicate radiance of satins and the whiteness of linen, with a tremendous unpacking in which furs were mixed with lace, fancy goods with oriental door-curtains. Slowly he walked amongst these riches strewn in disorder, piled up in their raw state. They would be taken upstairs and take fire from the displays, unleashing a flood of money through the departments; and no sooner were they taken upstairs than they were carried away on the tumultuous tide of buying and selling which swept through the shop. And he thought of how he had offered the girl silks, velvets, whatever she wanted to take, in any quantity, from those enormous heaps, and how she had refused with a little shake of her fair head.

Next he would proceed to the other end of the basement in order to pay his usual visit to the dispatch department. Endless corridors stretched out, lit by gas; to the right and left the stockrooms, shut off by wooden gates, were sleeping in the shadows like subterranean shops, a whole commercial district selling haberdashery, underwear, gloves, and knick-knacks. Further on there was one of the three heating installations; further on still a firemen's post was guarding the central gas meter, enclosed in its metal cage. In the dispatch department he found the sorting tables already loaded with parcels, cardboard boxes, and bandboxes, which were continually being brought down in baskets;

and Campion, the department manager, gave him details about the work in hand, while the twenty men under his command distributed the parcels into compartments, each bearing the name of a district of Paris, from which porters took them up to the vans drawn up along the pavement. People were calling out, names of streets were tossed about, instructions were shouted, there was all the din and bustle of a steamer about to weigh anchor. He stood there for a moment, motionless, watching the goods; he had just seen the shop gorging itself on them at the opposite end of the basement and now they were being disgorged in front of him: the enormous stream came to an end there and then went out into the street, after having filled the tills with gold. His eyes were becoming blurred; this colossal dispatch of goods no longer had any importance, and he was left with nothing but the idea of travelling, going away to distant countries, abandoning everything if she persisted in saying no.

Then he went upstairs again and continued his rounds, talking and getting more and more excited without being able to take his mind off his troubles. On the second floor he went into the forwarding department, picking quarrels and secretly getting exasperated by the perfect running of the machine which he had himself regulated. This was the department which was daily assuming the greatest importance: it already needed a staff of two hundred, some of whom were opening, reading, and sorting letters from the provinces and abroad, while others were putting on shelves the goods ordered in the letters. And the number of letters was increasing to such an extent that they were no longer counted; they were weighed, and up to a hundred pounds of them arrived every day. Mouret went feverishly through the three rooms occupied by the department, questioning Levasseur, who was in charge, about the weight of the mail: eighty pounds, ninety pounds, sometimes a hundred on Mondays. The figure was still rising; he should have been delighted. But he stood shuddering in the din made by a nearby team of packers nailing up cases. He was tramping the shop in vain: his obsession pursued him everywhere, and as his power unfolded before him, as the mechanism of the departments and the army of employees passed before his gaze, he felt the indignity of his powerlessness more keenly than ever. Orders from the whole of Europe were flowing in, a special mail van was required for his correspondence, and yet she said no, she still said no.

He went downstairs again, and inspected the main counting-house, where four cashiers were guarding the two giant safes, through which, in the previous year, eighty-eight million francs had passed. He glanced at the office where the invoices were checked, which kept twenty-five specially selected employees busy. He went into the accounts office, where thirty-five appren-tice accountants were occupied in checking the debit notes and calculating the salesmen's commissions. He returned to the main counting-house, and became irritated at the sight of the safes as he walked amidst these useless millions which were driving him mad. She still said no, always no.

Always no, in every department, in the galleries, in the halls, in every part of the shop! He would go from the silks to the drapery, from the household linens to the lace; he would go upstairs, and stop on the suspension bridges, prolonging his inspection with a painful, maniacal attention to detail. The shop had grown beyond measure, he had created department after department, he governed this new domain and was forever ex-tending his empire to some fresh industry; and still it was no, always no. His staff would now have peopled a small town: there were fifteen hundred salesmen, and a thousand other employees of every kind, including forty shopwalkers and seventy cashiers; the kitchens alone kept thirty-six men busy; ten clerks had been assigned to publicity; there were three hundred and fifty porters all wearing livery, and twenty-four resident firemen.* And in the stables, truly regal stables opposite the shop in the Rue Monsigny, there were a hundred and forty-five horses, magnifi-cent teams which had already become famous in Paris. The four original vehicles which had so upset the local tradesmen in the past, when the shop still only occupied one corner of the Place Gaillon, had gradually increased in number to sixty-two: there were small hand-carts, one-horse cabs, and heavy wagons drawn by two horses. They were continually ploughing through Paris, driven with great decorum by coachmen dressed in black, and bearing on their sides the gold and purple emblem of the Ladies' Paradise. They would even go outside the city walls, into the suburbs; they would be seen in the sunken lanes of Bicêtre, along the banks of the Marne, even beneath the shady trees of the forest of Saint-Germain; sometimes, from the depths of some sunny avenue, utterly deserted and silent, one of them would loom into sight, passing by with its superb animals at the trot, throwing the violent advertisement of its varnished panels over the mysterious peace of nature. He dreamed of sending them even further afield into neighbouring *départements*; he would have liked to hear them rattling along all the roads of France, from one frontier to the other. But he no longer even went to visit his horses, which he adored. What was the good of conquering the world, since it was no, still no?

Nowadays, in the evening, when he arrived at Lhomme's cash-desk he would still, from habit, look at the amount of the takings, written on a card which the cashier stuck on an iron spike at his side; this figure rarely fell below a hundred thousand francs, and sometimes it rose to eight or nine hundred thousand on days when there were special displays; but it no longer sounded in his ears like a trumpet call. He would regret having looked at it, for it left him with a feeling of bitterness, hatred, and contempt for money.

Yet Mouret's sufferings were to become even greater. He became jealous. One morning, in his office before the board meeting, Bourdoncle ventured to hint to him that that little girl in the ladieswear department was making a fool of him.

'What do you mean?' he asked, very pale.

'It's true! She has lovers right here in the shop.'

Mouret still had the strength to smile.

'I don't think about her any more, old man. You can tell me whatever you like . . . Who are they, these lovers?'

'Hutin, so I'm told, and a salesman in the lace department, Deloche, that big, stupid boy . . . I can't swear to it, I haven't seen them together. But apparently there's no doubt about it!'

There was a silence. Mouret pretended to arrange the papers on his desk so as to hide the trembling of his hands. Finally, without looking up, he said:

'We must have proof, try and get me some proof . . . As far as I'm concerned, as I said, I don't give a damn, I got fed up with her. But we can't tolerate that sort of thing in the shop.'

Bourdoncle simply replied:

'Don't worry, you'll have proof one of these days. I'm keeping my eyes open.'

After that Mouret's peace of mind was completely shattered. He did not have the courage to raise the matter again, and he lived in continuous expectation of a catastrophe which would really break his heart. His anguish made him quite terrifying; the whole shop trembled. He no longer wished to hide behind Bourdoncle and, feeling an urge to be spiteful, would carry out executions himself, relieving his feelings by abusing his power—that power which could do nothing to satisfy his sole desire. Each tour of inspection turned into a massacre; no sooner did he appear than a shudder of panic spread from counter to counter. The winter slack season was just beginning, and he made a clean sweep of the departments, piling up victims and pushing them out into the street. His first thought had been to get rid of Hutin and Deloche; then he had thought that if he did not keep them he would never discover anything; and so others suffered in their stead—the whole staff felt threatened. In the evening, when he was alone again, his eyes would fill with tears.

One day, in particular, terror reigned. A shopwalker thought he had seen Mignot, the glover, stealing. There were always a lot of strange-looking girls prowling around his counter, and one of them had just been arrested, her hips and bosom padded with sixty pairs of gloves. From then on a careful watch was kept, and the shopwalker caught Mignot red-handed, facilitating the sleight of hand of a tall blonde girl, a former salesgirl at the Louvre who had ended up on the street. Their technique was simple: he would pretend to be trying gloves on her, waiting until she had padded herself up, and would then conduct her to a cash-desk where she would pay for one pair only. Mouret happened to be there when this happened. Usually he preferred not to become involved in incidents of this kind, which were frequent; for, although it ran like a well-oiled machine, great disorder reigned in certain departments of the Ladies's Paradise, and not a week passed without an employee being dismissed for stealing. The management preferred to hush up these incidents, considering it pointless to call in the police, for by so doing they would have been exposing one of the fatal weaknesses of the big stores. But, on that particular day, Mouret had an urge to lose his temper, and he dealt very violently with the 'Handsome' Mignot who, his face pale and drawn, was trembling with fear.

'I ought to call a policeman,' Mouret was shouting, surrounded by the other salesmen. 'Answer me! Who is this woman? I swear I'll send for the police if you don't tell me the truth.'

The woman had been led away, and two salesgirls were undressing her. Mignot stammered:

'I've never seen her before, sir . . . She's the one who came . . .'

'Don't lie to me!' interrupted Mouret, becoming even more violent. 'And no one warned us! You're all in this together! We're in a regular den of thieves, robbed, pillaged, looted! It's enough to make me have everyone's pockets searched before they leave!'

There were audible murmurs. The three or four customers who were buying gloves looked on in amazement.

'Be quiet!' he went on furiously, 'or I'll clear the shop!'

But Bourdoncle had come running up, worried at the idea of a scandal. He murmured a few words in Mouret's ear, as the affair was becoming exceptionally serious; and he persuaded him to take Mignot into the shopwalkers' office, which was situated on the ground floor near the Rue Gaillon entrance. The woman was there, calmly putting her corset on again. She had just mentioned the name of Albert Lhomme. Mignot, questioned again, lost his head and began to sob: he was not to blame, it was Albert who sent his mistresses to him; to begin with, he had just given them preferential treatment, allowing them to take advantage of bargains; then, when they had ended up stealing, he was already too deeply involved to inform the management. Then they learned of a whole series of extraordinary thefts: how goods were carried off by prostitutes who went and attached them beneath their petticoats in the luxurious lavatories, surrounded by green plants, near the buffet; how a salesman would omit to call out a sale at a cash-desk when he was conducting a customer there, and how he would share the price of it with the cashier; how there were even false 'returns', goods which were said to have been sent back to the shop, so that the money falsely refunded could be pocketed; not to mention the classic technique of simply taking parcels out of the shop in the evening underneath an overcoat, twisted round a waist, or sometimes even hanging down someone's thighs. Thus, thanks to Mignot and doubtless to other salesmen whom he refused to name, Albert's cash-desk had been the focus for all sorts of shady dealings for the last fourteen months, a really shameless business, and the exact sums involved were never known.

Meanwhile, the news had spread through the departments. Uneasy consciences began to tremble, and even the most honest among them stood in dread of the clean sweep Mouret was making. Albert had been seen disappearing into the shopwalkers' office. Then Lhomme had gone in, red in the face, already choking with apoplexy. Next, Madame Aurélie herself had been summoned; she was holding her head high in her shame and her face was pale, with the flabby puffiness of a wax mask. The argument went on for some time; no one knew precisely what happened: it was said that the buyer from the ladieswear department had slapped her son's face, and that his poor old father had wept; while the governor, abandoning his usual graciousness and swearing like a trooper, had insisted on handing over the guilty parties to justice. However, the scandal was hushed up. Only Mignot was dismissed on the spot. Albert did not disappear until two days later; no doubt his mother had obtained a promise that the family should not be dishonoured by an immediate execution. But the panic had lasted for several more days, for after this scene Mouret had walked from one end of the shop to the other with a terrible look in his eye, firing immediately all those who dared even to raise their eyes.

'What are you doing there, sir, watching flies? Proceed to the pay-desk!'

One day the storm burst over the head of Hutin himself. Favier, appointed assistant buyer, was undermining the buyer so as to take over his position. He was using the usual tactics—sending secret reports to the management, taking advantage of every opportunity to have the head of the department caught doing something wrong. Thus, one morning as Mouret was going through the silk department, he stopped, surprised to see Favier altering the price tickets of a whole stock of black velvet.

'Why are you lowering the prices?' he asked. 'Who gave you the order to do that?'

The assistant buyer, who was making a great fuss over the job, as if he had wanted to catch the governor's attention as he went by, replied with an air of innocent surprise:

'Oh, it was Monsieur Hutin, sir.'

'Monsieur Hutin! Well, where is Monsieur Hutin?'

When the latter had returned from the reception desk downstairs, where a salesman had been sent to fetch him, he was immediately called to account. What! He was now reducing prices on his own initiative! But he appeared greatly astonished in his turn, having merely discussed the reduction with Favier, without giving a definite order. At this the latter put on the distressed air of an employee who feels obliged to contradict his superior. However, he would gladly take the blame, if it would get him out of a fix. Things now began to look very bad.

'You really must understand, Monsieur Hutin,' shouted Mouret, 'that I've never tolerated such attempts at independence . . . Only the management decides on prices!'

He continued to berate Hutin in a very harsh voice, which surprised the salesmen, for this kind of argument usually took place in private, and in any case it might really be the result of a misunderstanding. They could feel that he wanted to relieve some unavowed grudge. So at last he had caught him out, this man Hutin, who was supposed to be Denise's lover! Now he could relieve his feelings a bit, by making him fully aware that he was the master! And he exaggerated the whole affair, ending up by insinuating that the price reductions hid certain dishonest intentions.

'I intended to refer this reduction to you, sir,' repeated Hutin. 'It's really necessary, as you know, because these velvets haven't been selling well.'

Mouret cut him short with a final sharp remark.

'Very well, sir, we'll look into the matter . . . But don't do it again, if you value your job.'

And he walked off. Hutin, stunned and furious, had only Favier to relieve his feelings on; he swore to him that he would go and fling his resignation in that brute's face. Then he stopped talking about leaving, and merely raked up all the atrocious accusations which salesmen were always making against their employers. Favier, his eyes shining, defended himself, making a great show of his sympathy. He had been obliged to reply, hadn't he? And how could anyone have anticipated such a fuss about nothing? What was the matter with the governor lately? He really was impossible.

'Oh! We all know what's the matter with him,' Hutin went on. 'It isn't my fault if that whore in the ladieswear department is driving him crazy! . . . You see, old chap, that's what it's all about. He knows I've slept with her, and he doesn't like it; or else, she wants to have me kicked out because I make things difficult for her . . . I can tell you she'll know about it if she comes my way.'

Two days later, when Hutin had gone upstairs to the work-room, which was up in the attics, to give some instructions to a seamstress, he gave a slight start on seeing Denise and Deloche at the end of a corridor, leaning against an open window, and so deep in conversation that they did not look round. He noticed with surprise that Deloche was weeping, and it suddenly occurred to him that he'd caught them unawares. He withdrew silently, and, bumping into Bourdoncle and Jouve on the stairs, he told them some story about one of the fire-extinguishers which looked as if its door had been pulled off; this would make them go upstairs and run into the other two. Bourdoncle saw them first. He stopped short, and told Jouve to go and fetch the governor while he waited there. The shopwalker was forced to obey, very annoyed at finding himself involved in an affair of this kind.

They were in an out-of-the-way corner of the vast world in which the multitudes in the Ladies' Paradise came and went. It was reached by a complicated network of stairs and corridors. The series of work-rooms in the attics had low, sloping ceilings, lit by broad bay windows cut out of the zinc roof and furnished only with long tables and huge iron stoves; there were lingerie-makers, lace-makers, upholsterers, and dressmakers, who lived there winter and summer in stifling heat, in the midst of the smells peculiar to their trades; and in order to reach this remote part of the shop it was necessary to go right through that wing of the building, turn to the left after the dressmakers, and go up five steps. The rare customers who were sometimes taken there by a salesman for something they had ordered would recover their breath, exhausted and anxious, feeling that they had been going round and round for hours and were a hundred miles away from the street.

Several times already Denise had found Deloche waiting for her. As assistant buyer she was in charge of the department's dealings with the work-rooms where only models were made and alterations carried out; she was always going upstairs to give instructions. He would look out for her, inventing some pretext to walk after her; then he would pretend to be surprised when he met her at the work-room door. She had ended up by laughing about it; the meetings had become almost an accepted thing. The corridor ran along the side of the cistern, an enormous metal tank which contained sixty thousand litres of water; and there was another one of equal size on the roof, reached by an iron ladder. Deloche would stand talking for a moment, leaning one shoulder against the cistern, for his huge body was always exhausted and bent with fatigue. There were sounds of water, mysterious sounds which gave the metal of the tank a musical vibration. In spite of the utter silence Denise would look round anxiously, thinking she saw a shadow move across the bare walls covered in bright yellow paint. But soon the window would attract them; they would lean their elbows on the sill, and forget themselves in pleasant chatter, in endless reminiscences of the country where they had spent their childhood. Beneath them extended the immense glazed roof of the central gallery, a lake of glass bounded by the distant housetops, as if by rocky coasts. And beyond they could see nothing but the sky, an expanse of sky which, with its flights of clouds and its delicate azure blue, was mirrored in the still water of the window-panes.

On that particular day, as it happened, Deloche was talking about Valognes.

'I was six, and my mother used to take me in a cart to the market. You know it's a good eight miles; we had to leave Briquebec at five o'clock . . . It's very beautiful there. Do you know it?'

'Yes, yes,' replied Denise, slowly, gazing into the distance, 'I went there once, but I was very little . . . The roads have grass verges on either side, haven't they? And there are sheep, roaming about in pairs, trailing their tethering ropes . . .'

She was silent for a while, then resumed with a vague smile:

'In our part of the world, the roads run absolutely straight for miles, between trees which make them very shady . . . We have meadows surrounded by hedges which are taller than I am, where there are horses and cows . . . We've got a little river, and the water's very cold under the brushwood, in a spot I know very well.'

'It's just like that with us!' Deloche exclaimed in delight. 'There's nothing but grassland, and everyone surrounds his piece with hawthorns and elms and feels at home, and it's all green, a green you don't see in Paris . . . Oh! I used to play for hours at the bottom of the sunken path, on the left, on the way down from the mill!'

Their voices died away, and they remained there, gazing fixedly at the sunny lake of the window-panes. From this blinding water a mirage rose up before them; they could see endless pastures, the Cotentin soaked with breezes from the ocean, bathed in a luminous haze which was melting away on the horizon in the delicate grey of a water-colour. Below them, beneath the colossal iron framework, there was the roar of the buying and selling in the silk department, the reverberation of the machine at work, the whole shop vibrating with the trampling of the crowd, the bustle of salesmen, the life of the thirty thousand people packed together there; but, carried away by their dreams, they felt this deep, muffled roar with which the roofs were resounding, and thought they were listening to the wind from the sea blowing over the pastures, shaking the tall trees as it went.

'Mademoiselle Denise,' stammered Deloche, 'why aren't you kinder to me? I love you so much!'

Tears had come into his eyes, and when she tried to interrupt him with a gesture, he continued quickly:

'No, let me tell you this just once more . . . We'd get on so well together! There's always something to talk about when you come from the same part of the world.'

He was choking with tears and at last she was able to say gently:

'You're not being sensible; you promised not to talk about that any more . . . It's impossible. I'm very fond of you, because you're a very nice boy, but I want to stay free.'

'Yes, yes, I know,' he went on in a broken voice. 'You don't love me. Oh! You can say so, I understand, there's nothing to make you love me . . . I've only had one good hour in my life, that evening when I met you in Joinville, do you remember? For a moment, under the trees where it was so dark, I thought I felt your arm trembling. I was stupid enough to imagine . . .'

But she cut him short once more. Her sharp ears had just heard the footsteps of Bourdoncle and Jouve at the other end of the corridor.

'Listen, there's someone coming.'

'No,' he said, preventing her from leaving the window. 'It's in the cistern: it makes all sorts of strange noises; you'd think there were people inside it.'

He went on with his timid complaints. She was no longer listening to him, once more lulled into a day-dream by his talk of love, letting her glances stray over the roofs of the Ladies' Paradise. To the right and left of the glazed gallery, other galleries and other halls were gleaming in the sunshine, between gables pitted with windows and set out symmetrically like barrack wings. Metal structures rose up, ladders and bridges, whose lacework stood out against the blue sky; while the chimney from the kitchens was belching out enough smoke for a factory, and the great square cistern, supported in the air by iron pillars, seemed like some barbaric construction hoisted up there by the pride of one man. The roar of Paris could be heard in the distance.

When Denise returned from space, from this airy development of the Paradise where her thoughts had been floating as if in some vast retreat, she saw that Deloche had taken her hand. His face was so distressed that she did not take it back.

'Forgive me,' he murmured, 'it's all over now, it would make me too unhappy if you punished me by taking away your friendship . . . I swear to you that I didn't mean to say that to you. Yes, I'd promised myself to understand the situation, to be reasonable . . .'

His tears were flowing once more; he was trying to steady his voice.

'Because I know now what my lot in life is. And my luck isn't likely to change now. I was beaten back there at home, I'm beaten in Paris, I'm beaten everywhere. I've been here four years now, and I'm still on the bottom rung in the department . . . So I wanted to tell you that you shouldn't be upset on my account. I won't bother you any more. Try to be happy, love someone else; yes, that would make me happy. If you're happy, I'll be happy . . . That'll be my joy.'

He could not go on. As if to seal his promise, he had placed his lips on the girl's hand and was kissing it with the humble kiss of a slave. She was deeply touched, and with a sisterly tenderness which toned down the pity in her words, she said simply:

'You poor boy!'

But they gave a start and turned round. Mouret was standing there. For ten minutes Jouve had been looking for the governor in the shop. But the latter had been on the site for the new shopfront in the Rue du Dix-Décembre. He spent hours there every day, trying to take an interest in this work he had dreamed of for so long. He found a refuge from his torments among the masons laying the corner-stones and the metalworkers putting up great iron girders. Already the shop-front was rising up, outlining the vast porch, the bays on the first floor, the birth of a palace. He would go up ladders, discuss the decorations—which were to be something quite new—with the architect, climb over ironwork and bricks, and even go down into the cellars; and the roar of the steam-engine, the tick-tock of the winches, the banging of the hammers, and the clamour of the crowd of workmen in this huge cage surrounded by echoing boards succeeded in numbing his feelings for a few moments. He would leave white with plaster, black with iron filings, his feet splashed by the water from the pumps, his trouble so far from being cured that his anguish would return and make his heart beat even more loudly as the din of the building site died away behind him. It so happened, on that particular day, that a diversion had restored his gaiety: he had become fascinated by an album of drawings of the mosaics and terracotta tiles with which the friezes were to be decorated, when Jouve, out of breath and very annoyed at having to get his frock-coat dirty among the building materials, had come to fetch him. At first Mouret had shouted that they could wait for him; then, after the shopwalker had said a few words to him in an undertone, he had followed him, trembling, overwhelmed by his passion again. Nothing else existed; the shop-front was crumbling before it had been built: what was the good of this supreme triumph of his pride, if the mere name of a woman, murmured in an undertone, tortured him to this extent!

Upstairs Bourdoncle and Jouve thought it wise to disappear. Deloche had already fled. Denise stood facing Mouret alone, paler than usual, but looking straight up at him.

'Please follow me, miss,' he said in a hard voice.

She followed him; they went down two floors and crossed the furniture and carpet departments without saying a word. When he reached his office, he opened the door wide.

'Go in, please, miss.'

He closed the door and went straight to his desk. His new office was more luxurious than the old one: green velvet hangings had replaced the rep, a bookcase inlaid with ivory filled the whole of one wall; but, on the other walls, the only picture was still the portrait of Madame Hédouin, a young woman with a beautiful, calm face, smiling in her golden frame.

'Mademoiselle Baudu,' he said finally, trying to remain coldly severe, 'there are certain things we cannot tolerate . . . Good behaviour is compulsory here . . .'

He spoke slowly, choosing his words carefully in order not to give way to the rage which was mounting inside him. It was that boy she loved, that wretched salesman, the laughing-stock of his department! She preferred the humblest and clumsiest of them all to him, the master! For he had clearly seen them, Denise letting him take her hand, and Deloche covering that hand with kisses.

'I've been very good to you, Mademoiselle Baudu,' he continued, making a fresh effort. 'I hardly expected to be repaid in this way.'

From the moment she entered, Denise's eyes had been drawn to the portrait of Madame Hédouin; and, in spite of her great confusion, she remained preoccupied by it. Every time she went into Mouret's office her eyes met those of this lady. She was a little afraid of her, and yet she felt that she was very kind. This time, she felt as if, in her, she had a protector.

'You're right, sir,' she replied gently, 'it was wrong of me to stop and talk, and I apologize . . . That young man comes from my part of the country.'

'I'll throw him out!' shouted Mouret, putting all his suffering into this cry of fury.

And, completely distraught, abandoning his role as the general manager lecturing a salesgirl guilty of breaking the rules, he burst out in a torrent of violent words. Wasn't she ashamed? A girl like her giving herself to a creature like that! And he made all sorts of appalling accusations: he threw Hutin's name at her, and others as well, such a flood of words that she could not even defend herself. He was going to make a clean sweep; he would kick them all out. The telling-off which, as he had followed Jouve, he had promised himself he would give her was degenerating into a violent scene of jealousy.

'Yes, your lovers! I was told you had them, and I was stupid enough not to believe it . . . But I was the only one! I was the only one!'

Denise, stunned and bewildered, stood listening to these terrible reproaches. At first she had not understood. Did he really think she was immoral? He made a further remark, even more violent than before, upon which she turned silently towards the door. He made a movement to stop her, but she said:

'That's enough, sir, I must leave . . . If you think I'm what you say, I don't wish to remain in this shop another second.'

He rushed to the door.

'Defend yourself, at least! Say something!'

She stood very erect, in icy silence. For a long time he pressed her with questions, growing more and more anxious; and the virgin's silent dignity seemed once more to be the cunning ruse of a woman experienced in the tactics of passion. She could not have played a game more calculated to throw him at her feet, so torn with doubt was he, so anxious to be convinced.

'But you say he comes from your part of the world . . . Perhaps you met each other there . . . Swear to me that nothing's happened between you.'

And as she maintained an obstinate silence, and still wished to open the door and leave, he finally lost his head, and burst out in a climactic expression of his torment.

'My God! I love you, I love you . . . Why do you delight in tormenting me like this? You can see that nothing else exists, that the people I speak about to you only affect me through you, that you're the only person in the world who matters . . . I thought you were jealous, so I gave up my pleasures. People told you I had mistresses; well, I haven't any more, I hardly ever go out. Didn't I show my preference for you when we were in that lady's house? Didn't I break with her so that I could belong only to you? I'm still waiting for a word of thanks, a little gratitude. And if you're afraid that I'll go back to her you needn't worry: she's taking her revenge by helping one of our ex-assistants to set up a rival shop . . . Tell me! must I get down on my knees to move your heart?'

He had reached that point. He who would not tolerate his salesgirls making a slip, who threw them into the street at his slightest whim, found himself reduced to imploring one of them not to leave, not to abandon him to his misery. He was barring the door to her, he was ready to forgive her, to shut his eyes to everything if only she would condescend to lie about it. And it was true, he had become sick of girls picked up backstage in small theatres and night-clubs; he had given up Clara, he had not set foot again in Madame Desforges's house, where Bouthemont now reigned supreme, pending the opening of the new shop, the Quatre Saisons, for which the newspapers were already full of advertisements.

'Tell me, must I get down on my knees?' he repeated, choking back his tears.

She stopped him with a gesture, no longer able to hide her own confusion, deeply affected by this tortured passion.

'You're wrong to make yourself unhappy, sir,' she replied at last. 'I swear to you that all those wicked stories are just lies . . . That poor boy you saw a moment ago is no more guilty than I am.'

She was as wonderfully frank as ever and her clear eyes were looking him straight in the face.

'Very well, I believe you,' he murmured. 'I won't dismiss any of your friends, since you've taken them all under your wing . . . But why do you reject me, if you don't love anyone else?'

Denise was overcome with sudden embarrassment and anxious modesty.

'You do love someone, don't you?' he went on in a trembling voice. 'You can say so, I have no claim on your affections . . . You do love someone.'

She was blushing deeply; it was on the tip of her tongue to say what was in her heart, and she felt that, with her emotion betraying her and her repugnance for falsehood allowing the truth to show on her face in spite of everything, it would be impossible to lie.

'Yes,' she admitted weakly. 'Please let me go, sir, you're distressing me.'

She was now suffering in her turn. Wasn't it enough to have to defend herself against him? Would she also have to defend herself against herself, against the waves of tenderness which at times swept away all her courage? When he talked to her like that, when she saw him so deeply moved, so overcome, she didn't know why she still resisted him; and it was only afterwards that she rediscovered, at the very roots of her healthy temperament, the dignity and reason which maintained her virginal obstinacy. It was an instinctive desire for happiness that made her persist in refusing, to satisfy her need for a peaceful life, and not to conform to any idea of virtue. She would have fallen into his arms, her body overcome and her heart seduced, if she had not felt a resistance, almost a repulsion at the idea of giving herself to him, without knowing what might ensue. The thought of a lover frightened her, with that instinctive fear which makes a woman blanch at the approach of the male.

Meanwhile Mouret had made a gesture of complete discouragement. He did not understand. He turned round to his desk, where he shuffled some papers and put them down again immediately, saying:

'I won't detain you any longer, Mademoiselle Baudu; I can't keep you against your will.'

'But I'm not asking to leave,' she replied with a smile. 'If you think I'm respectable, I'll stay . . . You should always believe women to be respectable, sir. There are many who are, I assure you.'

Denise had, involuntarily, looked up at the portrait of Madame Hédouin, that lady so beautiful and wise, whose blood, so they said, brought luck to the shop. Mouret followed the girl's glance with a start, for he thought he'd heard his dead wife uttering this phrase; it was one of her phrases, which he recognized immediately. It was like a resurrection; he was rediscovering in Denise the good sense and sound balance of the woman he had lost, even down to the gentle voice, sparing of superfluous words. He was deeply struck by this resemblance, which made him sadder than ever.

'You know I belong to you,' he murmured in conclusion. 'Do what you like with me.'

At that she went on gaily:

'Very well, sir. A woman's opinion, however humble she may be, is always worth listening to, if she's got any sense . . . If you put yourself in my hands, I shall certainly make a decent man of you.'

She was joking, with her simple manner which was so charming. In his turn he gave a feeble smile and escorted her to the door as he would a lady.

The next day Denise was promoted to buyer. The management had split the dress and suit department into two, by creating specially for her a department for children's suits, which was set up near the ladieswear department. Since her son's dismissal Madame Aurélie lived in fear, for she could feel the management becoming cool towards her, and saw the girl's power growing daily. Were they going to sacrifice her to Denise, on some pretext or other? Her emperor-like mask, puffy with fat, seemed to have become thinner at the shame which now tainted the Lhomme dynasty; and she made a great show of going away every evening on her husband's arm, for they had become reconciled by misfortune, and understood that the trouble came from their home life being so messy; while her poor husband, who was even more affected than she was, and had a morbid fear of being suspected of theft too, would count the takings twice over, very noisily performing real miracles with his bad arm as he did so. And so, when she saw Denise promoted to buyer in the children's suit department, she felt such acute joy that she began to behave with the greatest affection towards her. It was really wonderful of her not to have taken her job away from her! She overwhelmed her with gestures of friendship; from then on she treated her as an equal and often went with a stately air to chat with her in the neighbouring department, like a queen mother visiting a young queen.

In any case, Denise now commanded great respect in the shop. Her appointment as buyer had broken down the last resistance around her. If some still talked, because of that itch for gossip which ravages any assembly of men and women, they nevertheless bowed very low before her, right down to the ground in fact. Marguerite, now assistant buyer in the ladieswear department, was full of praise for her. Even Clara, filled with secret respect before such good fortune, which she herself was incapable of attaining, had bowed her head. But Denise's victory was even more complete over the men—over Jouve, who now bent double whenever he addressed her; over Hutin, full of anxiety at feeling his job crumbling beneath him; over Bourdoncle, at last rendered powerless. When the latter had seen her coming out of Mouret's office, smiling, with her usual composed air, and when the next day the director had insisted that the board should create the new department, he had given in, conquered by a superstitious fear of Woman. He had always given in like that to Mouret's charm; he recognized him as his master, in spite of the wild flights of his genius and his idiotic impulsive actions. This time the woman had proved the stronger, and he was to be swept away by the disaster.

However, Denise responded to her triumph in a calm, charming manner. She was touched by these marks of consideration, and tried to see in them sympathy for the misery of her earlier days in the shop, and her final success after being courageous for so long. Therefore she welcomed the slightest gestures of friendship with joyful smiles, which made her really loved by some, for she had such a kind, sympathetic, and generous nature. The only person for whom she felt permanent repugnance was Clara, for she had learned that the girl had amused herself one evening by taking Colomban home as she had jokingly planned to do; and the assistant, carried away by this long-awaited satisfaction of his passion, now slept out all the time, while poor Geneviève was dying. They talked about it at the Paradise and thought it very amusing.

But this sorrow, the only one she had outside the shop, did not affect Denise's even temper. It was in her own department that she was seen at her best, surrounded by a crowd of little children of all ages. She adored children, and a better position could not have been found for her. Sometimes there would be as many as fifty little girls and the same number of boys there, a kind of boisterous boarding-school let loose in their growing coquettish desires. The mothers would lose their heads completely. She, soothing and smiling, would get all the youngsters lined up on chairs; and when she saw some rosy-cheeked little girl in the crowd whose pretty little face attracted her, she would serve her herself and would bring the dress and try it on the child's chubby shoulders with the tender care of a big sister. There would be peals of laughter, little cries of ecstasy in the midst of scolding voices. Sometimes a little girl of nine or ten, quite grown up already, when trying on a cloth coat would study it in front of a looking-glass, turning round with an absorbed look, her eyes shining with the desire to please. The counters were littered with unfolded goods, dresses in pink or blue tussore for children from one to five, zephyr sailor-suits, a pleated skirt and blouse trimmed with appliquéd cambric, Louis XV costumes, coats, jackets, a jumble of small garments, stiff in their childish grace, rather like the cloakroom of a collection of big dolls, taken out of cupboards and left to be ransacked. Denise always had some sweets in her pockets, and would soothe the tears of some infant in despair at not being able to take a pair of red trousers away with him; she lived there among the little ones as if they were her own family, and she herself felt younger because of all the innocence and freshness ceaselessly renewed around her.

She now had long friendly conversations with Mouret. When she had to go to his office for instructions or to give information he would keep her talking, enjoying the sound of her voice. This was what she laughingly called 'making a decent man of him'. In her shrewd, rational, Norman mind all sorts of projects were forming, ideas on modern business methods which she had already ventured to float at Robineau's, and some of which she had expressed on that fine evening when she and Mouret had walked together in the Tuileries Gardens. She could never do anything herself, or watch a task being carried out, without being obsessed with the need to put method into it, to improve the system. Thus, ever since she had been taken on at the Ladies' Paradise, she had been troubled above all by the precarious situation of the junior assistants. The sudden dismissals shocked her; she considered them clumsy and iniquitous, as harmful to the shop as they were to the staff. The sufferings of her early days in the shop were still fresh in her mind, and her heart was wrung with pity each time she met a newcomer in one of the departments, with sore feet and tears in her eyes, shuffling along miserably in her silk dress, persecuted constantly by the girls who had been there longer than she had. This dog's life made even the best of them turn bad, and their sad decline would begin. They were all worn out by their profession before they were forty; they would disappear, go off into the unknown, many would die in harness of consumption or anaemia, brought on by fatigue and bad air, and some would end up on the street, while the luckier ones would marry and be buried in some small provincial shop. Was it humane or right, this appalling consumption of human flesh every year by the big shops? She would plead the cause of the cogs in this great machine, not for sentimental reasons, but with arguments based on the employers' own interests. When one wants a sound machine one uses good metal; if the metal breaks or is broken there's a stoppage of work, repeated expense in getting it started again, a considerable wastage of energy. Sometimes she would become quite excited, imagining a huge, ideal emporium, a phalanstery of trade, in which everyone would have a fair share of the profits according to merit, and his or her future would be assured by a contract. Mouret would brighten up when she spoke like this, in spite of his misery. He would accuse her of socialism, and confuse her by pointing out the difficulties of putting it all into practice; for she spoke with the simplicity of her heart, and would bravely put her trust in the future whenever she perceived a dangerous pitfall in her own tender-hearted methods. He was disturbed and captivated, however, by her young voice, still trembling from the ills she had suffered, and so full of conviction when pointing out reforms which would benefit the shop; and although he laughed at her, he listened to her:

the salesmen's lot gradually improved, the mass dismissals were replaced by a system of leave given during the slack seasons, and there was also a plan to create a mutual aid society which would protect them against forced redundancy and would guarantee them a pension. This was the embryo of the vast trade unions of the twentieth century.

What is more, Denise did not confine herself to dressing the open wounds from which she herself had bled: the subtle, feminine ideas she whispered to Mouret delighted the customers. She also made Lhomme happy by supporting a plan he had had for some time, of forming a band from among the staff. Three months later Lhomme had a hundred and twenty musicians under his direction; his life's dream had come true. A big festival was organized in the shop, a concert and a ball, in order to introduce the band to the customers and to the whole world. The newspapers took it up, and even Bourdoncle, devastated by these innovations, had to acknowledge what superb advertising this was. Next, a games room for the assistants was installed, with two billiard tables as well as backgammon and chess boards. In the evenings, classes were held in the shop; there were English and German lessons, as well as lessons in grammar, arithmetic, and geography; there were even lessons in riding and fencing. A library was created, and ten thousand volumes were put at the disposal of the staff. A resident doctor gave free consultations, and there were baths, bars, and a hairdressing salon. Every need in life was provided for, everything was obtainable without leaving the building—study, refreshment, sleeping accommodation, clothing.* The Ladies' Paradise was self-sufficient in both pleasures and necessities, and the heart of Paris was filled with its din, with this city of labour which was growing so vigorously out of the ruins of the old streets which had at last been opened up to the sunlight.

There was a fresh wave of opinion in favour of Denise. Since Bourdoncle, now defeated, kept repeating in despair to his friends that he would have given a great deal to put her in Mouret's bed himself, it had been concluded that she had not yielded, and that her all-powerfulness resulted from her refusals. From then on, she became popular. People knew that they were indebted to her for various comforts, and she was admired for her strength of will. There was one person, at least, who knew how to hold the governor at her mercy, who was avenging them all, and who knew how to get something more than promises out of him! She had come at last, a woman who forced people to have some regard for the underprivileged! When she went through the departments, with her delicate but determined expression and her gentle yet invincible air, the salesmen would smile at her and feel proud of her, and would gladly have shown her off to the crowd. Denise was happy to allow herself to be swept along by this growing sympathy towards her. Could it really be true? She could see herself arriving in her shabby skirt, scared and lost among the gear-wheels of the terrifying machine; for a long time she had had the sensation of being nothing, hardly a grain of millet under the millstones crushing everyone beneath them. Now she was the very soul of that world, only she mattered, with a word she could speed up or slow down the colossus lying vanquished at her feet. And yet none of this had been premeditated; she had simply presented herself at the shop, with no ulterior motive and with nothing but her charming gentleness. Her supremacy sometimes caused her uneasy surprise: what was it that made them all obey her like that? She was not pretty, nor would she do them any harm. Then, her heart soothed, she would smile, for there was nothing in her but kindness and good sense and a love of truth and logic which was her great strength.

Now that she was in favour, one of Denise's joys was to be able to help Pauline. The latter was pregnant, and was very anxious, because two salesgirls in a fortnight had been forced to leave in the seventh month of their pregnancy. The management did not tolerate accidents of that kind; maternity was not allowed since it was considered cumbersome and indecent—marriage was occasionally allowed, but children were forbidden. Pauline's husband worked in the shop, of course; but she was very nervous all the same, for it did not make it any easier for her to appear in the department; and in order to delay her probable dismissal, she laced herself in till she could hardly breathe, determined to hide her condition as long as she could. One of the two salesgirls who had been dismissed had just had a stillborn child from having tortured her waist in this way; and there was little hope that she herself would recover. Meanwhile Bourdoncle was observing Pauline's complexion turning leaden, and thought he could see a painful stiffness in her gait. One morning he was standing near her in the trousseau department when a porter who was taking away a parcel bumped into her so hard that she gave a cry and put both hands on her stomach. He immediately led her away and made her confess, and then recommended to the board that she be dismissed, under the pretext that she needed some country air; the story of the blow she had received would get around, and if she had a miscarriage the effect on the public would be disastrous, as had occurred the year before with a girl from the babywear department. Mouret, who was not present at the board meeting, could only give his opinion in the evening. But Denise had had time to intervene, and he told Bourdoncle to keep quiet in the shop's own interest. Did they want to stir up the mothers against them, and offend all the young customers who had recently had babies? It was pompously decided that any married salesgirl who became pregnant would be entrusted to a special midwife as soon as her presence in the department became an offence to morality.

The next day, when Denise went up to the sick-room to see Pauline, who had had to go to bed as a result of the blow she had received, the latter kissed her violently on both cheeks.

'You're so kind! If it hadn't been for you they'd have thrown me out . . . Don't worry about me, the doctor says everything will be all right.'

Baugé, who had slipped away from his department, was also there, on the other side of the bed. He too stammered out his thanks, embarrassed in the presence of Denise, whom he now treated as someone who had made good and was in a superior class. Ah! If he heard any more nasty remarks about her he'd make sure that the jealous ones had their mouths shut for them! But Pauline sent him away with a friendly shrug of her shoulders.

'My poor darling, you're just talking nonsense . . . Off with you, leave us to have a chat.'

The sick-room was long and light, with twelve beds with white curtains. The assistants who lived in the shop were nursed there if they did not wish to go back to their families. But that day Pauline was the only person there, in a bed near one of the big windows which overlooked the Rue Neuve-Saint-Augustin. And they immediately began to exchange confidences, and fond, whispered phrases, in the midst of all that innocent linen, in the sleepy air perfumed with a vague smell of lavender.

'So he does everything you want? How cruel you are to make him so unhappy! Come on, explain, since I've dared to broach the subject. Can't you bear him?'

Pauline had kept Denise's hand in hers, for she was sitting by the bed, with her elbows on the bolster; and overcome with emotion at this blunt and unexpected question, she had a momentary weakness. She let out her secret, hiding her face in the pillow as she murmured:

'I love him!'

Pauline was dumbfounded.

'What! You love him? Then it's very simple: say yes.'

Denise, her face still hidden, shook her head vigorously. And she was refusing to say yes precisely because she loved him, although she did not say so. No doubt it was ridiculous, but that was how she felt, she couldn't change her nature. Her friend's surprise was increasing and she finally asked:

'So it's all to make him marry you?'

At that Denise sat up again. She was stunned.

'Marry me! Oh, no! Oh, I never wanted anything of the kind! No, the idea never entered my head, and you know how I hate any form of lying!'

'Well, my dear,' Pauline went on gently, 'if you had thought of making him marry you, you couldn't have gone about it better . . . It'll have to finish somehow, and there's nothing else except marriage, since you won't accept any other arrangement . . . I must tell you that everyone thinks the same thing: yes, they're all convinced that you're treating him like this so as to get him to the altar . . . You are a funny girl!'

She had to console Denise, who had let her head fall on the bolster again and was sobbing, declaring that she'd leave the shop in the end, since they were always attributing ideas to her which had never even crossed her mind. There was no doubt that when a man loved a woman he ought to marry her. But she did not want anything, she had no schemes, all she wanted was to be allowed to live in peace, with her sorrows and her joys, like everyone else. She would leave.

At that moment, downstairs, Mouret was walking through the shop. He had wanted to forget his thoughts by visiting the building work once again. Months had passed, and the monumental new façade now rose up behind the vast wooden hoardings which hid it from the public. A whole army of decorators was at work: marble-masons and specialists in ceramics and mosaics; the central group of figures above the door was being gilded, while on the acroterium* the pedestals which were to hold statues depicting the manufacturing towns of France were already being fixed in position. From morning till night, all along the newly opened Rue du Dix-Décembre, an inquisitive crowd stood looking up, seeing nothing, but imagining and talking to each other about this wondrous façade which was going to revolutionize Paris when it was opened. And it was precisely on that building site, with its feverish activity, among the artists who were putting the finishing touches to his dream which had been started by the builders, that Mouret had just felt more bitterly than ever the vanity of his fortune. The thought of Denise had suddenly troubled him, that thought which would shoot through him without respite like a flame, like the pain of an incurable disease. He had fled, unable to utter a word of satisfaction, afraid of showing his tears, turning his back on his triumph, which merely wearied him. The façade, built at last, seemed small to him, like a child's sand-castle, and even if it had extended from one end of the city to the other, or been as high as the stars, it would not have filled the emptiness of his heart, which only the 'yes' of a mere child could fill.

When Mouret returned to his office he was choking with tears. What did she want? He no longer dared to offer her money; the confused idea of marriage was beginning to dawn on him, although, as a young widower, he rebelled against it. His powerlessness made him weep with frustration. He was unhappy.

CHAPTER 13

ONE morning in November Denise was giving her first orders in the department when the Baudus' maidservant came to tell her that Mademoiselle Geneviève had had a very bad night, and that she wanted to see her cousin immediately. For some time the young girl had been getting weaker and weaker, and she had been obliged to take to her bed two days earlier.

'Tell her I'll come straight away,' Denise replied, very worried. It was the sudden disappearance of Colomban which was killing Geneviève. At first, because Clara had teased him, he had not returned home for several nights; then, yielding to the mad desire which can take possession of shifty, chaste young men, he had become her obedient slave, and one Monday had not returned, but had simply left a farewell letter for his employer, written in the studied terms of a man about to commit suicide. Perhaps one could also have read into this sudden passion the shrewd calculation of a young man delighted to escape from a disastrous marriage; the drapery shop was just as sick as his future wife and it was the right moment to break it all off by doing something foolish. Everyone cited him as a fatal victim of love.

When Denise arrived at the Vieil Elbeuf, Madame Baudu was there alone. She sat motionless behind the cash-desk, watching over the silent, empty shop, her little white face pallid with anaemia. There was no shop assistant now, so the maidservant would give the shelves an occasional whisk with a feather duster, and they were even thinking of replacing her with a charwoman. A dismal chill fell from the ceiling; hours passed without a customer coming to disturb the gloom, and the goods, which were no longer touched, were getting slowly covered with the saltpetre from the walls.

'What's wrong?' asked Denise anxiously. 'Is it serious?'

Madame Baudu did not reply at first. She began to cry. Then she stammered:

'I don't know, they don't tell me anything . . . Oh! It's all over, it's all over . . .'

Her eyes were full of tears. She gazed round the dark shop as if she felt her daughter and the shop departing together. The seventy thousand francs produced by the sale of the estate at Rambouillet had melted away in less than two years in the abyss of competition. In order to compete with the Paradise, which now stocked material for men's clothes, hunting velvets, and liveries, the draper had made considerable sacrifices. He had just been finally crushed by his rival's duffels and flannels, the most remarkable range ever to appear on the market. Little by little the debt had grown and, as a last resort, he had decided to mortgage the old building in the Rue de la Michodière, where old Finet, their ancestor, had founded the business. Now it was only a matter of days before everything finally crumbled; the very ceilings looked ready to collapse and be blown away as dust, like some barbarous, worm-eaten construction being carried away by the wind.

'Your uncle's upstairs,' Madame Baudu went on in her broken voice. 'We each spend two hours with her; someone has to keep an eye on the shop. Just as a precaution, because to be honest . . .'

Her gesture completed the sentence. They would have put up the shutters if it had not been for their ancient business pride, which made them still put a brave face on it for the neighbourhood.

'I'll go up then, Auntie,' said Denise, whose heart was aching at the resigned despair which even the lengths of cloth were exuding.

'Yes, go up, go up quickly, my dear . . . She's waiting for you, she was asking for you all night. There's something she wants to tell you.'

But just at that moment Baudu came downstairs. His bilious condition gave a greenish tinge to his sallow face, and his eyes were bloodshot. Still walking very softly, as he had done on leaving the sick-room, he murmured, as if he could have been heard upstairs:

'She's sleeping.'

And, his legs aching with tiredness, he sat down on a chair. With a mechanical gesture he wiped his brow, puffing like a man who has just finished some arduous task. Silence reigned. Finally he said to Denise:

'You can see her later . . . When she's asleep she looks as if she's recovered.'

Again there was a silence. The mother and father sat face to face, gazing at each other. Then, in undertones, he went over his troubles once more, without naming anyone or speaking to anyone in particular.

'I swear I wouldn't have believed it! He was the last person to do such a thing; I brought him up like my own son. If someone had come and said to me: "They'll take him away from you as well, you'll see him go over to the other side," I would have replied: "Well that would mean there's no longer any God!" And he's done it, he's gone over to the other side. Oh! The wretch, he knew so much about real business, he had the same ideas as me! And all for a dreadful woman like that, for one of those mannequins who flaunt themselves in the windows of houses of ill repute! No, really, it's beyond all reason!'

He shook his head, gazing blankly at the damp tiles which had been worn away by generations of customers.

'You know,' he went on in a lower voice, 'sometimes I feel that I'm the most to blame in our misfortune. Yes, it's my fault that our poor girl is lying up there, wasting away with fever. Shouldn't I have married them at once, without giving in to my stupid pride, my stubborn determination not to leave them the shop in a less prosperous state than when I started? She would have had the man she loves, and perhaps their youth would have been able to bring about the miracle I couldn't achieve . . . But I'm an old fool, I didn't understand anything; I didn't think people could fall ill over things like that . . . The boy was really extraordinary: a born salesman, and such integrity, such simple manners, such order in everything he did—in short, he was my pupil . . .'

He raised his head, still defending his own ideas in the assistant who had betrayed him. Denise could not bear to hear him accusing himself and was so carried away by emotion at the sight of this man who in the past had reigned there as absolute master, now so humble, with his eyes full of tears, that she told him everything.

'Please don't make excuses for him, Uncle, I beg you . . . He never loved Geneviève; he'd have run away earlier if you had tried to hasten the marriage. I talked to him about it myself; he knew perfectly well what my poor cousin was suffering on his account, and you can see that that didn't stop him from leaving . . . Ask Auntie.'

Without opening her lips, Madame Baudu confirmed these words with a nod. The draper became even paler, his tears now blinding him completely.

'It must be in the blood,' he stammered. 'His father died last summer from too much womanizing.'

He looked round the dark shop again, his eyes wandering from the bare counters to the full shelves, then returning to settle on his wife, still sitting at the cash-desk, waiting in vain for the vanished customers.

'It's all over,' he went on. 'They've killed our business, and now one of their girls is killing our daughter.'

They fell silent. In the stagnant air, stifling under the low ceiling, the rumbling of carriages, which from time to time made the tiles vibrate, sounded like a roll of funeral drums. Then, in the dismal sadness of the old shop in its death throes, muffled knocks could be heard coming from somewhere in the house. It was Geneviève, who had just woken up, and was banging with a stick which had been left near her bed.

'Quick, let's go up,' said Baudu, rising with a start. 'Try to laugh, she mustn't know.'

On the staircase he rubbed his eyes hard to remove the traces of his tears. As soon as he opened the door on the first floor, a feeble, distraught voice could be heard calling:

'I don't want to be alone . . . Don't leave me alone . . . Oh! I'm afraid to be left alone . . .'

Then, when she saw Denise, Geneviève became calmer, and gave a smile of joy.

'Ah! You've come! I've been longing to see you since yesterday! I was beginning to think you'd abandoned me as well!'

It was pitiful. The girl's room overlooked the yard, and only a livid glimmer of light penetrated it. At first her parents had put her bed in their own room, at the front of the house; but the sight of the Ladies' Paradise opposite had upset her so much that they had had to take her back to her own room again. There she lay, so slight that one could no longer sense the form and existence of a body under the blankets. Her thin arms, wasted with the burning fever of consumptives, moved restlessly over the covers, as if in search of something; while her black hair, heavy with passion, seemed to have become even thicker, to have taken on a voracious life of its own, and to be eating away her pathetic face—a face in which the ultimate degeneration of a long line grown in the dark, in that cellar of old commercial Paris, was dying out.

Denise, her heart bursting with pity, stood looking at her. She did not at first speak, for fear of not being able to control her tears. In the end she murmured:

'I came at once . . . Is there anything I can do for you? You were asking for me . . . Would you like me to stay?'

Geneviève, short of breath, her hands still wandering over the folds of the blanket, did not take her eyes off her.

'No, thank you, I don't need anything . . . I only wanted to embrace you.'

Her eyes filled with tears. At this Denise quickly bent down and kissed her on the cheeks, shuddering as she felt the fire of those hollow cheeks against her lips. But the sick girl had seized her, and was clasping her and holding on to her in a desperate embrace. Then she glanced at her father.

'Would you like me to stay?' Denise repeated. 'Is there nothing I can do for you?'

'No, no.'

Geneviève was still staring in the direction of her father, who was standing with a dazed look and a lump in his throat. Finally he understood, and withdrew without saying a word; they listened to his heavy footsteps as he went downstairs.

'Tell me, is he still with that woman?' the sick girl asked immediately, seizing her cousin's hand, and making her sit on the edge of the bed. 'Yes, I wanted to see you. You're the only person who can tell me . . . They're living together, aren't they?'

Denise, taken by surprise by these questions, had to admit the truth and blurted out the rumours which were circulating in the shop. Clara, who had grown tired of this lad who had now become a nuisance to her, had closed her door to him; and Colomban, in despair and with the humility of a beaten dog, was following her about everywhere, trying to obtain an occasional meeting with her. It was said that he was going to get a job at the Louvre.

'If you love him so much, he may still come back to you,' Denise continued, trying to lull the dying girl with this last hope. 'Get better quickly; he'll admit his mistake and marry you.'

Geneviève interrupted her. She had been listening with her whole being, with dumb passion which had made her raise herself up. But she fell back again immediately.

'No, don't say any more, I know it's all over . . . I don't say anything, because I hear Papa weeping, and I don't want to make Mamma more ill than she is. But I'm going, you see, and I was calling for you last night because I was afraid I would go before daylight . . . And to think he's not even happy!'

When Denise protested, assuring her that her condition was not as serious as she thought, Geneviève cut her short again, and suddenly threw back the blanket with the pure gesture of a virgin who, in death, has nothing more to hide. Uncovered to her waist, she murmured:

'Look at me! Isn't it all over?'

Trembling, Denise moved away from the bed as if afraid of destroying the girl's pitiful nakedness with a breath. It was the end of the flesh, a bride's body worn out with waiting, which had returned to the frail childishness of its earliest years. Slowly Geneviève covered herself again, repeating:

'You can see I'm no longer a woman . . . It would be wrong still to want him.'

They both fell silent. They continued to look at each other, finding nothing more to say. It was Geneviève who went on:

'There's no need to stay here, you've got your work to attend to. And thank you. I was tormented by not knowing; now I'm satisfied. If you see him again, tell him I forgive him . . . Farewell, dear Denise. Kiss me, it's the last time.'

Denise kissed her, protesting:

'No, no, don't lose heart, you need care and attention, that's all.'

But the sick girl shook her head obstinately. She was smiling; she knew for certain. And as her cousin finally turned towards the door, she said:

'Wait a minute, knock with this stick for Papa to come up . . . I'm too afraid to be on my own.'

Then, when Baudu arrived in the dismal little room where he would sit for hours, she put on a cheerful air and called to Denise:

'Don't come tomorrow, there's no point. I'll expect you on Sunday; you can spend the afternoon with me.'

The next day, at six o'clock in the morning, Geneviève died, after four hours of frightful agony. The funeral fell on a Saturday, in gloomy weather and with a black sky weighing down on the shivering city. The Vieil Elbeuf, draped with a white pall, lit up the street with a patch of white; and the candles, burning in the dim light, looked like stars drowning in twilight. Artificial wreaths and a big bouquet of white roses covered the coffin—a narrow child's coffin, which was placed in the dark alley beside the shop, level with the pavement, and so close to the gutter that passing carriages had already splashed the hangings. The whole neighbourhood was oozing with damp, exuding a smell of musty cellars, while there was a continual bustle of passers-by on the muddy pavement.

Denise had been there since nine o'clock, to keep her aunt company. But, as the procession was about to leave, Madame Baudu, no longer weeping but with her eyes inflamed by tears, asked Denise to follow the coffin and watch over her uncle, whose silent despair and almost insane grief was causing the family great concern. Downstairs, the girl found the street full of people. The small tradespeople of the neighbourhood wanted to show their sympathy to the Baudus; and their eagerness to do so was also a kind of demonstration against the Ladies' Paradise, which they held responsible for Geneviève's lingering death. All the monster's victims were there: Bédoré and his sister, the hosiers from the Rue Gaillon; the Vanpouille brothers, the furriers, Deslignières the fancy-goods dealer, and Piot and Rivoire the furniture dealers; even Mademoiselle Tatin the linen draper and Quinette the glover, who had been swept away long ago by bankruptcy, had made a point of coming, the former from the Batignolles and the latter from the Bastille, where they had been forced to take jobs in other people's shops. As they waited for the hearse, which had been held up because of some misunderstanding, these people, all dressed in black, walked up and down in the mud, glancing up in hatred at the Paradise, whose bright windows and gay displays seemed an insult to the Vieil Elbeuf, whose mourning appearance was casting a pall of gloom over the other side of the street. The faces of a few inquisitive assistants had appeared behind the windows; but the colossus was maintaining the indifference of a machine going full steam ahead, oblivious to the deaths it may cause on the way.

Denise looked round for her brother Jean. Finally she caught sight of him outside Bourras's shop, and she went over to tell him to walk close to his uncle and support him if he had difficulty in walking. For some weeks now Jean had been rather serious, as if tormented by some anxiety. That day, squeezed into a black frock-coat, now well established and earning twenty francs a day, he seemed so dignified and so sad that his sister was quite struck by it, for she had not suspected that he loved his cousin so much. She had wanted to spare Pépé any needless distress and so had left him with Madame Gras, planning to collect him in the afternoon and take him to see his uncle and aunt.

Meanwhile the hearse had still not arrived and Denise, very upset, was watching the candles burning when she was startled by a familiar voice behind her. It was Bourras. He had called over a chestnut-seller, who was installed opposite in a little booth that formed part of a wine merchant's shop, and was saying to him:

'Hey, Vigouroux, can you do something for me? I'm closing the shop for a little while . . . If anyone comes, can you tell them to come back? But don't worry, no one will come.'

Then he took up his position on the edge of the pavement, waiting like the others. Denise, feeling rather embarrassed, had glanced at his shop. He was letting it go now; in the window there was nothing but a pitiful array of rotting umbrellas and walking-sticks blackened by the gas. The improvements he had made, the light green paint, the mirrors, the gilded signboard, were all cracking and collecting dirt already, presenting a picture of the rapid and depressing decay of sham luxury plastered on top of ruins. But even though the old cracks were reappearing and the spots of damp were visible again beneath the gilding, the house was still stubbornly standing, stuck on to the side of the Ladies' Paradise like some shameful wart which, although it had cracked and come to a head, refused to fall off.

'Ah! The scoundrels!' growled Bourras. 'They won't even let her be taken away!'

The hearse, which had finally arrived, had just been run into by one of the Paradise's vans which, its varnished doors projecting their starry radiance in the mist, was disappearing at a brisk trot, pulled by two magnificent horses. The old shopkeeper cast a fiery sideways glance at Denise from beneath his bushy eyebrows.

The procession moved off slowly, splashing through the puddles amid the silence made by the cabs and omnibuses which had suddenly stopped to let them pass. When the coffin, draped in white, crossed the Place Gaillon, dark glances from the procession were cast once more in the direction of the windows of the great shop, where only two salesgirls had rushed to look out, glad of the distraction. Baudu was following the hearse with heavy, mechanical steps; he had refused with a gesture to take the arm of Jean, who was walking close beside him. Then, after the people bringing up the rear on foot, came three funeral carriages. As they were cutting across the Rue Neuve-des-Petits-Champs, Robineau, very pale, and looking greatly aged, ran up to join the procession.

At Saint-Roch a great many women were waiting, the small shopkeepers of the neighbourhood who had feared there would be a crush at the house of the deceased. The demonstration was turning into a riot; and when, after the service, the procession started off again once more all the men followed, although it was a long walk from the Rue Saint-Honoré to the Montmartre Cemetery. They had to go up the Rue Saint-Roch once more, and pass the Ladies' Paradise for the second time. It was like an obsession: the girl's pathetic body was carried round the big shop, as if she had been the first victim to fall under fire in time of revolution. At the door some red flannel was flapping in the wind like flags and a display of carpets was bursting out in a flowering of enormous blood-red roses and full-blown peonies.

Meanwhile Denise had got into a carriage, torn by bitter anxieties and her heart aching with such sadness that she no longer had the strength to walk. Just then there was a halt in the Rue du Dix-Décembre, opposite the scaffolding of the new shop-front, which was still obstructing the traffic. Then she noticed old Bourras lagging behind, limping along under the very wheels of the carriage in which she was sitting alone. He would never get as far as the cemetery, she thought. He raised his head and looked at her. Then he got into the carriage.

'It's these damned legs of mine,' he murmured. 'Don't you draw back like that. It isn't you we detest!'

She found him friendly but gruff, as he always had been in the past. He was grumbling, declaring that that old devil Baudu must be really tough to go on walking like that in spite of having suffered such blows. The procession had resumed its slow progress; and, leaning forward, she could see her uncle obstinately following the hearse with his heavy gait, which seemed to set the muffled, laborious pace of the procession. Then she sank back in her corner and listened to the endless complaints of the old umbrella dealer, to the accompaniment of the slow, melancholy swaying of the carriage.

'The police ought to keep public thoroughfares clear! They've been blocking up our streets for more than eighteen months with their new shop-front; only the other day another man was killed there. Never mind! When they want to expand in the future they'll have to throw bridges across the streets . . . They say you've got two thousand seven hundred employees, and that the turnover this year will reach a hundred million! A hundred million! Just imagine! A hundred million!'

Denise had nothing to say in reply. The procession was just turning into the Rue de la Chaussée-d'Antin, where it was held up by a group of carriages. Bourras went on, his eyes vacant, as if he was dreaming out loud. He still couldn't understand the triumph of the Ladies' Paradise, but he acknowledged the defeat of the old-fashioned shopkeepers.

'Poor Robineau's done for, he's got the look of a drowning man. And the Bédorés and the Vanpouilles, they can't keep going any more; they're like me, their legs are worn out. Deslignières will die from a stroke; Piot and Rivoire have had jaundice. We make a pretty sight—a lovely procession for the poor child! It must be funny for the people watching to see this string of failures going past . . . And it seems that the whole process is going to continue. The scoundrels are creating departments for flowers, millinery, perfume, shoes, and I don't know what else. Grognet, the perfumer in the Rue de Gramont, might as well pack up, and I wouldn't give ten francs for Naud's shoeshop in the Rue d'Antin. The plague's spread as far as the Rue Sainte-Anne, where Lacassagne at the feather and flower shop, and Madame Chadeuil, whose hats are so well known, will be swept away within two years . . . And after them, there'll be others, it'll go on and on! Every business in the neighbourhood will go the same way. When counter-jumpers start selling soap and galoshes, they're quite capable of wanting to sell fried potatoes. The world's really going quite mad!'

The hearse was now crossing the Place de la Trinité and, from the dark corner of the carriage where Denise, lulled by the funeral pace of the procession, was listening to the old shopkeeper's endless lamentations, she could see the coffin already going up the slope of the Rue Blanche, as they came out of the Rue de la Chaussée-d'Antin. Behind her uncle, who was trudging along blindly and dumbly like a stunned ox, she seemed to hear the trampling of a herd of cattle being led to the slaughterhouse, the destruction of the shops of a whole district, the small traders squelching along in their down-at-heel shoes, trailing ruin through the black mud of Paris. Bourras, meanwhile, was speaking in an even more hollow voice, as if slowed down by the steep incline of the Rue Blanche.

'As for me, I'm done for . . . But I'm hanging on to him all the same, and I won't let go. He's just lost another appeal. It's cost me a fortune: nearly two years of lawsuits and solicitors and barristers! It doesn't matter, he won't go underneath my shop; the judges have decided that work of that sort could never be considered as justified repairs. Just imagine, he was talking of creating, underneath me, a specially lit room where people could see the colours of materials by gaslight and which would have connected the hosiery and drapery departments! And he's furious about it; he can't accept that an old crock like me won't get out of his way, when everyone else goes down on their knees as soon as he shows them his money. Never! I won't! They'd better get that straight. It's very likely that I'll be destroyed in the process. Since I've had to contend with the bailiffs, I know the scoundrel's looking into my debts, no doubt so as to play a dirty trick on me. But it doesn't matter, he says yes, I say no, and I'll always say no, by God! Even when they nail me up in my little box like that poor girl over there.'

When they arrived at the Boulevard de Clichy the carriage picked up a little speed; one could hear the heavy breathing of the mourners and feel the unconscious haste of the procession, in a hurry to get it over. What Bourras did not mention outright was the terrible poverty into which he had fallen, bewildered as he was by the worries of a small shopkeeper going under yet persisting in holding out under a hail of refused bills. Denise, who knew what his circumstances were, finally broke the silence, murmuring in a pleading voice:

'Monsieur Bourras, please don't go on being difficult any longer. Let me settle things for you.'

He cut her short with a violent gesture.

'Be quiet, it's my business. You're a good little girl, I know you're giving him a hard time, that man who thought you were for sale like my house. But what would you say if I advised you to say yes? You'd tell me to get lost . . . So when I say no, just don't interfere.'

As the carriage had stopped at the cemetery gate, they both got out. The Baudus' family grave was in the first avenue on the left. The ceremony was over in a few minutes. Jean had taken his uncle, who was staring open-mouthed at the grave, to one side. The tail of the procession was spreading out among the neighbouring tombs, and the faces of all those shopkeepers, their blood impoverished from living in the depths of their unhealthy shops, were acquiring a sickly ugliness beneath the mud-coloured sky.

As the coffin sank slowly into the ground, their blotchy cheeks grew pale, their noses nipped with anaemia were lowered, and their eyes, yellow with biliousness and blinded with figures, turned away.

'We should all go and jump into the hole,' said Bourras to Denise, who had remained close to him. 'We're burying the whole neighbourhood with this child . . . Oh! I know what I'm saying, the old way of business might as well go and join those white roses they're throwing on her coffin.'

Denise took her uncle and her brother home in one of the funeral carriages. It had been a day of unrelieved sadness for her. First, she was beginning to worry about Jean's pallor, and when she realized that it was on account of yet another amorous affair, she tried to silence him by opening her purse; but he shook his head and refused: it was serious this time, the niece of a very rich pastry-cook, who would not even accept bunches of violets. Next, in the afternoon, when Denise went to fetch Pépé from Madame Gras, the latter declared that he was getting too big for her to keep any longer; this presented a new problem, for she would now have to find a school for him, perhaps even send him away. And finally, when she took Pépé back to see his aunt and uncle, her heart bled to see the bleak sorrow of the Vieil Elbeuf. The shop was closed; her uncle and aunt were at the back of the small dining-room, where they had forgotten to light the gas in spite of the total darkness of the winter day. They were now quite alone, face to face in the house which ruin had slowly emptied, and the death of their daughter was making the dark corners seem even more cavernous; it seemed the final blow which would make the old beams, eaten away with damp, fall to pieces. Crushed by his grief, her uncle kept walking blindly round the table, without saying anything, unable to stop himself, with the same gait he had had during the procession; while her aunt, silent too, was sunk in a chair, as white as though some wound was draining away her blood drop by drop. They didn't even weep when Pépé covered their cold cheeks with kisses. Denise choked back her tears.

That evening it so happened that Mouret sent for the girl in order to discuss a child's garment he wanted to put on the market, a cross between a kilt and the wide trousers of a zouave.* Still trembling with pity, shocked by so much suffering, she could not contain herself; she ventured first of all to speak of old Bourras, that poor, helpless old man whose throat they were about to slit. But at the name of the umbrella dealer, Mouret lost his temper. The crazy old man, as he called him, was spoiling his triumph by his ridiculous obstinacy in not parting with his house, that filthy hovel that spoiled the Ladies' Paradise, the only little corner of the vast block which had escaped conquest. The whole thing was becoming a nightmare; anyone but Denise who spoke in favour of Bourras would have risked being dismissed immediately, so tormented was Mouret by a morbid desire to kick down the hovel. After all, what did they want him to do? Could he leave that rubbish heap standing next to the Paradise? It would have to disappear in the end; the shop would have to pass over it. Too bad for the old fool! And he recalled his proposals, how he had offered him as much as a hundred thousand francs. Wasn't that reasonable? He wouldn't haggle, of course, he would give what was asked for it; but people should at least have a bit of intelligence, and let him complete his work! Did people interfere by trying to stop locomotives on railways? She listened to him, her eyes lowered, able to think only of sentimental reasons. Bourras was getting so old, they could at least have waited for him to die; if he went bankrupt it would kill him. At that Mouret declared that he was no longer even in a position to prevent things taking their course; Bourdoncle was dealing with it, for the board had decided to put an end to the matter. In spite of her tender-hearted and sorrowful compassion, she could think of nothing more to say.

After a painful silence it was Mouret himself who mentioned the Baudus. He began by saying how sorry he was for them at the loss of their daughter. They were excellent people, very worthy, and had been dogged by bad luck. Then he resumed his arguments: basically, they had brought their troubles on themselves by sticking obstinately to the old-fashioned ways in their worm-eaten hovel; it was hardly surprising that the house was falling on their heads. He had predicted it scores of times; she must remember how he had told her to warn her uncle that it would be fatal for him to go on clinging to his ridiculous old-fashioned ideas. The catastrophe had arrived, and no one in the world could prevent it now. They couldn't really expect him to ruin himself to spare the neighbourhood. In any case, if he had been foolish enough to close the Paradise, another big shop would have sprung up on its own next door, for the idea was gaining ground all over the world; the triumph of these great concentrations had been sown by the spirit of the times, which was sweeping away the crumbling edifice of past ages. Little by little Mouret was warming up, filled with eloquent emotion to defend himself against the hatred of his involuntary victims, against the clamour of small, moribund shops which he could hear rising around him. It was impossible to keep one's dead, after all, they must be buried; and with a gesture he swept away and threw into the paupers' grave the corpse of old-fashioned business, the greenish stinking remains of which were becoming the disgrace of the sunny streets of modern Paris. No, no, he felt no remorse; he was merely carrying out the task of his epoch, and she knew it, she who loved life and had a passion for big business deals settled in the glare of publicity. Reduced to silence, she listened to him for a long time and then withdrew, her heart full of confusion.

That night Denise hardly slept. Insomnia interspersed with nightmares made her toss and turn under the blankets. She thought she was quite small, and burst into tears in their garden at Valognes at the sight of warblers eating spiders who, in their turn, were eating flies. Was it really true then that death must fertilize the world, that the struggle for life propelled people towards the charnel-house of eternal destruction? Next, she saw herself again beside the grave into which Geneviève was being lowered, and she saw her uncle and aunt, alone in their dark dining-room. In the deep silence, the dull sound of something crumbling was echoing through the death-like air; it was Bourras's house collapsing, as if undermined by floods. The silence began again, more sinister than ever, and another crash was heard, then another, and another: the Robineaus, Bédoré and his sister, the Vanpouilles, were cracking up and collapsing one after another; the small businesses of the Saint-Roch district were disappearing under an invisible pickaxe, with sudden, thundering noises, like carts being unloaded. Then, a feeling of immense sorrow woke her with a start. My God! What tortures! Weeping families, old men thrown out into the street, all the poignant dramas associated with ruin! And she could not save anyone; she was even aware that it was a good thing: this manure of distress was necessary to the health of the Paris of the future. When morning came she grew calmer; a feeling of immense, resigned sadness kept her awake, her eyes turned towards the window as it grew lighter. Yes, it was the necessary sacrifice; every revolution demanded its victims, for it was only possible to advance over the bodies of the dead. Her fear of being an evil genius, and having helped in the murder of her relatives, was now dissolving into heartfelt pity at those irremediable misfortunes, the painful birth pangs of each new generation. She ended up by trying to think of possible alleviations; she thought for a long time of measures that might be taken to save at least her own family from the final collapse.

Mouret then rose up before her, with his passionate expression and his caressing eyes. He would surely not refuse her anything; she was certain he would grant her all reasonable compensation. And her thoughts strayed as she tried to understand him. She was familiar with his life, how calculating he had been in his affections, his continual exploitation of Woman, the mistresses he had taken in order to further his own ends, his liaison with Madame Desforges with the sole aim of keeping a hold on Baron Hartmann, and all the other women, the Claras he picked up, the pleasure which he bought, paid for, and threw back into the street. But these beginnings of a career of amorous adventure, which the shop joked about, came to be seen as part of the man's genius, his all-conquering charm. He was seduction personified. What she would never have forgiven him was the falsehood of his former behaviour, his coldness as a lover beneath the gallantry of his attentions. But now that he was suffering because of her, she felt no resentment towards him. His suffering had improved him. When she saw him tormented, paying so dearly for his contempt for women, she felt he was redeemed of his faults.

That very morning Denise obtained from Mouret the promise of such compensation, on the day when the Baudus and old Bourras succumbed, as she might judge legitimate. Weeks passed, and almost every afternoon she would slip out for a few minutes to go and see her uncle, taking with her laughter and her cheerful courage to brighten up the dark shop. She was especially worried about her aunt who, since Geneviève's death, had been in a dull stupor; it seemed as if her life was ebbing away all the time; and when questioned, she would reply with an air of surprise that she felt no pain, she just felt overcome with sleep. The neighbours shook their heads, saying that the poor woman would not pine for her daughter for long.

One day, Denise was coming out of the Baudus' house when, at the corner of the Place Gaillon, she heard a loud cry. People were rushing forward; there was panic in the air, the breath of fear and pity which can suddenly take hold of a crowd. A brown omnibus on the Bastille–Batignolles line had just run over a man at the corner of the Rue Neuve-Saint-Augustin, opposite the fountain. Standing on his seat and gesticulating furiously, the driver was reining in his two black horses, which were rearing; and he was swearing, shouting out furiously:

'Damn you! Can't you look where you're going, you idiot!'

By now the omnibus had stopped. A crowd had gathered round the injured man; a policeman happened by chance to be there. The driver was still standing up, calling the passengers upstairs as witnesses—for they had also stood up in order to lean out and see the blood—and was giving his version of the incident with exasperated gestures, choking with anger.

'He must have been mad! He just walked out into the road without looking. I shouted at him, and he just threw himself under the wheels!'

At that a workman, a house-painter who had rushed up with his brush in his hand, said in a piercing voice in the midst of the uproar:

'There's no need to get so worked up! I saw him, he obviously chucked himself under there deliberately! He dived forward head first. Someone else who was fed up with life, I suppose!'

Other people spoke up, agreeing that it was suicide, while the policeman was taking down particulars. Several ladies, quite pale, quickly got out of the omnibus without turning round, taking away with them the horror of the soft jolt which had made their stomachs turn when the vehicle had passed over the body. Meanwhile Denise approached, drawn by her compassionate impulses, which made her interfere in accidents of all kinds—dogs run over, fallen horses, tilers toppling off roofs. And she recognized the unfortunate man lying on the road, unconscious, his frock-coat covered with mud.

'It's Monsieur Robineau!' she exclaimed in painful astonishment. The policeman immediately questioned the girl. She gave Robineau's name, profession, and address. Thanks to the driver's efforts, the omnibus had swerved, and only Robineau's legs had been caught under the wheels. But it was to be feared that they were both broken. Four volunteers carried the injured man to a chemist's shop in the Rue Gaillon, while the omnibus slowly resumed its journey.

'God!' said the driver, cracking his whip round his horses. 'I've had enough for one day!'

Denise had followed Robineau to the chemist's shop. The chemist, while waiting for a doctor who could not be found, declared that there was no immediate danger, and that the best thing would be to carry the injured man to his own home, since he lived nearby. A man went off to the police station to ask for a stretcher. Then the girl had the bright idea of going on ahead so as to prepare Madame Robineau for the awful shock. But she had enormous difficulty in getting into the street through the crowd, which was milling round the door. This crowd, attracted by death, was increasing from minute to minute; children and women were craning their necks, standing their ground against violent pushing; and each newcomer had his own version of the accident; they were now saying that a husband had been thrown out of a window by his wife's lover.

In the Rue Neuve-des-Petits-Champs Denise caught sight of Madame Robineau in the distance, standing in the doorway of the silk-shop. This gave her an excuse to stop, and she chatted for a moment, trying to think of a way of breaking the terrible news gently. The shop's appearance revealed the disorder and abandon of the final struggles of a dying business. This was the expected outcome of the battle of the two rival silks; the Paris-Paradise had crushed all competition with a further reduction of five centimes: it was now selling at only four francs ninety-five, and Gaujean's silk had met its Waterloo. For the last two months Robineau, reduced to all sorts of expedients, had been leading a terrible life trying to prevent himself being declared bankrupt.

'I just saw your husband in the Place Gaillon,' murmured Denise, who'd finally stepped inside the shop.

'Ah! Just now? I'm expecting him; he should be back by now. Monsieur Gaujean came this morning, and they went out together.'

She was as charming as ever, delicate and cheerful; but her pregnancy, already well advanced, made her feel tired, and she was becoming more agitated, more at sea in business than ever, for her nature made it difficult for her to understand, and now it was all going badly. As she often said, what was the point of it all? Wouldn't it be nicer to live quietly and modestly in some little house somewhere?

'My dear,' she went on, her smile growing sad, 'we've nothing to hide from you . . . Things aren't going well; my poor darling doesn't sleep any more because of it. Today Gaujean tormented him again about some overdue bills . . . I thought I'd die of worry, all on my own here.'

She was moving back to the door when Denise stopped her. The latter had just heard the noise of the crowd in the distance. She imagined the stretcher they were bringing, and the stream of onlookers who were bent on following every stage of the accident. And then, her throat dry, unable to think of the consoling words she wanted, she was forced to tell her.

'You mustn't worry, there's no immediate danger . . . Yes, I saw Monsieur Robineau, he's had an accident . . . They're bringing him; don't worry, please.'

The young woman listened to her, as white as a sheet, without yet clearly understanding. The street was full of people, drivers of cabs were swearing, and the men had set down the stretcher outside the shop in order to open the double glass doors.

'It was an accident,' continued Denise, determined to conceal the attempt at suicide. 'He was on the pavement, and he slipped under the wheels of an omnibus. His feet got caught. They've sent for a doctor. You mustn't worry.'

A great shudder shook Madame Robineau. She made two or three inarticulate cries; then, no longer speaking, she ran to the stretcher and drew back the curtains with trembling hands. The men who had been carrying it were waiting outside the house in order to carry it away when a doctor had been found. They no longer dared touch Robineau, who had regained consciousness, and whose sufferings at the slightest movement were agonizing.

When he saw his wife, two huge tears ran down his cheeks. She kissed him, and wept as she knelt looking at him. There was still a crowd in the street, and faces were packed together as if at some show, their eyes shining; some girls who had left their work-room were in danger of breaking the glass of the shop-windows in their attempt to get a better view. In order to escape from this fever of curiosity, and thinking in any case that it was not advis-able to leave the shop open, Denise had the idea of lowering the metal shutters. She went to turn the crank-handle, the gear-wheels made a plaintive cry, and the iron plates slowly des-cended, like the heavy drapery of a theatre curtain coming down at the end of a play. When she came in again and had closed the little round door in the shutters, she found Madame Robineau still clasping her husband in her arms, in the sinister half-light coming from two stars cut in the metal. The ruined shop seemed to be sliding into the void; the two stars alone shone on this sudden, brutal catastrophe of the streets of Paris.

At last Madame Robineau found her voice again.

'Oh! My darling . . . Oh! My darling . . . Oh! My darling . . .'

This was all she could say, and, seeing her kneeling before him, her stomach pressed against the stretcher, he could bear it no longer and, in an attack of remorse, confessed. When he did not move he could only feel the burning leaden weight of his legs.

'Forgive me, I must have been mad . . . When the solicitor told me in front of Gaujean that the notices would be served tomorrow, I seemed to see flames dancing as if the walls were burning . . . After that I don't remember any more; I was walk-ing down the Rue de la Michodière, I thought the people in the Paradise were making fun of me, that great bitch of a shop was crushing me . . . Then, when the omnibus turned round I thought about Lhomme and his arm, and threw myself un-der it . . .'

Slowly, in horror at this confession, Madame Robineau sank down and sat on the floor. He had wanted to die! She grasped Denise's hand, for the girl had leaned towards her, deeply moved by the scene. The injured man, whose emotion was exhausting him, lost consciousness again. And still the doctor did not come!

Two men had already scoured the neighbourhood, and now the concierge had gone off in his turn.

'You mustn't worry,' Denise repeated mechanically, and she too was sobbing.

Then Madame Robineau, sitting on the floor, her head on the stretcher, her cheek against the webbing on which her husband was lying, unburdened her heart.

'Oh! I could tell you . . . It's for me that he wanted to die. He was always saying: "I've robbed you, it was your money." And at night he used to dream about those sixty thousand francs, he used to wake up in a sweat, saying he was useless and that if you didn't have a head for business, you shouldn't risk other people's money . . . You know he's always been a terrible worrier. In the end he used to see things that frightened me, he'd see me in the street in rags, begging, me whom he loved so much, whom he wanted to see rich and happy.'

But, turning her head, she saw that his eyes were open again; and she went on in a trembling voice:

'Oh! My darling, why did you do it? Did you really think I was so concerned about the money? I don't care if we're ruined, believe me. As long as we're together, we'll never be unhappy . . . Let them take everything. Let's go somewhere where you won't hear any more about them. You'll be able to work, you'll see how good everything can be.'

Her forehead had dropped down close to her husband's pale face, and both were silent in their distress. The shop seemed to be sleeping, numbed by the pale dusk which was flooding it; while behind the thin shutters, the din of the street could be heard—life passing by in the daylight, the rumbling of vehicles and the crowd bustling along the pavements. Finally Denise, who kept going to glance through the little hall door, came back crying:

'The doctor's here!'

The concierge showed him in. He was a young man with bright eyes. He preferred to examine Robineau before they put him to bed. Only one leg, the left one, turned out to be broken above the ankle. It was a simple fracture; there appeared to be no danger of complications. They were preparing to carry the stretcher into the bedroom, at the back, when Gaujean appeared. He was coming to report a final attempt he had made to avert the bankruptcy, but it had failed: the declaration of bankruptcy was now inevitable.

'What's this?' he murmured. 'What's happened?'

In a few words, Denise told him, and he became embarrassed. Robineau said to him in a feeble voice:

'I don't hold it against you, but all this is partly your fault.'

'Well, my dear fellow,' Gaujean replied, 'it needed stronger men than us . . . You know that I'm no better off than you are!'

They lifted the stretcher. Robineau found enough strength to say:

'No, no, stronger men would have fallen by the wayside as well . . . I can understand obstinate old men like Bourras and Baudu staying on; but you and I, who are young, and accepted the new ways of doing business! No, you know, Gaujean, it's the end of a world.'

They carried him away. Madame Robineau kissed Denise with an energy in which there was almost joy at being rid at last of the worries of their business affairs. As Gaujean was leaving with the girl, he confessed to her that that poor devil Robineau was right. It was idiotic to try to compete with the Ladies' Paradise. He knew that he himself was finished unless he could get into their good graces again. The day before he had secretly approached Hutin, who was about to leave for Lyons. But he was beginning to despair, and he tried to arouse Denise's interest, having no doubt heard about her influence.

'My word!' he was repeating. 'It's too bad for the manufacturers. People would laugh at me if I ruined myself fighting for other people's interests, when these fellows are quarrelling over who will manufacture at the cheapest rate . . . My goodness! As you used to say in the past, the manufacturers only need to keep up with progress by better organization and new methods. Everything will be all right, as long as the public's satisfied.'

'Just go and say that to Monsieur Mouret himself . . . He'll be pleased to see you; he's not a man to bear a grudge if you offer him even a centime's profit per metre.'

On a bright, sunny afternoon in January Madame Baudu died. For a fortnight she had no longer been able to go down into the shop, which a charwoman was looking after. She was sitting in the middle of her bed, propped up by pillows. In her white face only her eyes were still alive; and, her head erect, she gazed fixedly through the little curtains on the windows at the Ladies' Paradise opposite. Baudu, made ill himself by this obsession, by the despairing fixity of her gaze, would sometimes try to draw the big curtains. But, with an imploring gesture, she would stop him, determined to see it until her last breath. The monster had now taken everything from her, both her shop and her daughter; she herself had been gradually fading away with the Vieil Elbeuf, losing her life as it lost its customers; the day on which it was gasping its last breath, so too was she. When she felt she was dying, she still had enough strength to insist on her husband opening both windows. It was mild; a stream of bright sunshine was gilding the Paradise, whereas the bedroom of their old house shivered in the shade. Madame Baudu kept her gaze fixed on the Paradise, filled with the vision of the triumphant building, the clear glass behind which millions of francs were endlessly circulating. Slowly, her eyes grew dim, invaded by darkness, and when they were extinguished in death they remained wide open, still gazing, drowned in tears.

Once more all the ruined small shopkeepers of the neighbourhood walked in the funeral procession. The Vanpouille brothers were there, pale from their December bills, paid by a supreme effort which they would not be able to repeat. Bédoré, with his sister, was leaning on a cane, so full of worry and anxiety that his stomach trouble was getting worse. Deslignières had had a stroke; Piot and Rivoire were walking in silence, with downcast eyes, like men without hope. And no one dared ask about those who had disappeared, Quinette, Mademoiselle Tatin, and others who, from morning till night, were going under, being knocked over and swept away on the tide of disaster, to say nothing of Robineau lying in bed with his broken leg. But they were quick to point out to each other, with an air of special interest, the new shopkeepers stricken by the plague: Grognet the perfumer, Madame Chadeuil the milliner, Lacassagne the florist, and Naud the shoemaker, still on their feet, but filled with anxiety by the disease which would sweep them away in their turn. Baudu walked along behind the hearse with the same slow, heavy gait as when he had accompanied his daughter; while in the depths of the first mourning-carriage Bourras's glittering eyes could be seen under his bushy eyebrows and his thatch of snow-white hair.

Denise was in great trouble. For a fortnight she had been worn out with anxiety and fatigue. She had been forced to put Pépé in a school, and had had all sorts of trouble with Jean, who was so much in love with the pastry-cook's niece that he had begged his sister to ask for her hand in marriage. The death of her aunt had followed, and these repeated catastrophes had completely overwhelmed the girl. Mouret had once more offered his assistance, giving her permission to do whatever she wished for her uncle and the others. One morning, upon hearing that Bourras had been thrown into the street and Baudu was going to shut up shop, she had another interview with Mouret. Then after lunch she went out, in the hope of being of some help at least to them.

Bourras was standing in the Rue de la Michodière, on the pavement opposite his house, from which he had been expelled the day before following a fine trick, an idea the solicitor had thought up; as Mouret held some bills, he had easily had the umbrella dealer declared bankrupt and had then paid five hundred francs for the lease at the official receiver's sale; thus the obstinate old man had lost for five hundred francs what he had refused to part with for a hundred thousand. Furthermore, when the architect arrived with his demolition gang, he had had to call the police to get Bourras out. The goods were sold and the furniture removed from the rooms; but he stubbornly remained in the corner where he slept, from which, moved to pity at last, they did not dare drive him out. The demolition workers even attacked the roof over his head. They had removed the rotten slates, the ceilings were falling in, the walls were cracking, and there he remained, beneath the ancient beams which had been stripped bare, surrounded by the ruins of his shop. Finally, when the police came, he had left. But the very next morning he had reappeared on the pavement opposite, after spending the night in a nearby hotel.

'Monsieur Bourras,' said Denise gently.

He did not hear her; his blazing eyes were fixed on the demolition workers, who were attacking the front of his hovel with their pickaxes. Now, through the empty window-frames, the interior could be seen, the miserable rooms and the dark staircase where the sun had not penetrated for two hundred years.

'Ah! It's you,' he replied at last, when he recognized her. 'They're making a good job of it, aren't they, the robbers!'

Deeply moved by the terrible sadness of the old place, she no longer dared to say anything, and was herself unable to drag her eyes away from the mildewed stones that were falling. Upstairs, in a corner of the ceiling of her old room, she could still see the name 'Ernestine' written in shaky black letters with the flame of a candle; and the memory of her days of poverty came back to her, and filled her with pity for all suffering. The workmen, in order to knock down a section of wall all at once, had had the idea of attacking it at its base. It was tottering.

'I wish it would crush them all!' Bourras muttered savagely.

There was a terrible cracking noise. The terrified workmen ran out into the street. The wall was shaking and carrying the whole house with it as it crashed down. The hovel, with all its subsidences and cracks, could no longer stand the strain; one push had sufficed to split it from top to bottom. There was a pitiful landslide, the flattening of a mud hut sodden with rain. Not a board remained standing, and there was nothing left on the ground but a pile of rubbish, the refuse of the past heaped up by the roadside.

'My God!' the old man cried, as if the blow had reverberated in the very depths of his being.

He stood there gaping; he would never have thought it would be over so quickly. He gazed at the open gash, the open space which had at last been created on the flank of the Ladies' Paradise, which was now rid of the wart which had been disfiguring it. It was like the squashing of a gnat, the ultimate triumph over the bitter obstinacy of the infinitely small; the whole block had been overrun and conquered. Passers-by who had gathered on the pavement were talking in loud voices with the workmen, who were complaining angrily about these old buildings, which were quite liable to kill people.

'Monsieur Bourras,' repeated Denise, trying to draw him aside, 'you know you won't be abandoned. All your needs will be provided for . . .'

He drew himself up.

'I don't have any needs . . . They sent you, didn't they? Well, tell them that old Bourras still knows how to work, and that he can find work wherever he wants . . . Really, it would be too much to expect them to give charity to the people they murder!'

At that she implored him:

'Please accept, don't make me so unhappy.'

But he shook his white mane.

'No, no, it's all over. Goodbye. You're young; go and live happily, and don't stop old people from having their own ideas.'

He cast a last glance at the pile of rubbish, then hobbled away. She watched him disappear, jostled by the crowd on the pavement. He turned the corner of the Place Gaillon, and that was all.

For a moment Denise remained motionless, lost in thought. Then she went into her uncle's house. The draper was alone in the dark Vieil Elbeuf. The charwoman came only in the mornings and evenings to do a little cooking, and to help him take down and put up the shutters. He spent hours deep in solitude, often without anyone coming to disturb him for the whole day, and when a customer did venture in he became confused and unable to find the goods. He walked up and down continuously in the silence and half-light, still with his heavy funereal gait, giving way to a morbid need, to real paroxysms of forced marching, as if he wanted to lull and deaden his pain.

'Are you feeling better, Uncle?' asked Denise.

He only stopped for a second, and then started again, walking from the cash-desk to a dark corner.

'Yes, yes, very well . . . Thank you.'

She tried to think of something comforting to say, some cheerful remark, but found it impossible to do so.

'Did you hear the noise? The house has come down.'

'So it has!' he murmured with an astonished look. 'That must have been the house . . . I felt the ground tremble. I shut my door this morning when I saw them on the roof.'

He made a vague gesture, as if to say that such things no longer interested him. Each time he came back to the cash-desk, he looked at the empty bench, the bench covered with worn velvet on which his wife and daughter had grown up. Then, when his perpetual tramping brought him to the other end of the shop, he would look at the shelves drowned in shadow, in which a few pieces of cloth were being destroyed by mildew. It was a widowed shop: those whom he loved were gone, his business had come to a shameful end, he was left alone, carrying his dead heart and his broken pride about with him through these catastrophes. He looked up at the black ceiling, listening to the silence coming from the darkness in the little dining-room, the family nook he had loved so much, even down to its stale smell. Not a breath was left in the ancient dwelling, and his regular, heavy footsteps made the old walls echo, as if he was walking on the tomb of everything he had loved.

Finally Denise broached the subject which had brought her there.

'Uncle, you can't stay here like this. You must make up your mind.'

Without stopping, he replied:

'Of course, but what can I do? I've tried to sell, but no one came. My God! One day I'll just close the shop and go away.'

She knew that there was no longer any danger that he would be declared bankrupt. In the face of such relentless misfortune, his creditors had preferred to come to an agreement. Her uncle would simply find himself in the street, with everything paid.

'But what will you do, then?' she murmured, trying to find a way of coming to the offer she still could not bring herself to make.

'I don't know,' he replied. 'I'll manage somehow.'

He had changed his route, and was now walking from the dining-room to the shop-windows; each time he reached them, he gazed dejectedly at the pitiful windows and their forgotten display. He did not even look up at the triumphant façade of the Ladies' Paradise, its architectural lines stretching into the distance to right and left at both ends of the street. He was exhausted; he no longer had the strength to lose his temper.

'Listen, Uncle,' Denise said finally in embarrassment. 'Perhaps there might be a job for you . . .'

She began again, blurting out:

'Yes, I've been asked to offer you a job as a shopwalker.'

'Well, where?' asked Baudu.

'There! Opposite . . . At our place . . . Six thousand francs, it isn't very tiring work.'

Suddenly he came to a standstill, facing her. But, instead of flying into a rage as she had feared, he became very pale, overcome with emotion, with a feeling of resignation.

'Opposite, opposite,' he muttered several times. 'You want me to go and work opposite?'

Denise herself was overcome by the same emotion. She thought of the long struggle between the two shops, recalled the funeral processions of Geneviève and Madame Baudu, and saw before her the Vieil Elbeuf overthrown, utterly destroyed by the Ladies' Paradise. And the idea of her uncle going to work opposite, and walking about there in a white tie, made her feel sick with pity and resentment.

'But Denise, my dear, how could I?' he said simply, wringing his pathetic, trembling hands.

'No, no, Uncle!' she exclaimed, with an upsurge of her whole upright, generous being. 'It would be wrong . . . Forgive me, I beg of you.'

He had started walking up and down again; once more his tread was shaking the sepulchral emptiness of the house. And when she left him, he was still walking, walking with the obstinate restlessness of deep despair, which goes round and round in circles without ever being able to escape.

Denise had another sleepless night. She had now plumbed the depths of her impotence. She could do nothing to relieve the distress even of her own family. She had to witness to the bitter end the inexorable workings of life, which requires the seed of death for its continual renewal. She no longer fought against it; she accepted this law of the struggle; but her woman's heart was filled with compassion, moved to tears and brotherly love for the whole of suffering humanity. For years she had been caught in the wheels of the machine. Had she not shed her own blood in it? Had she not been bruised, driven out, heaped with insults? Even now she was frightened at feeling herself singled out by the logic of events. Why should it be her, a frail little girl? Why should her small hand suddenly become such a powerful part of the monster's work? And the force which was carrying everything before it was carrying her away too, she whose coming was to be a revenge. Mouret had invented this mechanism for crushing people, and its brutal operation shocked her. He had strewn the neighbourhood with ruins, he had despoiled some and killed others; yet she loved him for the grandeur of his achievement, and each time he committed some fresh excess of power, despite the flood of tears which overwhelmed her at the thought of the misery of the vanquished, she loved him even more.

CHAPTER 14

THE Rue du Dix-Décembre, brand new with its chalk-white houses and the last scaffoldings of a few buildings which were behind schedule, stretched out beneath a clear February sky; a stream of carriages was passing triumphantly along the middle of the new opening, full of light, which was cutting through the dank shade of the ancient Saint-Roch district; and between the Rue de la Michodière and the Rue de Choiseul there was almost a riot, the crush of a crowd of people excited by a month of advertising, and looking up open-mouthed at the monumental façade of the Ladies' Paradise. It was going to be opened that Monday, on the occasion of a great white sale.

There was a vast expanse of polychrome architecture, bright and new, and heightened with gold, which heralded the din and glare of the business inside, attracting the eye like a gigantic display blazing with the most brilliant colours. On the ground floor, so as not to kill the effect of the materials in the shop-windows, the decorations were sombre: the base of the building was of sea-green marble—the corner piles and supporting columns were inlaid with black marble, their severity lightened by gilded tablets; and everything else was of plate glass in a framework of metal—nothing but glass, which seemed to open up the depths of the galleries and halls to the daylight of the street. But, as the storeys rose up, the tones became brighter and brighter. Mosaics stretched out in the frieze on the ground floor—a garland of red and blue flowers alternating with slabs of marble on which the names of various wares were carved—encircling the colossus, disappearing into infinity. Next, the base of the first floor, made of glazed bricks, was in its turn supporting the glass of the broad bay windows as far up as the frieze, which consisted of gilded shields bearing the coats of arms of French towns, and designs in terracotta, the glazing of which repeated the clear tones of the base. Finally, at the very top, the entablature burst out as if it was a flamboyant blossoming of the whole shop-front, the mosaics and ceramics reappeared in warmer colouring, the zinc of the gutters was cut in a pattern and gilded, statues representing the great industrial and manufacturing cities were lined up on the acroterium, their delicate silhouettes standing out against the sky. The sightseers were especially impressed by the central door, which was as high as a triumphal arch, also decorated with an abundance of mosaics and ceramics, and surmounted by an allegorical group—Woman being dressed and embraced by a laughing flight of little Cupids—the fresh gilding of which glittered in the sun.

At about two o'clock the police were obliged to move the crowd on and to supervise the parking of carriages. The palace was built; the temple to Fashion's madness for spending had been set up. It dominated a whole neighbourhood and cast its shadow over it. Already the wound left on its flank by the demolition of Bourras's hovel had healed so completely that it would have been impossible to find the place where that ancient wart had been; in superb isolation the four shop-fronts now ran the length of the four streets. On the opposite pavement the Vieil Elbeuf, which had been closed since Baudu's admittance into a home for the elderly, was walled up like a tomb behind the shutters which were no longer taken down; the wheels of passing cabs splashed them with mud, while in the rising tide of publicity they were being drowned under posters which glued them together and seemed to be the final act in the burial of the old way of business. In the middle of the dead shop-window soiled by the street, motley with the rags and tatters of the life of the city, a huge yellow poster was displayed like a flag planted on a conquered empire. It was still wet, and in letters two feet high it announced the great sale at the Ladies' Paradise. It was as if, after its successive extensions, the colossus had been seized with shame and repugnance for the murky neighbourhood in which it had first sprung up and which it had later massacred, and had just turned its back on it, leaving the mud of the narrow streets behind it, presenting its upstart face to the sunny thoroughfare of the new Paris. Now, as it was represented in the picture on the advertisements, it had grown bigger and bigger, like the ogre in the fairy-tale whose shoulders threatened to break through the clouds. First, in the foreground of this picture, the Rue du Dix-Décembre, the Rue de la Michodière, and the Rue Monsigny were full of little black figures and stretched out inordinately, as if to open up the way for customers from all over the world. Then there was a bird's-eye view of the buildings themselves, of vastly exaggerated proportions, with their roofs indicating the position of the covered galleries and their courtyards with glass roofs through which the halls could be seen, an endless lake of glass and zinc shining in the sunshine. Beyond, Paris stretched out, but a Paris which was dwarfed and eaten up by the monster: the houses surrounding it had the humility of thatched cottages, and were scattered beyond it in a dust of blurred chimneys. The monuments seemed to be melting away: two marks on the left-hand side indicated Notre-Dame, there was a circumflex accent on the right for the Invalides, and in the background was the Panthéon lost and shamefaced, no bigger than a pea. The sky-line, crumbling into dust, had become nothing but a pathetic frame for the picture, and its distant blurred outlines indicated that it, too, as far away as the heights of Châtillon and the open country, was now enslaved.

The crowd had been growing throughout the morning. No shop had ever stirred up the city with such a mass of publicity. The Paradise was now spending nearly six hundred thousand francs a year on posters, advertisements, and appeals of every kind; the number of catalogues sent out was reaching four hundred thousand, and more than a hundred thousand francs' worth of materials was being cut up into patterns. Newspapers and walls were plastered with advertisements, and the public was assailed as if by a monstrous brass trumpet relentlessly amplifying the noise of the great sales to the four corners of the globe. And from now on the shop-front itself, which constantly attracted a milling crowd, would be a living advertisement, with its variegated and gilded luxury making it seem like a bazaar, its windows wide enough to display the entire range of women's clothes, its shop signs lavishly distributed everywhere, from the marble slabs on the ground floor to the sheets of iron arched over the roofs—signs which were painted, engraved, carved, unfolding the gold of their streamers on which the name of the shop could be read in sky-blue letters, cut out of the blue of the air. In order to celebrate the opening, banners and flags had been added as well: each storey was decked with banners and standards bearing the arms of the principal towns of France; while right at the top the flags of foreign nations, hoisted on flag-poles, were flapping in the wind. Finally, downstairs in the shop-windows, the display of household linen was blindingly intense. It was a strain on the eyes; everything was white: a complete trousseau and a mountain of sheets on the left, and curtains forming chapels and pyramids of handkerchiefs on the right; and, between the 'hangings' at the door—lengths of linen, calico, and muslin, hanging in sheets, like falls of snow—there were clothed figures made of sheets of bluish cardboard, a young bride and a lady in evening dress, both life-size and dressed in real lace and silk, smiling with their painted faces. A circle of gapers was constantly forming and reforming; desire and fascination were mingled in the excitement of the crowd.

The Ladies' Paradise was also arousing curiosity because of a calamity which was the talk of Paris, a fire which had burnt down the Quatre Saisons, the big shop Bouthemont had opened near the Opéra barely three weeks earlier. The newspapers were full of it: how the fire had been started by a gas explosion during the night, how the terrified salesgirls had fled in their night-dresses, the heroism of Bouthemont who had carried five of them to safety on his shoulders. The enormous losses were covered by insurance, and the public was beginning to shrug its shoulders, saying that it had been a splendid advertisement.* For the moment public attention, excited by the stories going round and preoccupied to the point of obsession by these emporiums which were acquiring such importance in public life, was flowing back to the Paradise. That man Mouret had nothing but luck! Paris was hailing his star and rushing to see him standing there erect, for the very flames of the fire seemed to raze all competition to the ground; people were already calculating the season's profits, estimating how much the forced closure of the rival shop would swell the tide of customers flowing through the doors of the Paradise. For a moment he had been anxious, worried at feeling that he had against him a woman—Madame Desforges, to whom he partly owed his fortune. The financial dilettantism of Baron Hartmann, who had put money into both businesses, also annoyed him. And he was especially exasperated at not having had the same inspired idea as Bouthemont, for that pleasure-lover had just had his shop blessed by the vicar of the Madeleine,

accompanied by all his clergy. It had been an astonishing ceremony: all the pomp of the Church was paraded through the silk
and glove departments, God circulated among women's knickers
and corsets; it is true that this had not prevented the whole shop
from being burnt down, but such had been its effect on society
customers that it had been worth a million advertisements. Ever
since then Mouret had been dreaming of getting hold of the
Archbishop.

Meanwhile, the clock over the door was striking three. It was
the afternoon crush: nearly a hundred thousand customers were
suffocating in the galleries and halls. Outside, from one end of
the Rue du Dix-Décembre to the other, carriages were waiting;
and, near the Opéra, another mass of vehicles was occupying the
blind alley where the new avenue was to start. Ordinary cabs
were mingled with gentlemen's broughams, coachmen were
waiting among the wheels, rows of horses were neighing and
shaking their glinting curbs, which were sparkling in the sun.
The ranks were endlessly reforming amidst the cries of the
ostlers and the jostling of the animals which closed in of their
own accord as fresh vehicles constantly arrived. Pedestrians were
fleeing to street-islands in startled bands and, in the vanishing
perspective of the broad, straight thoroughfare, the pavements
were black with people. The clamour was mounting between the
white buildings, and the soul of Paris seemed to rise from this
rolling human river, an enormous, gentle breath, like the kiss of
a giant.

Outside one of the windows Madame de Boves, accompanied
by her daughter Blanche and Madame Guibal, was looking at a
display of semi-made-up costumes.

'Oh, do look!' she said, 'those linen costumes, at nineteen
francs seventy-five!'

In their square cardboard boxes, the costumes, tied up with a
ribbon, were folded so as to show only the trimmings, embroidered with blue and red; and, across the corner of each box,
a picture showed the garment made up, being worn by a young
lady looking like a princess.

'I must say it isn't worth any more,' murmured Madame
Guibal. 'As soon as you pick it up you can see it's just made of
rags!' The two women had been on intimate terms ever since

Monsieur de Boves had become tied to an armchair by attacks of gout. The wife tolerated the mistress, preferring that the affair should take place in her own house, since this allowed her to make a little pocket-money by picking up sums of which her husband allowed himself to be robbed, for he knew that he needed indulgence.

'Well, let's go in,' Madame Guibal resumed. 'We must have a look at their exhibition . . . Didn't your son-in-law say he'd meet you inside?'

Madame de Boves did not reply; she was looking with fascination at the line of carriages which, one by one, were opening their doors and releasing more and more customers.

'Yes,' said Blanche at last, in her lifeless voice. 'Paul's going to pick us up at about four in the reading-room, when he leaves the Ministry.'

They had been married for a month, and Vallagnosc, following three weeks' leave in the Midi, had just returned to his post. The young woman already had her mother's heavy build; her flesh had become puffier and somehow coarsened by marriage.

'Look, there's Madame Desforges over there!' the Countess exclaimed, her eyes on a brougham which was just drawing up.

'Oh, do you think so?' murmured Madame Guibal. 'After that terrible business . . . She must still be mourning the fire at the Quatre Saisons.'

But it was indeed Henriette. She caught sight of the ladies, and went up to them gaily, hiding her defeat beneath the polished ease of her manners.

'Yes! Of course, I wanted to get an idea . . . It's better to see for oneself, isn't it? Oh! Monsieur Mouret and I are still good friends, although they say he's furious since I started to take an interest in the rival shop . . . As far as I'm concerned, there's only one thing I can't forgive him, and that's pushing, you know, that man Joseph and my protégée, Mademoiselle de Fontenailles, to get married . . .'

'What! Has it already happened?' interrupted Madame de Boves. 'How awful!'

'Yes, my dear, and just to assert his authority. I know him, he wanted to show that our society girls are only good for marrying his porters.'

She was becoming quite animated. All four of them were still standing on the pavement, in the middle of the great crush at the entrance. Little by little, however, they were being caught up in the stream, and they could do nothing but abandon themselves to the current; they went through the door as if they had been lifted up, without even realizing that they had done so, talking louder to make themselves heard. Now they were asking each other for news of Madame Marty. It was said that poor Monsieur Marty, following some violent family scenes, had been struck down with megalomania; he would extract treasures by the handful from the earth; he would empty gold-mines and load up tumbrels with diamonds and precious stones.

'Poor fellow!' said Madame Guibal. 'And he was always so shabby and humble, like the poor tutor he was! What about his wife?'

'She's living off an uncle at the moment,' Henriette replied. 'A nice old man who went to live in her house when he lost his wife . . . In any case, she should be here; we'll see her.'

The ladies stood rooted to the spot in surprise. Before them stretched the shop, the biggest shop in the world, as the advertisements said. The great central gallery now ran from one end to the other, opening into the Rue du Dix-Décembre and the Rue Neuve-Saint-Augustin; while to the right and left, like the side aisles in a church, the Monsigny Gallery and the Michodière Gallery, which were narrower, also ran the whole length of the two streets. Here and there, among the metal framework of the hanging staircases and suspension bridges, the halls widened out into squares. The interior plan had been changed round: now, the remnants were on the Rue du Dix-Décembre side, the silks were in the middle, the gloves occupied the Saint-Augustin Hall at the back; and when one looked up from the new main entrance hall one could still see the bedding, moved from one end of the second floor to the other. The number of departments had risen to fifty; several of them, brand new, were being opened that day; others, which had become too big, had simply had to be split up in order to facilitate selling; and, because of the continuous increase in business, the staff had just been brought up to three thousand and forty-five employees for the new season.

It was the stupendous sight of the great exhibition of household linen which had caused the ladies to stop. First of all, surrounding them, there was the entrance hall, with bright mirrors, and paved with mosaics, in which displays of inexpensive goods were drawing the voracious crowd. Then there were the galleries, dazzling in their whiteness like a polar vista, a snowy expanse unfolding with the endlessness of steppes draped with ermine, a mass of glaciers lit up beneath the sun. It was the same whiteness as that displayed in the outside windows, but heightened and on a colossal scale, burning from one end of the enormous nave to the other with the white blaze of a conflagration at its height. There was nothing but white, all the white goods from every department, an orgy of white, a white star whose radiance was blinding at first, and made it impossible to distinguish any details in the midst of this total whiteness. Soon the eye grew accustomed to it: to the left in the Monsigny Gallery there stretched out white promontories of linens and calicoes, white rocks of sheets, table-napkins, and handkerchiefs; while in the Michodière Gallery on the right, occupied by the haberdashery, hosiery, and woollens, white edifices were displayed made of pearl buttons, together with a huge construction of white socks, and a whole hall covered with white swansdown and illuminated by a distant shaft of light. But the light was especially bright in the central gallery, where the ribbons and fichus, gloves and silks were situated. The counters disappeared beneath the white of silks and ribbons, of gloves and fichus. Around the iron pillars were twined flounces of white muslin, knotted here and there with white scarves. The staircases were decked with white draperies, draperies of piqué alternating with dimity, running the whole length of the banisters and encircling the halls right up to the second floor; and the ascending whiteness appeared to take wing, merging together and disappearing like a flight of swans. The whiteness then fell back again from the domes in a rain of eiderdown, a sheet of huge snowflakes: white blankets and white coverlets were waving in the air, hung up like banners in a church; long streams of pillow-lace seemed suspended like swarms of white butterflies, humming there motionless; other types of lace were fluttering everywhere, floating like gossamer against a summer sky, filling the air with their white

breath. And over the silk counter in the main hall there was the
miracle, the altar of this cult of white—a tent made of white
curtains hanging down from the glass roof. Muslins, gauzes, and
guipures flowed in light ripples, while richly embroidered tulles
and lengths of oriental silk and silver lamé served as a background to this gigantic decoration, which was evocative both of
the tabernacle and of the bedroom. It looked like a great white
bed, its virginal whiteness waiting, as in legends, for the white
princess, for she who would one day come, all powerful, in her
white bridal veil.

'Oh! It's fantastic!' the ladies kept repeating. 'Amazing!'

They did not tire of this hymn of praise to white, which all the
materials in the shop were singing. It was the most immense
exhibition Mouret had mounted so far, the stroke of his genius
for display. Through the flow of all this white, and the apparent
disorder of the materials, there ran a harmonic phrase, white
maintained and developed in all its tones, which were introduced
and then grew and expanded with the complicated orchestration
of some masterly fugue, the continued development of which
carries the soul away in an ever-widening flight. There was
nothing but white, yet it was never the same white, but all the
different tones of white, competing together, contrasting with
and complementing each other, achieving the brilliance of light
itself. First came the mat whites of calico and linen, the dull
whites of flannel and cloth; next came the velvets, the silks, the
satins, a rising scale, the white gradually lighting up, finishing in
little flames around the breaks of the folds; and in the transparency of the curtains the white took wing, in the muslins and
laces it attained the freedom of light, and the tulles were so fine
that they seemed to be the ultimate note, dying away into nothing; while at the back of the gigantic alcove the silver in the
lengths of oriental silk sang out above everything else.

The shop was full of life: people were besieging the lifts, there
was a tremendous crush in the buffet and the reading-room; it
was as if the whole nation was travelling through those snow-
covered spaces. The crowd seemed black, like skaters on a Polish
lake in December. On the ground floor there was a dark swell
ebbing back, in which nothing but the delicate, enraptured faces
of the women could be seen. Along the fretwork of the iron
frames, all up the staircases, and on the suspension bridges, there

was an endless procession of little figures, as if lost among snowy mountain peaks. The suffocating hothouse heat which confronted them on those glacial heights came as a surprise. The buzz of voices made a deafening noise like a swiftly flowing river. On the ceiling the elaborate gilding, the glass inlaid with gold, and the golden roses were like a burst of sunshine shining on the Alps of the great exhibition of white.

'Well,' said Madame de Boves, 'we must move on. We can't stay here for ever.'

Jouve, standing near the door, had not taken his eyes off her since she had entered the shop. When she turned round their glances met. Then, as she started to walk off again, he let her get a little ahead, and followed her at a distance, without appearing to take any further notice of her.

'Look!' said Madame Guibal, stopping again at the first cash-desk. 'Those violets are a nice idea!'

She was referring to the Paradise's new free gift, little bunches of white violets, bought by the thousand in Nice, and distributed to every customer who made even the smallest purchase; it was one of Mouret's ideas which he was advertising in all the newspapers. Near each cash-desk messenger-boys in livery were handing out these free gifts, under the supervision of a shop-walker. Gradually the customers were becoming decked with flowers; the shop was filling with these white bridal bouquets; all the women were carrying around with them a penetrating perfume of flowers.

'Yes,' murmured Madame Desforges in a jealous voice, 'it's not a bad idea.'

But, just as they were about to move away, they heard two salesmen joking about the violets. One of them, tall and thin, was expressing his surprise: it was coming off then, was it, the boss's marriage with the buyer in the children's department? The other one, short and fat, was replying that no one knew for certain, but that they'd bought the flowers all the same.

'What!' said Madame de Boves, 'Monsieur Mouret is getting married?'

'It's the first I've heard of it,' Henriette replied, feigning indifference. 'But that's how we all end up.'

The Countess threw a sharp glance at her new friend. Now they both understood why Madame Desforges had come to the Ladies' Paradise, despite her rupture with Mouret. She was obviously giving way to an irresistible urge to see and to suffer.

'I'll stay with you,' said Madame Guibal, her curiosity aroused. 'We'll meet Madame de Boves in the reading-room.'

'Very well, let's do that!' the latter declared. 'There's something I want to do on the first floor . . . Are you coming Blanche?'

And she went upstairs, followed by her daughter, while Jouve, still following her, took a neighbouring staircase, in order not to attract her attention. The other two were soon lost in the dense crowd on the ground floor.

In the midst of the bustle of business all the departments were talking of nothing but the governor's love-affairs. The intrigue which for months had been giving the assistants, delighted by Denise's long resistance, something to talk about had suddenly come to a head: it had become known the day before that the girl wanted to leave the Paradise, in spite of Mouret's entreaties, on the pretext that she needed a long rest. Opinion was divided: would she or wouldn't she leave? From department to department bets of five francs were being laid that she would marry him the following Sunday. The crafty ones were staking a lunch on her marrying him in the end; yet the others, those who believed that she would leave, were not risking their money without good reason. Certainly, the young lady was in the strong position of an adored woman who refuses to yield; but the governor, on his side, was strong because of his wealth, his happiness as a widower, and his pride, which a final unreasonable demand might provoke beyond measure. In any case, they all agreed that the little salesgirl had conducted the affair with the skill of a courtesan of genius, and that she was playing her final card by offering him a deal; marry me, or I leave.

Denise, however, gave no thought to any of these things. She had never been either demanding or calculating. She had decided to leave precisely because of the opinions which, to her continual surprise, were being passed about her conduct. It was not as if she had willed it all, or had shown herself to be artful, flirtatious, or ambitious. She had simply turned up there, and she was the first to be surprised that anyone could love her like that. And why, even now, did people see cunning in her resolve to leave the Paradise? It was so natural! She was becoming most uncomfortable, she felt unbearable anguish, surrounded as she was by the continual gossip of the shop, by Mouret's burning obsession, and faced with the struggle she could not avoid within herself; she preferred to go away, fearing that she might give in one day and regret it for the rest of her life. If these were skilful tactics, she was not aware of it, and she would ask herself in despair what she could do to avoid giving the impression that she was trying to catch a husband. The idea of marriage now irritated her; she was resolved to go on saying no, always no, if he persisted in his madness. She alone should suffer. The need for the separation reduced her to tears; but, courageous as she was, she told herself that it was necessary, and that she would have no peace or happiness if she acted in any other way.

When Mouret received her resignation, in his effort to contain himself he remained silent and apparently unmoved. Then he curtly declared that he would give her a week to think it over before allowing her to do anything so silly. At the end of a week, when she brought the subject up again and confirmed her resolve to leave after the big sales, he did not lose his temper, but attempted to appeal to her reason: she would be throwing away all she had achieved, she would never find another position equal to the one she occupied in his shop. Had she got another job in view, then? He was quite ready to offer her the advantages she was hoping to find elsewhere. When she replied that she had not yet looked for another job, but that, thanks to the money she had been able to save, she intended to have a month's rest at Valognes before looking for something, he asked what would prevent her from coming back to the Paradise after that, if it was only concern for her health which was obliging her to leave. She remained silent, tortured by this interrogation. This made him imagine that she was going to join a lover, perhaps a husband. Hadn't she confessed to him, one evening, that there was someone she loved? From that moment onwards he had carried the avowal he had dragged from her in a moment of distress deep in his heart, plunged in like a knife. If this man was going to marry her, she was giving up everything in order to follow him: that explained her obstinacy. It was all over, and he simply added in his icy voice that he would detain her no longer, since she could not tell him the real reasons for her leaving. These crisp words, spoken without anger, upset her more than the violent scene she had expected.

During the week which Denise still had to spend in the shop Mouret remained pale and impassive. When he walked through the departments he pretended not to see her; never had he seemed more detached, more buried in his work; and the bets began again, but only the bravest dared risk a lunch on marriage. Meanwhile, beneath this coldness, which was so unusual for him, Mouret was hiding a terrible crisis of indecision and suffering. Fits of anger made the blood rush to his head: he saw red, he dreamed of taking Denise by force, of keeping her by stifling her cries. Then he would try to reason, he would try to think of practical ways of preventing her from going out of the door; but he was always confronted with his own powerlessness, filled with fury by the uselessness of his power and money. Nevertheless, in the midst of these mad projects, an idea was growing and imposing itself little by little in spite of his resistance. After the death of Madame Hédouin he had sworn not to remarry; having owed his initial good luck to a woman, he was resolved from then on to make his fortune out of all women. It was a superstition with him, as it was with Bourdoncle, that the manager of a big drapery store should be a bachelor if he wished to retain his masculine power over the scattered desires of his nation of customers: once a wife was introduced, the atmosphere would change; her smell would drive the others away. He was resisting the irresistible logic of facts; he would rather have died than give in, overcome with sudden bouts of rage against Denise, sensing that she was the revenge, and afraid that, on the day he married her, he would be broken like a straw by the Eternal Feminine. Then he would gradually become faint-hearted again and would argue his reluctance away: what was there to be afraid of? She was so gentle, so sensible, that he could surrender himself to her without fear. Twenty times an hour the struggle would begin again in his tormented mind. Pride was irritating the wound, and he was finally losing what little reason he had left at the thought that, even after his final surrender, she might say no, still no, if she loved someone else. On the morning of the big sale he had still not come to a decision, and Denise was leaving the next day.

On that day, when Bourdoncle went into Mouret's office at about three o'clock, as was his custom, he caught him with his elbows on the desk, his hands over his eyes, so absorbed that he had to touch him on the shoulder. Mouret looked up, his face wet with tears, and they looked at each other; then these men, who had fought so many commercial battles together, reached out and gripped each other by the hand. For the past month Bourdoncle's attitude had completely changed: he was giving way to Denise, he was even secretly pushing his chief into marriage. No doubt he was manœuvring in that way to save himself from being swept away by a force which he now recognized to be superior. But, at the root of this change, there could also be found the awakening of an old ambition, the nervous but growing hope that he might devour Mouret, to whom he had been subservient for so long. Such a thought was always in the air, in the struggle for existence, the continual massacres of which boosted the sales around him. He was carried away by the workings of the machine, seized by the same appetite as the others, by the voraciousness which, throughout the shop, drove the thin to exterminate the fat. Only a sort of religious fear, the religion of luck, had so far prevented him from taking his bite. And now the governor was becoming childish again, was slipping into an idiotic marriage, was going to kill his luck, destroy his charm with the customers. Why should he dissuade him from it, when it would then be so easy for him to pick up the inheritance of a man who was finished, who had fallen into the arms of a woman? Thus it was with the emotion of a farewell, the compassion of a long comradeship, that he shook his chief's hand, repeating as he did so:

'Come on, cheer up, damn it! Marry her, and have done with it.'

Mouret was already ashamed of his moment of weakness. He stood up, protesting.

'No, no, it's really stupid . . . Come on, we'll do our tour of the shop. Things are going well, aren't they? I think we'll have a magnificent day.'

They went out and began their afternoon inspection, making their way through the crowded departments. Bourdoncle cast sideways glances at him, worried by this last burst of energy, watching his lips in order to catch the slightest sign of suffering.

The sale was indeed roaring away at an infernal pace, making the shop shake like a great ship going at full speed. In Denise's department was a gaggle of mothers, trailing hordes of little girls and boys who were drowning beneath the garments which were being tried on them. The department had brought out all its white things, and there, as everywhere else, there was an orgy of white, enough white to clothe a whole troupe of cupids feeling the cold: there were overcoats in white cloth, dresses in piqué and nainsook and white cashmere, sailor suits, and even white zouave suits. Although it was not yet the season, in the centre, as a decoration, was a display of first communion dresses and veils in white muslin, white satin shoes, a spectacular florescence, as if an enormous bouquet of innocence and guileless ecstasy had been planted there. Madame Bourdelais, facing her three children who were sitting in order of size—Madeline, Edmond, Lucien—was losing her temper with the smallest because he was struggling while Denise was trying to put a mousseline-de-laine jacket on him.

'Keep still! Don't you think it's a little tight, miss?'

With the sharp look of a woman who cannot be deceived she was examining the material, criticizing the cut, and looking at the stitching.

'No, it's fine,' she went on, 'it's quite a job dressing these youngsters . . . Now, I need a coat for this young lady.'

The department was being taken by storm and Denise had had to lend a hand at the counters. She was looking for the coat she needed, when she gave a little cry of surprise.

'What! You! What on earth's the matter?'

Her brother Jean, holding a parcel in his hands, was standing in front of her. He had been married for a week, and on the preceding Saturday his wife—who was small and dark with a charming, anxious little face—had paid a long visit to the Ladies' Paradise to make some purchases. The young couple were going to accompany Denise to Valognes; it was to be a real honeymoon, a month's holiday which would remind them of old times.

'Just fancy,' he repeated, 'Thérèse forgot a lot of things. There are some to be changed and others to be bought . . . So, since she's busy, she sent me with this parcel . . . I'll explain . . .'

But, catching sight of Pépé, she interrupted him.

'What! Pépé too! What about school?'

'Well,' said Jean, 'after dinner on Sunday, yesterday, I didn't have the heart to take him back. He'll go back tonight . . . The poor kid's very sad at being shut up in Paris while we go back home on a holiday.'

In spite of her troubles, Denise was smiling. She handed Madame Bourdelais over to one of her salesgirls, then came back to them in a corner of the department which was fortunately becoming less crowded. The children, as she still called them, had become great strapping fellows. Pépé, who was now twelve, was already taller than she was; he was still very quiet, and craved affection, and in his school uniform he had a sweet gentleness about him; whereas Jean was broad-shouldered, and was a full head taller than his sister; and with his blond hair swept back in the windswept style of artisans, he still had the beauty of a woman. And she, as slim as ever, no fatter than a sparrow as she said, had retained her authority over them like an anxious mother, treated them like little boys who needed looking after, and would re-button Jean's coat so that he would not look like a tramp, and make sure that Pépé had a clean handkerchief. When she saw Pépé looking at her with his big, reproachful eyes, she gently lectured him.

'You must be reasonable, my darling. You can't interrupt your studies. I'll take you there in the holidays . . . Is there anything you'd like to have now? Perhaps you'd rather I gave you some money?'

She turned back to Jean again.

'You know, you get him excited by making him think we're going to have a good time. Do try to be more sensible.'

She had given Jean four thousand francs, half of her savings, to enable him to set up house. Her younger brother's schooling was costing her a good deal and, as in the past, all her money was spent on them. They were her only reason for living and working, for she had again sworn that she would never marry.

'Well,' Jean resumed, 'first of all in this parcel there's the tan coat which Thérèse . . .'

But he stopped short, and on turning round to see what was intimidating him, Denise caught sight of Mouret standing behind them. For a few moments he had been watching her standing in her motherly way between the two big lads, scolding them and kissing them, turning them round like babies having their clothes changed. Bourdoncle had remained in the background, apparently more interested in the sale; but he lost nothing of the scene.

'They're your brothers, aren't they?' asked Mouret after a silence.

He spoke in his icy voice, with the stiff manner he used with her nowadays. Denise herself was making an effort to remain cold. Her smile disappeared, she replied:

'Yes, sir . . . I've married off the eldest, and his wife has sent him to buy a few things.'

Mouret continued looking at the three of them. Finally he said:

'The younger one has grown a lot. I recognize him, I remember seeing him in the Tuileries one evening, with you.'

His voice, which was growing more hesitant, shook slightly. Denise, very nervous, bent down, pretending to adjust Pépé's belt. The two brothers, red in the face, stood smiling at their sister's employer.

'They're like you,' Mouret added.

'Oh!' she exclaimed, 'they're better-looking than I am!'

For a moment he seemed to be comparing their faces. But he was at the end of his tether. How she loved them! He walked a few steps away; then he came back and said in her ear:

'Come to my office after the sale. I want to talk to you before you leave.'

This time Mouret did walk away and resumed his tour of inspection. The battle within him was starting again, for now he was annoyed that he had arranged a meeting. To what feeling had he yielded on seeing her with her brothers? It was crazy; he no longer had the strength to have a will of his own. However, he could put an end to it by saying a word of farewell to her. Bourdoncle, who had rejoined him, seemed less anxious, though he was still studying him with sly glances.

Meanwhile Denise had gone back to Madame Bourdelais.

'How is the coat?'

'Oh, it's excellent . . . Well, that's enough for today. These little ones are ruining me!'

Denise was able to slip away and listen to Jean's explanations, and then accompanied him through the departments, where he would certainly have lost his head without her. First there was the tan coat which Thérèse, after thinking it over, wanted to change for a white cloth coat of the same size and shape. Having taken the parcel, Denise proceeded to the ladieswear department, followed by her two brothers.

The department had laid out all its light-coloured garments, summer jackets and mantillas made of fine silk and fancy woollens. But the sale had moved elsewhere, and most of the customers had left. Almost all the salesgirls were new. Clara had disappeared a month ago; according to some, she had run off with the husband of a customer, and according to others, she had gone on the streets. As for Marguerite, she was at last going back to run the little shop in Grenoble, where her cousin was waiting for her. Madame Aurélie alone remained there, unchanging in the rounded armour of her silk dress, and with her imperial mask which had the yellowish fleshiness of antique marble. Nevertheless, her son Albert's bad behaviour still troubled her greatly, and she would have retired to the country but for the holes made in the family savings by that good-for-nothing, whose terrible extravagance was threatening to eat away little by little their estate at Les Rignolles. It was like a punishment for their broken home, for the mother had started giving tasteful parties for women only again, while the father continued to play the horn. Bourdoncle was already beginning to look disapprovingly at Madame Aurélie, surprised that she had not had the tact to retire: too old for selling! That knell would soon be tolling, sweeping away the Lhomme dynasty.

'It's you!' she said to Denise with exaggerated friendliness. 'You want this coat changed, do you? Of course, straight away . . . Ah! So there are your brothers. They've really grown up!'

In spite of her pride, she would have gone down on her knees to do homage to Denise. In the ladieswear department, as in the other departments, they were talking of nothing but Denise's departure; and the buyer was quite ill over it, for she had counted on the protection of her former salesgirl. She lowered her voice.

'They say you're leaving us . . . It can't be true, surely?'

'Yes, it is,' replied the girl.

Marguerite was listening. Since the date of her marriage had been fixed, she had been going about with a more disdainful expression than ever on her pasty face. She came up to them, saying:

'You're quite right. Self-respect is the most important thing, isn't it? I bid you farewell, my dear.'

Some customers were arriving. Madame Aurélie sternly asked her to attend to the sale. Then, seeing Denise take the coat so as to make the 'return' herself, she protested, and called an assistant. It so happened that this was an innovation which Denise had suggested to Mouret: the use of female employees whose duty was to carry the goods so that the salesgirls would be less tired.

'Please accompany this young lady,' said the buyer, handing the coat over to her.

And, returning to Denise, she said:

'Do think it over, won't you? We're all really sorry that you're leaving.'

Jean and Pépé, who were waiting, smiling in the midst of the overflowing stream of women, once more followed their sister. They now had to go to the trousseau department to get six chemises just like the half-dozen Thérèse had bought on Saturday. But in the lingerie department, where a display of white was snowing from every shelf, there was a tremendous crush, and it was becoming very difficult to get through.

First of all, in the corsets, a slight disturbance was making a crowd collect. Madame Boutarel, who had arrived from the Midi this time with her husband and daughter, had been scouring the galleries since the morning in quest of a trousseau for the girl, who was getting married. The father had to be consulted all the time, and it seemed as if they would never be able to choose anything. They had just found themselves in the lingerie department; and, while the young lady was engrossed in a close study of knickers, the mother, having taken a fancy to some corsets, had disappeared. When Monsieur Boutarel, a big red-faced man, abandoned his daughter in order to go and look for his wife, he finally found her in a fitting-room at the door of which he was politely asked to sit down. These rooms were narrow cells shut off with frosted glass doors; because of the exaggerated prudery of the management, men, even husbands, were not allowed to enter. Salesgirls were going in and out of them quickly, and each time they slammed the door those outside were given a rapid glimpse of ladies in their chemises and petticoats, with bare necks and arms, of fat women whose flesh was fading, and of thin women the colour of old ivory. A row of men sat waiting on chairs, looking bored: Monsieur Boutarel, when he grasped the situation, lost his temper, and shouted that he wanted his wife, he insisted on knowing what they were doing to her, and he would certainly not allow her to undress without him. Vainly they tried to calm him down: he seemed to believe that something improper was going on inside. While the crowd discussed the matter and laughed about it, Madame Boutarel was forced to reappear.

Denise and her brothers were now able to get through. Every type of women's linen, all the white things which are hidden underneath, were displayed in a succession of rooms divided into different departments. The corsets and bustles occupied one counter; there were stitched corsets, long-waisted corsets, armour-like boned corsets, above all white silk corsets with coloured fan-stitching on them, of which a special display had been arranged that day; there was an army of mannequins without heads or legs, nothing but torsos lined up, their dolls' breasts flattened under the silk; they had the disturbing lewdness of the disabled. Close by, on neighbouring stands, there were bustles of horsehair and jaconet, their enormous taut rumps forming extensions to the long rods and their outlines appearing grotesquely indecent. But beyond them the luxury *déshabillé* began, a *déshabillé* strewn across the vast galleries, as if an army of pretty girls had undressed as they went from department to department, down to their satiny skin. On one side there were fine linen goods, white cuffs and scarves, fichus and white collars, an infinite variety of frills and flounces, a white froth escaping from the boxes and rising like so much snow. On the other side there were jackets, little bodices, tea-gowns, dressing-gowns, made of linen, nainsook, and lace, and long white garments, loose and diaphanous, which evoked visions of languorous, lazy mornings after nights of love. And the underclothes appeared, falling one by one: white petticoats of every length, petticoats tight across the knees, and petticoats with a train that swept on the ground, a rising tide of petticoats in which legs were drowning; bloomers in cambric, linen, and piqué; broad white bloomers in which a man's hips would be lost; finally, the chemises, buttoned up to the neck for the night, and leaving the bosom bare during the day, held up only by narrow shoulder-straps, and made of plain calico, Irish linen, and cambric, the last veil slipping from the breasts and down the hips. In the trousseau department all discretion was abandoned: women were turned round and viewed from below, from the ordinary housewife with her common calicoes to the rich lady smothered in lace; it was an alcove open to the public, whose hidden luxury, its plaitings and embroideries and Valenciennes lace, depraved the senses as it overflowed in costly fantasies. Woman dressed herself again, and the white waves of this flood of linen again became hidden beneath the quivering mystery of skirts; the chemise stiffened by the dressmaker's fingers, the frigid bloomers retaining the creases from the box, and all that dead cambric and muslin lying dishevelled, strewn about, and piled up on the counters were soon to become alive with the life of the flesh, scented and warm with the fragrance of love, a cloud of white which would become sacred, steeped in night, and of which the slightest flutter, the pink of a knee glimpsed in the depths of the whiteness, played havoc with the world. There was still one more room, devoted to baby linen, where the voluptuous white of Woman led to the guileless white of children: innocence, joy, the young wife who wakes up a mother, infants' vests made of fluffy quilting, flannel hoods, chemises, and bonnets no bigger than toys, and christening robes, and cashmere shawls, the white down of birth like a shower of fine white feathers.

'You know, they're like chemises in the theatre,' said Jean, who was delighted at this unrobing, this rising tide of clothes into which he was sinking.

In the trousseau department Pauline ran up immediately when she saw Denise. And before she even asked what the latter wanted, she spoke to her in an undertone, showing her agitation at the rumours which were circulating throughout the shop. In her department, two salesgirls had even quarrelled, one insisting that Denise would leave, the other denying it.

'You're staying with us, I've staked everything on it . . . What would become of me if you left?'

And when Denise replied that she was leaving the next day, she said;

'No, no, you think you will, but I know you won't . . . Now I've got a baby, you must get me promoted assistant buyer. Baugé's counting on it, my dear.'

Pauline was smiling with an air of conviction. Then she gave them the six chemises; and as Jean had said that they were now going on to the handkerchiefs, she called another assistant to carry the chemises and the coat left by the assistant from the ladieswear department. The girl who happened to be there was Mademoiselle de Fontenailles, who had recently married Joseph. She had just obtained this menial job as a favour, and was wearing a big black overall marked on the shoulder with a number in yellow wool.

'Would you please follow this young lady?' said Pauline.

Then, coming back and again lowering her voice, she said to Denise:

'I'll be assistant buyer, won't I? It's agreed!'

Joking in her turn, Denise laughingly gave her promise. Then she moved on and went downstairs with Pépé and Jean, the three of them accompanied by the assistant. On the ground floor they suddenly found themselves in the woollens: one corner of a gallery was entirely hung with white duffel and flannel. Liénard, whose father was vainly summoning him back to Angers, was talking with the 'Handsome' Mignot, who had become a broker, and who had had the nerve to reappear in the Ladies' Paradise. No doubt they were talking about Denise, for they both fell silent in order to greet her obsequiously. Indeed, as she advanced through the departments, the salesmen became quite excited and bowed down before her, uncertain as to what she might be the next day. They whispered, saying that she looked triumphant; and there was a fresh wave of betting: people began staking a bottle of Argenteuil wine and some fried fish on her. She had entered the household linen gallery in order to get to the hand-kerchief department, which was at the further end. There was an endless array of white: the white of cotton, of dimity, of piqués, of calicoes; the white of madapollam, nainsook, muslin, and tarlatan; then, in enormous piles built of lengths of material alternating like stones hewn in cubes, came the linens, coarse linens and fine linens of every width, white and unbleached, made from pure flax bleached in the meadows; then the whole thing began all over again and departments for every kind of made-up linen succeeded each other; there was household linen, table linen, kitchen linen, an endless avalanche of white, there were sheets and pillow-cases, innumerable different kinds of table-napkins and table-cloths, aprons and dishcloths. And the greetings continued as they fell back while Denise passed by. In the linen department Baugé had dashed forward to give her a smile, as if she was the beloved queen of the shop. Finally, after having gone through the blankets department, a room decked with white banners, she went into the handkerchiefs, where the ingenious decorations were sending the crowd into ecstasies— there were white columns, white pyramids, white castles, com-plicated architecture built up of nothing but handkerchiefs, handkerchiefs made of lawn, cambric, Irish linen, and Chinese silk, initialled handkerchiefs, handkerchiefs embroidered with satin-stitch, trimmed with lace, hemstitched, and with woven designs, a whole town of white bricks of infinite variety, standing out like a mirage against an oriental sky warmed to white heat.

'Another dozen, you say?' Denise asked her brother. 'It's Cholets you want, isn't it?'

'Yes, I think so, the same as this one,' he replied, showing her a handkerchief in the parcel.

Jean and Pépé had not left her side, but were staying close to her as they had in the past when, worn out from the journey, they had arrived in Paris. This vast shop, where she was so at home, was disturbing them; they sheltered behind her and, their childhood instinctively reawakening, once more placed them-selves under the protection of the sister who was a mother to them. People were watching them, smiling at these two strap-ping lads—Jean who was scared in spite of the fact that he had a beard, and Pépé bewildered in his tunic—following in the footsteps of the slight, serious-looking girl, all three of them now with the same fair hair, which made people from one end of the department to the other whisper as they passed:

'They're her brothers . . . they're her brothers . . .'

While Denise was looking for a salesman, an encounter took place. Mouret and Bourdoncle entered the gallery; and just as the former came to a halt before the girl without, however, saying a word to her, Madame Desforges and Madame Guibal passed by. Henriette repressed the shudder which had passed through her whole body. She looked at Mouret; then she looked at Denise. They, too, looked at her; it was like a silent denouement, the common end of violent emotional dramas, a glance exchanged in the middle of a crowd. Mouret had already moved on, while Denise, still searching for a free salesman, disappeared with her brothers at the far end of the department. Then Henriette, who had recognized the assistant following the three of them, with a yellow number on her shoulder and her mask-like face coarse and cadaverous like that of a servant, to be Mademoiselle de Fontenailles, relieved her feelings by saying to Madame Guibal in an irritated voice:

'Just look what he's done to that poor girl. Isn't it shameful? A marchioness! And he forces her to follow the creatures he's picked up off the pavements as if she were a dog.'

She tried to regain her composure, and putting on an air of indifference she added:

'Let's go and have a look at their silk display.'

The silk department was like a huge bedroom dedicated to love, hung with white by the whim of a woman in love who, snowy in her nudity, wished to compete in whiteness. All the milky tones of an adored body were there, from the velvet of the hips to the fine silk of the thighs and the shining satin of the breasts. Lengths of velvet were hung between the columns, and against this creamy-white background silks and satins stood out in hangings of metallic whiteness and the whiteness of porcelain; and falling in arches there were also silk poults and Sicilian grosgrains, light foulards and surahs, ranging from the heavy white of a Norwegian blonde to the transparent white, warmed by the sun, of a redhead from Italy or Spain.

Favier was just measuring some white foulard for the 'pretty lady', that elegant blonde who was a regular customer in the department and to whom the salesmen never referred except by that name. She had been coming there for years, and they still knew nothing about her, neither what sort of life she led, nor her address, nor even her name. None of them ever tried to find out, although all of them made guesses each time she appeared, just for something to talk about. She was getting thinner, she was getting fatter, she had slept well, or she must have gone to bed late the night before; and each small incident in her unknown life—domestic events, external dramas—therefore had reper-cussions which would be commented on at length. On that day she seemed very happy. And Favier, when he came back from the cash-desk where he had accompanied her, suggested to Hutin:

'She may be getting married again.'

'Why, is she a widow?' asked the other.

'I don't know . . . But don't you remember the time she was in mourning? . . . Unless she's made some money on the Stock Exchange.'

There was a silence. Then he concluded:

'It's her business. It wouldn't do if we became familiar with all the women who come here . . .'

But Hutin was looking very thoughtful. Two days earlier he had had an argument with the management, and he felt himself condemned. After the big sale his dismissal was certain. His job had been at risk for a long time; at the last stock-taking he had been reproached for not having reached the turnover fixed in advance; and, above all, there was still the slow pressure of appetites devouring him in his turn, a whole secret war in the department throwing him out, forming part of the very motion of the machine. Favier's hidden work could now be heard; there was a loud sound of hungry jaws, muffled underground. The latter had already been promised the job of buyer. Hutin, who was aware of all this, instead of punching his old friend, now considered him to be very clever. Such a cold fish, with such a docile manner, whom he had himself used to wear down Robineau and Bouthemont! He was overcome with surprise mingled with respect.

'By the way,' Favier went on, 'you know she's staying. The governor was just seen making sheep's eyes at her . . . I stand to lose a bottle of champagne.'

He was referring to Denise. Gossip was raging more than ever round the counters, across the endlessly swelling stream of customers. The silk department, especially, was in an uproar, for heavy bets had been laid there.

'Damn it!' Hutin blurted out, waking as if from a dream. 'What a fool I was not to sleep with her! I'd be well off today if I had!'

Then, seeing Favier laughing, he blushed at his confession. He pretended to laugh too, and added, in order to make up for what he had said, that it was that creature who had done for him in the eyes of the management. However, a need for violent action seized him, and he lost his temper with the salesmen, who had dispersed under the assault of the customers. But suddenly he began to smile again: he had just caught sight of Madame Desforges and Madame Guibal walking slowly through the department.

'There's nothing you need today, madam?'

'No, thank you,' Henriette replied. 'I'm just walking round; I only came today out of curiosity.'

Having stopped her, he lowered his voice. A whole plan was springing up in his head, and he humoured her by running down the shop: he had had quite enough of it; he would rather leave than stay on any longer in such chaos. She listened to him, delighted. It was she who, thinking she was stealing him from the Paradise, offered to get him taken on by Bouthemont as buyer in the silk department when the Quatre Saisons was re-fitted. The deal was clinched in whispers, while Madame Guibal was looking at the displays.

'May I offer you one of these bunches of violets?' Hutin resumed, pointing to a table where there were three or four gift bunches, which he had procured for his own personal presents from one of the cash-desks.

'Oh, no!' exclaimed Henriette, stepping back. 'I don't want to take any part in the wedding!'

They understood each other. They separated, still laughing and exchanging knowing glances.

Madame Desforges, looking for Madame Guibal, gave an exclamation of surprise when she saw her with Madame Marty. The latter, followed by her daughter Valentine, had already been in the shop for two hours, carried away by one of those fits of spending which always left her exhausted and confused. She had made a thorough inspection of the furniture department, which had been transformed by a display of white lacquered furniture into a young girl's bedroom, and the ribbon and fichu department, where there were colonnades covered with white awnings; and the haberdashery and trimming departments, where white fringes framed ingenious trophies carefully built up out of cards of buttons and packets of needles; and finally the hosiery, where that year there was a tremendous crush of people wanting to see an immense decorative design: the glorious name of the Ladies' Paradise in letters three metres high, made of white socks against a background of red socks. But Madame Marty was especially excited by the new departments; a department could not be opened without her going to inaugurate it: she would rush in and buy something indiscriminately. She had spent an hour in the millinery department, installed in a new salon on the first floor, having cupboards emptied for her, taking hats from the rosewood stands with which the two tables there were decked, and trying them all on with her daughter—white hats, white bonnets, white toques. Then she had gone downstairs again to the shoe department at the far end of one of the galleries, beyond the ties, a department which had been opened that very day; she had ransacked the show-cases, seized with morbid desire at the sight of white silk mules trimmed with swansdown and shoes and boots of white satin with high Louis XV heels.

'Oh, my dear!' she stammered, 'you've no idea! They've got a wonderful assortment of bonnets. I've chosen one for myself and one for my daughter . . . And what about the shoes, eh? Valentine . . .'

'It's fantastic!' added the girl, who was as self-possessed as a mature woman. 'There are some wonderful boots at twenty francs fifty!'

A salesman was following them, dragging the eternal chair on which a heap of goods was already piling up.

'How is Monsieur Marty?' asked Madame Desforges.

'Quite well, I believe,' replied Madame Marty, startled by this sudden question which disturbed her fever of spending. 'He's still away; my uncle was supposed to go to see him this morning . . .'

But she broke off and let out a cry of ecstasy:

'Oh, look! Isn't that adorable?'

The ladies, who had walked on a little, were now standing opposite the new flower and feather department, which had been installed in the central gallery between the silks and gloves. Endless blooms lay under the bright light from the glass roof, a white sheaf as tall and broad as an oak tree. Clusters of flowers decorated the base—violets, lilies-of-the-valley, hyacinths, daisies, all the delicate whites of a flower-bed. Then, higher up, there were bunches of white roses softened with a fleshy tint, huge white peonies lightly shaded with carmine, white chrysanthemums in delicate sprays starred with yellow. The flowers went up and up: there were great mystical lilies, branches of apple blossom, sheaves of fragrant lilac, and endless blossoming which, on a level with the first floor, was crowned with plumes of ostrich feathers, white feathers which seemed to be the breath floating away from this crowd of flowers. A whole corner was devoted to a display of trimmings and wreaths made of orange blossom. There were flowers made of metal, silver thistles, and silver ears of corn. In the foliage and the petals, in the midst of all this muslin, silk, and velvet, in which drops of gum were like drops of dew, there flew birds of paradise for hats, purple tangaras with black tails and septicolours with shimmering breasts, shot with all the colours of the rainbow.

'I'm going to buy a branch of apple blossom,' Madame Marty went on. 'It's lovely, isn't it . . . And that little bird, do look, Valentine. Oh! I'll get it!'

Madame Guibal was getting bored at just standing there, in the swirl of the crowd. Finally she said:

'Well, we'll leave you to your purchases. We're going upstairs.'

'Oh no, wait for me!' Madame Marty exclaimed. 'I'm going upstairs again too . . . The perfume department's up there. I must go and visit it.'

This department, which had been created the day before, was next door to the reading-room. Madame Desforges, in order to avoid the crush on the stairs, spoke of taking the lift, but they had to abandon the idea, as there was a queue waiting to go up. They got there in the end by going through the buffet, where there was such a crowd that a shopwalker had been obliged to curb people's appetites by only allowing the gluttonous customers to enter in small groups at a time. Even in the buffet the ladies began to smell the perfume department; the penetrating scent of sachets pervaded the gallery. There was quite a struggle over a particular soap, the Paradise soap, a speciality of the shop. Inside the display counters and on the small crystal shelves of the show-cases pots of pomades and creams were lined up, boxes of powder and rouge, phials of oils and toilet waters; while the fine brushes, combs, scissors, and pocket flasks occupied a special cupboard. The salesmen had used their ingenuity to decorate the display with all their white china pots and all their white glass phials. The customers were delighted by a silver fountain in the centre, a shepherdess standing in a harvest of flowers, from which a continuous trickle of violet water was flowing, tinkling musically in the metal basin. An exquisite scent was spreading everywhere, and the ladies soaked their handkerchiefs in it as they passed.

'There!' said Madame Marty, when she had loaded herself with lotions, toothpastes, and cosmetics. 'That's enough, now I'm at your disposal. Let's go and find Madame de Boves.'

But on the landing of the big, central staircase she was distracted again by the Japanese department. This counter had grown since the day when Mouret had amused himself by setting up in the same place a little auction stall, covered with a few shop-soiled trinkets, without foreseeing its enormous success. Few departments had had such modest beginnings, but now it was overflowing with old bronzes, old ivories, and old lacquers. His turnover there was fifteen thousand francs a year, and he was ransacking the whole Far East, where travellers were pillaging palaces and temples for him. And new departments were still being opened: they had tried two new ones in December, in order to fill the gaps during the winter off-season—a book department and a children's toy department, which would certainly also grow and sweep away more businesses in the neighbourhood. In four years the Japanese department had succeeded in attracting all the artistic clientele of Paris.*

This time Madame Desforges herself, in spite of the grudge she bore which had made her swear not to buy anything, succumbed to a delicately carved ivory.

'Send it to me,' she said quickly, at a nearby cash-desk. 'Ninety francs, isn't it?'

And, seeing Madame Marty and her daughter engrossed in a selection of trashy china, she said as she led Madame Guibal away: 'You'll find us in the reading-room . . . I really must sit down for a little while.'

In the reading-room the ladies had to remain standing. All the chairs round the big table covered with newspapers were taken. Portly men were reading, leaning back, displaying their stomachs, without it occurring to them that it would be polite to give up their seats. A few women were writing, their noses buried in their letters, as if they were trying to hide the paper with the flowers on their hats. In any case, Madame de Boves was not there, and Henriette was getting impatient when she noticed Vallagnosc, who was also looking for his wife and mother-in-law. He greeted her, and finally said:

'They're bound to be in the lace department, they just can't be dragged away . . . I'll go and see.'

He gallantly procured them two chairs before he disappeared.

In the lace department the crush was increasing every minute. It was the crowning glory of the great display of white, the most delicate and costly whites that could be seen. The temptation was acute; mad desires were driving all the women crazy. The department had been transformed into a white chapel. Tulle and guipure lace were falling from above, forming a white sky, as if veiled by clouds, its flimsy gossamer paling the early morning sun. Round the columns flounces of Mechlin and Valenciennes lace were hanging down like the white skirts of ballerinas, falling to the ground in a shiver of whiteness. And everywhere, on all the counters, there was a snowy whiteness, Spanish blond-lace as light as air, Brussels appliqué with large flowers on fine mesh, needle-point and Venetian lace with heavier designs, Alençon and Bruges lace of regal and almost religious richness. It seemed as if the God of Fashion had set up his white tabernacle there.

Madame de Boves, after walking about with her daughter for a long time, prowling about in front of the displays and feeling a sensual urge to bury her hands in the materials, had just decided to get Deloche to show her some Alençon lace. At first he had brought out the imitation; but she had wanted to see some real Alençon, and was not content with little trimmings at three hundred francs a metre, but insisted on the big flounces at a thousand francs, and handkerchiefs and fans at seven and eight hundred francs. Soon the counter was covered with a fortune. In one corner of the department Jouve the shopwalker, who had not let Madame de Boves out of his sight in spite of her apparent dawdling, was standing motionless in the midst of the seething crowd, looking quite detached, but still keeping his eye on her.

'Do you have any berthas* in needle-point?' the Countess asked Deloche. 'Would you show them to me, please?'

She looked so imposing, with her build and voice of a princess, that the assistant, whom she had been monopolizing for twenty minutes, dared not resist. He did, however, hesitate, for the salesmen were advised not to pile up valuable laces like that, and the week before he had let himself be robbed of ten metres of Mechlin. But she was making him flustered; he gave way and abandoned the pile of Alençon for a moment in order to take the berthas for which she had asked from a drawer behind him.

'Look, Mamma,' said Blanche, who was rummaging through a box full of little pieces of inexpensive Valenciennes. 'You could get some of this for our pillows.'

Madame de Boves did not reply. Then her daughter, looking round with her podgy face, saw her mother with her hands deep in the lace and in the act of making some flounces of Alençon disappear up the sleeve of her coat. Blanche did not seem surprised, and moved forward instinctively to hide her, when Jouve suddenly appeared between them. He leaned forward and murmured politely in the Countess's ear:

'Would you be so kind as to follow me, madam?'

She hesitated for a moment.

'But what for, sir?'

'Would you be so kind as to follow me?' the shopwalker repeated, without changing his tone.

She cast a rapid glance around her, her face contorted with anguish. Then, recovering her haughty bearing, she submitted, and walked beside him like a queen who deigns to entrust herself to the care of an aide-de-camp. Not a single customer had even noticed the scene. Deloche, who had returned to the counter with the berthas, watched open-mouthed as she was led away: What? Her too! That lady who looked so aristocratic! They might as well have them all searched! Blanche, who was left at liberty, followed her mother at a distance, lingering in the midst of the surge of shoulders with a ghastly expression, torn between her duty not to abandon her and her terror of being detained with her. She saw her go into Bourdoncle's office, and was content to wait outside the door.

Bourdoncle, from whom Mouret had just succeeded in escaping, happened to be there. He usually dealt with thefts of this sort, committed by respectable people. Jouve, who had had his eye on Madame de Boves, had told him long ago that he had his doubts about her; therefore he was not surprised when the shopwalker briefly explained the matter to him; besides, such extraordinary cases passed through his hands that he declared that women were capable of anything when they got carried away by their passion for clothes. As he was aware of Mouret's social connection with the thief, he treated her with the utmost politeness.

'Madam, we forgive these moments of weakness . . . But I beg you to reflect where forgetting yourself like this might lead you. If someone else had seen you slipping that lace . . .'

But she interrupted him indignantly. She, a thief! Who did he take her for? She was the Comtesse de Boves, her husband, Inspector-General of the Stud, was received at Court.

'I know, I know, madam,' Bourdoncle calmly repeated. 'I have the honour of being acquainted with you . . . But would you first of all please return the lace you have on you . . .'

She protested again, did not allow him to say another word, magnificent in her violence, even going so far as to shed the tears of a great lady who has been insulted. Anyone else but he would have been shaken, fearing some deplorable mistake, for in order to avenge such slander she was threatening to take him to court.

'Be careful, sir! My husband will go to the Minister!'

'Come on, you've got no more sense than the rest of them,' declared Bourdoncle, losing his patience. 'We'll have to search you.'

Still she did not flinch, but said with superb assurance:

'Very well, search me . . . But I warn you, you're putting the shop at risk.'

Jouve went to fetch two salesgirls from the corset department. When he came back he told Bourdoncle that the lady's daughter had been left at liberty and had not left the door, and asked if he should arrest her too, although he had not seen her take anything. Bourdoncle, always correct in his behaviour, decided in the name of good morals that she should not be brought in, so that a mother should not be forced to blush in front of her daughter. The two men retired to a neighbouring room while the salesgirls searched the Countess, even taking off her dress to inspect her bosom and hips. Apart from the Alençon flounces, twelve metres at a thousand francs a metre, which were hidden in the depths of a sleeve, they found a handkerchief, a fan, and a scarf hidden squashed and warm in her bosom, making a total of about fourteen thousand francs' worth of lace. Ravaged by a furious, irresistible urge, Madame de Boves had been stealing like this for a year. The attacks had been getting worse, increasing until they had become a sensual pleasure necessary to her existence, sweeping away all the reasonings of prudence and giving her enjoyment which was all the more keen because she was risking, under the very eyes of the crowd, her name, her pride, and her husband's important position. Now that her husband let her take money from his drawers, she was stealing with her pockets full of money, stealing for stealing's sake as people love for the sake of loving, spurred on by desire, possessed by the neurosis which had been developed within her in the past by her unsatisfied desire for luxury when confronted by the enormous, violent temptation of the big stores.

'It's a trap!' she cried, when Bourdoncle and Jouve came back in. 'Someone planted this lace on me, I swear!'

Now she was weeping tears of rage, and had fallen on to a chair, sobbing in her half-fastened dress. Bourdoncle sent the salesgirls away. Then he resumed in his calm manner:

'We are quite prepared to hush this up, madam, out of consideration for your family. But, first of all, you will have to sign a statement saying: "I have stolen lace from the Ladies' Paradise," with details of the lace, and the date . . . And I'll let you have this paper back as soon as you bring me two thousand francs for the poor.'

She had risen to her feet again; and declared in a fresh burst of indignation:

'I'll never sign such a thing; I'd rather die.'

'You won't die, madam. But I warn you that I'm going to send for the police.'

This provoked a terrible scene. She insulted him, telling him that it was cowardly of men to torture a woman like that. Her Junoesque beauty and her tall majestic body were suffused with the fury of a fishwife. Then she tried pity: she begged them in the name of their mothers, she talked of crawling at their feet. And as they remained unmoved, their hearts hardened from practice, she suddenly sat down and with a trembling hand began to write. The pen sputtered; at the words: 'I have stolen' she pressed with such fury that she almost tore the thin paper; and she kept repeating in a choking voice:

'There you are, sir, there you are, sir . . . I yield to force . . .'

Bourdoncle took the paper, folded it carefully, and locked it in a drawer as she looked on, saying as he did so:

'You can see it won't be alone; for ladies, having talked of dying rather than signing, generally forget to come and collect their love letters . . . I'll keep it at your disposal, however. You'll be able to think about whether it's worth two thousand francs.'

She finished buttoning up her dress; now that she had paid she was recovering all her arrogance.

'Can I go now?' she asked curtly.

Bourdoncle was already busy with other matters. On hearing Jouve's report, he decided on Deloche's dismissal: he was stupid; he was continually letting himself be robbed, and would never have any control over the customers. Madame de Boves repeated her question, and when they had dismissed her with a nod, she enveloped them both with a murderous glance. From the stream of coarse words she was choking back a melodramatic cry rose to her lips:

'Scoundrels!' she said, banging the door.

Meanwhile, Blanche had not moved from the door of the office. Her ignorance of what was taking place inside, and the comings and goings of Jouve and the two salesgirls, had upset her, making her conjure up visions of the police, the assizes, prison. But suddenly she stared open-mouthed: Vallagnosc, her husband of a month, whose use of the familiar second person singular still made her feel awkward, was standing before her; surprised at her dazed state, he began to ask her questions.

'Where's your mother? Have you lost each other? Answer me, I'm concerned . . .'

She could think of no plausible lie. In her distress, she told him everything in a whisper.

'Mamma, Mamma . . . She stole something . . .'

What! Stole something! At last he understood. His wife's bloated face, that pale mask ravaged with fear, terrified him.

'Some lace, like this, up her sleeve,' she stammered.

'So you saw her do it; you were watching?' he murmured, chilled at the thought that she had been an accomplice.

They had to stop talking; people were already turning round to look at them. For a moment Vallagnosc remained motionless, paralysed by agonized hesitation. What was to be done? He was on the point of going in to see Bourdoncle when he caught sight of Mouret crossing the gallery. He told his wife to wait for him, seized his old friend's arm, and told him about the affair in broken phrases. The latter took him immediately to his office, where he put his mind at rest about the possible consequences. He assured him that there was no need to intervene, and explained the way things would certainly turn out, without appearing at all disturbed about the theft himself, as if he had foreseen it for a long time. But Vallagnosc, now that he no longer feared an immediate arrest, did not react to the incident with the same coolness. He had thrown himself into an armchair and, now that he could discuss the matter, began to lament his lot. Could it be true? So he had married into a family of thieves! It was a stupid marriage he had fallen into just to please her father! Surprised by this violence, which was like that of a sickly child, Mouret watched him weep, thinking of the pessimistic pose he had always adopted in the past. Hadn't he heard him affirm the pointlessness of life scores of times; hadn't he considered misfortune alone to be interesting? And so, in order to take his mind off his own troubles, Mouret amused himself for a moment by preaching indifference to him, in a friendly, bantering tone. At this Vallagnosc lost his temper: he was quite unable to regain his now compromised philosophy; the whole of his middle-class upbringing recoiled from his mother-in-law in virtuous indignation. As soon as he experienced something personally, at the slightest contact with human misery, at which he had always sneered, the braggart sceptic in him collapsed in suffering. It was abominable, the honour of his ancestry was being dragged through the mud, and the world seemed to be coming to an end.

'Come on, calm down,' Mouret said, overcome with pity. 'I won't tell you that everything happens and nothing happens, because that wouldn't console you at the moment. But I think you ought to go and offer your arm to Madame de Boves—that would be more sensible than creating a scandal . . . Damn it! You who professed such scorn at the universal baseness of mankind!'

'Of course!' exclaimed Vallagnosc naïvely. 'When it affects other people!'

However, he stood up and followed his old school-friend's advice. They were both going back to the gallery when Madame de Boves came out of Bourdoncle's office. She majestically accepted her son-in-law's arm, and, as Mouret bowed to her with an air of courteous respect, he heard her say:

'They gave me an apology. Really, mistakes like that are appalling.'

Blanche had rejoined them, and was walking behind them. They slowly disappeared in the crowd.

Then Mouret, alone and pensive, went through the shop once more. This scene, which had taken his mind off the conflict within him, was now increasing his fever, bringing the final struggle to a head. In his mind he felt that everything was vaguely connected: that unfortunate woman's theft, the final act of madness of his clientele which lay vanquished, prostrate at its tempter's feet, evoked the proud avenging image of Denise, whose victorious foot he could feel planted on his chest. He stopped at the top of the central staircase, and gazed for a long time at the immense nave, at his nation of women swarming beneath him.

Six o'clock was about to strike; the light which was fading outside was leaving the covered galleries, which were dark already, and was waning in the depths of the halls flooded with long shadows. In this lingering daylight, electric lamps* were lighting up one by one, and their opaque white globes studded the distant depths of the departments with bright moons. They shed a white brightness of blinding fixity, like the reflection of some colourless star, which was killing the dusk. Then, when all the lamps were lit, there was a rapturous murmur from the crowd; the great display of white took on fairy-like splendour beneath this new lighting. It seemed as if the colossal orgy of white was burning too, was itself becoming changed into light. The song of white was taking wing in the blazing whiteness of a dawn. A white gleam was projected from the linens and calicoes in the Monsigny Gallery, like the first bright streak which whitens the sky in the east; while, along the Michodière Gallery, the haberdashery and trimmings, the fancy goods and ribbons, were casting reflections of distant slopes—the flashing white of mother-of-pearl buttons, silvered bronze, and pearls. In the central nave, above all, there was an explosion of white bathed in flames: the froth of white muslin round the pillars, the white dimities and piqués draping the staircase, the white coverlets hanging like banners, the guipures and white lace floating in the air—all this opened up a dream firmament, a glimpse into the dazzling whiteness of a paradise, where the marriage of the unknown queen was being solemnized. The pavilion in the silk hall, with its white curtains, white gauzes, and white tulles, was like a gigantic bedroom whose brilliance protected the white nudity of the bride from onlookers. There was nothing left but a blinding white light in which every tone of white was dissolving, a dusting of stars snowing in the general whiteness.

In the midst of this blazing scene Mouret was still looking down at his nation of women. Black shadows stood out strongly against a pale background. Long eddies were breaking up the crowd; the fever of the great sale was passing away over the disordered swirl of heads. People were beginning to leave, a mess of materials was littering the counters, gold was clinking in the cash-desks; while the customers, despoiled and violated, were going away in disarray, their desires satisfied, and with the secret shame of having yielded to temptation in the depths of some sleazy hotel. And it was he who possessed them all like that, who held them at his mercy by his continual accumulation of goods, by his price reductions and his 'returns', his charm and his publicity. He had even conquered the mothers themselves; he reigned over them all with the brutality of a despot, whose whims were wrecking families. His creation was producing a new religion; churches, which were being gradually deserted by those of wavering faith, were being replaced by his bazaar. Women came to spend their hours of leisure in his shop, the thrilling, disturbing hours which in the past they'd spent in the depths of a chapel; for this expenditure of nervous passion was necessary, it was part of the recurring struggle between a god and a husband, the ceaselessly renewed cult of the body, with the divine future life of beauty. If he had closed his doors, there would have been a rising in the street, a desperate outcry from the worshippers whose confessional and altar he would have abolished. In spite of the lateness of the hour he could still see them in their luxury, which in the last ten years had increased so much, clinging stubbornly to the enormous metal framework, along the staircases and suspension bridges. Madame Marty and her daughter, swept up to the very top, were wandering about among the furniture. Madame Bourdelais, held back by her children, could not get away from the fancy goods. Then came another group: Madame de Boves, still on Vallagnosc's arm, was followed by Blanche, and was stopping in every department, still examining the materials in her arrogant manner. In the mass of customers, the sea of bosoms bursting with life, beating with desire, all decked with bunches of violets as if they were celebrating some royal wedding, he could no longer distinguish anything but the bare bosom of Madame Desforges, who had stopped in the glove department with Madame Guibal. In spite of her jealousy and resentment, she too was buying, and he felt himself the master one last time; under the dazzle of the electric lights they were all at his feet, like cattle from which he had extracted his fortune.

Mechanically Mouret went along the galleries, so deep in thought that he let himself be carried along by the crowd. When he looked up he found himself in the new millinery department, the windows of which looked out on to the Rue du Dix-Décembre. There, his forehead pressed against the glass, he made a fresh halt and watched the people leaving. The setting sun was spreading a yellow sheen over the tops of the white houses, the blue sky was paling, cooled by a strong fresh breeze; while, in the dusk which was already enveloping the boulevard, the electric lights of the Ladies' Paradise were casting the steady brilliance of stars lit up on the horizon at the decline of day. Towards the Opéra and the Bourse the three rows of waiting carriages were sunk in darkness, though the harness still reflected the bright lights—the gleam of a lantern, the flash of a silvered bit. The cries of liveried ostlers were ringing out all the time, and a cab would advance, a brougham would move forward and pick up a customer, then depart at a resounding trot. The queues were growing smaller now; six carriages went off at a time, occupying the whole street, to the sound of banging doors, the cracking of whips, and the buzz of pedestrians overflowing between the wheels. There seemed to be a continual expansion of customers as they spread out and were carried away to the four corners of the city, emptying the shop with the roaring noise of a sluice-gate. The roofs of the Paradise, the great golden letters on the signboards and the banners hoisted up in the sky, were still flaming with the reflection of the sunset, and seemed so colossal in this oblique lighting that they conjured up the monster on the advertisements, the phalanstery with its proliferating buildings, which were swallowing whole districts as far away as the distant woods of the suburbs. The soul of Paris, like an enormous, gentle breath, was falling asleep in the serenity of the evening, covering the last carriages with long, soft caresses, hastening down the street which was gradually becoming deserted, and disappearing in the darkness of the night.

Mouret, gazing into the distance, felt that something immense had just taken place within him; and in the thrill of triumph with which his flesh was trembling, faced with Paris devoured and

Woman conquered, he experienced a sudden weakness, a failure of his will by which he was being overthrown in his turn as if by a superior force. In his victory he felt an irrational need to be conquered; it was the irrationality of a warrior yielding on the morrow of his conquest to the whim of a child. He who, for months, had been struggling, who only that morning had still been swearing that he would stifle his passion, was suddenly giving in, overcome with vertigo, and happy to commit what he believed was an act of folly. His decision, so rapidly taken, had gathered such momentum from one minute to the next that he no longer considered anything else in the world to have any importance or to be necessary.

That evening, after the last meal service, he waited in his study. He was trembling like a young man about to stake his life's happiness; he could not stay in one spot, but kept going to the door to listen to the noises coming from the shop, where the assistants, up to their shoulders in the chaos from the sale, were folding up the goods. His heart beat at each sound of footsteps. Suddenly he felt a violent emotion and rushed forward, for he had heard in the distance a muffled murmur, which became gradually louder.

It was Lhomme, slowly approaching with the day's takings. On that day they were so heavy, there was so much copper and silver in the cash taken, that he had asked two porters to accompany him. Behind him, Joseph and one of his colleagues were bending under the sacks, enormous sacks thrown over their shoulders like sacks of cement, while he walked on ahead carrying the notes and the gold in a wallet bulging with paper, and in two bags hung round his neck, the weight pulling him down on his right-hand side, the side of his lost arm. Slowly, sweating and puffing, he had come from the other end of the shop, through the growing excitement of the salesmen. Those in the glove and silk departments had laughingly offered to relieve him of his burden; those in the cloths and woollens had wanted him to take a false step which would have scattered the gold all over the department. Then he had had to go up a staircase, cross a suspension bridge, go up more stairs, turning through the girders, followed by the gazes of the salesmen in the household linen, the hosiery, and the haberdashery, who stood gaping with ecstasy at the sight of such a fortune travelling through the air. On the first floor the ladieswear, the perfumes, the laces, and the shawls had lined up with devotion as if God himself was passing by. With every step he took the noise increased, becoming the uproar of a nation bowing down to the golden calf.

Mouret had opened his door. Lhomme appeared, followed by the two porters, who were staggering; and although he was out of breath, he still had the strength to shout:

'One million, two hundred and forty-seven francs, ninety-five centimes!'

A million had been reached at last, a million collected in one day, the figure of which Mouret had dreamed for so long!* But he made an angry gesture, and, with the disappointed air of a man disturbed by an unwelcome intruder, he said impatiently:

'A million? Very well, put it there.'

Lhomme knew that he liked to see big takings on his desk, before they were deposited in the central counting-house. The million covered the desk, crushing the papers and almost upsetting the ink; and the gold, silver, and copper, overflowing from the sacks and bursting out of the bags, made a great heap, a heap of raw takings, just as they had left the customers' hands, still warm and alive.

Just as the cashier was withdrawing, deeply hurt by his employer's indifference, Bourdoncle arrived, exclaiming gaily:

'Well, we've done it this time! We've reached a million!'

But, noticing Mouret's agitated state, he understood and calmed down. He was beaming with joy, and after a short silence he resumed:

'You've made up your mind, haven't you? You know, I think you're right.'

Suddenly Mouret planted himself in front of him, and, in the terrifying voice he used on days of crisis, he said:

'I say, my good fellow, you're rather too pleased . . . You think I'm finished, don't you, and you're feeling hungry. Well, be careful! People don't eat me up!'

Disconcerted by the sudden attack from this amazing man who always guessed everything, Bourdoncle stammered:

'What? You're joking! I've always admired you very much!'

'Don't lie,' replied Mouret, becoming even more violent. 'Listen, we were stupid to have that superstition that marriage would ruin us. After all, isn't it the health necessary to life, its very strength and order? Well! Yes, my dear fellow, I'm going to marry her, and I'll kick you all out if you do so much as lift a finger. Yes! You'll proceed to the pay-desk just like anyone else, Bourdoncle!'

He dismissed him with a gesture. Bourdoncle felt himself condemned, swept away by the victory of Woman. He took his leave. Denise arrived just at that moment, and he greeted her with a deep bow, having lost all his self-possession.

'You've come at last,' said Mouret gently.

Denise was pale with emotion. She had just suffered further grief, for Deloche had told her of his dismissal; and when she had tried to keep him back by offering to speak on his behalf, he had clung to his misfortune, saying he wanted to disappear: what was the good of staying? Why should he stand in the way of those more fortunate than himself? Denise, overcome with tears, had bade him a sisterly farewell. Wasn't she herself hoping to forget? Soon it would all be over, and all she asked of her exhausted powers was courage for the separation. In a few minutes, if she was valiant enough to break her own heart, she would be able to go away on her own and weep somewhere far away.

'You said you wanted to see me, sir,' she said in her calm way. 'I'd have come in any case, to thank you for all your kindness.'

As she came in she caught sight of the million on the desk, and the display of all that money distressed her. Above her, as if watching the scene, the portrait of Madame Hédouin in its golden frame had that eternal smile on its painted lips.

'You're still resolved to leave us?' asked Mouret, whose voice was trembling.

'Yes, sir, I must.'

Then he seized her hands and, his tenderness bursting out after the coldness he had forced himself to show towards her for so long, he said:

'And if I married you, Denise, would you still leave?'

But she had drawn her hands away; she was struggling as if under the weight of some great sorrow.

'Oh! Monsieur Mouret, please don't say any more, I beg you! Don't make me even more unhappy! . . . I can't! I can't! God is my witness that I was going away to avoid a misfortune like that!'

She went on defending herself in broken phrases. Hadn't she already suffered too much from the gossip of the shop? Did he want her to seem a woman of easy virtue in other people's eyes as well as in her own? No, no, she would be strong, she would prevent him from doing such a silly thing. He was listening to her in torment, repeating passionately:

'I want to . . . I want to . . .'

'No, it's impossible . . . And what about my brothers? I've sworn never to marry. I can't bring you two children, can I?'

'They'll be my brothers too . . . say yes, Denise!'

'No, no, leave me, you're tormenting me!'

Little by little he was losing heart, driven mad by this final obstacle. What! Even at this price she still refused! In the distance he could hear the din of his three thousand employees, shifting his regal fortune about by the armful. And that idiotic million lying there on his desk! He could not bear the irony of it; he would gladly have thrown it into the street.

'Go, then!' he exclaimed in a flood of tears. 'Go and join the man you love . . . That's the reason, isn't it? You warned me; I ought to have known, and not tormented you any further.'

She stood there dazed, astonished at the violence of this despair. Her heart was bursting. Then, with the impetuosity of a child, she threw her arms round his neck, sobbing too, and exclaimed:

'Oh! Monsieur Mouret, it's you I love!'

A last murmur, the distant acclamation of the crowd, rose from the Ladies' Paradise. The portrait of Madame Hédouin was still smiling with its painted lips. Mouret had collapsed on to the desk, and was sitting there in the middle of his million which he no longer even noticed. He was still holding Denise, clasping her tightly to his breast, telling her that she could go away now, that she could spend a month in Valognes, which would end the gossip, and that then he would go and fetch her himself, and bring her back, all powerful, on his arm.

EXPLANATORY NOTES

3 *Rue Neuve-Saint-Augustin*: the Ladies' Paradise is situated in the Opéra district of Paris, which was largely rebuilt by Baron Haussmann in the final years of the Second Empire (1852–70). Many of the streets whose names recur in the text (Rue de Choiseul, Rue Gaillon, Rue de la Michodière, Rue Monsigny, Rue Neuve-des-Petits-Champs, Rue Neuve-Saint-Augustin, Rue Sainte-Anne, Rue Saint-Roch) are situated in this area.

11 *Mexico*: French troops fought in Mexico from 1862 to 1865 in support of the Austrian Archduke Maximilian as emperor of that country. In 1867 Maximilian was shot and a republic set up in Mexico. Allusions of this kind enable Zola to situate his novels historically.

Rambouillet: some 35 miles south-west of Paris, well known for its forest and palace.

13 *shop*: the description of the Baudus and their shop is highly reminiscent of Balzac's descriptions in *La Maison du Chat-qui-pelote* (1829) and *Grandeur et décadence de César Birotteau* (1837), in which he chronicled the predecessors of the department store, the *magasins de nouveauté*.

14 *Seine-et-Oise*: a former *département* encompassing most of greater Paris; in 1964 it was divided into three smaller *départements* (Essonne, Val d'Oise, Yvelines).

18 *Vabre*: an allusion to Auguste Vabre, a character (a silk merchant) in *Pot-Bouille*, the novel Zola wrote immediately before *The Ladies' Paradise* and which features the young Octave Mouret, who has an affair with Vabre's wife.

21 *Midi*: the South of France; Mouret comes from Zola's fictional 'Plassans' (i.e. Aix-en-Provence).

23 *business*: Aristide Boucicaut, the founder of the Bon Marché, had encouraged his employees to invest their money in his shop, giving them 6 per cent interest on their investment.

32 *supervision*: although the character of Octave Mouret is based largely on Aristide Boucicaut, the relationship between Mouret and Bourdoncle was suggested by the partnership between Alfred Chauchard and Auguste Hériot, founders of the Grands Magasins du Louvre (1855).

35 *father*: Octave's father was François Mouret, son of Ursule Macquart and the hatter Mouret, and husband of Marthe Rougon, the daughter of Pierre and Félicité Rougon: see *La Fortune des Rougon* (1871) and *La Conquête de Plassans* (1874).

37 *voices*: the details contained in the preceding pages (the counterfoil book, the system of commissions and percentages, the counting-house, the receiving department) are based (like many others in the novel, but very systematically here) on the notes Zola took on Boucicaut's innovations at the Bon Marché.

44 *Chablis*: a small town in Burgundy famous for its dry white wine.

Port-aux-Vins: the Port-aux-Vins, where the boats that trans-ported wines and spirits to Paris docked, was situated on the Quai Saint-Bernard between the Rue des Fossés-Saint-Bernard and the Rue Cuvier.

46 *Auvergne*: a region of south central France.

Constantine: a town captured by the French on 13 Oct. 1837 dur-ing the conquest of Algeria.

50 *crinolines*: a hooped skirt which became fashionable in France after 1855.

59 *Rue de Rivoli and the Rue d'Alger*: a well-to-do area in the first *arrondissement*.

Baron Hartmann, director of the Crédit Immobilier: the historical reference here is to the great modernizer of Paris, Baron Haussmann (1809–91), Napoleon III's Prefect of the Seine (1853–70). In seventeen years he was responsible for a vast trans-formation of the city. By 1870 one-fifth of the streets in central Paris were his creation, and the acreage of the city had been dou-bled by annexation. At the height of the reconstruction, one in five Parisian workers was employed in the building trade. In the name of slum clearance, some 350,000 people (on Haussmann's own estimation) were displaced from the *quartiers* of old Paris to make way for the new boulevards, parks, and 'pleasure grounds'. Zola's reference to Haussmann is conflated with the operations of the Société des Immeubles Rivoli, founded by the Péreire brothers (and soon renamed the Compagnie Immobilière), which in 1855 built many of the buildings along the Rue de Rivoli. The 'Haussmanization' of Paris, and the speculative frenzy it provoked, are described in Zola's novel *La Curée* ('The Kill', 1872).

61 *Luc*: probably Luc-sur-Mer, in the *département* of Calvados in Normandy.

62 *Lycée Bonaparte*: now the Lycée Condorcet, situated in the Opéra district.

63 *imperial*: a small beard.

Plassans: Zola's fictional name for Aix-en-Provence, his own birthplace and the origin of the Rougon-Macquart family (see *La Fortune des Rougon* and *La Conquête de Plassans*).

64 *baccalauréat*: the important examination taken at the end of high school.

66 *the four rules*: adding, subtracting, multiplying, dividing.

67 *doing wrong*: the character of Vallagnosc represents the disciples of the German pessimist writer Arthur Schopenhauer (1788–1860), whose influence in France was widespread in the 1880s. This type of character is portrayed more fully in Lazare Chanteau, the protagonist of Zola's novel *La Joie de vivre* (1884), and the aristocratic *fin de siècle* figures of whom Des Esseintes, the protagonist of J.-K. Huysmans's novel *A rebours* ('Against Nature', 1884), is the supreme embodiment.

71 *the new street*: the Rue du Dix-Décembre (later renamed the Rue du 4 Septembre) was in fact declared available for public purposes on 24 Aug. 1864, and officially expropriated in two stages, in Sept. 1867 and Mar. 1868; construction work began at the end of 1868 and it was opened at the end of 1869. Thus there are some slight anachronisms in Zola's account.

73 *Grand Hotel*: a sumptuous new hotel near the Opéra, the largest and grandest in Paris.

134 *guinguettes*: open-air cafés with dancing.

phalanstery: a reference to the utopian social theories of Charles Fourier (1772–1837), who wanted a perfect community set apart from the rest of society. He introduced the idea of the self-sufficient, co-operative community (the 'phalanstery'), free from the constraints and trials of urban industrial civilization. This community was to be based on agriculture and craftsmanship rather than on industrialization, and all members would share equally in the communal life. Rather than have the individual adjust to society, Fourier wished to create a community which responded to individual needs. A number of co-operative communities were formed in Europe and the United States on the principles outlined by Fourier; all were ultimately unsuccessful.

139 *Cotentin*: peninsular region of Normandy.

175 *the Madeleine district*: the Madeleine church, standing at the west end of the *grands boulevards*, is the grandest and smartest of modern Paris churches.

182 *Hôtel Duvillard*: the word 'Hôtel' is used here in the sense of private mansion.

193 *the Gard . . . the Isère*: *départements* in the south of France.

208 *the new Opéra*: Garnier's grandiose Opera House (the one we know today) was built between 1862 and 1874.

Rue Monsigny: the Bon Marché, the Louvre, and the Printemps were all substantially extended in stages: the Bon Marché between 1869 and 1872, the Louvre in 1869, the Printemps in 1880.

211 *the Halles*: the great central food market of Paris, designed by the architect Victor Baltard (1805–74) and built in iron between 1851 and 1857. The Halles form the focus of Zola's *Le Ventre de Paris* ('The Belly of Paris', 1873). They were demolished in 1971.

216 *Bois de Vincennes*: wooded area to the east of Paris.

234 *metal naves*: Frantz Jourdain, Zola's friend and the future designer of La Samaritaine, who had provided Zola with an imaginary layout for his fictional store, shared the general enthusiasm for iron and glass in the second half of the nineteenth century. The triumph of these new architectural materials permitted new forms that met the need of large-scale commerce for more space, light, and ventilation. The man Boucicaut chose as his engineer in the expansion of his shop was Gustave Eiffel (1832–1923), renowned as the builder of the Eiffel Tower—the world's most famous symbol of the nineteenth century's enthusiasm for industrial and technological progress.

exhibitions: Boucicaut opened a picture and sculpture gallery at the Bon Marché in March 1875.

248 *Blois, Libourne, and Tarbes*: provincial towns.

the Batignolles . . .: a district in the north-west of Paris.

255 *the big shops*: while the expansion of commerce was greeted by many as a mark of progress benefiting the consumer and contributing to the economic health of the nation, it was also perceived to possess a darker side in its encouragement of pleasure-seeking and narcissistic self-gratification, a temptation to which women were particularly prone. The emergence of kleptomania, a disease that was seen as both feminine and modern, was a particularly striking instance of the sexual disorder that was seen to lie at the very heart of consumer culture. See Elaine S. Abelson, *When*

Ladies Go A-thieving: Middle-Class Shoplifters in the Victorian Department Store (Oxford: Oxford University Press, 1989).

274 *Le Roi Dagobert*: a very popular comic song; King Dagobert was the last Frankish king of the Merovingian dynasty, and ruled all France from AD 628 to 638.

279 *Poitou*: a region in the south-west of France.

284 *the Gros-Caillou*: an area near the École Militaire and the Invalides on the right bank of the Seine.

289 *Bullier*: a very well-known dance-hall in the Latin Quarter, at the end of the Boulevard Saint-Michel.

311 *King of Prussia*: Wilhelm I (1798–1888) visited Paris for the World Fair (l'Exposition Universelle) of 1867.

314 *twelve times*: annual turnover at the Bon Marché in 1869 was 22 million; in 1877 (the year of Boucicaut's death) it was 67 million; it reached 100 million (with figures of over one million for the busiest sales days) in 1881–2.

328 *trowel*: Marguerite Boucicaut laid the first stone of the new sections of the Bon Marché on 9 Sept. 1869. Work on the extension continued until 1872; on completion it occupied a whole city block.

337 *firemen*: the documentation Zola collected in the spring of 1882 included statistical details of the Bon Marché and the Louvre: the former, for example, had 11 directors, 36 department heads, and 2,500 employees, including 152 salesgirls and 30 shopwalkers.

356 *clothing*: Denise's humanitarian social initiatives recall those inspired by Marguerite Boucicaut. During the 1870s Boucicaut established a library for his employees, provided evening classes in foreign languages, music, and fencing, and instituted a pension fund financed entirely from store revenues. By the early years of the twentieth century, paternalist concern for the 'great family' had produced paid sick leave and free health care, paid maternity leave, gifts at the birth of each child and family allowances for employees with three children or more, relief for widows and orphans, and even paid annual holidays.

360 *acroterium*: in classical architecture, any of the pedestals, usually without a base, placed at the two extremes or in the middle of pediments or frontispieces, serving to support statues, etc.

373 *zouave*: member of a body of French infantry, originally composed of Algerians, characterized by a colourful uniform of gaiters,

baggy trousers, short and open-fronted jacket, and tasselled cap or turban.

393 *advertisement*: the Printemps was destroyed by a fire (caused by an accident with a gas-lamp) on 9 Mar. 1881, and was largely rebuilt by the beginning of 1882. The incident was widely reported in the newspapers, which stressed the 'heroism' of Jules Jaluzot, the owner of the shop, who had gone to wake up his salesgirls in their attic rooms.

419 *Paris*: all aspects of Japanese art were highly fashionable during the second half of the nineteenth century. Zola, Manet, and the Goncourt brothers were all enthusiasts.

420 *berthas*: wide round collars covering the shoulders (as for a dress or blouse).

426 *electric lamps*: in fact electric lighting was fully introduced into the big stores only after 1880. See Wolfgang Schivelbusch, *Disenchanted Night: The Industrialization of Light in the Nineteenth Century* (Berkeley, Calif.: University of California Press, 1988).

430 *so long*: see note to p. 314.

American Literature

British and Irish Literature

Children's Literature

Classics and Ancient Literature

Colonial Literature

Eastern Literature

European Literature

Gothic Literature

History

Medieval Literature

Oxford English Drama

Poetry

Philosophy

Politics

Religion

The Oxford Shakespeare

A complete list of Oxford World's Classics, including Authors in Context, Oxford English Drama, and the Oxford Shakespeare, is available in the UK from the Marketing Services Department, Oxford University Press, Great Clarendon Street, Oxford OX2 6DP, or visit the website at www.oup.com/uk/worldsclassics.

In the USA, visit www.oup.com/us/owc for a complete title list.

Oxford World's Classics are available from all good bookshops. In case of difficulty, customers in the UK should contact Oxford University Press Bookshop, 116 High Street, Oxford OX1 4BR.

ÉMILE ZOLA

L'Assommoir
The Attack on the Mill
La Bête humaine
La Débâcle
Germinal
The Kill
The Ladies' Paradise
The Masterpiece
Nana
Pot Luck
Thérèse Raquin

A SELECTION OF OXFORD WORLD'S CLASSICS

LUDOVICO ARIOSTO	**Orlando Furioso**
GIOVANNI BOCCACCIO	**The Decameron**
MATTEO MARIA BOIARDO	**Orlando Innamorato**
LUÍS VAZ DE CAMÕES	**The Lusíads**
MIGUEL DE CERVANTES	**Don Quixote de la Mancha** **Exemplary Stories**
DANTE ALIGHIERI	**The Divine Comedy** **Vita Nuova**
BENITO PÉREZ GALDÓS	**Nazarín**
LEONARDO DA VINCI	**Selections from the Notebooks**
NICCOLÒ MACHIAVELLI	**Discourses on Livy** **The Prince**
MICHELANGELO	**Life, Letters, and Poetry**
PETRARCH	**Selections from the *Canzoniere* and** **Other Works**
GIORGIO VASARI	**The Lives of the Artists**